ARTHUR
KING *of* BRITAIN

History, Chronicle, Romance & Criticism

WITH TEXTS IN MODERN ENGLISH, FROM GILDAS TO MALORY

Edited by

Richard L. Brengle
Indiana University Southeast

Prentice-Hall, Inc., Englewood Cliffs, New Jersey

Printed in the United States of America

ISBN: 0-13-049270-1

Library of Congress Catalog Card Number: 64-17761

9 8 7 6 5 4

PRENTICE-HALL INTERNATIONAL, INC., London
PRENTICE-HALL OF AUSTRALIA, PTY. LTD., Sydney
PRENTICE-HALL OF CANADA, LTD., Toronto
PRENTICE-HALL OF INDIA PRIVATE LIMITED, New Delhi
PRENTICE-HALL OF JAPAN, INC., Tokyo

ARTHUR

KING *of* BRITAIN

To

TERRY

and Her Court of Four

PREFACE

Peering back nearly fifteen hundred years to the momentous "Birth of Britain," the twentieth century's greatest knight and war leader, Sir Winston Churchill, has this to say about the story of King Arthur: "If we could see exactly what happened we should find ourselves in the presence of a theme as well founded, as inspired, and as inalienable from the inheritance of mankind as the *Odyssey* or the Old Testament. It is all true, or it ought to be; and more and better besides." No doubt the legendary figure of Arthur has loomed large in the minds of Western men ever since the dimly-lit days of Castle Guinnion and Mount Badon; and no doubt he is as close to the hearts of Englishmen and Frenchmen today as St. George and Charlemagne. For Arthur is both the hero and the human: a towering commander with a tragic destiny, a matchless champion with failing strength against the wearing of time.

The vast and unique body of history, pseudo-history, chronicle, and romance of King Arthur has fascinated poets, storytellers, scholars, and readers for centuries. His vogue in Britain and especially in France during the Middle Ages was immense; it spread all over the face of Europe, even to the Middle East and to Iceland. From its beginnings, probably in Wales and Ireland, the story of the fabulous monarch and his men crossed to France in the twelfth century where the genius of Chrétien de Troyes brought to it the full force of courtly love; then sometime within the next hundred years it went on to Germany where the Grail quest was brilliantly handled by Wolfram von Eschenbach and the love story of Tristan and Isolt was further immortalized by Gottfried von Strassburg.

Meanwhile, in the early thirteenth century, the story of Arthur returned to its native land. Despite its novel and often inconsistent developments, the British welcomed the legend back with renewed pleasure. They saw that the King's court had grown from a small, fierce band of Roman Briton warriors repelling the hated Saxons to a large, chivalrous entourage of British and Continental knights searching for love or mere adventure. And they listened enthralled to what was new: the doctrines of *l'amour courtois,* and certain Christian motifs, particularly the mysterious Grail quest—both of which profoundly altered the original, rather simple themes of defense and conquest. With light hearts and bright armor, the paladins gathered at the Round Table of Caerleon with Arthur and his Queen Guinevere. Here sat Sir Gawain and Sir Lancelot, surpassing all others, and the lesser characters, among them Kay, Mordred, Galahad, Yvain, Perceval, Tristan, Cligés, Erec, Agravain, Lot, Bors, Gareth, Gaheris, Lionel, Hoel, Bedivere, and a host more —while in the shadows stood the enigmatic Merlin and Morgan le Fay. Now there were entire cycles and endless stories to relate about Gawain, Tristan, Perceval, Merlin, and Lancelot; there were fantastic lands to describe, and superhuman emprises, enchanted castles, magic horns and springs, evil giants and crafty dwarfs, distressed damsels, "and more and better besides." The mighty King, as noble and generous as ever, became more and more a part of the setting in which his knights begged boons, quested, jousted, loved, and triumphed.

Yet, withal, Arthur has always remained at the very center of the legend which bears his name. It is the intent of this book to concentrate on him as he appears in history, pseudo-history, chronicle, and romance, from Gildas to Malory, to try to see in these documents and literary works "exactly what happened." Once the reader gets a reasonably clear—and chiefly English—picture of his character, achievement, and fate, the boundless domain over which he ruled becomes easier to survey and explore. For this reason certain masterpieces of medieval Arthurian literature are not included here, ones such as Chrétien de Troyes' *Lancelot* and *Perceval, or the Story of the Grail,* the *Lais* of Marie de France, Wolfram von Eschenbach's *Parzival,* Gottfried von Strassburg's *Tristan and Isolt,* and the faultless *Sir Gawain and the Green Knight.* To the student engaged in research or undertaking serious study, this focus will be especially helpful. Did Arthur really exist? Did his legend begin in Welsh folklore or in the gifted imaginations of early chroniclers? Did his military exploits have any historical foundations or parallels? What kind of a man was he at first? What changes took place in his character and court as his story traveled through Europe?

What human or symbolic significance can be found in his victories, betrayals, and death?

These are only a few of the questions this book enables the reader to begin to answer. Here is Arthur, valiant King of Britain, from the beginning to the end of the Middle Ages, from the time he slaughters invaders in early history (Part I) until he succumbs through treachery in late romance (Part II). In between is a great wealth of materials for investigation and interpretation. To aid in both these important endeavors, Part III consists of criticism, carefully selected essays by leading Arthurian scholars. After the student has read the primary texts in translation, he can turn to these pages to broaden and deepen his knowledge and understanding, as well as to sharpen his critical perception through varying analytical approaches. As a guide throughout, study questions on the materials in Parts I, II, and III are contained in Part IV, along with suggestions for short and long investigative papers. These topics for research allow the reader to leave Arthur if he chooses and follow in library resources the outstanding personages of that glittering court. Moreover, broad historical, geographical, and mythical subjects are included for possible examination. A selective bibliography in Part V contains a list of translations, text and author studies, and critical items for use in the various research topics. Finally, there is a brief Glossary at the end to assist the student with certain Middle English and Latin words or expressions, and to identify a few geographical locations and real or imaginary persons.

Though it is primarily designed as a controlled research materials text, this book has other uses. It can serve as a supplement to history of English literature courses; and it can be adopted as a primary reader in advanced classes in medieval literature. Lastly, it contains significant examples of the workings of history, legend, and myth for courses investigating such aspects of world culture. Students of all levels will find here that the story of King Arthur does indeed embody a well-founded and inspired theme which is "inalienable from the inheritance of mankind"—and perhaps they will discover, besides, that "it is all true, or it ought to be."

No book of this type is done alone. Professor William Matthews of the University of California read the work through in manuscript and offered invaluable suggestions for improving both its scope and form. It is a pleasure also to express my gratitude for the assistance and interest of my former colleagues, Miss Elizabeth Eley Wright, Dr. Robert B. Lloyd, and Dr. David K. Cornelius. The staff of Lipscomb Library at Randolph-Macon Woman's College has been more than patient with my demands, particularly Miss Ruth Paris; and I have been kindly accorded use of the facilities of the Alderman Library at the University of Virginia and the Library of the State University of Iowa. My parents, as always, have helped me beyond measure: to them, and to Mrs. Evelyn Eaton, Barbara and Walter Wriston, and Helen and Barry Emmert, I owe more than I can ever say.

R. L. B.

CONTENTS

xi

PART II: CHRONICLE AND ROMANCE

Contents

PART III: CRITICISM

CONTENTS

PART ONE

History and Pseudo-History

GILDAS

De Excidio et Conquestu Britanniae *(c. 540)*

Translated by the editor from the Latin text in E. K. Chambers *Arthur of Britain* (London: Sidgwick & Jackson, Ltd., 1927).

From CHAPTER 25:

And thus some of the wretched remnants [of the Britons], caught in the mountains, were slaughtered in large numbers; others, weakened by hunger, came forward and surrendered to their enemies [the Saxons] to be slaves forever, if for all that they were not immediately cut to pieces, which was the greatest kindness that remained to them; others went to lands across the sea with loud lamentation, just as if in the manner of the chief oarsman intoning in this way under the billows of the sails: "Thou hast made us like sheep for slaughter, and hast scattered us among the nations" [Psalms 44:11]; others, entrusting life always with suspicious mind to the mountainous country, overhanging hills, steep fortified places, densest forests, and sea caverns, stood firm on their native soil, although in a state of fear. Then, some time intervening, when these most cruel plunderers [236] had gone back home, under the leader Ambrosius Aurelianus, a moderate man, who by chance alone of the Roman nation had survived in the shock of so great a calamity —his parents, undoubtedly of royal rank, having perished in the same disaster, his progeny today having very much degenerated from the excellence of their ancestors—[the remnants of the Britons] gained strength and challenging the conquerors to battle, by God's favor the victory fell to them.

From CHAPTER 26:

Since that period, at one time our countrymen, at another the enemy, were victorious . . . up to the year of the besieging of Mount Badon, when almost the last but not the least slaughter of these hangdogs took place, and which, as I know, begins the forty-fourth year (one month having passed already), which is also the year of my birth.[237]

BEDE

Historia Ecclesiastica Gentis Anglorum (731)

Translated by the editor from the Latin text in E. K. Chambers, *Arthur of Britain* (London: Sidgwick & Jackson, Ltd., 1927).

From BOOK I, CHAPTER 16:

They [the Britons] had at that time for their leader Ambrosius Aurelianus, a moderate man, who by chance alone of the Roman nation had survived the previously mentioned calamity, his parents, bearing the name and insignia of kings, having perished in the same disaster. Therefore, with this leader, the Britons took up arms, and challenging the [Saxon] conquerors to battle, by God's favoring themselves attained the victory. And since that period, at one time our countrymen, at another the enemy, were victorious, up to the year of the besieging of Mount Badon, when they gave these enemies no less slaughter, about forty-four years after their arrival in Britain.[238]

NENNIUS

Historia Brittonum (c. 800)

Translated by the editor from the Latin text in E. K. Chambers, *Arthur of Britain* (London: Sidgwick & Jackson, Ltd., 1927).

From CHAPTER 56:

At that time the Saxons grew powerful in great numbers and increased in Britain. But now that Hengist was dead, his son Octha crossed over from the left side of Britain to the kingdom of the Kentishmen, and from him are sprung the kings of the Kentishmen. Then Arthur fought against them [the Saxons] in those days together with the kings of Britain, but he was himself the leader of battles. The first battle was [238] at the mouth of the river which is called Glein; the second, third, fourth, and fifth on another river, which is called Dubglas and is in the region of Linnuis; the sixth battle on a river which is called Bassas. The seventh was the battle in the wood of Celidon, that is Cat Coit Celidon. The eighth was the battle at the castle Guinnion, in which Arthur carried the image of Saint Mary, the perpetual Virgin, on his shoulders and the pagans were put to flight on that day, and there was great slaughter of them by the virtue of our Lord, Jesus Christ, and by the virtue of Saint Mary the Virgin, His Mother.

The ninth battle was fought in the city of the Legion. The tenth
battle he fought on the shore of the river, which is called Tribruit.
The eleventh was the battle waged on the mountain, which is
called Agned. The twelfth was the battle at Mount Badon, in which
on one day nine hundred and sixty men fell to the ground during
one onset of Arthur; and no one overthrew them save himself alone,
and in all the battles he emerged the victor.[239]

From CHAPTER 73:

There is another marvelous thing in the region which
is called Buelt. There is at that place a pile of stones and one stone
placed over and above this heap with the footprint of a dog on it.
When he was hunting the boar Troynt, Cabal, who was the dog of
Arthur [239] the soldier, impressed his footprint on the stone, and
Arthur afterwards gathered together a pile of stones under the one
on which was the footprint of his dog, and it is called Carn Cabal.
And men come and carry the stone away in their hands for the
space of a day and a night, and on the next day it is found back on
its pile.

There is another marvel in the region which is called Ercing.
There is found at that place a tomb near a fountain, which is
called Licat Anir, and the name of the man who is buried in the
sepulchral mound was thus designated Anir. He was the son of
Arthur the soldier, and he was the one who killed him in the same
place and buried him. And men come to measure the sepulchral
mound, sometimes six, sometimes nine, sometimes twelve, sometimes fifteen feet in length. Whatever way you measure it in alternation, the second time you will not find its measurement the same,
and I have tested it myself.[240]

"ANNALES CAMBRIAE" (c. 950)

Three entries

Translated by the editor from the Latin text in E. K. Chambers, *Arthur of Britain* (London: Sidgwick & Jackson, Ltd., 1927).

Year [516]　The Battle of Badon, in which Arthur carried the Cross of our Lord Jesus Christ on his shoulders for three days and three nights, and the Britons were victorious. . . .
Year [537]　The Battle of Camlann, in which Arthur and Medraut fell; and there was death in Britain and in Ireland. . . .
Year [570]　Gildas died.[241]

WILLIAM OF MALMESBURY

Gesta Regum Anglorum (c. 1125)

Translated by the editor from the Latin text in E. K. Chambers, *Arthur of Britain* (London: Sidgwick & Jackson, Ltd., 1927).

From BOOK I:

But when he [Vortimer, son of Vortigern] died, the strength of the Britons dwindled away, hopes diminishing and fleeting; and indeed they would have then immediately perished had not Ambrosius—alone of the Romans [249] surviving, who reigned as king after Vortigern—overpowered the presumptuous barbarians with the distinguished service of the warlike Arthur. This is the Arthur about whom the trifles of the Bretons* rave even now, one certainly not to be dreamed of in false myths, but proclaimed in truthful histories—indeed, who for a long time held up his tottering fatherland, and kindled the broken spirits of his countrymen to war. At last, at the siege of Mount Badon, trusting in the image of our Lord's Mother which he had sewn on his armor, rising alone against nine hundred of the enemy he dashed them to the ground with incredible slaughter.[250]

From BOOK III:

At that time [c. 1066-1087], in a province of Wales which is called Ros, was found the tomb of Walwen, who was not unworthy of Arthur—a nephew through his sister. He reigned in that part of Britain which is still called Walweitha, a soldier highly celebrated for his deeds of bravery, but who was driven from the kingdom by the brother and nephew of Hengist (of whom I have spoken in my first book), first making them pay dearly for his banishment. He deservedly shared in his uncle's praising, because he prevented the fall of his collapsing country for many years. But the tomb of Arthur is nowhere seen, whence ancient dirges still fable his coming. Yet the sepulchre of the other, as I said before, was found above the seacoast in the time of King William, fourteen feet long. There, as certain people claim, he [Walwen] was wounded by his enemies, and cast forth from a shipwreck; by others it is said that he was killed by his fellow citizens at a public feast. Therefore, knowledge of the truth falls in doubt, although neither of these stories would fail as a defense of his fame.[250]

---

* **Bretons.** The Latin text reads *Britonum*, "of the Britons," but by the twelfth century when William of Malmesbury was writing the word always meant the Bretons of Armorica or Brittany in France, not the insular Roman Britons, Welsh, or Cornish. *Editor's note.*

GIRALDUS CAMBRENSIS

De Principis Instructione (c. 1195)

From *The Autobiography of Giraldus Cambrensis,* ed. and trans. H. E. Butler (London: Jonathan Cape, 1937).

Now the body of King Arthur, which legend has feigned to have been transferred at his passing, as it were in ghostly form, by spirits to a distant place and to have been exempt from death, was found in these our days at Glastonbury deep down in earth and encoffined in a hollow oak between two stone pyramids erected long ago in the consecrated graveyard, the site being revealed by strange and almost miraculous signs; and it was afterwards transported with honour to the Church and decently consigned to a marble tomb. Now in the grave there was found a cross of lead, placed under a stone and not above it, as is now customary, but fixed on the lower side. This cross I myself have seen; for I have felt the letters engraved thereon, which do not project or stand out, but are turned inwards toward the stone. They run as follows.

HERE LIES BURIED THE RENOWNED KING ARTHUR
WITH GUENEVERE HIS SECOND WIFE
IN THE ISLE OF AVALON

Now in regard to this there are many things worthy of note. For he had two wives, the last of whom was buried with him, and her bones were found together with his, but separated from them as thus; two parts of the tomb, to wit, the head, were allotted to the bones of the man, while the remaining third towards the foot contained [119] the bones of the woman in a place apart; and there

was found a yellow tress of woman's hair still retaining its colour
and its freshness; but when a certain monk snatched it and lifted
it with greedy hand, it straightway all of it fell into dust. Now
whereas there were certain indications in their writings that the
body would be found there, and others in the letters engraven upon
the pyramids, though they were much defaced by their extreme
age, and others again were given in visions and revelations vouchsafed to good men and religious, yet it was above all King Henry
II of England that most clearly informed the monks, as he had
heard from an ancient Welsh bard, a singer of the past, that they
would find the body at least sixteen feet beneath the earth, not in
a tomb of stone, but in a hollow oak. And this is the reason why
the body was placed so deep and hidden away, to wit, that it might
not by any means be discovered by the Saxons who occupied the
island after his death, whom he had so often in his life defeated
and almost utterly destroyed; and for the same reason those letters,
witnessing to the truth, that were stamped upon the cross, were
turned inwards towards the stone, that they might at that time
conceal what the tomb contained, and yet in due time and place
might some day reveal the truth.

Now the place which is now called Glaston, was in ancient
times called the isle of Avalon. For it is as it were an isle, covered
with marshes, wherefore in the British tongue it was called Inis
Avallon, that is 'the apple-bearing isle'. Wherefore Morganis, a
noble matron and the ruler and lady of those parts, who moreover
was kin by blood to King Arthur, carried him away after the war
of Camlan to the island that is now called Glaston that she might
heal his wounds. It was also once called 'Inis gutrin' in the British
tongue, that is, the glassy isle,[120] wherefore when the Saxons afterwards came thither they call that place Glastingeburi. For 'Glas' in
their language has the same meaning as *uitrum*, while 'buri' means
castrum or *ciuitas*.

You must also know that the bones of Arthur thus discovered
were so huge that the words of the poet seemed to be fulfilled:

> 'And he shall marvel at huge bones
> In tombs his spade has riven' (*Virg. Georg.* I, 497).

For his shank-bone, when placed against that of the tallest man
in that place and planted in the earth near his foot, reached (as

the Abbot showed us) a good three inches above his knee. And the skull was so large and capacious as to be a portent or prodigy; for the eyesocket was a good palm in width. Moreover, there were ten wounds or more, all of which were scarred over, save one larger than the rest, which had made a large hole.[121]

RALPH HIGDEN

Polychronicon (c. 1327)

Translated from the Latin into Middle English by an unknown writer (c. 1440) and modernized by Richard L. Brengle from *Polychronicon Ranulphi Higden*, ed. Joseph Rawson Lumby, Rolls Series, Volume V (London: Longmans & Co., 1874).

. . . Many men wonder about this Arthur, whom Geoffrey [333] extols so much singly, how the things that are said of him could be true, for, as Geoffrey repeats, he conquered thirty realms. If he subdued the king of France to him, and did slay Lucius the Procurator of Rome, Italy, then it is astonishing that the chronicles of Rome, of France, and of the Saxons should not have spoken of so noble a prince in their stories, which mentioned little things about men of low degree. Geoffrey says that Arthur overcame Frollo, King of France, but there is no record of such a name among men of France. Also, he says that Arthur slew Lucius Hiberius, Procurator of the city of Rome in the time of Leo the Emperor, yet according to all the stories of the Romans Lucius did not govern in that time—nor was Arthur born, nor did he live then, but in the time of Justinian, who was the fifth emperor after Leo. Geoffrey says that he has marveled that Gildas and Bede make no mention

of Arthur in their [335] writings; however, I suppose it is rather
to be marveled why Geoffrey praises him so much, whom old
authors, true and famous writers of stories, leave untouched. But
perhaps it is the custom of every nation to extol some of their
blood-relations excessively, as the Greeks great Alexander, the
Romans Octavian, Englishmen King Richard, Frenchmen Charles;
and so the Britons extolled Arthur. Which thing happens, as Jose-
phus says, either for fairness of the story, or for the delectation of
the readers, [337] or for exaltation of their own blood. [339]

PART TWO

Chronicle and Romance

"THE MABINOGION"

"Culhwch and Olwen" (c. 1100)

Translated by Gwyn Jones and Thomas Jones, Everyman's Library (London: J. M. Dent & Sons, Ltd., 1949).

Cilydd son of Cyleddon Wledig wished for a wife as wellborn as himself. The wife that he took was Goleuddydd daughter of Anlawdd Wledig. After his stay with her the country went to prayers whether they might have offspring, and they got a son through the prayers of the country. But from the time she grew with child, she went mad, without coming near a dwelling. When her time came upon her, her right sense came back to her; it came in a place where a swineherd was keeping a herd of swine, and through terror of the swine the queen was delivered. And the swineherd took the boy until he came to the court. And the boy was baptized, and the name Culhwch given to him because he was found in a pig-run. Nonetheless the boy was of gentle lineage: he was first cousin to Arthur. And the boy was put out to nurse.

And after that the boy's mother, Goleuddydd daughter of Anlawdd Wledig, grew sick. She called her husband to her, and quoth she to him, 'I am going to die of this sickness, and thou wilt wish for another wife. And these days wives are the dispensers of gifts, but it is wrong for thee to despoil thy son. I ask of thee that thou take no wife till thou see a two-headed briar on my grave.' That he promised her. She summoned her preceptor to her and bade him strip the grave each year, so that nothing might grow on it. The queen died. The king would send an attendant every morning to see whether anything was growing on the grave. At the end of seven

15

years the preceptor neglected that which he had promised the queen. One day when the king was hunting, he drew near the graveyard; he wanted to see the grave whereby he was to take a wife. He saw the [95] briar. And when he saw it the king took counsel where he might get a wife. Quoth one of the counsellors, 'I could tell of a woman would suit thee well. She is the wife of king Doged.' They decided to seek her out. And they slew the king, and his wife they brought home with them, and an only daughter she had along with her; and they took possession of the king's lands.

Upon a day as the good lady went walking abroad, she came to the house of an old crone who was in the town, without a tooth in her head. Quoth the queen: 'Crone, wilt thou for God's sake tell me what I ask of thee? Where are the children of the man who has carried me off by force?' Quoth the crone: 'He has no children.' Quoth the queen: 'Woe is me that I should have come to a childless man!' Said the crone: 'Thou needst not say that. It is prophesied that he shall have offspring. 'Tis by thee he shall have it, since he has not had it by another. Besides, be not unhappy, he has one son.'

The good lady returned home joyfully, and quoth she to her husband, 'What reason hast thou to hide thy child from me?' Quoth the king, 'I will hide him no longer.' Messengers were sent after the boy, and he came to the court. His stepmother said to him, 'It were well for thee to take a wife, son, and I have a daughter meet for any nobleman in the world.' Quoth the boy, 'I am not yet of an age to take a wife.' Said she in reply: 'I will swear a destiny upon thee, that thy side shall never strike against woman till thou win Olwen daughter of Ysbaddaden Chief Giant.' The boy coloured, and love of the maiden entered into every limb of him, although he had never seen her. Quoth his father to him, 'How, son, why dost thou colour? What ails thee?' 'My stepmother has sworn on me that I shall never win a wife until I win Olwen daughter of Ysbaddaden Chief Giant.' 'It is easy for thee to achieve that, son,' said his father to him. 'Arthur is thy first cousin. Go then to Arthur to trim thy hair, and ask that of him as his gift to thee.' [96]

Off went the boy on a steed with light-grey head, four winters old, with well-knit fork, shell-hoofed, and a gold tubular bridle-bit in its mouth. And under him a precious gold saddle, and in his hand two whetted spears of silver. A battle-axe in his hand, the fore-

arm's length of a full grown man from ridge to edge. It would draw
blood from the wind; it would be swifter than the swiftest dewdrop
from the stalk to the ground, when the dew would be heaviest in
the month of June. A gold-hilted sword on his thigh, and the blade
of it gold, and a gold-chased buckler upon him, with the hue of
heaven's lightning therein, and an ivory boss therein. And two grey-
hounds, whitebreasted, brindled, in front of him, with a collar of
red gold about the neck of either, from shoulder-swell to ear. The
one that was on the left side would be on the right, and the one
that was on the right side would be on the left, like two seaswallows
sporting around him. Four clods the four hoofs of his steed would
cut, like four swallows in the air over his head, now before him,
now behind him. A four-cornered mantle of purple upon him, and
an apple of red gold in each of its corners; a hundred kine was the
worth of each apple. The worth of three hundred kine in precious
gold was there in his foot gear and his stirrups, from the top of his
thigh to the tip of his toe. Never a hair-tip stirred upon him, so
exceeding light his steed's canter under him on his way to the gate
of Arthur's court.

Quoth the youth, 'Is there a porter?' 'There is. And thou, may
thy head not be thine, that thou dost ask! I am porter to Arthur
each first day of January, but my deputies for the year save then,
none other than Huandaw and Gogigwr and Llaesgymyn, and Pen-
pingion who goes upon his head to spare his feet, neither heaven-
wards not earthwards, but like a rolling stone on a court floor.'
'Open the gate.' 'I will not.' 'Why wilt thou not open it?' 'Knife
has gone into meat, and drink into horn, and a thronging in
Arthur's hall. Save the son of a king of a rightful dominion, or a
craftsman who [97] brings his craft, none may enter. Meat for thy
dogs and corn for thy horse, and hot peppered chops for thyself,
and wine brimming over, and delectable songs before thee. Food
for fifty men shall come to thee in the hospice; there men from afar
take their meat, and the scions of other countries who do not proffer
a craft in Arthur's court. It will be no worse for thee there than for
Arthur in the court: a woman to sleep with thee, and delectable
songs before thee. To-morrow at tierce, when the gate is opened
for the host that came here to-day, for thee shall the gate be opened
first, and thou shalt sit wherever thou wilt in Arthur's hall, from
its upper end to its lower.' The youth said, 'I will do nothing of

that. If thou open the gate, it is well. If thou open it not, I will bring dishonour upon thy lord and ill report upon thee. And I will raise three shouts at the entrance of this gate, so that it shall not be less audible on the top of Pengwaedd in Cornwall and in the depths of Dinsel in the North, and in Esgeir Oerfel in Ireland. And every woman with child that is in this court shall miscarry, and such of them as are not with child their wombs shall turn to a burden within them, so that they may never bear child from this day forth.' Quoth Glewlwyd Mighty-grasp, 'Shout as much as thou wilt about the laws of Arthur's court, thou shalt not be let in till first I go and have word with Arthur.'

And Glewlwyd came into the hall. Quoth Arthur to him, 'Thou hast news from the gate?' 'I have. Two-thirds of my life are past, and two-thirds of thine own. I was of old in Caer Se and Asse, in Sach and Salach, in Lotor and Ffotor. I was of old in India the Great and India the Lesser. I was of old in the contest between the two Ynyrs, when the twelve hostages were brought from Llychlyn. And of old I was in Egrop, and in Africa was I, and in the islands of Corsica, and in Caer Brythwch and Brythach, and Nerthach. I was there of old when thou didst slay the war-band of Gleis son of Merin, when thou didst slay Mil the Black,[98] son of Dugum; I was there of old when thou didst conquer Greece unto the east. I was of old in Caer Oeth and Anoeth, and in Caer Nefenhyr Nineteeth. Fair kingly men saw we there, but never saw I a man so comely as this who is even now at the entrance to the gate.' Quoth Arthur, 'If thou didst enter walking go thou out running. And he that looks upon the light, and opens his eye and shuts it, an injunction upon him. And let some serve with golden drinking horns, and others with hot peppered chops, so that there be ample meat and drink for him. A shameful thing it is to leave in wind and rain a man as thou tellest of.' Quoth Cei: 'By the hand of my friend, if my counsel were acted upon, the laws of court would not be broken for his sake.' 'Not so, fair Cei. We are noble men so long as we are resorted to. The greater the bounty we show, all the greater will be our nobility and our fame and our glory.'

And Glewlwyd came to the gate and opened the gate to him. And what every man did, to dismount at the gate on the horse-block, he did not do; but on his steed he came inside. Quoth Culhwch, 'Hail, sovereign prince of this Island! Be it no worse unto the lower

half of the house than unto the upper. Be this greeting equally to
thy nobles, and thy retinue, and thy leaders of hosts. May there be
none without his share of it. Even as I gave thee full greeting, may
thy grace and thy faith and thy glory be in this Island.' 'God's truth,
so be it, chieftain! Greeting to thee too. Sit thou between two of
the warriors, and delectable song before thee, and the privilege of
an atheling for thee, an heir to a throne, for as long as thou shalt
be here. And when I dispense my gifts to guests and men from afar,
it shall be at thy hand that I so begin in this court.' Quoth the
youth: 'I have not come here to wheedle meat and drink. But if I
obtain my boon, I will repay it, and I will praise it. If I obtain it
not, I will bear hence thine honour as far as thy renown was farthest
in the four corners of the world.' Quoth Arthur, 'Though thou bide
not here, chieftain, thou [99] shalt obtain the boon thy head and
thy tongue shall name, as far as wind dries, as far as rain wets, as
far as sun runs, as far as sea stretches, as far as earth extends, save
only my ship and my mantle, and Caledfwlch my sword, and Rhongomyniad my spear, and Wynebgwrthucher my shield, and Carnwennan my dagger, and Gwenhwyfar my wife.' 'God's truth
thereon?' 'Thou shalt have it gladly. Name what thou wilt.' 'I will.
I would have my hair trimmed.' 'That thou shalt have.' Arthur
took a golden comb and shears with loops of silver, and he combed
his head.

And he asked who he was. Quoth Arthur: 'My heart grows
tender towards thee: I know thou art sprung from my blood. Declare who thou art.' 'I will: Culhwch son of Cilydd son of Cyleddon
Wledig, by Goleuddydd daughter of Anlawdd Wledig, my mother.'
Quoth Arthur: 'True it is. Thou art then my first cousin. Name
what thou wilt, and thou shalt have it, whatever thy mouth and
thy tongue shall name.' 'God's truth thereon to me, and the truth
of thy kingdom?' 'Thou shalt have it gladly.' 'My claim on thee is
that thou get me Olwen daughter of Ysbaddaden Chief Giant. And
I invoke her in the name of thy warriors.' [100]

Arthur said, 'Ah, chieftain, I have never heard tell of the
maiden thou tellest of, nor of her parents. I will gladly send messengers to seek her.' From that night till the same night at the end
of a year the messengers were a-wandering. At the end of the year,
when Arthur's messengers had found nothing, said the chieftain,
'Every one has obtained his boon, yet am I still lacking. I will

away and take thine honour with me.' Said Cei, 'Ah, chieftain, overmuch dost thou asperse Arthur. Come thou with us. Till thou shalt say she exists not in the world, or till we find her, we will not be parted from thee.'

Then Cei arose. Cei had this peculiarity, nine nights and nine days his breath lasted under water, nine nights and nine days would he be without sleep. A wound from Cei's sword no physician might heal. A wondrous gift had Cei: when it pleased him he would be as tall as the tallest tree in the forest. Another peculiarity had he: when the rain was heaviest, a handbreadth before his hand and another behind his hand what would be in his hand would be dry, by reason of the greatness of his heat; and when the cold was hardest on his comrades,, that would be to them kindling to light a fire.

Arthur called on Bedwyr, who never shrank from an [107] enterprise upon which Cei was bound. It was thus with Bedwyr, that none was so handsome as he in this Island, save Arthur and Drych son of Cibddar, and this too, that though he was one-handed no three warriors drew blood in the same field faster than he. Another strange quality was his; one thrust would there be of his spear, and nine counter-thrusts.

Arthur called on Cynddylig the Guide. 'Go thou for me upon this enterprise along with the chieftain.' He was no worse a guide in the land he had never seen than in his own land.

He called Gwrhyr Interpreter of Tongues: he knew all tongues.

He called Gwalchmei son of Gwyar, because he never came home without the quest he had gone to seek. He was the best of walkers and the best of riders. He was Arthur's nephew, his sister's son, and his first cousin.

Arthur called on Menw son of Teirgwaedd, for should they come to a heathen land he might cast a spell over them, so that none might see them and they see every one.

Away they went till they came to a wide open plain and saw a fort, the greatest of forts in the world. That day they journeyed. When they thought they were near to the fort they were no nearer than at first. And the second and the third day they journeyed, and with difficulty did they get thereto. However, as they were coming to the same plain as it, they could see a great flock of sheep without limit or end to it, and a shepherd tending the sheep on top of a mound, and a jerkin of skins upon him, and at his side a shaggy mastiff which was bigger than a nine year old stallion. It was the way of him that never a lamb had he lost, much less a grown beast. No company had ever fared past him that he did not do it harm or deadly hurt; every dead tree and bush that was on the plain, his breath would burn them to the very ground.

Quoth Cei: 'Gwrhyr Interpreter of Tongues, go and have [108] word with yonder man.' 'Cei, I made no promise to go save as far as thou thyself wouldst go.' 'Then let us go there together.' Quoth Menw son of Teirgwaedd: 'Have no qualms to go thither. I will cast a spell over the dog, so that he shall do harm to none.'

They came to where the shepherd was. Quoth they, 'Things are well with thee, shepherd.' 'May things never be better with you than with me.' 'Yea, by God, for thou art chief.' 'There is no affliction to do me harm save my wife.' 'Whose are the sheep thou tendest, or whose is the fort?' 'Fools of men that you are! Throughout the world it is known that this is the fort of Ysbaddaden Chief Giant.' 'And thou, who art thou?' 'Custennin son of Mynwyedig am I, and because of my wife Ysbaddaden Chief Giant has wrought my ruin. You too, who are you?' 'Messengers of Arthur are here, to seek Olwen.' 'Whew, men! God protect you! For all the world, do not that. Never a one has come to make that request that went away with his life.'

The shepherd arose. As he arose Culhwch gave him a ring of gold. He sought to put on the ring, but it would not go on him, and he placed it in the finger of his glove and went home and gave the glove to his wife. And she took the ring from the glove. 'Whence came this ring to thee, husband? 'Twas not often that thou hast had treasure-trove.' 'I went to the sea, to find sea-food. Lo! I saw a body coming in on the tide. Never saw I body so beautiful as that, and on its finger I found this ring.' 'Alas, husband, since sea does not tolerate a dead man's jewel therein, show me that body.' 'Wife, the one whose body that is, thou shalt see him here presently.' 'Who is that?' the woman asked. 'Culhwch son of Cilydd son of Cyleddon Wledig, by Goleuddydd daughter of Anlawdd Wledig, his mother, who is come to seek Olwen.' Two feelings possessed her: she was glad that her nephew, her sister's son, was coming to her; and she was sad because she had never seen any depart with his life that had come to make that request.[109]

They came forward to the gate of the shepherd Custennin's court. She heard the noise of their coming. She ran with joy to meet them. Cei snatched a log out of the wood-pile, and she came to meet them, to try and throw her arms about their necks. Cei thrust a stake between her two hands. She squeezed the stake so that it became a twisted withe. Quoth Cei, 'Woman, had it been I thou didst squeeze in this wise, there were no need for another to love me ever. An ill love, that!'

They came into the house and their needs were supplied. After a while, when all were letting themselves be busied, the woman opened a coffer alongside the hearth, and out of it arose a lad with curly yellow hair. Quoth Gwrhyr, ' 'Twere pity to hide a lad like this. I know that it is no fault of his own that is visited upon him.' Quoth the woman, 'He is all that is left. Three-and-twenty sons of mine has Ysbaddaden Chief Giant slain, and I have no more hope of this one than of the others.' Quoth Cei, 'Let him keep company with me, and we shall not be slain save together.'

They ate. Quoth the woman, 'On what errand are you come hither?' 'We are come to seek Olwen.' 'For God's sake, since none from the fort has yet seen you, get you back!' 'God knows we will not get us back till we have seen the maiden. Will she come to where she may be seen?' 'She comes hither every Saturday to wash her head; and in the bowl where she washes she leaves all her rings. Neither she nor her messenger ever comes for them.' 'Will she come hither if she is sent for?' 'God knows I will not slay my soul. I will not betray the one who trusts in me. But if you pledge your word you will do her no harm, I will send for her.' 'We pledge it,' said they.

She was sent for. And she came, with a robe of flame-red silk about her, and around the maiden's neck a torque of red gold, and precious pearls thereon and rubies. Yellower was her head than the flower of the broom, whiter was her [110] flesh than the foam of the wave; whiter were her palms and her fingers than the shoots of the marsh trefoil from amidst the fine gravel of a welling spring. Neither the eye of the mewed hawk, nor the eye of the thrice-mewed falcon, not an eye was there fairer than hers. Whiter were her breasts than the breast of the white swan, redder were her cheeks than the reddest foxgloves. Whoso beheld her would be filled with love of her. Four white trefoils sprang up behind her wherever she went; and for that reason was she called Olwen.

She entered the house and sat between Culhwch and the high seat, and even as he saw her he knew her. Said Culhwch to her, 'Ah maiden, 'tis thou I have loved. And come thou with me.' 'Lest sin be charged to thee and me, that I may not do at all. My father has sought a pledge of me that I go not without his counsel, for he shall live only until I go with a husband. There is, however, counsel I will give thee, if thou wilt take it. Go ask me of my father. And however much he demand of thee, do thou promise to get it, and me too shalt thou get. But if he have cause to doubt at all, get me thou shalt not, and 'tis well for thee if thou escape with thy life.' 'I promise all that, and will obtain it,' said he.

She went to her chamber. They then arose to go after her to the fort, and slew nine gatemen who were at nine gates without a man crying out, and nine mastiffs without one squealing. And they went forward to the hall.

Quoth they, 'In the name of God and man, greeting unto thee, Ysbaddaden Chief Giant.' 'And you, where are you going?' 'We are going to seek Olwen thy daughter for Culhwch son of Cilydd.' 'Where are those rascal servants and those ruffians of mine?' said he. 'Raise up the forks under my two eyelids that I may see my future son-in-law.' That was done. 'Come hither to-morrow. I will give you some answer.' [111]

They rose, and Ysbaddaden Chief Giant snatched at one of the three poisoned stone-spears which were by his hand and hurled it after them. And Bedwyr caught it and hurled it back at him, and pierced Ysbaddaden Chief Giant right through the ball of his knee. Quoth he, 'Thou cursed savage son-in-law! I shall walk the worse up a slope. Like the sting of a gadfly the poisoned iron has pained me. Cursed be the smith who fashioned it, and the anvil on which it was wrought, so painful it is!'

That night they lodged in the house of Custennin. And on the morrow with pomp and with brave combs set in their hair they came into the hall. They said, 'Ysbaddaden Chief Giant, give us thy daughter in return for her portion and her maiden fee to thee and her two kinswomen. And unless thou give her, thou shalt meet thy death because of her.' 'She and her four great-grandmothers and her four great-grandfathers are yet alive. I must needs take counsel with them.' 'So be it with thee,' said they. 'Let us go to our meat.' As they arose he took hold of the second stone-spear which was by his hand and hurled it after them. And Menw son of Teirgwaedd caught it and hurled it back at him, and pierced him in the middle of his breast, so that it came out in the small of his back. 'Thou cursed savage son-in-law! Like the bite of a big-headed leech the hard iron has pained me. Cursed be the forge wherein it was heated. When I go uphill, I shall have tightness of chest, and bellyache, and a frequent loathing of meat.' They went to their meat.

And the third day they came to court. Quoth they, 'Ysbaddaden Chief Giant, shoot at us no more. Seek not thy harm and deadly hurt and death.' 'Where are my servants? Raise up the forks —my eyelids have fallen over the balls of my eyes—so that I may take a look at my future son-in-law.' They arose, and as they arose he took the third poisoned stone-spear and hurled it after them. And Culhwch caught it and hurled it back, even as he wished, and pierced him through the ball of the eye, so that it came [112] out through the nape of the neck. 'Thou cursed savage son-in-law! So long as I am left alive, the sight of my eyes will be the worse. When I go against the wind they will water, a headache I shall have, and a giddiness each new moon. Cursed be the forge wherein it was heated. Like the bite of a mad dog to me the way the poisoned iron has pierced me.' They went to their meat.

On the morrow they came to court. Quoth they, 'Shoot not at us. Seek not the harm and deadly hurt and martyrdom that are upon thee, or what may be worse, if such be thy wish. Give us thy daughter.' 'Where is he who is told to seek my daughter?' ' 'Tis I who seek her, Culhwch son of Cilydd.' 'Come hither where I may see thee.' A chair was placed under him, face to face with him.

Said Ysbaddaden Chief Giant, 'Is it thou that seekest my daughter?' ' 'Tis I who seek her.' 'Thy pledge would I have that thou wilt not do worse by me than is just.' 'Thou shalt have it.' 'When I have myself gotten that which I shall name to thee, then thou shalt get my daughter.' 'Name what thou wouldst name.'

'I will,' said he. 'Dost see the great thicket yonder?' 'I see.' 'I must have it uprooted out of the earth and burnt on the face of the ground so that the cinders and ashes thereof be its manure; and that it be ploughed and sown so that it be ripe in the morning against the drying of the dew, in order that it may be made into meat and drink for thy wedding guests and my daughter's. And all that I must have done in one day.'

'It is easy for me to get that, though thou think it is not easy.'

'Though thou get that, there is that thou wilt not get. A husbandman to till and prepare that land, other than Amaethon son of Dôn. He will not come with thee of his own free will, nor canst thou compel him.'

'It is easy for me to get that, though thou think it is not easy.' [113]

'Though thou get that, there is that thou wilt not get. Gofannon son of Dôn to come to the headland to set the irons. He will not do work of his own free will, save for a king in his own right, nor canst thou compel him.'

'It is easy for me to get that, though thou think it is not easy.'

'Though thou get that, there is that thou wilt not get. The two oxen of Gwlwlydd Wineu, both yoked together to plough well the rough ground yonder. He will not give them of his own free will, nor canst thou compel him.'

'It is easy for me to get that, though thou think it is not easy.'

'Though thou get that, there is that thou wilt not get. The Melyn Gwanwyn and the Ych Brych, both yoked together, must I have.'

"It is easy for me to get that, though thou think it is not easy.'

'Though thou get that, there is that thou wilt not get. The two horned oxen, one of which is beyond Mynydd Bannawg, and the other this side—and to fetch them together in the one plough. Nyniaw and Peibiaw are they, whom God transformed into oxen for their sins.'

'It is easy for me to get that, though thou think it is not easy.'

'Though thou get that, there is that thou wilt not get. Dost see the hoed tilth yonder?' 'I see.' 'When first I met the mother of that maiden, nine hestors of flax seed were sown therein; neither black nor white has come out of it yet, and I have that measure still. I must have that in the new-broken ground yonder, so that it may be a white veil for my daughter's head on the day of thy wedding-feast.'

'It is easy for me to get that, though thou think it is not easy.'

'Though thou get that, there is that thou wilt not get.[114]

Honey that will be nine times sweeter than the honey of a virgin swarm, without drones and without bees, to make bragget for the feast.'

'It is easy for me to get that, though thou think it is not easy.'

'Though thou get that, there is that thou wilt not get. The cup of Llwyr son of Llwyrion, in which is the best of all drink; for there is no vessel in the world which can hold that strong drink, save it. Thou shalt not have it of his own free will, nor canst thou compel him.'

'It is easy for me to get that, though thou think it is not easy.'

'Though thou get that, there is that thou wilt not get. The hamper of Gwyddneu Long-shank: if the whole world should come around it, thrice nine men at a time, the meat that every one wished for he would find therein, to his liking. I must eat therefrom the night my daughter sleeps with thee. He will give it to no one of his own free will, nor canst thou compel him.'

'It is easy for me to get that, though thou think it is not easy.'

'Though thou get that, there is that thou wilt not get. The horn of Gwlgawd Gododdin to pour out for us that night. He will not give it of his own free will, nor canst thou compel him.'

'It is easy for me to get that, though thou think it is not easy.'

'Though thou get that, there is that thou wilt not get. The harp of Teirtu to entertain me that night. When a man pleases, it will play of itself; when one would have it so, it will be silent. He will not give it of his own free will, nor canst thou compel him.'

'It is easy for me to get that, though thou think it is not easy.'

'Though thou get that, there is that thou wilt not get. The birds of Rhiannon, they that wake the dead and lull the [115] living to sleep, must I have to entertain me that night.'

'It is easy for me to get that, though thou think it is not easy.'

'Though thou get that, there is that thou wilt not get. The cauldron of Diwrnach the Irishman, the overseer of Odgar son of Aedd king of Ireland, to boil meat for thy wedding guests.'

'It is easy for me to get that, though thou think it is not easy.'

'Though thou get that, there is that thou wilt not get. I must needs wash my head and shave my beard. The tusk of Ysgithyrwyn Chief Boar I must have, wherewith to shave myself. I shall be none the better for that unless it be plucked from his head while alive.'

'It is easy for me to get that, though thou think it is not easy.'

'Though thou get that, there is that thou wilt not get. There is no one in the world can pluck it from his head save Odgar son of Aedd king of Ireland.'

'It is easy for me to get that, though thou think it is not easy.'

'Though thou get that, there is that thou wilt not get. I will not entrust the keeping of the tusk to any save Cadw of Prydein. The threescore cantrefs of Prydein are under him. He will not come out of his kingdom of his own free will, nor can he be compelled.'

'It is easy for me to get that, though thou think it is not easy.'

'Though thou get that, there is that thou wilt not get. I must needs dress my beard for me to be shaved. It will never settle unless the blood of the Black Witch be obtained, daughter of the White Witch, from the head of the Valley of Grief in the uplands of Hell.'

'It is easy for me to get that, though thou think it is not easy.' [116]

'Though thou get that, there is that thou wilt not get. The blood will be of no use unless it be obtained while warm. There is no vessel in the world will keep heat in the liquid that is put therein save the bottles of Gwyddolwyn the Dwarf, which keep their heat from the time when the liquid is put into them in the east till one reaches the west. He will not give them of his own free will, nor canst thou compel him.'

'It is easy for me to get that, though thou think it is not easy.'

'Though thou get that, there is that thou wilt not get. Some will wish for milk, but there will be no way to get milk for every one until the bottles of Rhynnon Stiff-beard are obtained. In them no liquid ever turns sour. He will not give them of his own free will, nor can he be compelled.'

'It is easy for me to get that, though thou think it is not easy.'

'Though thou get that, there is that thou wilt not get. There is no comb and shears in the world wherewith my hair may be dressed, so exceeding stiff it is, save the comb and shears that are between the two ears of Twrch Trwyth son of Taredd Wledig. He will not give them of his own free will, nor canst thou compel him.'

'It is easy for me to get that, though thou think it is not easy.'

'Though thou get that, there is that thou wilt not get. Twrch Trwyth will not be hunted till Drudwyn be obtained, the whelp of Greid son of Eri.'

'It is easy for me to get that, though thou think it is not easy.'

'Though thou get that, there is that thou wilt not get. There is no leash in the world may hold on him, save the leash of Cors Hundred-claws.'

'It is easy for me to get that, though thou think it is not easy.'

'Though thou get that, there is that thou wilt not get.[117] There is no collar in the world can hold the leash, save the collar of Canhastyr Hundred-hands.'

'It is easy for me to get that, though thou think it is not easy.'

'Though thou get that, there is that thou wilt not get. The chain of Cilydd Hundred-holds to hold the collar along with the leash.'

'It is easy for me to get that, though thou think it is not easy.'

'Though thou get that, there is that thou wilt not get. There is no huntsman in the world can act as houndsman to that hound, save Mabon son of Modron, who was taken away when three nights old from his mother. Where he is is unknown, or what his state is, whether alive or dead.'

'It is easy for me to get that, though thou think it is not easy.'

'Though thou get that, there is that thou wilt not get. Gwyn Dun-mane, the steed of Gweddw (as swift as the wave is he!), under Mabon to hunt Twrch Trwyth. He will not give him of his own free will, nor canst thou compel him.'

'It is easy for me to get that, though thou think it is not easy.'

'Though thou get that, there is that thou wilt not get. Mabon will never be obtained, where he is is unknown, till his kinsman Eidoel son of Aer be first obtained; for he will be untiring in quest of him. He is his first cousin.'

'It is easy for me to get that, though thou think it is not easy.'

'Though thou get that, there is that thou wilt not get. Garselit the Irishman, chief huntsman of Ireland is he. Twrch Trwyth will never be hunted without him.'

'It is easy for me to get that, though thou think it is not easy.'

'Though thou get that, there is that thou wilt not get. A [118] leash from the beard of Dillus the Bearded, for save that there is nothing will hold those two whelps. And no use can be made of it unless it be twitched out of his beard while he is alive, and he be plucked with wooden tweezers. He will not allow any one to do that to him while he lives, but it will be useless if dead, for it will be brittle.'

'It is easy for me to get that, though thou think it is not easy.'

'Though thou get that, there is that thou wilt not get. There is no huntsman in the world will hold those two whelps, save Cynedyr the Wild son of Hetwn the Leper. Nine times wilder is he than the wildest wild beast on the mountain. Him wilt thou never get, nor wilt thou get my daughter.'

'It is easy for me to get that, though thou think it is not easy.'

'Though thou get that, there is that thou wilt not get. Thou wilt not hunt Twrch Trwyth until Gwyn son of Nudd be obtained, in whom God has set the spirit of the demons of Annwn, lest this world be destroyed. He will not be spared thence.'

'It is easy for me to get that, though thou think it is not easy.'

'Though thou get that, there is that thou wilt not get. There is no horse in the world that will avail Gwyn to hunt Twrch Trwyth, save Du the horse of Moro Oerfeddawg.'

'It is easy for me to get that, though thou think it is not easy.'

'Though thou get that, there is that thou wilt not get. Until Gwilenhin king of France come, Twrch Trwyth will never be hunted without him. It is improper for him to leave his kingdom, and he will never come hither.'

'It is easy for me to get that, though thou think it is not easy.'

'Though thou get that, there is that thou wilt not get.[119] Twrch Trwyth will never be hunted without the son of Alun Dyfed be obtained. A good unleasher is he.'

'It is easy for me to get that, though thou think it is not easy.'

'Though thou get that, there is that thou wilt not get. Twrch Trwyth will never be hunted until Aned and Aethlem be obtained. Swift as a gust of wind would they be; never were they unleashed on a beast they did not kill.'

'It is easy for me to get that, though thou think it is not easy.'

'Though thou get that, there is that thou wilt not get. Arthur and his huntsmen to hunt Twrch Trwyth. A man of might is he, and he will not come with thee—the reason is that he is a man of mine.'

'It is easy for me to get that, though thou think it is not easy.'

'Though thou get that, there is that thou wilt not get. Twrch Trwyth can never be hunted until Bwlch and Cyfwlch and Syfwlch be obtained, sons of Cilydd Cyfwlch, grandsons of Cleddyf Difwlch. Three gleaming glitterers their three shields; three pointed piercers their three spears; three keen carvers their three swords; Glas, Glesig, Gleisad, their three dogs; Call, Cuall, Cafall, their three horses; Hwyrddyddwg and Drwgddyddwg and Llwyddyddwg, their three wives; Och and Garym and Diasbad, their three witches; Lluched and Neued and Eisywed, their three daughters; Drwg and Gwaeth and Gwaethaf Oll, their three maid-servants. The three men shall wind their horns, and all the others will come to make outcry, till none would care though the sky should fall to earth.'

'It is easy for me to get that, though thou think it is not easy.'

'Though thou get that, there is that thou wilt not get. The sword of Wrnach the Giant; never can he be slain save with that. He will not give it to any one, neither for price nor for favour, nor canst thou compel him.' [120]

'It is easy for me to get that, though thou think it is not easy.'

'Though thou get that, there is that thou wilt not get. Wakefulness without sleep at night shalt thou have in seeking those things. And thou wilt not get them, nor wilt thou get my daughter.'

'Horses shall I have and horsemen, and my lord and kinsman Arthur will get me all those things. And I shall win thy daughter, and thou shalt lose thy life.'

'Set forward now. Thou shalt not be answerable for food or raiment for my daughter. Seek those things. And when those things are won, my daughter too thou shalt win.'

That day they journeyed till evening, until there was seen a great fort of mortared stone, the greatest of forts in the world. Lo, they saw coming from the fort a black man, bigger than three men of this world. Quoth they to him: 'Whence comest thou, fellow?' 'From the fort you see yonder.' 'Whose is the fort?' 'Fools of men that you are! There is none in the world does not know whose fort this is. It belongs to Wrnach the Giant.' 'What usage is there for a guest and far-comer alighting at this fort?' 'Ah, chieftain, God protect you! No guest has ever come thence with his life. None is permitted therein save him who brings his craft.'

They made their way to the gate. Quoth Gwrhyr Interpreter of Tongues, 'Is there a porter?' 'There is. And thou, may thy head not be thine, that thou dost ask!' 'Open the gate.' 'I will not.' 'Why wilt thou not open it?' 'Knife has gone into meat, and drink into horn, and a thronging in Wrnach's hall. Save for a craftsman who brings his craft, it will not be opened again this night.' Quoth Cei, 'Porter, I have a craft.' 'What craft hast thou?' 'I am the best furbisher of swords in the world.' 'I will go and tell that to Wrnach the Giant and will bring thee an answer.' [121]

The porter came inside. Said Wrnach the Giant, 'Thou hast news from the gate?' 'I have. There is a company at the entrance to the gate who would like to come in.' 'Didst thou ask if they had a craft with them?' 'I did, and one of them declared he knew how to furbish swords.' 'I had need of him. For some time I have been seeking one who should polish my sword, but I found him not. Let that man in, since he had a craft.'

The porter came and opened the gate, and Cei came inside all alone. And he greeted Wrnach the Giant. A chair was placed under him. Said Wrnach, 'Why, man, is this true which is reported of thee, that thou knowest how to furbish swords?' 'I do that,' said Cei. The sword was brought to him. Cei took a striped whetstone from under his arm. 'Which dost thou prefer upon it, white-haft or dark-haft?' 'Do with it what pleases thee, as though it were thine own.' He cleaned half of one side of the blade for him and put it in his hand. 'Does that content thee?' 'I would rather than all that is in my dominions that the whole of it were like this. It is a shame a man as good as thou should be without a fellow.' 'Oia, good sir, I have a fellow, though he does not practise this craft.' 'Who is he?' 'Let the porter go forth, and I will tell his tokens: the head of his spear will leave its shaft, and it will draw blood from the wind, and settle upon the shaft again.' The gate was opened and Bedwyr entered in. Said Cei, 'A wondrous gift has Bedwyr, though he does not practise this craft.'

And there was great debate concerning the entry of Cei and Bedwyr betwixt those men outside, and a young lad who came in with them, the shepherd Custennin's only son. He and his comrades with him, as though it were nothing out of the way, crossed the three baileys until they came inside the fort. Quoth his comrades of Custennin's son, 'Best of men is he.' From then on he was called Goreu son of Custennin. They dispersed to their lodgings that they [122] might slay those who lodged them, without the Giant knowing.

The furbishing the sword was done, and Cei gave it into the hand of Wrnach the Giant, as though to see whether the work was to his satisfaction. Said the giant, 'The work is good, and I am content with it.' Quoth Cei, 'It is thy scabbard has damaged thy sword. Give it to me to take out the wooden side-pieces, and let me make new ones for it.' And he took the scabbard, and the sword in the other hand. He came and stood over the giant, as if he would put the sword into the scabbard. He sank it into the giant's head and took off his head at a blow. They laid waste the fort and took away what treasures they would. To the very day at the end of a year they came to Arthur's court, and the sword of Wrnach the Giant with them.

They told Arthur how it had gone with them. Arthur said, 'Which of those marvels will it be best to seek first?' 'It will be best,' said they, 'to seek Mabon son of Modron, and there is no getting him until his kinsman Eidoel son of Aer is got first.' Arthur rose up, and the warriors of the Island of Britain with him, to seek for Eidoel; and they came to Glini's outer wall, to where Eidoel was in prison. Glini stood on the rampart of the fort, and he said, 'Arthur, what wouldst thou have of me, since thou wilt not leave me alone on this crag? I have no good herein and no pleasure, neither wheat nor oats have I, without thee too seeking to do me harm.' Arthur said, 'Not to thy hurt have I come hither, but to seek out the prisoner that is with thee.' 'I will give thee the prisoner, though I had not bargained to give him up to any one. And besides this, my aid and my backing thou shalt have.'

The men said to Arthur, 'Lord, get thee home. Thou canst not proceed with thy host to seek things so petty as these.' Arthur said, 'Gwrhyr Interpreter of Tongues, it is right for thee to go on this quest. All tongues hast thou,[123] and thou canst speak with some of the birds and the beasts. Eidoel, it is right for thee to go along with my men to seek him—he is thy first cousin. Cei and Bedwyr, I have hope that whatever you go to seek will be obtained. Go then for me on this quest.'

They went on their way as far as the Ouzel of Cilgwri. 'For God's sake,' Gwrhyr asked her, 'knowest thou aught of Mabon son of Modron, who was taken when three nights old from betwixt his mother and the wall?' The Ouzel said, 'When first I came hither, there was a smith's anvil here, and as for me I was a young bird. No work has been done upon it save whilst my beak was thereon every evening. To-day there is not so much of it as a nut not worn away. God's vengeance on me if I have heard aught of the man you are asking after. Nevertheless, that which it is right and proper for me to do for Arthur's messengers, I will do. There is a kind of creature God made before me; I will go along as your guide thither.'

They came to the place where the Stag of Rhedynfre was. 'Stag of Rhedynfre, here we have come to thee, Arthur's messengers, since we know of no animal older than thou. Say, knowest thou aught of Mabon son of Modron, who was taken away from his mother when three nights old?' The Stag said, 'When first I came hither, there was but one tine on either side of my head, and there were no trees here save a single oak-sapling, and that grew into an oak with a hundred branches, and the oak thereafter fell, and to-day there is naught of it save a red stump; from that day to this I have been here. I have heard naught of him you are asking after. Nevertheless I will be your guide, since you are Arthur's messengers, to the place where there is an animal God made before me.'

They came to the place where the Owl of Cwm Cawlwyd was. 'Owl of Cwm Cawlwyd, here are Arthur's messengers. Knowest thou aught of Mabon son of Modron, who was taken away from his mother when three nights old?' 'If I [124] knew it, I would tell it. When first I came hither, the great valley you see was a wooded glen, and a race of men came thereto and it was laid waste. And the second wood grew up therein, and this wood is the third. And as for me, why! the roots of my wings are mere stumps. From that day to this I have heard naught of the man you are asking after. Nevertheless I will be a guide to Arthur's messengers until you come to the place where is the oldest creature that is in this world, and he that has fared furthest afield, the Eagle of Gwernabwy.'

Gwrhyr said, 'Eagle of Gwernabwy, we have come to thee, Arthur's messengers, to ask whether thou knowest aught of Mabon son of Modron who was taken away from his mother when three nights old?' The Eagle said, 'I came here a long time ago, and when first I came hither I had a stone, and from its top I pecked at the stars each evening; now it is not a hand-breadth in height. From that day to this I have been here, but have heard naught of him you are asking after. Save that at one faring I went to seek my meat as far as Llyn Llyw, and when I came there I sank my claws into a salmon, thinking he would be meat for me many a long day, and he drew me down into the depths, so that it was with difficulty I got away from him. And my whole kindred and I went after him, to seek to destroy him. But he sent messengers to make peace with me, and came to me in person to have fifty tridents taken out of his back. Unless he knows something of what you seek, I know none who may. Nevertheless, I will be your guide to the place where he is.'

They came to the place where he was. The Eagle said, 'Salmon of Llyn Llyw, I have come to thee with Arthur's messengers to ask whether thou knowest aught of Mabon son of Modron who was taken away from his mother when three nights old?' 'As much as I know, I will tell. With every tide I go up along the river till I come to the bend of the wall of Caer Loyw; and there I found such distress that [125] I never found its equal in all my life; and, that you may believe, let one of you come here on my two shoulders.' And Cei and Gwrhyr Interpreter of Tongues went upon the salmon's two shoulders, and they journeyed until they came to the far side of the wall from the prisoner, and they could hear wailing and lamentation on the far side of the wall from them. Gwrhyr said, 'What man laments in this house of stone?' 'Alas, man, there is cause for him who is here to lament. Mabon son of Modron is here in prison; and none was ever so cruelly imprisoned in a prison house as I; neither the imprisonment of Lludd Silver-hand nor the imprisonment of Greid son of Eri.' 'Hast thou hope of getting thy release for gold or for silver or for worldly wealth, or by battle and fighting?' 'What is got of me, will be got by fighting.'

They returned thence and came to where Arthur was. They told where Mabon son of Modron was in prison. Arthur summoned the warriors of this Island and went to Caer Loyw where Mabon was in prison. Cei and Bedwyr went upon the two shoulders of the fish. Whilst Arthur's warriors assaulted the fort, Cei broke through the wall and took the prisoner on his back; and still he fought with the men. Arthur came home and Mabon with him, a free man.

Arthur said, 'Which of the marvels is it now best to seek first?' 'It is best to seek for the two whelps of the bitch Rhymhi.' 'Is it known where she is?' asked Arthur. 'She is,' said one, 'at Aber Deu Gleddyf.' Arthur came to the house of Tringad in Aber Cleddyf and asked him, 'Hast thou heard of her in these parts? In what shape is she?' 'In the shape of a she-wolf,' answered he, 'and she goes about with her two whelps. Often has she slain my stock, and she is down in Aber Cleddyf in a cave.'

Arthur went to sea in his ship Prydwen, and others by land to hunt the bitch, and in this wise they surrounded her and her two whelps, and God changed them back into their own [126] semblance for Arthur. Arthur's host dispersed, one by one, two by two.

And as Gwythyr son of Greidawl was one day journeying over a mountain, he heard a wailing and a grievous lamentation, and these were a horrid noise to hear. He sprang forward in that direction, and when he came there he drew his sword and smote off the anthill level with the ground, and so saved them from the fire. And they said to him, 'Take thou God's blessing and ours, and that which no man can ever recover, we will come and recover it for thee.' It was they thereafter who came with the nine hestors of flax seed which Ysbaddaden Chief Giant had named to Culhwch, in full measure, with none of it wanting save for a single flax seed. And the lame ant brought that in before night.

As Cei and Bedwyr were sitting on top of Pumlumon on Carn Gwylathyr, in the highest wind in the world, they looked about them and they could see a great smoke towards the south, far off from them, and not blowing across with the wind. And then Cei said, 'By the hand of my friend, see yonder the fire of a warrior.' They hastened towards the smoke and approached thither, watching from afar as Dillus the Bearded was singeing a wild boar. Now, he was the mightiest warrior that ever fled from Arthur. Then Bedwyr said to Cei, 'Dost know him?' 'I know him,' said Cei; 'that is Dillus the Bearded. There is no leash in the world may hold Drudwyn the whelp of Greid son of Eri, save a leash from the beard of him thou seest yonder. And that too will be of no use unless it be plucked alive with wooden tweezers from his beard; for it will be brittle, dead.' 'What is our counsel concerning that?' asked Bedwyr. 'Let us suffer him,' said Cei, 'to eat his fill of meat and after that he will fall asleep.' Whilst he was about this, they busied themselves making tweezers. When Cei knew for certain that he was asleep, he dug a pit under his feet, the biggest [127] in the world, and he struck him a blow mighty past telling, and pressed him down in the pit until they had entirely twitched out his beard with the tweezers; and after that they slew him outright.

And then the two of them went to Celli Wig in Cornwall, and a leash from Dillus the Bearded's beard with them. And Cei gave it into Arthur's hand, and thereupon Arthur sang this englyn:

> Cei made a leash
> From Dillus' beard, son of Eurei.
> Were he alive, thy death he'd be.

And because of this Cei grew angry, so that it was with difficulty the warriors of this Island made peace between Cei and Arthur. But nevertheless, neither for Arthur's lack of help, nor for the slaying of his men, did Cei have aught to do with him in his hour of need from that time forward.

And then Arthur said, 'Which of the marvels will it now be best to seek?' 'It will be best to seek Drudwyn the whelp of Greid son of Eri.'

A short while before this Creiddylad daughter of Lludd Silverhand went with Gwythyr son of Greidawl; and before he had slept with her there came Gwyn son of Nudd and carried her off by force. Gwythyr son of Greidawl gathered a host, and he came to fight with Gwyn son of Nudd. And Gwyn prevailed, and he took prisoner Greid son of Eri, Glinneu son of Taran, and Gwrgwst the Half-naked and Dyfnarth his son. And he took prisoner Pen son of Nethawg, and Nwython, and Cyledyr the Wild his son, and he slew Nwython and took out his heart, and compelled Cyledyr to eat his father's heart; and because of this Cyledyr went mad. Arthur heard tell of this, and he came into the North and summoned to him Gwyn son of Nudd and set free his noblemen from his prison, and peace was made between Gwyn son of Nudd and Gwythyr son of Greidawl. This is [128] the peace that was made: the maiden should remain in her father's house, unmolested by either side, and there should be battle between Gwyn and Gwythyr each May-calends for ever and ever, from that day till doomsday; and the one of them that should be victor on doomsday, let him have the maiden.

And when those lords had been thus reconciled, Arthur obtained Dun-mane the steed of Gweddw, and the leash of Cors Hun dred-claws.

After that Arthur made his way to Llydaw, and with him Mabon son of Mellt and Gware Golden-hair, to seek the two dogs of Glythfyr Ledewig. And when he had obtained them, Arthur went to the west of Ireland to seek out Gwrgi Seferi, and Odgar son of Aedd king of Ireland along with him. And after that Arthur went into the North and caught Cyledyr the Wild; and he went after Ysgithyrwyn Chief Boar. And Mabon son of Mellt went, and the two dogs of Glythfyr Ledewig in his hand, and Drudwyn the whelp of Greid son of Eri. And Arthur himself took his place in the hunt, and Cafall, Arthur's dog, in his hand. And Cadw of Prydein mounted Llamrei, Arthur's mare, and he was the first to bring the boar to bay. And then Cadw of Prydein armed him with a hatchet, and boldly and gallantly set upon the boar and split his head in two. And Cadw took the tusk. It was not the dogs which Ysbaddaden had named to Culhwch which killed the boar, but Cafall, Arthur's own dog.

And after Ysgithyrwyn Chief Boar was slain, Arthur and his host went to Celli Wig in Cornwall; and thence he sent Menw son of Teirgwaedd to see whether the treasures were between the two ears of Twrch Trwyth—so mean a thing would it be to go to fight with him, had he not those treasures. However, it was certain that he was there; he had already laid waste the third part of Ireland. Menw went [129] to seek them out. He saw them in Esgeir Oerfel in Ireland. And Menw transformed himself into the likeness of a bird and alighted over his lair and sought to snatch one of the treasures away from him. But for all that he got nothing save one of his bristles. The other arose in his might and shook himself so that some of his poison caught him. And after that Menw was never without scathe.

After that Arthur sent a messenger to Odgar son of Aedd king of Ireland, to ask for the cauldron of Diwrnach the Irishman, his overseer. Odgar besought him to give it. Said Diwrnach, 'God knows, though he should be the better for getting one glimpse of it, he should not have it.' And Arthur's messenger came back from

Ireland with a nay. Arthur set out and a light force with him, and
went in Prydwen his ship, and came to Ireland, and they made for
the house of Diwrnach the Irishman. The hosts of Odgar took note
of their strength; and after they had eaten and drunk their fill
Arthur demanded the cauldron. He made answer that were he to
give it to any one, he would have given it at the word of Odgar
king of Ireland. When he had spoken them nay, Bedwyr arose and
laid hold of the cauldron and put it on the back of Hygwydd,
Arthur's servant; he was brother by the same mother to Cacamwri,
Arthur's servant. His office was always to carry Arthur's cauldron
and to kindle fire under it. Llenlleawg the Irishman seized Caledfwlch and swung it in a round and he slew Diwrnach the Irishman
and all his host. The hosts of Ireland came and fought with them.
And when the hosts were utterly routed Arthur and his men went
on board ship before their very eyes, and with them the cauldron
full of the treasures of Ireland. And they disembarked at the house
of Llwydeu son of Cel Coed, at Porth Cerddin in Dyfed. And
Mesur-y-Peir is there.[130]

And then Arthur gathered together what warriors there were
in the Island of Britain and its three adjacent islands, and what
there were in France and Brittany and Normandy and the Summer
Country, and what there were of picked dogs and horses of renown.
And with all those hosts he went to Ireland, and at his coming there
was great fear and trembling in Ireland. And when Arthur had
come to land, there came to him the saints of Ireland to ask his
protection. And he granted them protection, and they gave him
their blessing. The men of Ireland came to Arthur and gave him a
tribute of victuals. Arthur came to Esgeir Oerfel in Ireland, to the
place where Twrch Trwyth was, and his seven young pigs with
him. Dogs were let loose at him from all sides. That day until
evening the Irish fought with him; nevertheless he laid waste one
of the five provinces of Ireland. And on the morrow Arthur's war-
band fought with him: save for what evil they got from him, they
got nothing good. The third day Arthur himself fought with him,
nine nights and nine days: he slew of his pigs but one pigling. His
men asked Arthur what was the history of that swine, and he told
them: 'He was a king, and for his wickedness God transformed him
into a swine.'

Arthur sent Gwrhyr Interpreter of Tongues to seek to have

word with him. Gwrhyr went in the form of a bird and alighted above the lair of him and his seven young pigs. And Gwrhyr Interpreter of Tongues asked him, 'For His sake who made thee in this shape, if you can speak, I beseech one of you to come and talk with Arthur.' Grugyn Silver-bristle made answer. Like wings of silver were all his bristles; what way he went through wood and meadow one could discern from how his bristles glittered. This was the answer Grugyn gave: 'By Him who made us in this shape, we will neither do nor say aught for Arthur. Harm enough hath God wrought us, to have made us in this shape, without you too coming to fight with us.' 'I tell you, Arthur will fight for the comb, the razor and the shears which are [131] between the two ears of Twrch Trwyth.' Said Grugyn, 'Until first his life be taken, those treasures will not be taken. And to-morrow in the morning we will set out hence and go into Arthur's country, and there we will do all the mischief we can.'

They set out by sea towards Wales; and Arthur and his hosts, his horses and his dogs, went aboard Prydwen, and in the twinkling of an eye they saw them. Twrch Trwyth came to land at Porth Cleis in Dyfed. That night Arthur came as far as Mynyw. On the morrow Arthur was told they had gone by, and he overtook him killing the cattle of Cynwas Cwryfagyl, after slaying what men and beasts were in Deu Gleddyf before the coming of Arthur.

From the time of Arthur's coming, Twrch Trwyth made off thence to Preseleu. Arthur and the hosts of the world came thither. Arthur sent his men to the hunt, Eli and Trachmyr, and Drudwyn the whelp of Greid son of Eri in his own hand; and Gwarthegydd son of Caw in another quarter, with the two dogs of Glythfyr Ledewig in his hand; and Bedwyr with Arthur's dog Cafall in his hand. And he ranged all the warriors on either side the Nyfer. There came the three sons of Cleddyf Difwlch, men who had won great fame at the slaying of Ysgithyrwyn Chief Boar. And then he set out for Glyn Nyfer and came to Cwm Cerwyn, and there he stood at bay. And he then slew four of Arthur's champions, Gwarthegydd son of Caw, Tarawg of Allt Clwyd, Rheiddwn son of Eli Adfer, and Isgofan the Generous. And after he had slain those men, again he stood at bay against them there, and slew Gwydre son of Arthur, Garselit the Irishman, Glew son of Ysgawd, and Isgawyn son of Banon. And then he himself was wounded.

And the morrow's morn at point of day some of the men
caught up with him. And then he slew Huandaw and Gogigwr
and Penpingon, the three servants of Glewlwyd Mighty-grasp, so
that God knows he had never a servant [132] left to him in the
world, save only Llaesgymyn, a man for whom none was the
better. And over and above those he slew many a man of the country, and Gwlyddyn the Craftsman, Arthur's chief builder. And then
Arthur caught up with him at Peluniawg, and he then slew
Madawg son of Teithion, and Gwyn son of Tringad son of Neued,
and Eiriawn Penlloran. And thence he went to Aber Tywi. And
there he stood at bay against them, and he then slew Cynlas son of
Cynan and Gwilenhin king of France. Thereafter he went to Glyn
Ystun, and then the men and dogs lost him.

Arthur summoned to him Gwyn son of Nudd and asked him
whether he knew aught of Twrch Trwyth. He said he did not.
Thereupon all the huntsmen went to hunt the pigs as far as Dyffryn Llychwr. And Grugyn Silver-bristle and Llwydawg the Hewer
dashed into them and slew the huntsmen so that not a soul of them
escaped alive, save one man only. So Arthur and his hosts came to
the place where Grugyn and Llwydawg were. And then he let loose
upon them all the dogs that had been named to this end. And at
the clamour that was then raised, and the barking, Twrch Trwyth
came up and defended them. And ever since they had crossed the
Irish Sea, he had not set eyes on them till now. Then was he beset
by men and dogs. With might and with main he went to Mynydd
Amanw, and then a pigling was slain of his pigs. And then they
joined with him life for life, and it was then Twrch Llawin was
slain. And then another of his pigs was slain, Gwys was his name.
And he then went to Dyffryn Amanw, and there Banw and Benwig
were slain. Not one of his pigs went with him alive from that place,
save Grugyn Silver-bristle and Llwydawg the Hewer.

From that place they went to Llwch Ewin, and Arthur caught
up with him there. Then he stood at bay. And then he slew Echel
Big-hip, and Arwyli son of [133] Gwyddawg Gwyr, and many a man
and dog besides. And after that they went on to Lywch Tawy.
Grugyn Silver-bristle then parted from them, and Grugyn thereafter
made for Din Tywi. And he proceeded then into Ceredigiawn, and
Eli and Trachmyr with him, and a multitude along with them
besides. And he came as far as Garth Grugyn. And there Grugyn

was slain in their midst, and he slew Rhuddfyw Rhys and many a man with him. And then Llwydawg went on to Ystrad Yw. And there the men of Llydaw met with him, and he then slew Hir Peisawg king of Llydaw, and Llygadrudd Emys and Gwrfoddw, Arthur's uncles, his mother's brothers. And there he himself was slain.

Twrch Trwyth went then between Tawy and Ewyas. Arthur summoned Cornwall and Devon to meet him at the mouth of the Severn. And Arthur said to the warriors of this Island: 'Twrch Trwyth has slain many of my men. By the valour of men, not while I am alive shall he go into Cornwall. I will pursue him no further, but I will join with him life for life. You, do what you will.' And by his counsel a body of horsemen was sent, and the dogs of the Island with them, as far as Ewyas, and they beat back thence to the Severn, and they waylaid him there with what tried warriors there were in this Island, and drove him by sheer force into Severn. And Mabon son of Modron went with him into Severn, on Gwyn Dun-mane the steed of Gweddw, and Goreu son of Custennin and Menw son of Teirgwaedd, between Llyn Lliwan and Aber Gwy. And Arthur fell upon him, and the champions of Britain along with him. Osla Big-knife drew near, and Manawydan son of Llŷr, and Cacamwri, Arthur's servant, and Gwyngelli, and closed in on him. And first they laid hold of his feet, and soused him in Severn till it was flooding over him. On the one side Mabon son of Modron spurred his horse and took the razor from him, and on the other Cyledyr the Wild, on another horse, plunged into Severn with him and took from him [134] the shears. But or ever the comb could be taken he found land with his feet; and from the moment he found land neither dog nor man nor horse could keep up with him until he went into Cornwall. Whatever mischief was come by in seeking those treasures from him, worse was come by in seeking to save the two men from drowning. Cacamwri, as he was dragged forth, two quernstones dragged him into the depths. As Osla Big-knife was running after the boar, his knife fell out of its sheath and he lost it; and his sheath thereafter being full of water, as he was dragged forth, it dragged him back into the depths.

Then Arthur went with his hosts until he caught up with him in Cornwall. Whatever mischief was come by before that was play to what was come by then in seeking the comb. But from mischief to mischief the comb was won from him. And then he was forced out of Cornwall and driven straight forward into the sea. From that time forth never a one has known where he went, and Aned and Aethlem with him. And Arthur went thence to Celli Wig in Cornwall, to bathe himself and rid him of his weariness.

Said Arthur, 'Is there any of the marvels still unobtained?' Said one of the men, 'There is: the blood of the Black Witch, daughter of the White Witch, from the head of the Valley of Grief in the uplands of Hell.' Arthur set out for the North and came to where the hag's cave was. And it was the counsel of Gwyn son of Nudd and Gwythyr son of Greidawl that Cacamwri and Hygwydd his brother be sent to fight with the hag. And as they came inside the cave the hag grabbed at them, and caught Hygwydd by the hair of his head and flung him to the floor beneath her. And Cacamwri seized her by the hair of her head, and dragged her to the ground off Hygwydd, but she then turned on Cacamwri and dressed them down both and disarmed them, and drove them out squealing and squalling. And Arthur was angered to see his two servants well nigh [135] slain, and he sought to seize the cave. And then Gwyn and Gwythyr told him, 'It is neither seemly nor pleasant for us to see thee scuffling with a hag. Send Long Amren and Long Eiddil into the cave.' And they went. But if ill was the plight of the first two, the plight of those two was worse, so that God knows not one of the whole four could have stirred from the place, but for the way they were all four loaded on Llamrei, Arthur's mare. And then Arthur seized the entrance to the cave, and from the entrance he took aim at the hag with Carnwennan his knife, and struck her across the middle until she was as two tubs. And Cadw of Prydein took the witch's blood and kept it with him.

And then Culhwch set forth, and Goreu son of Custennin with him, and every one that wished ill to Ysbaddaden Chief Giant, and those marvels with them to his court. And Cadw of Prydein came to shave his beard, flesh and skin to the bone, and his two ears outright. And Culhwch said, 'Hast had thy shave, man?' 'I have,' said he. 'And is thy daughter mine now?' 'Thine,' said he. 'And thou needst not thank me for that, but thank Arthur who has secured her for thee. Of my own free will thou shouldst never have had her. And it is high time to take away my life.' And then Goreu son of Custennin caught him by the hair of his head and dragged him behind him to the mound, and cut off his head, and set it on the bailey-stake. And he took possession of his fort and his dominions.

And that night Culhwch slept with Olwen, and she was his only wife so long as he lived. And the hosts of Arthur dispersed, every one to his country.

And in this wise did Culhwch win Olwen daughter of Ysbaddaden Chief Giant.[136]

GEOFFREY OF MONMOUTH

Historia Regum Britanniae (c. 1136)

From *History of the Kings of Britain,* trans. Sebastian Evans, rev. Charles W. Dunn (New York: E. P. Dutton & Co., Inc., 1958).

BOOK I, CHAPTER 1:

EPISTLE DEDICATORY TO ROBERT, EARL OF GLOUCESTER

Oftentimes in turning over in mine own mind the many themes that might be subject-matter of a book, my thoughts would fall upon the plan of writing a history of the Kings of Britain, and in my musings thereupon meseemed it a marvel that, beyond such mention as Gildas and Bede have made of them in their luminous tractate, nought could I find as concerning the kings that had dwelt in Britain before the Incarnation of Christ, nor nought

even as concerning Arthur and the many others that did succeed
him after the Incarnation, albeit that their deeds be worthy of
praise everlasting and be as pleasantly rehearsed from memory by
word of mouth in the traditions of many peoples as though they
had been written down. Now, whilst I was thus thinking upon
such matters, Walter, Archdeacon of Oxford, a man learned not
only to the art of eloquence, but in the histories of foreign lands,
offered me a certain most ancient book in the British language that
did set forth the doings of them all in due succession and order
from Brute, the first King of the Britons, onward to Cadwallader,
the son of Cadwallo, all told in stories of exceeding beauty. At
his request, therefore, albeit that never have I gathered gay flowers
of speech in other men's little gardens, and am content with mine
own rustic manner of speech and mine own writing-reeds, have I
been at the pains to translate this volume into the Latin tongue.
For had I besprinkled my page [3] with high-flown phrases, I should
only have engendered a weariness in my readers by compelling
them to spend more time over the meaning of the words than upon
understanding the drift of my story.

Unto this my little work, therefore, do thou, Robert, Earl of
Gloucester, show favour in such wise that it may be so corrected
by thy guidance and counsel as that it may be held to have sprung,
not from the poor little fountain of Geoffrey of Monmouth, but
rather from thine own deep sea of knowledge, and to savour of thy
salt. Let it be held to be thine own offspring, as thou thyself art offspring of the illustrious Henry, King of the English. Let it be thine,
as one that hath been nurtured in the liberal arts by philosophy,
and called unto the command of our armies by thine own inborn
prowess of knighthood; thine, whom in these our days Britain
haileth with heart-felt affection as though in thee she had been
vouchsafed a second Henry.[4]

BOOK VI, CHAPTER 9:

Now Vortigern, when he saw that there was none his
peer in the kingdom, set the crown thereof upon his own head
and usurped precedence over all his fellow-princes. Howbeit, his
treason at last being publicly known, the people of the neighbour-

ing out-islands, whom the Picts had led with them into Scotland, raised an insurrection against him. For the Picts, indignant that their comrades-in-arms had been thus put to death on account of Constans, were minded to revenge them upon Vortigern, who was thereby not only sore troubled in his mind, but suffered heavy loss amongst his fighting-men in battle. On the other hand, he was still more sorely troubled in his mind by his dread of Aurelius Ambrosius and his brother Uther Pendragon, who, as hath been said, had fled into Little Britain for fear of him. For day after day was it noised in his ears that they were now grown men, and had builded a passing huge fleet, being minded to adventure a return unto the kingdom that of right was their own.[120]

CHAPTER 15:

After the death of his son, Vortigern was restored unto his kingdom, and at the earnest instance of his wife sent his envoys to Hengist in Germany, bidding him to come back again to Britain, but privily and with but few men only, as he was afeard, in case he came over otherwise, a quarrel might arise betwixt the barbarians and the men of the country. Howbeit, Hengist, hearing of Vortimer's death, raised an army of three hundred thousand armed men, and fitting out a fleet returned unto Britain. But as soon as the arrival of so huge a host was reported to Vortigern and the princes of the realm, they took it in high dudgeon, and taking counsel together, resolved to give them battle and drive them forth of their coasts. Tidings of this resolve were at once sent to Hengist by messengers from his daughter, and he forthwith bethought him what were best to do by way of dealing a counter-stroke. After much brooding over divers devices, the one that he made choice of in the end was to betray the people of the [129] kingdom by approaching them under a show of peace. He accordingly sent messengers unto the King, bidding them bear him on hand that he had not brought with him so mighty an armament either with any purpose that they should remain with him in the country, or in any way do violence unto any that dwelt therein. The only reason he had brought them with him was that he believed Vortimer to be still alive, and that in case Vortimer had opposed his return he was minded to be able to withstand him. Howbeit, now that he had no longer any doubt as to Vortimer being dead, he committed himself and his people unto Vortigern to dispose of as he should think best. So many of their number as he might wish to retain with him in the kingdom might stay, and so many as he might desire to dismiss he was quite willing should return to Germany forthwith. And, in case Vortigern were willing to accept these terms, he himself besought him to name a day and place for them to meet, and they would then settle everything in accordance with his wishes. When such a message was brought unto Vortigern, passing well pleased was he, for he had no mind that Hengist should again depart. So at last he bade that the men of the country and the Saxons should meet together nigh the monastery of Ambrius on the Kalends of May, then just drawing on, that then and there the matter might be solemnly settled. When this had been agreed on both sides, Hengist, having a mind to put in use a new manner of treason, made ordinance unto his comrades that every single one of them should have a long knife hidden in his legging, and when the Britons were without any suspicion discussing the business of the meeting, he himself would give the signal, "Nimeth eoure saxas" ("Take your daggers"), whereupon each of them should be ready to fall boldly upon the Briton standing next him, and drawing forth his knife to cut his throat as swiftly as might be. Accordingly on the day appointed all met together in the city [130] aforesaid, and began to talk together over the terms of peace, and when Hengist espied that the hour had come when his treachery might most meetly be carried into effect he shouted out, "Nimeth eoure saxas!" and forthwith laid hold on Vortigern and held him fast by his royal robe. The moment the Saxons heard the signal they drew forth their long knives and set upon the princes that stood around, thinking of nought less at the instant, and cut the throats of about four hundred and sixty amongst the barons and earls, whose bodies the blessed Eldad did afterward bury and place in the ground after Christian fashion not far from Kaercaradoc, that is now called Salisbury, within the church-yard that lieth about the monastery of Abbot Ambrius, who of yore had been the founder thereof. For all of them had come unarmed, nor never deemed of aught save treating as touching the peace. Whence it came to pass that the others, which had come for nought but treachery, could lightly slay them as having done off their arms. Howbeit the Paynims wrought not their treason un-avenged, for many of themselves were slain whilst that they were putting the others to death the Britons snatching the stones and sticks that were on the ground, and in self-defence doing no little execution upon their betrayers.

CHAPTER 16:

Among others that were there was Eldol, Earl of Gloucester, who, seeing this treachery, took up a stake that he had found by chance and defended himself therewithal. Whomsoever he got at, he brake him the limb he struck and sent him to hell forthwith. Of some the head, of others the arms, of others the shoulders, and of many more the legs did he shatter, causing no small terror wheresoever he laid about him, nor did he stir from the place before he had slain seventy men [131] with the stake he wielded. But when he could no longer stand his ground against so great a multitude, he made shift to get away and betook him to his own city. Many fell on the one side and the other, but the Saxons had the upper hand, as well they might, seeing that the Britons, never suspecting aught of the kind, had come without arms and so were the less able to defend them. Natheless, they were not minded to slay Vortigern, but bound him and threatened him with death, and demanded his cities and strong places as ransom for his life; he straightway granting all they had a mind to, so he were allowed to escape on live. And when he had confirmed this unto them by oath, they loosed him from his fetters, and marching first of all upon London, took that city, taking next York and Lincoln as well as Winchester, and ravaging the country at will, slaying the country folk as wolves do sheep forsaken of their shepherd. When therefore Vortigern beheld so terrible a devastation, he betook him privily into the parts of Wales, not knowing what to do against this accursed people.

CHAPTER 17:

Howbeit, he at last took counsel of his wizards, and bade them tell him what he should do. They told him that he

ought to build him a tower exceeding strong, as all his other castles
he had lost. He sought accordingly in all manner of places to find
one fit for such a purpose and came at last unto Mount Snowden,
where, assembling a great gang of masons from divers countries,
he bade them build the tower. The stonemasons, accordingly, came
together and began to lay the foundations thereof, but whatsoever
they wrought one day was all swallowed up by the soil the next,
in such sort as that they knew not whither their work had van- [132]
ished unto. And when word was brought hereof unto Vortigern,
he again held counsel with his wizards to tell him the reason
thereof. So they told him that he must go search for a lad that had
never a father, and when he had found him should slay him and
sprinkle his blood over the mortar and the stones, for this, they
said, would be good for making the foundation of the tower hold
firm. Forthwith messengers are sent into all the provinces to look
for such manner of man, and when they came into the city that was
afterward called Carmarthen, they saw some lads playing before the
gate and went to look on at the game. And being weary with travel,
they sate them down in the ring and looked about them to see if
they could find what they were in quest of. At last, when the day
was far spent, a sudden quarrel sprang up betwixt a couple of
youths whose names were Merlin and Dinabutius. And as they
were wrangling together, saith Dinabutius unto Merlin: "What a
fool must thou be to think thou art a match for me! Keep thy
distance, prithee! Here am I, born of the blood royal on both sides
of the house; and thou? None knoweth what thou art, for never a
father hadst thou!" At that word the messengers lifted up their
faces, and looking narrowly upon Merlin, asked the bystanders
who he might be. They told them that none knew his father, but
that his mother was daughter of the King of South Wales, and that
she lived along with the nuns in St. Peter's Church in that same
city.

CHAPTER 18:

The messengers hurried off to the reeve of the city,
and enjoined him in the King's name that Merlin and his mother
should be sent unto the King. The reeve, accordingly, so soon as

he knew the errand whereon [133] they came, forthwith sent Merlin and his mother unto Vortigern for him to deal withal as he might list. And when they were brought into his presence, the King received the mother with all attention as knowing that she was of right noble birth, and afterward began to make inquiry as to who was the father of the lad. Unto whom she made answer: "As my soul liveth and thine, O my lord the King, none know I that was his father. One thing only I know, that on a time whenas I and the damsels that were about my person were in our chambers, one appeared unto me in the shape of a right comely youth and embracing me full straitly in his arms did kiss me, and after that he had abided with me some little time did as suddenly vanish away so that nought more did I see of him. Natheless, many a time and oft did he speak unto me when that I was sitting alone, albeit that never once did I catch sight of him. But after that he had thus haunted me of a long time, he lay with me for some while in the shape of a man and left me heavy with child. So much, my lord King, is my true story, and so much leave I unto thee to interpret aright, for none other have I known that is father unto this youth." Amazed at her words, the King commanded that Maugantius should be called unto him to declare whether such a thing might be as the lady had said. Maugantius was brought accordingly, and when he had heard the story from first to last, said unto Vortigern: "In the books of our wise men and in many histories have I found that many men have been born into the world on this wise. For, as Apuleius in writing as touching the god of Socrates doth make report, certain spirits there be betwixt the moon and the earth, the which we do call incubus dæmons. These have a nature that doth partake both of men and angels, and whensoever they will they do take upon them the shape of men, and do hold converse with mortal women. Haply one of these hath appeared unto this lady, and is the father of the youth." [134]

CHAPTER 19:

And when Merlin had hearkened unto all this, he came unto the King and said: "Wherefore have I and my mother been called into thy presence?" Unto whom Vortigern: "My wizards have declared it unto me as their counsel that I should seek out one that had never a father, that when I shall have sprinkled his blood upon the foundation of the tower my work should stand firm." Then said Merlin: "Bid thy wizards come before me, and I will convict them of having devised a lie." The King, amazed at his words, straightway bade his wizards come and set them down before Merlin. Unto whom spake Merlin: "Since ye know not what it is that doth hinder the foundation being laid of this tower, ye have given counsel that the mortar thereof should be slacked of my blood, that so the tower should stand forthwith. Now tell me, what is it that lieth hid beneath the foundation, for somewhat is there that doth not allow it to stand?" But the wizards were adread and held their peace. Then saith Merlin, that is also called Ambrosius: "My lord the King, call thy workmen and bid delve the soil, and a pool shalt thou find beneath it that doth forbid thy tower to stand." And when this was done, straightway a pool was found under the earth, the which had made the soil unconstant. Then Ambrosius Merlin again came nigh unto the wizards and saith: "Tell me now, ye lying flatterers, what is it that is under the pool?" But they were all dumb and answered unto him never a word. And again spake he unto the King, saying: "Command, O King, that the pool be drained by conduits, and in the bottom thereof shalt thou behold two hollow stones and therein two dragons asleep." The King, believing his words for that he had spoken true as touching the pool, commanded also that the pool should be drained. And when he [135] found that it was even as Merlin had said he marvelled greatly. All they that stood by were no less astonished at such wisdom being found in him, deeming that he was possessed of some spirit of God.[136]

BOOK VIII, CHAPTER 8:

Then Aurelius led his army unto York to beleaguer Octa, Hengist's son. And when he laid siege unto the city, Octa misdoubted whether he might withstand him and hold the city against so huge a host. After taking counsel thereupon, he issued forth along with the more noble of them that were with him, bearing a chain in his hand and with dust upon his head, and presented him before the King with these words: "My gods be vanquished, nor do I falter to acknowledge that it is thy God which reigneth and hath compelled so many nobles to come unto thee on this wise. Wherefore do thou accept of us and of this chain, and, save thou have mercy upon us, have us bound and doom us unto any punishment thou wilt." Aurelius was thereby moved to pity, and taking counsel, bade declare what should be done unto them. And when divers of them had delivered divers counsel, Eldad the Bishop rose up and spake his mind after this fashion: "The Gibeonites of their own will did come unto the children of Israel,[161] and beseeching mercy did obtain mercy. Shall we Christians, therefore, be worse than Jews and deny mercy unto these? Mercy is that they beseech, mercy let them have! Broad is this island of Britain, and in many places void of inhabitants. Let us therefore make covenant with them that, so we suffer them to dwell at least in our desert places, they shall be vassal unto us for ever." The King thereupon agreed unto Eldad's proposal, and had mercy upon them. Moreover, moved thereto by the ensample of Octa, came Eosa and the rest of them that had fled and begged for mercy. He assigned unto them, therefore, the country upon the borders of Scotland, and confirmed a covenant with them.

CHAPTER 9:

Having now triumphed over all his enemies, the King called together the earls and princes of the realm to meet him at York, and gave ordinance unto them to restore the churches which the Saxon people had destroyed. Howbeit, he himself began to rebuild the Metropolitan church of that city and the rest of the cathedral churches of the province. After a space of fifteen days, when he had stablished a gang of workmen in the several places, he repaired unto London, which the ravages of the enemy had not spared, and sore grieved at the destruction that had been wrought, recalled the residue of the citizens from all parts and set him to bring about their restoration. There also he made ordinance for the government of the kingdom, renewing the laws that had dropped on sleep, and allotting unto the grandchildren the possessions that their grandsires had lost. Whatsoever estates had lost all heirs he shared amongst his fellow-soldiers. For all his thought and intention was turned upon the restitution of the realm, the reformation of the churches, the renewal of [162] peace and law, and the administering of justice. He next went on to Winchester to restore it the same as the other cities, and when he had there established all that had to be stablished toward the restoration thereof, by advice of Bishop Eldad, he went unto the monastery nigh Kaercaradoc, that is now called Salisbury, where the earls and princes lay buried whom the accursed Hengist had betrayed. There was there a convent of three hundred brethren upon the Mount of Amesbury, who, as is said, was the founder thereof in days of old. When he looked around upon the place where they lay dead, he was moved to pity and tears began to flow. At last he fell to pondering within himself in what wise he might best make the place memorable, for worthy of remembrance did he deem the green turf that covered so many noble warriors that had died for their country.

CHAPTER 10:

Accordingly he called together from all quarters the master craftsmen in stone and wood, and bade them put forth their utmost skill to contrive some new kind of building that should stand for ever in memory of men so worthy. But all of them, mistrusting their own mastery in such a matter, were only able to meet him with a "Nay." Whereupon Tremorinus, Archbishop of Caerleon, came unto the King and saith he: "If man there be anywhere strong enow to carry out this ordinance into effect, let Merlin, Vortigern's prophet, set hand thereunto. For well I wot that never another man in thy kingdom is there that is brighter of wit than he, whether it be in foretelling that which shall be or in devising engines of artifice. Bid him come hither and set his wits to work, and I warrant he shall build thee a memorial to last!" Accordingly, when Aurelius had asked many questions about him, he sent [163] divers messengers through the divers countries of the kingdom to find and fetch him; and after they had journeyed throughout the provinces they found him in the country of Gwent, at the fountain of Galabes that he wont to haunt, and, telling him what it was they wanted, brought him unto the King. The King received him gladly, and bade him declare the future, being fain to hear marvellous things. Unto whom Merlin: "Mysteries of such kind be in no wise to be revealed save only in sore need. For, and I were to utter them lightly or to make laughter, the spirit that teacheth me would be dumb and would forsake me in the hour of need." At last, when he had in like manner denied them all, the King was not minded to ask him further about the future, but spake unto him of the work he did propose to construct. Unto whom Merlin:

"If thou be fain to grace the burial-place of these men with a work that shall endure for ever, send for the Dance of the Giants that is in Killare, a mountain in Ireland. For a structure of stones is there that none of this age could arise save his wit were strong enough to carry his art. For the stones be big, nor is there stone anywhere of more virtue, and, so they be set up round this plot in a circle, even as they be now there set up, here shall they stand for ever."

CHAPTER 11:

At these words of Merlin, Aurelius burst out laughing, and quoth he: "But how may this be, that stones of such bigness and in a country so far away may be brought hither, as if Britain were lacking in stones enow for the job?" Whereunto Merlin made answer: "Laugh not so lightly, King, for not lightly are these words spoken. For in these stones is a mystery, and a healing virtue against many ailments. Giants of old did carry them from the furthest ends of Africa and [164] did set them up in Ireland what time they did inhabit therein. And unto this end they did it, that they might make them baths therein whensoever they ailed of any malady, for they did wash the stones and pour forth the water into the baths, whereby they that were sick were made whole. Moreover, they did mix confections of herbs with the water, whereby they that were wounded had healing, for not a stone is there that lacketh in virtue of leechcraft." When the Britons heard these things, they bethought them that it were well to send for the stones, and to harry the Irish folk by force of arms if they should be minded to withhold them. At last they made choice of Uther Pendragon, the King's brother, with fifteen thousand men, to attend to this business. They made choice also of Merlin, so that whatsoever might have to be done should be dealt with according his wit and counsel. Then, as soon as the ships are ready, they put to sea and make for Ireland with a prosperous gale.

CHAPTER 12:

At that time was Gilloman King in Ireland, a youth of marvellous prowess, who, so soon as ever he heard of the Britons having landed in Ireland, got together a huge army and started forth to meet them. And when he had learned the reason wherefore they had come, he laughed, and saith he unto them that stood by:

"No wonder the craven Saxon folk were strong enough to lay waste the island of Britain when the Britons themselves are such gross-witted wiseacres. Who hath ever heard of such folly? Are the stones of Ireland any better than those of Britain that our kingdom should thus be challenged to fight for them? Arm yourselves, men, and defend your country, for never while life is in me shall they carry off from us the very smallest stone of the Dance." [165]

Uther accordingly, seeing that they were ready to fight, fell upon them straightway at the double-quick. Forthwith the Britons prevailed, and, his Irishmen all cut up and slain, forced Gilloman to flee for his life. When they had won the day they pressed forward to Mount Killare, and when they reached the structure of stones rejoiced and marvelled greatly. Whilst they were all standing around, Merlin came unto them and said: "Now, my men, try what ye can do to fetch me down these stones! Then may ye know whether strength avail more than skill, or skill than strength." Thereupon at his bidding they all with one accord set to work with all manner devices, and did their utmost to fetch down the Dance. Some rigged up huge hawsers, some set to with ropes, some planted scaling ladders, all eager to get done with the work, yet natheless was none of them never a whit the forwarder. And when they were all weary and spent, Merlin burst out on laughing and put together his own engines. At last, when he had set in place everything whatsoever that was needed, he laid the stones down so lightly as none would believe, and when he had laid them down, bade carry them to the ships and place them inboard, and on this wise did they again set sail and returned unto Britain with joy, presently with a fair wind making land, and fetching the stones to the burial-place ready to set up. When this was reported unto Aurelius, he sent messengers throughout the countries of Britain, bidding summon clergy and laity, and enjoining them when summoned to assemble at the Mount of Amesbury with rejoicing and honour to set up the stones again round the foresaid burial-place. Accordingly, in obedience to the edict, came pontiffs and abbots and folk of every single order that were his subjects, and when all were met together on the day appointed, Ambrosius set the crown upon his own head and celebrated the Whitsuntide festival right royally, giving up the three following days running to the holiday. Mean- [166] while such honours as lacked a holder he distributed as bounties unto them of his household as rewards for their toil in his service. At that time two of the Metropolitan Sees, York, to wit, and Caerleon, were vacant without their shepherds. Wherefore, being minded to consult the common wish of his peoples, he gave York unto Samson, a man of high dignity and illustrious by the depth of his piety; and Caerleon unto Dubric, whom the providence of God had before singled out as like to be right serviceable in that same place. And when he had settled these and other matters in his realm, he bade Merlin set up the stones that he had brought from Ireland around the burial-place. Merlin accordingly obeyed his ordinance, and set them up about the compass of the burial-ground in such wise as they had stood upon Mount Killare in Ireland, and proved yet once again how skill surpasseth strength.[167]

CHAPTER 19:

After this victory Uther marched unto the city of Dumbarton and made ordinance for settling that province, as well as for restoring peace everywhere. He also went round all the nations of the Scots, and made that rebellious people lay aside their savage ways, for such justice did he execute throughout the lands as never another of his predecessors had ever done before him. In his days did misdoers tremble, for they were dealt punishment without mercy. At last, when he had stablished his peace in the parts of the North, he went to London and bade that Octa and

Eosa should be kept in prison there. And when the Easter festival drew nigh, he bade the barons of the realm assemble in that city that he might celebrate so high holiday with honour by assuming the crown thereon. All obeyed accordingly, and repairing thither from the several cities, assembled together on the eve of the festival. The King, accordingly, celebrated the ceremony as he had proposed, and made merry along with his barons, all of whom did make great cheer for that the King had received them in such joyful wise. For all the nobles that were there had come with their wives and daughters as was meet on so glad a festival. Among the rest, Gorlois, Duke of Cornwall, was there, with his wife Igerna, that in beauty did surpass all the other dames of the whole of Britain. And when the King espied her amidst the others, he did suddenly wax so fain of her love that, paying no heed unto none of the others, he turned all his attention only upon her. Only unto her did he send [174] dainty tit-bits from his own dish; only unto her did he send the golden cups with messages through his familiars. Many a time did he smile upon her and spake merrily unto her withal. But when her husband did perceive all this, straightway he waxed wroth and retired from the court without leave taken. Nor was any that might recall him thither, for that he feared to lose the one thing that he loved better than all other. Uther, waxing wroth hereat, commanded him to return and appear in his court that he might take lawful satisfaction for the affront he had put upon him. And when Gorlois was not minded to obey the summons, the King was enraged beyond all measure and sware with an oath that he would ravage his demesnes so he hastened not to make him satisfaction. Forthwith, the quarrel betwixt the two abiding unsettled, the King gathered a mighty army together and went his way into the province of Cornwall and set fire to the cities and castles therein. But Gorlois, not daring to meet him in the field for that he had not so many armed men, chose rather to garrison his own strong places until such time as he obtained the succour he had besought from Ireland. And, for that he was more troubled upon his wife's account than upon his own, he placed her in the Castle of Tintagel on the seacoast, as holding it to be the safer refuge. Howbeit, he himself betook him into the Castle of Dimilioc, being afeard that in case disaster should befall him both might be caught in one trap. And when message of this was brought unto the King, he went unto the castle wherein Gorlois had ensconced him, and beleaguered him and cut off all access unto him. At length, at the end of a week, mindful of his love for Igerna, he spake unto one of his familiars named Ulfin of Rescraddeck: "I am consumed of love for Igerna, nor can I have no joy, nor do I look to escape peril of my body save I may have possession of her. Do thou therefore give me counsel in what wise I may fulfil my desire, for, and I do not, of [175] mine inward sorrow shall I die." Unto whom Ulfin: "And who shall give thee any counsel that may avail, seeing that there is no force that may prevail whereby to come unto her in the Castle of Tintagel? For it is situate on the sea, and is on every side encompassed thereby, nor none other entrance is there save such as a narrow rock doth furnish, the which three armed knights could hold against thee, albeit thou wert standing there with the whole realm of Britain beside thee. But, and if Merlin the prophet would take the matter in hand, I do verily believe that by his counsel thou mightest compass thy heart's desire."

The King, therefore, believing him, bade Merlin be called, for he, too, had come unto the leaguer. Merlin came forthwith accordingly, and when he stood in presence of the King, was bidden give counsel how the King's desire might be fulfilled. When he found how sore tribulation of mind the King was suffering, he was moved at beholding the effect of a love so exceeding great, and saith he: "The fulfilment of thy desire doth demand the practice of arts new and unheard of in this thy day. Yet know I how to give thee the semblance of Gorlois by my leechcrafts in such sort as that thou shalt seem in all things to be his very self. If, therefore, thou art minded to obey me, I will make thee like unto him utterly, and Ulfin will I make like unto Jordan of Tintagel his familiar. I also will take upon me another figure and will be with ye as a third, and in such wise we may go safely unto the castle and have access unto Igerna." The King obeyed accordingly, and gave heed strictly unto that which Merlin enjoined him. At last, committing the siege into charge of his familiars, he did entrust himself unto the arts and medicaments of Merlin, and was transformed into the semblance of Gorlois. Ulfin was changed into Jordan, and Merlin into Brithael in such sort as that none could have told the one from the other. They then went their way toward Tintagel, and at dusk hour ar- [176] rived at the castle. The porter, weening that the Duke had arrived, swiftly unmade the doors, and the three were admitted.

For what other than Gorlois could it be, seeing that in all things it seemed as if Gorlois himself were there? So the King lay that night with Igerna and enjoyed the love for which he had yearned, for as he had beguiled her by the false likeness he had taken upon him, so he beguiled her also by the feigned discourses wherewith he did full artfully entertain her. For he told her he had issued forth of the besieged city for naught save to see to the safety of her dear self and the castle wherein she lay, in such sort that she believed him every word, and had no thought to deny him in aught he might desire. And upon that same night was the most renowned Arthur conceived, that was not only famous in after years, but was well worthy of all the fame he did achieve by his surpassing prowess.

CHAPTER 20:

In the meantime, when the beleaguering army found that the King was not amongst them, they did unadvisedly make endeavour to breach the walls and challenge the besieged Duke to battle. Who, himself also acting unadvisedly, did straightway sally forth with his comrades in arms, weening that his handful of men were strong enow to make head against so huge a host of armed warriors. But when they met face to face in battle, Gorlois was amongst the first that were slain, and all his companies were scattered. The castle, moreover, that they had besieged was taken, and the treasure that was found therein divided, albeit not by fair casting of lots, for whatsoever his luck or hardihood might throw in his way did each man greedily clutch in his claws for his own. But by the time that this outrageous plundering had at last come to an end messengers had come unto Igerna to tell her of the Duke's [177] death and the issue of the siege. But when they beheld the King in the likeness of the Duke sitting beside her, they blushed scarlet, and stared in amazement at finding that he whom they had just left dead at the leaguer had thus arrived hither safe and sound, for little they knew what the medicaments of Merlin had accomplished. The King therefore, smiling at the tidings, and embracing the countess, spake saying: "Not slain, verily, am I, for lo, here thou seest me alive, yet, natheless, sore it irketh me of the destruction of my castle and the slaughter of my comrades, for that which next is to dread is lest the King should overtake us here and make us prisoners in this castle. First of all, therefore, will I go meet him and make my peace with him, lest a worst thing befall us." Issuing forth accordingly, he made his way unto his own army, and putting off the semblance of Gorlois again became Uther Pendragon. And when he understood how everything had fallen out, albeit that he was sore grieved at the death of Gorlois, yet could he not but be glad that Igerna was released from the bond of matrimony. Returning, therefore, to Tintagel, he took the castle, and not the castle only, but Igerna also therein, and on this wise fulfilled he his desire. Thereafter were they linked together in no little mutual love, and two children were born unto them, a son and a daughter, whereof the son was named Arthur and the daughter Anna.[178]

BOOK IX, CHAPTER 1:

After the death of Uther Pendragon, the barons of Britain did come together from the divers provinces unto the city of Silchester, and did bear on hand Dubric, Archbishop of Caerleon, that he should crown as king, Arthur, the late King's son. For sore was need upon them; seeing that when the Saxons heard of Uther's death they had invited their fellow-countrymen from Germany, and under their Duke Colgrin were bent upon exterminating the Britons. They had, moreover, entirely subdued all that part of the island which stretcheth from the river Humber, as far as the sea of Caithness. Dubric, therefore, sorrowing over the calamities of the country, assembled the other prelates, and did invest Arthur with the crown of the realm. At that time Arthur was a youth of fifteen years, of a courage and generosity beyond compare, whereunto his inborn goodness did lend such grace as that he was beloved of wellnigh all the peoples in the land. After he had been invested with the ensigns of royalty, he abided by his ancient wont, and was so prodigal of his bounties as that he began to run short of wherewithal to distribute amongst the huge multitude of knights that made repair unto him. But he that hath within him a bountiful nature along with prowess, albeit that he be lacking for a time,

natheless in no wise shall poverty be his bane for ever. Wherefore
did Arthur, for that in him did valour keep company with largesse,
make resolve to harry the Saxons, to the end that with their treasure he might make rich the retainers that [183] were of his own
household. And herein was he monished of his own lawful right,
seeing that of right ought he to hold the sovereignty of the whole
island in virtue of his claim hereditary. Assembling, therefore, all
the youth that were of his allegiance, he made first for York. And
when Colgrin was ware of this, he got together his Saxons, Scots,
and Picts, and came with a mighty multitude to meet him nigh the
river Douglas, where, by the time the battle came to an end, the
more part of both armies had been put to the sword. Natheless,
Arthur won the day, and after pursuing Colgrin's flight as far as
York, did beleaguer him within that city. Thereupon, Baldulf,
hearing of his brother's flight, made for the besieged city with six
thousand men to relieve him. For, at the time his brother had
fought the battle, he himself was upon the seacoast awaiting the
arrival of Duke Cheldric, who was just coming from Germany to
their assistance. And when he had come within ten miles of the
city, he was resolved to make a night march and fall upon them by
surprise. Howbeit, Arthur was ware of his purpose, and bade
Cador, Duke of Cornwall, go meet him that same night with six
hundred horse and three thousand foot. He, choosing a position on
the road whereby the enemy were bound to march, surprised them
by an assault on the sudden, and cutting up and slaying the
Saxons, drave Baldulf off in flight. Baldulf, distressed beyond measure that he could convey no succour to his brother, took counsel
with himself in what wise he might have speech of him, for he
weened that so he might get at him, they might together devise
some shift for the safety of them both. Failing all other means of
access unto him, he shaved off his hair and his beard, and did upon
him the habit of a jongleur with a ghittern, and walking to and fro
within the camp, made show as had he been a minstrel singing unto
the tunes that he thrummed the while upon his ghittern. And, for
that none suspected him, by little and little he [184] drew nigh unto
the walls of the city, ever keeping up the disguise he had taken
upon him. At last he was found out by some of the besieged, who
thereupon drew him up with cords over the wall into the city and
brought him unto his brother, who, overjoyed at the sight of him,

greeted him with kisses and embraces. At last, after talking over every kind of shift, when they had fallen utterly into despair of ever issuing forth, the messengers they had sent into Germany returned, bringing with them unto Scotland six hundred ships full of stout warriors under Duke Cheldric; and when Arthur's counsellors heard tell of their coming, they advised him to hold the leaguer no longer, for that sore hazard would it be to do battle with so mighty a multitude of enemies as had now arrived.

CHAPTER 2:

Arthur, therefore, in obedience to the counsel of his retainers, retired him into the city of London. Hither he summoned all the clergy and chief men of his allegiance and bade them declare their counsel as to what were best and safest for him to do against this inroad of the Paynim. At last, by common consent of them all, messengers are sent unto King Hoel in Brittany with tidings of the calamitous estate of Britain. For Hoel was sister's son unto Arthur, born unto Budicius, King of the Bretons. Where, so soon as he heard of the invasion wherewith his uncle was threatened he bade fit out his fleet, and mustering fifteen thousand men-at-arms, made for Southampton with the first fair wind. Arthur received him with all honour due, and the twain embraced the one the other over and over again.[185]

CHAPTER 3:

A few days later they set forth for the city of Kaerliud-coit, then besieged by the Paynim already mentioned, the which city lieth upon a hill betwixt two rivers in the province of Lindsey, and is otherwise called Lincoln. Accordingly, when they had come thither with their whole host, they did battle with the Saxons and routed them with no common slaughter, for upon that day fell six thousand of them, some part drowned in the rivers and some part smitten of deadly weapons. The residue, in dismay, forsook the siege and fled, but Arthur stinted not in pursuit until they had reached the forest of Caledon, wherein they assembled again after the fight and did their best to make a stand against him. When the battle began, they wrought sore havoc amongst the Britons, defending themselves like men, and avoiding the arrows of the Britons in the shelter afforded by the trees. When Arthur espied this he bade the trees about that part of the forest be felled, and the trunks set in a compass around them in such wise as that all ways of issuing forth were shut against them, for he was minded to beleaguer them therein until they should be starven to death of hunger. This done, he bade his companies patrol the forest, and abode in that same place three days. Whereupon the Saxons, lacking all victual and famishing to death, besought leave to issue forth upon covenant that they would leave all their gold and silver behind them so they might return unto Germany with nought but their ships only. They promised further to give them tribute from Germany and to leave hostages for the payment thereof. Arthur, taking counsel thereupon, agreed unto their petition, retaining all their treasure and the hostages for payment of the tribute, and granting only unto them bare permission to depart. Natheless, whilst [186] that they were ploughing the seas as they returned homeward, it repented them of the covenant they had made, and tacking about, they returned into Britain, making the shore at Totnes. Taking possession of the country, they devastated the land as far as the Severn sea, slaying the husbandmen with deadly wounds. Marching forth from thence they made for the country about Bath and besieged that city. When word of this was brought unto the King, astonied beyond measure at their wicked daring, he bade judgment be done upon their hostages and hanged them out of hand, and, abandoning the expedition whereby he intended to repress the Picts and Scots, hurried away to disperse the leaguer. Howbeit, that which did most sorely grieve him in this strait was that he was compelled to leave his nephew Hoel behind him lying sick in the city of Dumbarton. When at last he arrived in the province of Somerset, and beheld the leaguer nigh at hand, he spake in these words: "For that these Saxons, of most impious and hateful name, have disdained to keep faith with me, I, keeping my faith unto my God, will endeavour me this day to revenge upon them the blood of my countrymen. To arms, therefore, ye warriors, to arms, and fall upon yonder traitors like men, for, of a certainty, by Christ's succour, we cannot fail of victory!"

CHAPTER 4:

When he had thus spoken, the holy Dubric, Archbishop of Caerleon, went up on to the top of a certain mount and
cried out with a loud voice:

"Ye men that be known from these others by your Christian
profession, take heed ye bear in mind the piety ye owe unto your
country and unto your fellow-countrymen, whose slaughter by the
treachery of the Paynim shall be unto ye a disgrace everlasting save
ye press hardily forward to defend them. Fight ye there- [187] fore
for your country, and if it be that death overtake ye, suffer it willingly for your country's sake, for death itself is victory and a healing
unto the soul, inasmuch as he that shall have died for his brethren
doth offer himself a living sacrifice unto God, nor is it doubtful that
herein he doth follow in the footsteps of Christ who disdained not
to lay down His own soul for His brethren. Whosoever, therefore,
amongst ye shall be slain in this battle, unto him shall that death be
as full penance and absolution of all his sins, if so be he receive it
willingly on this wise."

Forthwith, thus cheered by the benison of the blessed man,
each one hastened to arm him to do his bidding, and Arthur himself doing upon him a habergeon worthy of a king so noble, did set
upon his head a helm of gold graven with the semblance of a
dragon. Upon his shoulders, moreover, did he bear the shield that
was named Pridwen, wherein, upon the inner side, was painted the
image of holy Mary, Mother of God, that many a time and oft did
call her back unto his memory. Girt was he also with Caliburn,
best of swords, that was forged within the Isle of Avallon; and the
lance that did grace his right hand was called by the name Ron, a
tall lance and a stout, full meet to do slaughter withal. Then, sta-
tioning his companies, he made hardy assault upon the Saxons that
after their wont were ranked wedge-wise in battalions. Natheless,
all day long did they stand their ground manfully maugre the Britons that did deliver assault upon assault against them. At last, just
verging upon sundown, the Saxons occupied a hill close by that
might serve them for a camp, for, secure in their numbers, the hill
alone seemed all the camp they needed. But when the morrow's

sun brought back the day, Arthur with his army clomb up to the
top of the hill, albeit that in the ascent he lost many of his men.
For the Saxons, dashing down from the height, had the better advantage in dealing their wounds, whilst they could also run far [188]
more swiftly down the hill than he could struggle up. Howbeit,
putting forth their utmost strength, the Britons did at last reach
the top, and forthwith close with the enemy hand to hand. The
Saxons, fronting them with their broad chests, strive with all their
endeavour to stand their ground. And when much of the day had
been spent on this wise, Arthur waxed wroth at the stubbornness
of their resistance, and the slowness of his own advance, and drawing forth Caliburn, his sword, crieth aloud the name of Holy Mary,
and thrusteth him forward with a swift onset into the thickest press
of the enemy's ranks. Whomsoever he touched, calling upon God,
he slew at a single blow, nor did he once slacken in his onslaught
until that he had slain four hundred and seventy men single-
handed with his sword Caliburn. This when the Britons beheld,
they followed him up in close rank dealing slaughter on every side.
Colgrin and Baldulf his brother fell amongst the first, and many
thousands fell besides. Howbeit, as soon as Cheldric saw the jeopardy
of his fellows, he turned to flee away.

CHAPTER 5:

The King having won the victory, bade Cador, Duke
of Cornwall, pursue the enemy, while he himself hastened his
march into Scotland, for word had thence been brought him that
the Scots and Picts were besieging Hoel in the city of Dumbarton,
wherein, as I have said, he was lying afflicted of grievous sickness,
and sore need it was he should come swiftly to his succour lest he
should be taken by the barbarians along with the city. The Duke
of Cornwall, accordingly, accompanied by ten thousand men, was
not minded, in the first place, to pursue the fleeing Saxons, deeming it better to make all speed to get hold of their ships and thus
forbid their embarking therein. As soon as he had taken possession [189] of the ships, he manned them with his best soldiers, who
could be trusted to take heed that no Paynim came aboard, in case
they should flee unto them to escape. Then he made best haste to

obey Arthur's orders by following up the enemy and slaying all he overtook without mercy. Whereupon they, who but just now had fallen upon the Britons with the all fury of a thunderbolt, straightway sneak off, faint of heart, some into the depths of the forest, others into the mountains and caves, anywhither so only they may live yet a little longer. At last, when they found all shelter failing, they march their shattered companies into the Isle of Thanet. Thither the Duke of Cornwall follows hard upon their heels, smiting them down without mercy as was his wont; nor did he stay his hand until after Cheldric had been slain. He compelled them to give hostages for the surrender of the whole residue.

CHAPTER 6:

Having thus established peace, he marched towards Dumbarton, which Arthur had already delivered from the oppression of the barbarians. He next led his army into Moray, where the Scots and Picts were beleaguered, for after they had thrice been defeated in battle by Arthur and his nephew they had fled into that province. When they had reached Loch Lomond, they occupied the islands that be therein, thinking to find safe refuge; for this lake doth contain sixty islands and receiveth sixty rivers, albeit that but a single stream doth flow from thence unto the sea. Upon these islands are sixty rocks plain to be seen, whereof each one doth bear an eyrie of eagles that there congregating year by year do notify any prodigy that is to come to pass in the kingdom by uttering a shrill scream all together in concert. Unto these islands accordingly the enemy had fled in order to avail them of the protection of the lake. But [190] small profit reaped they thereby, for Arthur collected a fleet and went round about the inlets of the rivers for fifteen days together, and did so beleaguer them as that they were famished to death of hunger by thousands. And whilst that he was serving them out on this wise arrived Gillamaur, King of Ireland, with a mighty host of barbarians in a fleet, to bring succour unto the wretched islanders. Whereupon Arthur left off the leaguer and began to turn his arms against the Irish, whom he forced to return unto their own country, cut to pieces without mercy. When he had won the victory, he again gave all his thoughts to doing away utterly the race of the Scots and Picts, and yielded him to treating them with a cruelty beyond compare. Not a single one that he could lay hands on did he spare, insomuch as that at last all the bishops of the miserable country assembled together with all the clergy of their obedience, and came unto him barefoot, bearing relics of the saints and the sacred objects of the church, imploring the King's mercy for the safety of their people. As soon as they came into his presence, they prayed him on their bended knees to have pity on the down-trodden folk, for that he had visited them with pains and penalties enow, nor was any need to cut off the scanty few that still survived to the last man. Some petty portion of the country he might allot unto them whereon they might be allowed to bear the yoke of perpetual bondage, for this were they willing to do. And when they had besought the King on this wise, he was moved unto tears for very pity, and, agreeing unto the petition of the holy men, granted them his pardon.

CHAPTER 7:

These matters ended, Hoel did explore the site of the foresaid lake, and marvelled greatly to behold how so many rivers, so many islands, so many rocks and so [191] many eyries of eagles did all so exactly agree in number. And while he thus marvelled, holding the same for a miracle, Arthur came unto him and told him there was another lake in the same province even yet more marvellous. "It lieth," saith he, "not far hence, and it hath twenty foot in breadth and the same measure in length, with but five foot of depth. Howbeit, within this square, whether it be by artifice of man or by ordinance of nature, do breed four manner fishes in the four corners thereof; nor never is a fish of one quarter found in any of the others. Moreover," saith he, "another lake is there in the parts of Wales nigh the Severn, which the men of that country do call Linligwan, whereinto when the sea floweth it is received as into a whirlpool or swallow, in suchwise as that the lake is never the fuller for the waters it doth ingulf so as to cover the margent of the banks thereof. Natheless, when the sea ebbeth again, it does spout forth the waters it hath sucked in as it were a mountain, and overplasheth and covereth the banks. At such a time, were the folk of all that country to stand anigh with their faces toward the lake and should be sprinkled of the spray of the waves upon their garments, they should scarce escape, if indeed they did at all escape, being swallowed up of the lake. Natheless, should they turn their back to the lake, they need have no fear of being sprinkled, even though they should stand upon the very brink."

CHAPTER 8:

Pardon granted unto the Scottish people, the King made for York, there to celebrate the forthcoming Christmas festival. And when he was entered into the city and beheld the desolation of the holy churches, he was sore grieved and moved unto compassion. For Samson the Archbishop had been driven forth along with all the other holy men of religion, and the half-burnt [192] churches had ceased from the offices of God, so fiercely had the fury of the Paynim prevailed. Forthwith he summoned a convocation of the clergy and people, and appointed Pyramus his chaplain unto the Metropolitan See; restored the churches that were cast down even to the ground, and did grace them with convents of religious both men and women. The barons also that had been driven out by the incursions of the Saxons did he restore unto their former honours.

CHAPTER 9:

In that city were three brethren born of blood royal, Loth, to wit, and Urian and Angusel, that had held the principality of those parts before the Saxons had prevailed. Being minded, therefore, to grant unto them as unto the others their hereditary rights, he restored unto Angusel the kingly power of the Scots, and conferred the sceptre of the people of Moray upon Urian. Howbeit, Loth, who in the days of Aurelius Ambrosius had married Arthur's own sister, who had borne unto him Gawain and Modred, he did reinstate in the Dukedom of Lothian and of the other provinces thereby that had appertained unto him aforetime. At last, when he had re-established the state of the whole country in its ancient dignity, he took unto him a wife born of a noble Roman family, Guenevere, who, brought up and nurtured in the household of Duke Cador, did surpass in beauty all the other dames of the island.

CHAPTER 10:

When the next summer came on he fitted out his fleet and sailed unto the island of Ireland, that he desired to subdue unto himself. No sooner had he landed than Gillamaur, beforementioned, came to meet him with [193] a host past numbering, purposing to do battle with him. But as soon as the fight began, his folk, naked and utterly unarmed, fled whithersoever they might find a place of refuge. Gillamaur was forthwith taken prisoner and compelled to surrender, and the rest of the princes of the country, smitten with dismay, likewise surrendered them after their King's ensample. All parts of Ireland thus subdued, he made with his fleet ifor Iceland, and there also defeated the people and subjugated the island. Next, for far and wide amongst the other islands it was rumoured that no country could stand against him, Doldavius, King of Gothland, and Gunvasius, King of the Orkneys, came of their own accord, and promising a tribute, did homage unto him. At the end of winter he returned into Britain, and re-establishing his peace firmly throughout the realm, did abide therein for the next twelve years.

CHAPTER 11:

At the end of this time he invited unto him all soever of most prowess from far-off kingdoms and began to multiply his household retinue, and to hold such courtly fashion in his household as begat rivalry amongst peoples at a distance, insomuch as the noblest in the land, fain to vie with him, would hold himself as nought, save in the cut of his clothes and the manner of his arms he followed the pattern of Arthur's knights. At last the fame of his bounty and his prowess was upon every man's tongue, even unto the uttermost ends of the earth, and a fear fell upon the Kings of realms oversea lest he might fall upon them in arms and they might lose the nations under their dominion. Grievously tormented of these devouring cares, they set them to repairing their cities and the towers of their cities, and builded them strongholds in places meet for defence, to the end that in case Arthur should lead an [194] expedition against them they might find refuge therein should need be. And when this was notified unto Arthur, his heart was uplifted for that he was a terror unto them all, and he set his desire upon subduing the whole of Europe unto himself. Fitting forth his fleets accordingly, he made first of all for Norway, being minded to set the crown thereof upon the head of Loth, his sister's son. For Loth was grandson of Sichelm, King of Norway, who at that time had died leaving the kingdom unto him. But the Norwegians disdained to receive him, and had raised one Riculf to the kingly power, deeming that, so they garrisoned their cities, he would be able to withstand Arthur himself. At that time Gawain, the son of Loth, was a youth of twelve years, and had been sent by his uncle to be brought up as a page in the service of Pope Sulpicius, from whom he had received arms. Accordingly, when Arthur, as I had begun to tell, landed upon the coast of Norway, King Riculf met him with the whole people of the Kingdom and did battle; but after much blood had been shed upon both sides, the Britons at last prevailed, and making an onset, slew Riculf with a number of his men. When they had won this victory they overran and set fire to the cities, scattering the country folk, nor did they cease to give full loose to their cruelty until they had submitted the whole of Norway as well as Denmark unto the dominion of Arthur. These countries thus conquered, as soon as Arthur had raised Loth to be King of Norway Arthur sailed for Gaul, and dividing his force into companies began everywhere to lay the country waste. The province of Gaul at that time had been committed to the charge of Flollo, tribune of Rome, who ruled it under the Emperor Leo. He, when he was aware of Arthur's arrival, summoned every soldier in arms that owned his allegiance and fought against Arthur, but in no wise might he stand against him. For the youth of all the islands he had conquered were in Arthur's company, whence it was [195] of common report that his army was so great that scarce of any the greatest might he be overcome. In his retinue, moreover, was the better part of the knighthood of Gaul, whom by his much largesse he had bound unto himself.

Flollo, therefore, when he saw that he had been worsted in the battle, forthwith forsaking the field, fled with a few of his men unto Paris. There, reassembling his straggling army, he put the city in estate of defence and again was fain to do battle with Arthur. But whilst he was thinking of strengthening his army by auxiliaries from the neighbouring countries, Arthur came upon him at unawares and besieged him in the city. At the end of a month, Flollo, taking it grievously to heart that his people should be famished to death, sent unto Arthur challenging him to single combat on condition that whichsoever of the twain should be conqueror should have the kingdom of the other. For he was of great stature, hardihood, and valour, and of his overweening confidence herein had sent this challenge hoping that it might open unto him a door of safety. When the message was brought unto Arthur, mightily was he rejoiced at Flollo's proposal, and sent back word that he was ready and willing to abide by the conditions thereof. Thereupon each did duly enter into covenant with the other, and the twain met in an island that is without the city, all the folk watching to see what might be the issue. Both were armed full seemly, and each bestrode a destrier of marvellous swiftness; nor was it easy to forecast which of the twain were most like to win the day. Taking their stand opposite each other, and couching lance in rest, they forthwith set spur to their steeds and smote together with a right mighty shock. But Arthur, who bare his spear the more heedfully, thrusted the same into the top of Flollo's breast, and shielding off the other's blow with all the force he might, bare him to the ground. Then, unsheathing his sword, he was hastening to smite him, when Flollo, on his legs again in an instant, ran upon [196] him with his spear levelled, and with a deadly thrust into his destrier's chest brought both horse and rider to the ground. When the Britons saw their King lying his length on the field, they thought he was slain and could scarce be withholden from breaking the covenant and setting on the Gauls with one accord. But before they had resolved to transgress the bounds of peace Arthur was quickly on his legs again, and, covering him with his shield, was hastily stepping up to meet Flollo, who was bearing down upon him. And now, standing up to each other man to man, they redouble buffet on buffet, each bent upon fighting it out to the death. At last Flollo found an opening and smote Arthur on the forehead, and, had not the crash of the stroke on the helmet blunted the edge of his sword, the wound might well have been Arthur's death. But when the blood welled forth, and Arthur saw his habergeon and shield all red therewithal, his wrath waxed yet more burning hot, and raising Caliburn aloft, with all his force he brought it down through the helmet on to the head of Flollo and clove it sheer in twain. With this stroke, Flollo fell, and beating the ground with his heels, gave up his ghost to the winds.

When the tidings was known throughout the army, the citizens all ran together, and, opening the gates, delivered themselves up unto Arthur. He, after thus achieving the victory, divided his army into two commands, giving one into commission unto Duke Hoel, and bidding him go conquer Guitard, Duke of the Poitevins, whilst he himself with the other command busied him with subduing the other provinces. Thereupon Hoel marched into Aquitaine, invaded the cities of the country, and after harassing Guitard in a number of battles, compelled him to surrender. He next laid waste Gascony with fire and sword, and subjugated the princes thereof. After a space of nine years, when he had subdued all the parts of Gaul unto his dominion, Arthur again came unto Paris and there held his court.[197] He there also summoned a convocation of the clergy and people, and did confirm the stablishment of the realm in peace and law. At that time, moreover, he made grant of Neustria, which is now called Normandy, unto Bedevere his butler, and the province of Anjou unto Kay his seneschal. Many other provinces also did he grant unto the noblemen that did him service in his household. At last, when all the states and peoples were stablished in his peace, he returned into Britain at the beginning of spring.

CHAPTER 12:

When the high festival of Whitsuntide began to draw nigh, Arthur, filled with exceeding great joy at having achieved so great success, was fain to hold high court, and to set the crown of the kingdom upon his head, to convene the Kings and Dukes that were his vassals to the festival so that he might the more worshipfully celebrate the same, and renew his peace more firmly amongst his barons. Howbeit, when he made known his desire unto his

familiars, he, by their counsel, made choice of Caerleon wherein to
fulfil his design. For, situate in a passing pleasant position on the
river Usk in Glamorgan, not far from the Severn sea, and abound-
ing in wealth above all other cities, it was the place most meet for
so high a solemnity. For on the one side thereof flowed the noble
river aforesaid whereby the Kings and Princes that should come
from oversea might be borne thither in their ships; and on the
other side, girdled about with meadows and woods, passing fair
was the magnificence of the kingly palaces thereof with the gilded
verges of the roofs that imitated Rome. Howbeit, the chiefest glories
thereof where the two churches, one raised in honour of the Martyr
Julius, that was right fair graced by a convent of virgins that had
dedicated them unto God, and the second, founded in the [198]
name of the blessed Aaron, his companion, the main pillars whereof
were a brotherhood of canons regular, and this was the cathedral
church of the third Metropolitan See of Britain. It had, moreover,
a school of two hundred philosophers learned in astronomy and in
the other arts, that did diligently observe the courses of the stars,
and did by true inferences foretell the prodigies which at that time
were about to befall unto King Arthur. Such was the city, famed
for such abundance of things delightsome, that was now busking
her for the festival that had been proclaimed. Messengers were sent
forth into the divers kingdoms, and all that owed allegiance
throughout the Gauls and the neighbour islands were invited unto
the court. Came accordingly Angusel, King of Albany, that is now
called Scotland; Urian, King of them of Moray; Cadwallo Lawirh,
King of the Venedotians, that now be called the North Welsh;
Stater, King of the Demeti, that is, of the South Welsh; Cador, King
of Cornwall; the Archbishops of the three Metropolitan Sees, to
wit, of London and York, and Dubric of Caerleon. He, Primate of
Britain and Legate of the Apostolic See, was of so meritorious a
piety that he could make whole by his prayers any that lay oppressed of any malady. Came also the Earls of noble cities; Morvid,
Earl of Gloucester; Mauron of Worcester; Anaraut of Salisbury;
Arthgal of Cargueir, that is now called Warwick; Jugein from
Leicester; Cursalem from Caichester; Kimmarc, Duke of Canterbury; Galluc of Salisbury; Urbgennius from Bath; Jonathal of
Dorset; Boso of Rhydychen, that is Oxford. Besides the Earls came
champions of no lesser dignity, Donaut map Papo; Cheneus map

Coil; Peredur map Eridur; Grifuz map Nogoid; Regin map Claud; Eddelein map Cledauc; Kincar map Bangan; Kimmarc; Gorbonian map Goit; Clofaut; Run map Neton; Kimbelin map Trunat; Cathleus map Catel; Kinlith map Neton, and many another beside, the names whereof be too long to tell. From the neighbour islands came [199] likewise Gillamaur, King of Ireland; Malvasius, King of Iceland; Doldavius, King of Gothland; Gunvasius, King of the Orkneys; Loth, King of Norway; Aschil, King of the Danes. From the parts oversea came also Holdin, King of Flanders; Leodegar, Earl of Boulogne; Bedevere the Butler, Duke of Normandy; Borel of Maine; Kay the Seneschal, Duke of Anjou; Guitard of Poitou; the Twelve Peers of the Gauls whom Guerin of Chartres brought with him; Hoel, Duke of Brittany, with the Barons of his allegiance, who marched along with such magnificence of equipment in trappings and mules and horses as may not easily be told. Besides all these, not a single Prince of any price on this side Spain remained at home and came not upon the proclamation. And no marvel, for Arthur's bounty was of common report throughout the whole wide world, and all men for his sake were fain to come.

CHAPTER 13:

When all at last were assembled in the city on the high day of the festival, the archbishops were conducted unto the palace to crown the King with the royal diadem. Dubric, therefore, upon whom the charge fell, for that the court was held within his diocese, was ready to celebrate the service. As soon as the King had been invested with the ensigns of kingship, he was led in right comely wise to the church of the Metropolitan See, two archbishops supporting him, the one upon his right hand side the other upon his left. Four Kings, moreover, to wit, those of Scotland, Cornwall, and North and South Wales, went before him, bearing before him, as was their right, four golden swords. A company of clerics in holy orders of every degree went chanting music marvellous sweet in front. Of the other party, the archbishops and pontiffs led the Queen, crowned with laurel and wearing her own ensigns, unto the church [200] of the virgins dedicate. The four Queens, moreover, of the four Kings already mentioned, did bear before her according to wont and custom four white doves, and the ladies that were present did follow after her rejoicing greatly. At last, when the procession was over, so manifold was the music of the organs and so many were the hymns that were chanted in both churches, that the knights who were there scarce knew which church they should enter first for the exceeding sweetness of the harmonies in both. First into the one and then into the other they flocked in crowds, nor, had the whole day been given up to the celebration, would any have felt a moment's weariness thereof. And when the divine services had been celebrated in both churches, the King and Queen put off their crowns, and doing on lighter robes of state, went to meat, he to his palace with the men, she to another palace with the women. For the Britons did observe the ancient custom of the Trojans, and were wont to celebrate their high festival days, the men with the men and the women with the women severally. And when all were set at table according as the rank of each did demand, Kay the Seneschal, in a doublet furred of ermines, and a thousand youths of full high degree in his company, all likewise clad in ermines, did serve the meats along with him. Of the other part, as many in doublets furred of vair did follow Bedevere the Butler, and along with him did serve the drinks from the divers ewers into the manifold-fashioned cups. In the palace of the Queen no less did numberless pages, clad in divers brave liveries, offer their service each after his office, the which were I to go about to describe I might draw out my history into an endless prolixity. For at that time was Britain exalted unto so high a pitch of dignity as that it did surpass all other kingdoms in plenty of riches, in luxury of adornment, and in the courteous wit of them that dwelt therein. Whatsoever knight in the land was of renown for his prowess did wear his clothes and his arms all of [201] one same colour. And the dames, no less witty, would apparel them in like manner in a single colour, nor would they deign have the love of none save he had thrice approved him in the wars. Wherefore at that time did dames wax chaste and knights the nobler for their love.

CHAPTER 14:

Refreshed by their banqueting, they go forth into the fields without the city, and sundry among them fall to playing at sundry manner games. Presently the knights engage in a game on horseback, making show of fighting a battle whilst the dames and damsels looking on from the top of the walls, for whose sake the courtly knights make believe to be fighting, do cheer them on for the sake of seeing the better sport. Others elsewhere spend the rest of the day in shooting arrows, some in tilting with spears, some in flinging heavy stones, some in putting the weight; others again in playing chess or at the dice or in a diversity of other games, but all without wrangling; and whosoever had done best in his own game was presented by Arthur with a boon of price. And after the first three days had been spent on this wise, upon the fourth day all they that had done service in virtue of the office they held were summoned, and unto each was made grant of the honour of the office he held, in possession, earldom, to wit, of city or castle, archbishopric, bishopric, abbacy, or whatsoever else it might be.

CHAPTER 15:

Now the blessed Dubric, piously yearning after the life of a hermit, did depose himself from the archiepiscopal See, and David, the King's uncle, was consecrated in his [202] place, whose life was an ensample of all goodness unto them whom he had instructed in his doctrine. In the place, moreover, of the holy Samson, Archbishop of Dol, was appointed Teliau, an illustrious priest of Llandaff, with the consent of Hoel, King of Brittany, unto whom the good life and conditions of the man had commended him. The Bishopric of Silchester also was assigned to Maugan, and that of Winton unto Durian, and the pontifical mitre of Dumbarton unto Eleden. And whilst Arthur was allotting these benefices amongst them, behold, twelve men of ripe age and worshipful aspect, bearing branches of olive in their right hands in token of embassy, approach anigh the King with quiet step and words as quiet, and after saluting him, present unto him a letter on behalf of Lucius Hiberius conceived in these words:

"Lucius, Procurator of the Republic, unto Arthur, King of Britain, wisheth that which he hath deserved.

"With much marvel do I marvel at the insolence of thy tyranny. I do marvel, I say, thereat, and at the injury that thou hast done unto Rome. When I recall it to remembrance, I am moved unto wrath for that thou art so far beside thyself as not to acknowledge it, and art in no hurry to perceive what it is to have offended the Senate by thy wrongful deeds, albeit none better knoweth than thou that the whole world oweth vassalage thereunto. For the tribute of Britain that the Senate hath commanded thee to pay, and that hath been paid these many ages unto Gaius Julius, and unto his successors in the dignity of Rome, thou hast presumed to hold back in contempt of an empire of so lofty rank. Thou hast, moreover, seized from them Gaul, seized from them the province of the Burgundians, seized from them all the islands of the Ocean sea, the Kings whereof have paid tribute unto our forefathers from the time that the Roman power did in those parts prevail. Now, therefore, seeing that the Senate hath decreed to demand lawful redress of thee for heaping [203] so huge a pile of injuries upon them, I do command thee that thou appear in Rome, and do appoint the middle day of August in the year next coming as the term of thine appearance, there to make satisfaction unto thy lords, and to abide by such sentence as their justice shall decree. Wherein if thou dost make default, I myself will enter into thy dominions and will take heed by means of the sword to restore unto the Republic all those lands whereof thy mad presumption hath plundered her."

When this letter was read in presence of the King and his earls, Arthur went apart with them into the Giants' Tower, that is at the entrance of the palace, to treat with them as to what ordinance they ought to make as against a mandate of the kind. But, just as they had begun to mount the stair, Cador, Duke of Cornwall, that was ever a merry man, burst out on laughing before the King, and spake unto him on this wise:

"Until now it hath been my fear that the easy life the Britons have led this long time they have been at peace might make them wax craven, and utterly do away in them their renown in knighthood wherein they have ever been held to excel all other nations. For where use of arms is none, and nought is there to do but to toy with women and play at the dice and such like follies, none need doubt but that cowardice will tarnish all they once had of valour and honour and hardihood and renown. For nigh upon five year is it since we took to junketings of the kind for lack of the sports of Mars. Wherefore, methinks, God Himself hath put the Romans upon this hankering, that so He may deliver us from our cowardize and restore us to our prowess as it wont to be in the old days."

And whilst he was saying this and more to the same purpose, they were come to their seats, and when they were all set, Arthur spake unto them thus: [204]

CHAPTER 16:

"Comrades," saith he, "alike in adversity and in prosperity, whose prowess I have made proof of in giving of counsel no less than in deeds of arms, now earnestly bethink ye all in common, and make ye wise provision as to what ye deem best for us to do in face of such mandate as is this, for that which is diligently provided for by a wise man aforehand is the more easily borne withal when it cometh to the act. The more easily therefore shall we be able to withstand the attack of Lucius, if we shall first with one accord have applied us to weighing heedfully the means whereby we may best enfeeble the effect thereof. Which, verily, I deem not greatly to be dreaded of us, seeing that he doth with so unreasonable cause demand the tribute that he desireth to have from Britain. For he saith that we ought of right to give it unto him, for that it was paid unto Julius Caesar and the other his successors, who, invited by the discords of the ancient Britons, did of old invade Britain by force of arms, and did thus by violence subdue unto their power the country tottering as it then was with evil dissensions. But, forasmuch as it was on this wise that they possessed them of the country, it hath been only by an injustice that they have taken tribute thereof. For nought that is taken by force and violence can be justly possessed by him that did the violence. Wherefore a cause without reason is this that he pretendeth whereby he assumeth that we are of right his tributaries. Howbeit, sith that he thus presumeth to demand of us that which is unjust, let us also, by like reasoning, ask tribute of Rome from him, and let him that is the better man of the twain carry off that which he hath demanded to have. For, if it be that because Julius Caesar and the rest of the Roman Kings did conquer Britain in old days, he doth therefore de- [205] cree that tribute ought now to be paid unto him therefrom, in like manner do I now decree that Rome ought of right to pay tribute unto me, forasmuch as mine ancestors did of yore obtain possession of Rome. For Belinus, that most high and mighty King, did, with the assistance of his brother, Brennius, to wit, Duke of the Burgundians, take the city, and in the midmost of the market-place thereof did hang a score of the most noble Romans; and moreover, after they had taken it, did for many a year possess the same. Constantine, also, the son of Helena, no less than Maximian, both of them nigh of kindred unto myself, and both of whom, the one after the other, wore the crown of Britain, did also obtain the throne of the Roman empire. Bethink ye, therefore, whether we should ask tribute of Rome? But as to Gaul or the neighbour islands of the Ocean, no need is there of answer, inasmuch as he shrank from defending them at the time we took them out of his dominion."

And when he had thus spoken with more to the same effect, Hoel, King of Brittany, rising up in precedence of all the rest, made answer unto him on this wise:

CHAPTER 17:

"Were each one of us to take thought within himself, and were he able to turn over in his mind all the arguments upon every point in question, I deem that no better counsel could he find than this which the wise discretion of thy policy hath thus proposed unto our acceptance. For so exactly hath thy provident forethought anticipated our desire, and with such Tullian dew of eloquence hast thou besprinkled it withal, that we ought all of us to praise without ceasing the affection of a man so constant, the power of a mind so wise, the profit of counsel so exceeding apt to the occasion.[206] For if, in accordance with thine argument, thou art minded to go to Rome, I doubt not that the victory shall be ours, seeing that what we do justly demand of our enemies they did first begin to demand of us. For whosoever doth seek to snatch away from another those things that be his own doth deserve to lose his own through him whom he seeketh to wrong. Wherefore, sith that the Romans do desire to take from us that which is our own, beyond all doubt we shall take their own from them, so only we be allowed to meet them in the field. Behold, this is the battle most to be desired by all Britons. Behold the prophecies of the Sibyl that are witnessed by tokens true, that for the third time shall one of British race be born that shall obtain the empire of Rome. Already are the oracles fulfilled as to the two, sith that manifestly, as thou hast said, the two illustrious princes, Belinus and Constantine have worn the imperial crown of the Roman empire. And now in thee have we the third unto whom is promised that highest height of honour. Hasten thou, therefore, to receive that which God tarrieth not to grant. Hasten to subjugate that which doth desire to be subjugated! Hasten to exalt us all, who, in order that thou thyself mayst be exalted, will shrink not from receiving wounds, nay, nor from losing our very lives. And that thou mayst carry this matter through I will accompany thy presence with ten thousand men-at-arms."

CHAPTER 18:

When Hoel had made an end of his speech, Angusel also, King of Scotland, went on to declare what was his mind in the matter on this wise:

"From the moment that I understood my lord to be so minded as he hath said, such gladness hath entered into my heart that I know not how to utter it at this present. For in all our past campaigns that we have [207] fought against kings so many and so mighty, all that we have done meseemeth as nought so long as the Romans and the Germans remain unharmed, and we revenge not like men the slaughter they have formerly inflicted upon our fellow-countrymen. But now that leave is granted us to meet them in battle, I rejoice with exceeding great joy, and do yearn with desire for the day to come when we shall meet. I am athirst for their blood, even as for a well-spring when I had for three days been forbidden to drink. O, may I see that morrow! How sweet will be the wounds whether I give them or receive! when the right hand dealeth with right hand. Yea, death itself will be sweet, so I may suffer it in revenging our fathers, in safeguarding our freedom, in exalting our King! Let us fall upon these half men, and falling upon them, tread them under foot, so that when we have conquered them we may spoil them of their honours and enjoy the victory we have won. I will add two thousand horsemen to our army besides those on foot."

CHAPTER 19:

Thereafter the rest said what there was left to say. Each promised the knight's service that was due from him, so that besides those that the Duke of Brittany had promised, sixty thousand were reckoned from the island of Britain alone of armed men with all arms. But the Kings of the other islands, inasmuch as they had not yet taken up with the custom of having knights, promised foot soldiers as many as were due from them, so that out of the six islands, to wit, Ireland, Iceland, Gothland, the Orkneys, Norway, and Denmark, were numbered six score thousand. From the duchies of the Gauls, Flanders, Ponthieu, Normandy, Maine, Anjou, and Poitou, eighty thousand; from the twelve earldoms of those who came along with Guerin of Chartres,[208] twelve hundred. Altogether they made one hundred and eighty-three thousand two hundred besides those on foot, who were not so easy to reckon.

CHAPTER 20:

King Arthur, seeing that all those of his allegiance were ready with one accord, bade them return quickly unto their own countries and call out the armies they had promised; so that in the Kalends of August they might hasten unto the haven of Barfleur, and from thence advance with him to the frontiers of the Burgundians to meet the Romans. Howbeit, he sent word unto the Emperors through their ambassadors that in no wise would he pay the tribute, nor would go to Rome for the sake of obeying their decree, but rather for the sake of demanding from them what they had by judicial sentence decreed to demand from him. Thereupon the ambassadors depart, the Kings depart, the barons depart, nor are they slow to perform what they had been bidden to do.[209]

BOOK X, CHAPTER 1:

Lucius Hiberius, when he learnt that such answer had been decreed, by command of the Senate called forth the Kings of the Orient to make ready their armies and come with him to the conquest of Britain. In haste accordingly came Epistrophus, King of the Greeks; Mustensar, King of the Africans; Alifatima, King of Spain; Hirtacius, King of the Parthians; Boccus of the Medes; Sertorius of Libya; Serses, King of the Ituraeans; Pandrasus, King of Egypt; Micipsa, King of Babylon; Politetes, Duke of Bithynia; Teucer, King of Phrygia; Evander of Syria; Echion of Bœotia; Hippolytus of Crete, with the dukes and barons of their allegiance. Of the senatorial order, moreover, Lucius Catellus, Marius Lepidus, Gaius Metellus Cotta, Quintus Milvius Catulus, Quintus Carucius, and so many others as were reckoned to make up a total of forty thousand one hundred and sixty.

CHAPTER 2:

All needful ordinance made, they started on their expedition Britainwards at the beginning of the Kalends of August. When Arthur learned that they were upon the march, he made over the charge of defending Britain unto his nephew Mordred and his Queen Guenevere, he himself with his army making for Southampton, where he embarked with a fair breeze of wind. And whilst that he was thronged about with his [210] numberless ships, and was cleaving the deep with a prosperous course and much rejoicing, a passing deep sleep as about the middle of the night did overtake him, and in his sleep he saw in dream a certain bear flying in the air, at the growling whereof all the shores did tremble. He saw, moreover, a dreadful dragon come flying from the West that did enlumine the whole country with the flashing of his eyes. And when the one did meet the other there was a marvellous fight betwixt them, and presently the dragon leaping again and again upon the bear, did scorch him up with his fiery breath and cast down his shrivelled carcass to the earth. And thereby awakened, Arthur did relate his dream unto them that stood by, who expounded the same unto him saying that the dragon did betoken himself, but the bear some giant with whom he should encounter; that the fight did foretoken a battle that should be betwixt them, and that the dragon's victory should be his own. Natheless, Arthur did conjecture otherwise thereof, weening that such vision as had befallen him was more like to have to do with himself and the Emperor. At last, when the night had finished her course and the dawn waxed red, they came to in the haven of Barfleur, and pitching their tents thereby, did await the coming of the Kings of the islands and the Dukes of the neighbour provinces.

CHAPTER 3:

Meanwhile tidings are brought unto Arthur that a certain giant of marvellous bigness hath arrived out of the parts of Spain, and, moreover, that he hath seized Helena, niece of Duke Hoel, out of the hands of them that had charge of her, and hath fled with her unto the top of the mount that is now called of Michael, whither the knights of the country had pursued him. Howbeit, nought might they prevail against him, neither by sea [211] nor by land, for when they would attack him, either he would sink their ships with hugeous rocks, or slay the men with javelins or other weapons, and, moreover, devour many half-alive. Accordingly, in the following night at the second hour, he took with him Kay the Seneschal and Bedevere the Butler, and issuing forth of the tents, unknown to the others, started on his way towards the mount. For of such puissance was his own valour that he deigned not lead an army against such monsters, as holding himself singly enow for their destruction, and being minded to spirit up his men to follow his ensample. Now, when they came anigh the mount, they espied a great fire of wood a-blazing thereupon, and another smaller fire upon a smaller mount not far away from the first. So, being in doubt which were the one whereupon the giant had his wone, they sent Bedevere to spy out the certainty of the matter. He, therefore, finding a little boat, oared him first unto the smaller mount, for none otherwise might he attain thereunto, seeing that it was set in the sea. And when he began to climb up towards the top he heard above him the ullaloo of a woman wailing above him, and at first shuddered, for he misdoubted him the monster might be there. But quickly recovering his hardihood, he drew his sword from the scabbard and mounted to the very top, whereon nought found he save the fire of wood they had espied. But close thereby he saw a newly-made grave-mound, and beside it an old woman weeping and lamenting, who, so soon as she beheld him, stinted her tears forthwith and spake unto him on this wise: "O, unhappy man, what evil doom hath brought thee unto this place? Oh, thou that must endure the pangs unspeakable of death, woe is me for thee! Woe is me that a monster so accurst must this night consume the flower of thine youth! For that most foul and impious giant of execrable name shall presently be here, that did carry hither unto this mount the niece of our Duke, whom I have but just now sithence buried in [212] this grave, and me, her nurse, along with her. On what unheard of wise will he slay thee and tarry not? Alas for the sorrow and the doom! This most queenly foster-child of mine own, swooning with terror when this abhorred monster would fain have embraced her, breathed forth the life that now can never know the longer day that it deserved! But, as he could not with his foul lechery despoil her who was mine other soul, mine other life, mine other sweetness of gladness, so now inflamed with a detestable lust, he has pressed his force and violence upon me, all unwilling, as may God and mine eld bear witness! Flee thou, my beloved, flee lest he return to use me after his wont and find thee here, and rend thee limb from limb by a pitiable death!" But Bedevere, moved to the heart deeply as heart of man may be moved, soothed her with words of comfort, and promising her such cheer as speedy succour might bring, returned unto Arthur and told him the story of what he had found. Howbeit, Arthur, grieving over the damsel's hapless fate, bade them that they should allow him to attack the monster singly, but if need were should come unto his rescue and fall upon the giant like men. They made their way from thence unto the greater mount, and giving their horses in charge to their squires, began to climb the mount, Arthur going first. Just then that unnatural monster was by the fire, his chops all besmeared with the clotted blood of half-eaten swine, the residue whereof he was toasting on spits over the live embers. The moment he espied them, when nought was less in his thought, he hastened him to get hold of his club, which two young men could scarce have lifted from the ground. The King forthwith unsheathed his sword, and covering him with his shield, hurried as swiftly as hurry he might to be beforehand with him, and prevent his getting hold of the club. But the giant, not unaware of his intention, had already clutched it and smote the King upon the cover of his shield with such a buffet as that [213] the sound of the stroke filled the whole shore, and did utterly deafen his ears. But Arthur, thereupon blazing out into bitter wrath, lifted his sword and dealt him a wound upon his forehead, from whence the blood gushed forth over his face and eyes in such sort as wellnigh blinded his sight. Howbeit, the blow was not deadly, for he had warded his forehead with his club in such wise as to scape being killed outright. Natheless, blinded as he was with the blood welling forth, again he cometh on more fiercely than ever, and as a wild boar rusheth from his lay upon a huntsman, so thrust he in within the sweep of Arthur's sword, gripped him by the loins, and forced him to his knees upon the ground. Howbeit, Arthur, nothing daunted, soon slipped from out his clutches, and swiftly bestirring him with his sword, hacked the accursed monster first in one place and then in another, and gave him no respite until at last he smote him a deadly buffet on the head, and buried the whole breadth of his sword in his brain-pan. The abhorred beast roared aloud and dropped with a mighty crash like an oak torn up by the roots in the fury of the winds. Thereupon the King brake out on laughing, bidding Bedevere strike off his head and give it to one of the squires to carry to the camp as a rare show for sightseers. Natheless, said he, never had he forgathered with none other of so puissant hardihood since he slew the giant Ritho upon Mount Aravius, that had challenged him to fight with him. For this Ritho had fashioned him a furred cloak of the beards of the kings he had slain, and he had bidden Arthur heedfully to flay off his beard and send it unto him with the skin, in which case, seeing that Arthur did excel other kings, he would sew it in his honor above the other beards on his cloak. Howbeit, in case he refused, he challenged him to fight upon such covenant, that he which should prove the better man of the twain should have the other's beard as well as the furred cloak. So when it came to the scratch Arthur [214] had the best of it and carried off Ritho's beard and his cloak, and sithence that time had never had to do with none so strong until he lighted upon this one, as he is above reported as asserting. After he had won this victory as I have said, they returned just after daybreak to their tents with the head; crowds coming running up to look upon it and praising the valour of the man that had delivered the country from so insatiable a man. But Hoel, grieving over the loss of his niece, bade build a church above her body upon the mount where she lay, the which was named after the damsel's grave, and is called the Tomb of Helena unto this day.

CHAPTER 4:

When all were come together that Arthur had expected, he marched from thence to Autun, where he thought the Emperor was. But when he had come as far as the river Aube, tidings were brought him that he had pitched his camp not far away, and was marching with an army so huge that it was impossible, so they said, to withstand him. Howbeit, so little was Arthur affrighted thereat, that no change made he in his plans, but pitched his camp upon the river bank, from whence he could freely lead forth his army, and whither in case of need he could as easily repair. He then sent two of his earls, Boso of Oxford and Guerin of Chartres, together with his nephew Gawain, unto Lucius Hiberius, to intimate unto him that either he must retire forthwith beyond the frontier of Gaul or come next day to try conclusions with him as to which of the twain had the better right to the country. Thereupon the young men of the court, rejoicing exceedingly at the prospect, began to egg on Gawain to start the quarrel before leaving the Emperor's camp, so that they might have occasion to come to blows with the Romans forthwith. Away went the envoys accordingly [215] to Lucius, and bade him retreat from Gaul at once or come out next day to fight. And when he made them answer that he had not come thither to retreat, but on the contrary to command, a nephew of his that was there, one Gaius Quintillianus, took occasion to say that the Britons were better men at bragging and threatening than in deeds of hardihood and prowess. Gawain thereat waxing wroth, drew his sword wherewith he was girt, and running upon him smote off his head, coming swiftly away with his companions to their horses. The Romans, some on foot and some on horse, start in hot pursuit, straining their utmost to wreak revenge for their fellow-countryman upon the fleeing legates. But Guerin of Chartres, when one of them was almost nigh enow to touch him, wheeled round of a sudden and couching his spear thrust him through the armour and right through the middle of the body, and stretched him out as flat as he might upon the ground. Boso of Oxford, waxing jealous at seeing Guerin do so daring a deed, turned back his own destrier and thrust his spear into the gullet of the first man he met, and forced him, mortally wounded, to part company with the hackney whereon he was pursuing him. Meanwhile, Marcellus Mucius, burning to be first to avenge Quintillianus, was hard upon the back of Gawain and had begun to lay hold upon him, when Gawain suddenly turning round, clove him with the sword he still held in his hand sheer through helmet and skull down to the breast. Gawain, moreover, bade him when he should meet Quintillianus, whom he had slain in the camp, in hell, to tell him that in such manner of bragging and threatening were none better men than the Britons.

Gawain then, reassembling his comrades, counselled that all should turn back, and that in charging all together each should do his best to slay his man. All agreed accordingly; all turned back; and each killed his man. Howbeit, the Romans kept on pursuing them [216] and now and again with spear or sword made shift to wound some few of them, but were unable either to hold or to unhorse any. But whilst they were following up the pursuit nigh a certain wood, straightway forth issue therefrom about six thousand Britons, who having intelligence of the flight of the earls, had hidden them therein for the purpose of bringing them succour. Sallying forth, they set spur to their horses, and rending the air with their shouts and covering them with their shields, attack the Romans on the sudden, and presently drive them in flight before them. Pursuing them with one accord, they smite some from their horses with their spears, some they take prisoner, some they slay. When word of this was brought to the Senator Petreius, he took with him a company of ten thousand men, and hastened to succour his comrades, and compelled the Britons to hasten back to the wood from whence they had made the sally, not without some loss of his own men. For in their flight the Britons turned back, and knowing the ground well, did inflict passing heavy slaughter upon their pursuers. Whilst the Britons were thus giving ground, Hider, the son of Nun, with five thousand men, hurried to their assistance. They now make a stand, and whereas they had afore shown their back to the Romans, they now show their front and set to work to lay about them like men as stoutly as they might. The Romans also stand up to them stiffly, and one while it is Briton that gets stricken down and another while Roman. But the Britons were yearning with all their soul for a fight, and cared not greatly whether they won or lost in the first bout so long as the fighting were really begun, whereas the Romans went to work more heedfully, and Petreius Cotta, like a good captain as he was, skilfully instructed them how and when to advance or retreat, and thus did the greater damage to the Britons. Now, when Boso took note of this, he called a number of them that he knew to be the hardiest aside from the others,[217] and spake unto them on this wise: "Seeing that we began this battle without Arthur's knowledge, we must take right good heed that we get not the worst of it in our adventure. For and if it be that we come to grief herein, we shall not only do heavy damage to our men, but we shall have the King cursing us for our foolhardiness. Wherefore, pluck up your courage, and follow me into the Roman ranks, and if that we have any luck we will either slay Petreius or take him prisoner." So they all set spur to their horses, and charging with one accord into the enemies' ranks, came to where Petreius was giving orders to his men. Boso rushed in upon him as swiftly as he might, grasped him round the neck, and, as he had made up his mind to do aforehand, dropped down with him to the ground. Thereupon the Romans come running up to rescue him from the enemy, and the Britons as quickly run up to succour Boso. A mighty slaughter is made betwixt them, with mighty shouting and uproar as the Romans struggle to deliver the duke and the Britons to hold him. On both sides were wounders and wounded, strikers and stricken to the ground. There, moreover, could it be seen which was the better man at thrust of spear and stroke of swords and fling of javelin. At last the Britons falling upon them in close rank, unbroken by the Roman charge, move off into the safety of their own lines along with Petreius.

From thence forthwith they again charge upon the Romans, now bereft of their captain and for the most part enfeebled and dispirited and beginning to turn tail. They press forward and strike at them in the rear, cut down them they strike, plunder them they cut down, and pass by them they have plundered to pursue the rest. Howbeit, a number of them they take prisoner whom they are minded to present unto the King. In the end, when they had inflicted mischief enow upon them, they made their way back to the camp with their spoil and their captives, and, relating all that had befallen them pre- [218] sented Petreius Cotta and the rest of the prisoners unto Arthur and wished him joy of the victory. He, in return, did bid them joy, and promised them honours and increase of honours seeing that they had done deeds of such prowess in his absence. Being minded, moreover, to thrust the captives into prison, he called unto him certain of his sergeants to bring them on the morrow unto Paris, and deliver them unto the charge of the reeves of the city until further ordinance should be made on their behalf. He further commanded Duke Cador, Bedevere the Butler and the two Earls Borel and Richer, with their retinues, to convoy them so far on their way as that they need be under no fear of molestation by the Romans.

CHAPTER 5:

But the Romans happening to get wind of this arrangement, by command of the Emperor made choice of fifteen thousand of their men to march that very night so as to be beforehand, and to rescue the prisoners after defeating the convoy. These were to be under the command of the Senators Vulteius Catellus and Quintus Carucius, besides Evander, King of Syria, and Sertorius, King of Libya, who started on the appointed march with the said soldiers at night, and hid them in a position convenient for an ambuscade upon the road they weened that the party would travel by. On the morrow the Britons begin their march with the prisoners, and had well-nigh reached the place, not knowing what snares the crafty enemy had set for them. Howbeit, no sooner had they entered that part of the road than the Romans sallied forth of a sudden and surprised and broke the ranks of the British who were quite unprepared for an attack of the kind. Natheless, albeit they were thus taken aback, they soon drew together again and made a stout defence, setting some to [219] guard the prisoners whilst the rest divided into companies to do battle with the enemy. Richer and Bedevere were in command of the company that kept guard over the prisoners, Cador, Duke of Cornwall, with Borel, taking command of the rest. But the Romans had all burst in upon them disorderly, and took no heed to dispose their men in companies, their one care, indeed, being which should be first to slaughter the Britons before they could form their ranks and marshal them so as to defend themselves. By reason of this the Britons were reduced to so sore straits that they would shamefully have lost the prisoners they were convoying had not good luck swiftly brought them the succour they needed. For Guitard, Duke of the Poitevins, who had discovered the stratagem, had arrived with three thousand men, by whose timely assistance the Britons did at last prevail and pay back the evil turn of the slaughter upon the insolent brigands that had assaulted them. But many of their own men did they lose in the first onset, for among others they lost Borel, the renowned Earl of Maine, who, while battling with Evander, King of Syria, was pierced through the throat with his spear, and poured forth his life with his blood. They lost, moreover, four barons, Hirelglas, of Periron, Maurice of Cahors, Aliduc of Tintagel, and Her, the son of Hider, than whom none hardier were easy to be found. Natheless, the Britons stinted nought of their hardihood nor gave them up to despair, but straining every endeavour determined to keep safe their prisoners and cut down their enemies to the last. In the end the Romans, unable to stand up against them, hastily retreated from the field and began to make for their camp. But the Britons, still pursuing them, slew many and took more prisoners, nor did they rest until Vulteius Catellus and Evander, King of Syria, were slain and the rest utterly scattered. When they had won the victory, they sent the prisoners they were convoying on to Paris, and marching back unto their King with them [220] that they had lately taken, promised him hope of supreme victory, seeing that so few had won the day against so many enemies that had come against them.

CHAPTER 6:

Lucius Hiberius, meanwhile, taking these disasters sorely to heart, was mightily perplexed and distressed to make resolve whether it were better for him to hazard a general engagement with Arthur, or to throw himself into Autun and there await assistance from the Emperor Leo. In the end he took counsel of his fears, and on the night following marched his armies into Langres on his way to Autun. As soon as Arthur discovered this scheme, he determined to be beforehand with him on the march, and that same night, leaving the city on his left, he took up a position in a certain valley called Soissie, through which Lucius would have to pass. Disposing his men in companies as he thought best, he posted one legion close by under the command of Morvid, Earl of Gloucester, so that, if need were, he would know whither to betake him to rally his broken companies and again give battle to the enemy. The rest of his force he divided into seven battalions, and in each battalion placed five thousand five hundred and fifty-five men, all fully armed. One division of each consisted of horse and the remainder of foot, and order was passed amongst them that when the infantry advanced to the attack, the cavalry advancing in close line slantwise on their flanks should do their best to scatter the enemy. The infantry divisions, British fashion, were drawn up in a square with a right and left wing. One of these was commanded by Angusel, King of Scotland, and Cador, Duke of Cornwall, the one in the right wing and the other in the left. Another was in command of two earls of renown, to wit, Guerin of Chartres, and Boso of Rhydychen,[221] which in the tongue of the Saxons is called Oxford. A third was commanded by Aschil, King of the Danskers, and Loth, King of the Norwegians. The fourth by Hoel, Duke of Brittany, and Gawain, the King's nephew. After these four were four others stationed in the rear, one of which was in the command of Kay the Seneschal and Bedevere the Butler. Holdin, Duke of the Flemings, and Guitard, Duke of the Poitevins, commanded the second; Jugein of Leicester, Jonathal of Dorset, and Cursalem of Caichester the third, and Urbgenius of Bath the fourth. To the rear of all these he made choice of a position for himself and one legion that he designed to be his bodyguard, and here he set up the golden dragon he had for standard, whereunto, if need should be, the wounded and weary might repair as unto a camp. In that legion which was in attendance upon himself were six thousand six hundred and sixty-six men.

CHAPTER 7:

When all these dispositions were made, Arthur spake unto his fellow-soldiers on this wise:—

"Lieges mine, ye that have made Britain Lady of thirty realms, I do bid ye joy of your prowess, that meseemeth hath in nowise failed ye, but rather hath waxed the stronger albeit that for five years no occasion have ye had to put it to the proof, and hitherto have given more thought unto the disports of an easy life than unto the practice of arms. Natheless, in no wise have ye degenerated from the inborn valour of your race, but staunch as ever, have scattered in flight before ye these Romans that pricked by the spur of their own pride would fain curtail ye of your freedom. Already, marching with a host larger than your own, have they ventured to begin the attack, and failing to withstand your advance, have taken refuge with shame [222] in yonder city. At this moment they are ready to issue forth from thence upon their march towards Autun. Through this valley must they pass, and here falling upon them when they least expect it, may you meet and slaughter them like sheep. Surely they deemed that the cowardize of the nations of the East was in ye when they were minded to make your country tributary and yourselves bond-slaves! What! have they heard not of the battles ye fought with the Danskers and Norwegians and the Dukes of the Gauls, when ye delivered them from their shameful yoke and gave them into my allegiance? We, therefore, that were strong enow to subdue the mightier, shall doubtless prove stronger yet against this feebler foe, so we only take the same pains in the same spirit to crush these emasculate cravens. Only obey my will and command as loyal comrades of mine own, and what honours, what treasures await each one of ye! For so soon as we have put these to the rout, forthwith we start for Rome. For us to march upon Rome is to take it and possess. Yours shall be the gold and silver, the palaces and castles, the towns and cities and all the riches of the vanquished!"

Whilst he yet spake thus all unite in a mighty cheer, ready to meet death rather than flee from the field leaving him there alive.

CHAPTER 8:

Now Lucius Hiberius, who had been warned of their design and the trap that was laid for him, was not minded to flee as he had at first proposed, but plucking up his courage to march to the valley and meet them. With this design he called his Dukes together and spake unto them thus:—

"Venerable Fathers, unto whose empire the realms of the East and of the West do owe their allegiance, call ye now your fathers unto remembrance, how they [223] shrank not from shedding their blood to vanquish the enemies of the Commonweal, but leaving unto their children an ensample of prowess and knightly hardihood, did so bear them in the field as though God had decreed that none of them should die in battle. Wherefore full oft did they achieve the triumph, and in the triumph avoidance of death, for that unto none might aught else befall than was ordained by the providence of God. Hence sprang the increase of the Commonweal; hence the increase of their own prowess; hence, moreover, came it that the uprightness, the honour, and the bounty that are wont to be in them of gentle blood, ever flourishing amongst them from age to age, have exalted them and their descendants unto the dominion of the whole world. This is the spirit I would fain arouse within ye. I do appeal unto ye that ye be mindful of your ancient valour, and be staunch thereunto. Let us seek out our foemen in the valley wherein they now lurk in ambush for us, and fight to win from them that which is our own of right! Nor deem ye that I have made repair unto this city for refuge as though I would shrink from them or their invasions. On the contrary, I reckoned upon their foolishly pursuing us, and believed that we might surprise them by suddenly falling upon them when they were scattered in pursuit so as to put them to the rout with a decisive slaughter. But now that they have done otherwise than we expected, let us also do otherwise. Let us seek them out and fall upon them hardily, or, if so be that they are strong enow to fall upon us first, let us stand our ground with one accord and abide their first onset. On this wise, without doubt, we shall win the day, for in most battles he that hath been able to withstand the first charge hath most often come off the conqueror."

So when he had made an end of speaking thus, with much more to the same effect, all with one assent agreeing and pledging them by oath with joining of hands, they all hastened to do on their armour, and [224] when they were armed at last, sally forth from Langres and march to the valley where Arthur had stationed his men. They, likewise, had marshalled their men in twelve wedge-shaped battalions, all infantry, and formed, Roman fashion, in the shape of a wedge, so that when the army was in full array each division contained six thousand six hundred and sixty-six soldiers. Unto each, moreover, they appointed captains to give orders when to advance and when to stand their ground against the enemy's onset. Unto one they appointed Lucius Catellus, the senator, and Alifatima, King of Spain, commanders. Unto the second, Hirtacius, King of the Parthians, and Marius Lepidus, the senator; upon the third, Boccus, King of the Medes, and Gaius Metellus, the senator; unto the fourth, Sertorius, King of Libya, and Quintus Milvius, senator. These four divisions were placed in the vanguard of the army. In their rear came another four, whereof one was under the command of Serses, King of the Ituraens; the second under Pandrasus, King of Egypt; the third under Politetes, Duke of Bithynia; the fourth under Teucer, Duke of Phrygia. Behind these again were other four battalions, one captained by Quintus Carucius, senator; the second by Lellius of Hostia; the third by Sulpicius Subuculus; the fourth by Mauricius Silvanus. Lucius himself was moving hither and thither amongst them giving orders and instructions how they should behave them. In their midst he bade set up firmly the golden eagle that he had brought with him for standard, and warned the men that should any by misadventure be separated from the ranks, he should endeavour to return thereunto.

CHAPTER 9:

After that they were arrayed the one against the other, Britons on this side and Romans on that, javelins up- [225] right, forthwith upon hearing the blare of the trumpets the battalion under the command of the King of Spain and Lucius Catellus fell hardily upon the division led by the King of Scotland and the Duke of Cornwall, but could in no wise make any breach in the close ranks of them that opposed them. And whilst they were still struggling most fiercely to make head against them, up came the division captained by Guerin and Boso, who, spurring their horses to a gallop, charged against the assailants, and breaking right through and beyond them came face to face with the battalion that the King of the Parthians was leading against Aschil, King of the Danes. Straight, the battalions fling them the one upon another, burst through each other's ranks and batter together in a general melly. Pitiable is the slaughter wrought betwixt them amidst the din as one after another droppeth on both sides, beating the ground with head or heels and retching forth his life with his blood. But the first grave disaster fell upon the Britons, for Bedevere the Butler was slain and Kay the Seneschal wounded unto the death. For Bedevere when he met Boccus, King of the Medes, fell dead, smitten through by his spear amidst the ranks of the enemy, and Kay the Seneschal, in attempting to avenge him, was surrounded by the Median troops and received a deadly hurt. Natheless, after the wont of good knight, opening a way with the wing that he led, he slew and scattered the Medes, and would have brought off his company unharmed and returned with them to their own ranks had he not been met by the division of the King of Libya, the assault whereof dispersed all his men. Natheless, still retreating, albeit with but four of his followers, he made shift to flee unto the Golden Dragon, bearing with him the corpse of Bedevere. Alas! what lamentation was there amongst the Normans when they beheld the body of their Duke rent by so many wounds! Alas, what wailing was there amongst the Angevins when they searched with all the arts of [226] leechcraft the wounds of Kay their earl! But no time was that for sorrowing when the blood-bespattered ranks rushing one upon another scarce allowed space for a sigh ere they were forced to turn to defend their own lives. And now Hirelglas, the nephew of Bedevere, wroth beyond measure at his death, took with him a company of three hundred men of his own, and like a wild boar amidst a pack of hounds dashed with a sudden gallop of their steeds right through the ranks of the enemy towards the place where he had espied the standard of the King of the Medes, little reckoning of aught that might befall himself so only he might avenge his uncle. Gaining the place he desired, he slew the King and carried him off to his comrades, and laying the corpse by the side of that of the Butler, hewed it utterly to pieces. Then, with a mighty shout cheering on the troops of his fellow-countrymen, he called upon them to fall upon the enemy and harass them with charge after charge now, whilst their courage was still hot, whilst the hearts of their foes were still quaking with terror; whilst they had the advantage in bearing down upon them hand to hand through their companies being more skilfully ordered than those of the enemy, and being thus able to renew the attack more often and to inflict a deadlier damage. Thus cheered by his counsel, they made a general charge upon the enemy from every quarter, and the slaughter on both sides waxed exceeding heavy. For on the side of the Romans, besides numberless others, fell Alifatima, King of Spain, and Micipsa of Babylon, as well as the senators Quintus Milvius and Marius Lepidus. On the side of the Britons fell Holdin, King of Flanders, and Leodegar of Boulogne, besides three Earls of Britain, Cursalem of Caichester, Galluc of Salisbury, and Urbgennius of Bath. The troops they led thus, sore enfeebled, retreated until they came upon the battalion of the Bretons commanded by Hoel and Gawain. But the Bretons thereupon, like a fire bursting into a blaze,[227] made a charge upon the enemy, and rallying them that had retreated, soon compelled those that but just before had been the pursuers to flee in their turn, and ever followed them up, slaying some and stretching others on the ground, nor ceased from their slaughter until they reached the bodyguard of the Emperor, who, when he saw the disaster that had overtaken his comrades, had hastened to bring them succour.

CHAPTER 10:

In the first onset the Bretons suffered great loss. For Kimmarcoch, Earl of Tréguier, fell, and with him two thousand men. Fell also three barons of renown, Richomarch, Bloccovius, and Iaguvius of Ballon, who, had they been princes of kingdoms, would have been celebrated by fame to all after-ages for the passing

great prowess that was in them. For when they were charging along
with Hoel and Gawain, as hath been said, not an enemy escaped
that came within their reach, but either with sword or with spear
they sent the life out of him. But when they fell in with the bodyguard of Lucius, they were surrounded on all sides by the Romans,
and fell along with Kimmarcoch and his followers. But Hoel and
Gawain, than whom have no better knights been born in later ages,
were only spurred to keener endeavour by the death of their comrades, and rode hither and thither, one in one direction and the
other in another searching the companies of the Emperor's guards
for occasion to do them a hurt. And now Gawain, still glowing with
the fire kindled by his former exploits, endeavoured to cleave an
opening, whereby he might come at the Emperor himself and forgather with him. Like a right hardy knight as he was, he made a
dash upon the enemy, bearing some to the ground and slaying them
in the fall, while Hoel, in no wise less hardy than he, fell like [228]
a thunderbolt upon another company, cheering on his men, and
smiting the enemy undaunted by their blows, not a moment passing
but either he struck or was stricken. None that beheld them could
have said which of the twain was the doughtier knight or quitted
him better that day.

CHAPTER 11:

Howbeit, Gawain thus dashing amidst the companies,
found at last the opening he longed for, and rushing upon the
Emperor forgathered with him man to man. Lucius, then in the
flower and prime of youth, had plenty of hardihood, plenty of
strength and plenty of prowess, nor was there nought he did more
desire than to encounter such a knight as would compel him to
prove what he was worth in feats of arms. Wherefore, standing up
to Gawain, he rejoiceth to begin the encounter and prideth him
therein for that he hath heard such renown of him. Long while did
the battle last betwixt them, and mighty were the blows they dealt
one upon other or warded with the shields that covered them as
each strove for vantage to strike the death-blow on the other. But
whilst that they were thus in the very hottest of the fight, behold
the Romans, suddenly recovering their vigour, make a charge upon

the Bretons and come to their Emperor's rescue. Hoel and Gawain and their companies are driven off and sore cut up, until all of a sudden they came up over against Arthur and his company. For Arthur, hearing of the slaughter just inflicted upon his men, had hurried forward with his guard, and drawing forth Caliburn, best of swords, had cheered on his comrades, crying out in a loud voice and hot words: "What be ye men doing? Will ye let these womanish knaves slip forth of your hands unharmed? Let not a soul of them escape alive! Remember your own right hands that have fought in [229] so many battles and subdued thirty realms to my dominion! Remember your grandsires whom the Romans stronger than themselves made tributaries! Remember your freedom that these half men feebler than yourselves would fain reave away from ye! Let not a single one escape alive—not a single one escape! What be ye doing?" Shouting out these reproaches and many more besides, he dashed forward upon the enemy, flung them down, smote them— never a one did he meet but he slew either him or his horse at a single buffet. They fled from him like sheep from a fierce lion madly famishing to devour aught that chance may throw in his way. Nought might armour avail them but that Caliburn would carve their souls from out them with their blood. Two Kings, Sertorius of Libya, and Politetes of Bithynia did their evil hap bring in front of him, whom he despatched to hell with their heads hewn off. And when the Britons beheld in what wise their King did battle, they took heart and hardihood again, and fell with one accord upon the Romans, pressing forward in close rank, so that whilst they afoot cut them down on this wise, they a-horseback did their best to fling them down and thrust them through. Natheless, the Romans made stout resistance, and, urged on by Lucius, strove hard to pay back the Britons for the slaughter inflicted on the guard of their renowned King. On both sides the battle rageth as though it had been but just begun. On this side, as hath been said, Arthur many a time and oft smiting the enemies, exhorted the Britons to stand firm; on the other, Lucius Hiberius exhorted his Romans, and gave them counsel, and led them in many a daring exploit of prowess. Nor did he himself cease to fight with his own hand, but going round from one to another amongst his companies slew every single enemy that chance threw in his way, either with his spear or his sword. Thus a most unconscionable slaughter took place on

either side, for at one time the Britons and at another the
Romans [230] would have the upper hand. In the end, while the
battle was still going on thus, lo and behold, Morvid, Earl of
Gloucester, with the legion which as I have said above was posted
betwixt the hills, came up full speed and fell heavily on the enemy's
rear just at a moment they least expected it, broke through their
lines, scattering them in all directions, with exceeding great slaughter. Many thousand Romans fell in this onslaught, and amongst
them even the Emperor himself, slain in the midst of his companies
by a spear-thrust from a hand unknown. And thus, ever following
up their advantage, the Britons, albeit with sore travail, won the
victory that day.

CHAPTER 12:

The Romans, thus scattered, betook them, some to
the waste-lands and forests, some to the cities and towns, each fleeing to the refuge he deemed safest. The Britons pursue them, take
them prisoner, plunder them, put them miserably to the sword,
insomuch as that the more part of them stretch forth their hands
womanishwise to be bound so only they might have yet a little
space longer to live. The which, verily, might seem to have been
ordained by providence divine, seeing that whereas in days of
yore the Romans had persecuted the grandsires of the Britons with
their unjust oppressions, so now did the Britons in defence of the
freedom whereof they would have bereft them, and refusing the
tribute that they did unrighteously demand, take vengeance on the
grandchildren of the Romans.

CHAPTER 13:

The victory complete, Arthur bade the bodies of his
barons be separated from the carcasses of the enemy,[231] and
embalmed in kingly wise, and borne when enbalmed into the abbeys
of the province. Bedevere the Butler was carried unto Bayeux, his
own city that was builded by Bedevere the first, his great-grand-
father, and loud was the lamentation that the Normans made over

him. There, in a certain churchyard in the southern part of the city, was he worshipfully laid next, the wall. But Kay, grievously wounded, was borne in a litter unto Chinon, a town he himself had builded, and dying a brief space after of the same wound, was buried, as became a Duke of Anjou, in a certain forest in a convent of brethren hermit that dwelt there no great way from the city. Holdin, likewise, Duke of the Flemings, was borne into Flanders and buried in his own city of Thérouanne. Howbeit, the rest of the earls and barons were carried, as Arthur had enjoined, unto the abbeys in the neighbourhood. Having pity, moreover, upon his enemies, he bade the folk of the country bury them. But the body of Lucius he bade bear unto the Senate with a message to say that none other tribute was due from Britain. Then he abode in those parts until after the following winter, and busied him with bringing the cities of the Burgundians into his allegiance. But the summer coming on, at which time he designed to march unto Rome, he had begun to climb the passes of the mountains, when message was brought him that his nephew Modred, unto whom he had committed the charge of Britain, had tyrannously and traitorously set the crown of the kingdom upon his own head, and had linked him in unhallowed union with Guenevere the Queen in despite of her former marriage.[232]

BOOK XI, CHAPTER 1:

Hereof, verily, most noble Earl, will Geoffrey of Monmouth say nought. Natheless, according as he hath found it in the British discourse aforementioned, and hath heard from Walter of Oxford, a man of passing deep lore in many histories, in his own mean style will he briefly treat of the battles which that renowned King upon his return to Britain after this victory did fight with his nephew. So soon therefore as the infamy of the aforesaid crime did reach his ears, he forthwith deferred the expedition he had emprised against Leo, the King of the Romans, and sending Hoel, Duke of Brittany, with the Gaulish army to restore peace in those parts, he straightway hastened back to Britain with none save the island Kings and their armies. Now, that most detestable traitor Modred had despatched Cheldric, the Duke of the Saxons, into

Germany, there to enlist any soever that would join him, and hurry
back again with them, such as they might be, the quickest sail he
could make. He pledged himself, moreover, by covenant to give
him that part of the island which stretcheth from the river Humber
as far as Scotland, and whatsoever Horsus and Hengist had possessed in Kent in the time of Vortigern. Cheldric, accordingly, obeying his injunctions, had landed with eight hundred ships full of
armed Paynims, and doing homage unto this traitor did acknowledge him as his liege lord and king. He had likewise gathered into
his company the Scots, Picts, and Irish, and whomsoever else he
knew bare hatred unto his uncle. All told, they numbered [233]
some eight hundred thousand Paynims and Christians, and in their
company and relying on their assistance he came to meet Arthur
on his arrival at Richborough haven, and in the battle that ensued
did inflict sore slaughter on his men when they were landed. For
upon that day fell Angusel, King of Scotland, and Gawain, the
King's nephew, along with numberless other. Iwen, son of Urian
his brother, succeeded Angusel in the kingdom, and did afterward
win great renown for his prowesses in those wars. At last, when with
sore travail they had gained possession of the coast, they revenged
them on Modred for this slaughter, and drove him fleeing before
them. For inured to arms as they had been in so many battles, they
disposed their companies right skilfully, distributing horse and foot
in parties, in such wise that in the fight itself, when the infantry
were engaged in the attack or defence, the horse charging slantwise
at full speed would strain every endeavour to break the enemies'
ranks and compel them to take to flight. Howbeit, the Perjurer
again collected his men together from all parts, and on the night
following marched into Winchester. When this was reported unto
Queen Guenevere, she was forthwith smitten with despair, and fled
from York unto Caerleon, where she purposed thenceforth to lead
a chaste life amongst the nuns, and did take the veil of their order
in the church of Julius the Martyr.

CHAPTER 2:

But Arthur, burning with yet hotter wrath for the loss
of so many hundred comrades-in-arms, after first giving Christian

burial to the slain, upon the third day marched upon that city and beleaguered the miscreant that had ensconced him therein. Natheless, he was not minded to renounce his design, but encouraging his adherents by all the devices he could, marched forth with [234] his troops and arrayed them to meet his uncle. At the first onset was exceeding great slaughter on either side, the which at last waxed heavier upon his side and compelled him to quit the field with shame. Then, little caring what burial were given unto his slain, "borne by the swift-oared ferryman of flight," he started in all haste on his march toward Cornwall. Arthur, torn by inward anxiety for that he had so often escaped him, pursued him into that country as far as the river Camel, where Modred was awaiting his arrival. For Modred, being, as he was, of all men the boldest and ever the swiftest to begin the attack, straightway marshalled his men in companies, preferring rather to conquer or to die than to be any longer continually on the flight in this wise. There still remained unto him out of the number of allies I have mentioned sixty thousand men, and these he divided into six battalions, in each of which were six thousand six hundred and sixty-six men-at-arms. Besides these, he made out of the rest that were over a single battalion, and appointing captains to each of the others, took command of this himself. When these were all posted in position, he spake words of encouragement unto each in turn, promising them the lands and goods of their adversaries in case they fought out the battle to a victory. Arthur also marshalled his army over against them, which he divided into nine battalions of infantry formed in square with a right and left wing, and having appointed captains to each, exhorted them to make an end utterly of these perjurers and thieves, who, brought from foreign lands into the island at the bidding of a traitor, were minded to reave them of their holdings and their honours. He told them, moreover, that these motley bar-barians from divers kingdoms were a pack of raw recruits that knew nought of the usages of war, and were in no wise able to make stand against valiant men like themselves, seasoned in so many battles, if they fell upon them hardily and fought like men. And whilst the twain were still [235] exhorting their men on the one side and the other, the battalions made a sudden rush each at other and began the battle, struggling as if to try which should deal their blows the quicker. Straight, such havoc is wrought upon both sides, such groaning is there of the dying, such fury in the onset, as it would be grievous and burdensome to describe. Everywhere are wounders and wounded, slayers and slain. And after much of the day had been spent on this wise, Arthur at last, with one battalion wherein were six thousand six hundred and sixty-six men, made a charge upon the company wherein he knew Modred to be, and hewing a path with their swords, cut clean through it and inflicted a most grievous slaughter. For therein fell that accursed traitor and many thousands along with him. Natheless not for the loss of him did his troops take to flight, but rallying together from all parts of the field, struggle to stand their ground with the best hardihood they might. Right passing deadly is the strife betwixt the foes, for well-nigh all the captains that were in command on both sides rushed into the press with their companies and fell. On Modred's side fell Cheldric, Elaf, Egbricht, Bruning, that were Saxons, Gilla-patric, Gillamor, Gillasel, Gillarn, Irish. The Scots and Picts, with well-nigh all that they commanded, were cut off to a man. On Arthur's side, Odbricht, King of Norway, Aschil, King of Denmark, Cador Limenic, Cassibelaunus, with many thousands of his lieges as well Britons as others that he had brought with him. Even the renowned King Arthur himself was wounded deadly, and was borne thence unto the Isle of Avallon for the healing of his wounds, where he gave up the crown of Britain unto his kinsman, Constantine, son of Cador, Duke of Cornwall, in the year of the Incarnation of Our Lord five hundred and forty-two.[236]

ROBERT BIKET

"The Lay of the Horn" (c. 1150)

From *Tales from the Old French*, trans. Isabel Butler (Boston and New York: Houghton Mifflin Co., 1910).

Once upon a time, King Arthur held a mighty feast at Carlion. Our tale saith that the king hath sent through all his realm; and from Esparlot in Bretagne into Alemaigne, from the city of Boillande down even into Ireland, the king, for fellowship, hath summoned his barons, that they be at Carlion at Ascension tide. On this day all came, both high and low; twenty thousand knights sat at the board, and thereto twenty thousand damoiselles, maidens and dames. It was of great mark that each man had his mate, for he who had no wife yet sat with a woman, whether sister or friend: and herein lay great courtesy. But before they may eat one and all shall be sore angered; for now, lo you, a youth, fair and pleasing and mounted upon a swift horse, who cometh riding into the palace.

In his hand he held a horn banded about four times with gold. Of ivory was [93] that horn, and wrought with inlay wherein amid the gold were set stones of beryl and sardonyx and rich chalcedony; of elephant's ivory was it made, and its like for size and beauty and strength was never seen. Upon it was a ring inlaid with silver, and it had a hundred little bells of pure gold,—a fairy, wise and skilful, wrought them in the time of Constantine, and laid such a spell upon the horn as ye shall now hear: whoever struck it lightly with his finger, the hundred bells rang out so sweetly that neither harp nor viol, nor mirth of maidens, nor syren of the sea were so joyous to hear. Rather would a man travel a league on foot than lose that sound, and whoso hearkeneth thereto straightway forgetteth all things.

So the messenger came into the palace and looked upon that great and valiant company of barons. He was clad in a bliaut, and the horn was hung about his neck, and he took it in his hand and raised it on high, and struck upon it that all the palace resounded. The bells rang out in so sweet accord that all the knights left eating. Not a damsel looked down at her [94] plate; and of the ready varlets who were serving drink, and bore about cups of maplewood and beakers of fine gold filled with mulled wine and hippocrass, with drinks spiced and aromatic, not one of these but stopped where he was, and he who held aught scattered it abroad. Nor was there any seneschal so strong or so skilful but if he carried a plate, let it tremble or fall. He who would cut the bread cut his own hand. All were astounded by the horn and fell into forgetfulness; all ceased from speech to hearken to it; Arthur the great king grew silent, and by reason of the horn both king and barons became so still that no word was spoken.

The messenger goeth straightway to the king, bearing in his hand the ivory horn; well knew he the ten kings by their rich array; and still because of the horn's music all were silent about King Arthur. The comely youth addressed him, greeted him fairly, and laughing, bespoke him: "King Arthur, may God who dwells above save you and all your baronage I see here assembled." And Arthur answered him: "May he give you joy like- [95] wise." Saith the messenger: "Lord, now give heed to me for a little space. The king of Moraine, the brave and courteous, sendeth you this horn from out his treasure, on such a covenant—hearken to his desire herein—that you give him neither love nor hate therefor." "Friend," then saith the king, "courteous is thy lord, and I will take the horn with its four bands of gold, but will return him neither love nor hate therefor." So King Arthur took the horn which the varlet proffered him: and he let fill with wine his cup of pure gold, and then bespoke the youth: "Take this beaker, sit you down before me, and eat and drink; and when we have eaten I will make you a knight, and on the morrow I will give you a hundred *livres* of pure gold." But laughing the youth maketh answer: "It is not meet that the squire sit at table with the knight, rather will I go to the inn and repose me; and then when I am clothed and equipped and adorned I will come again to you, and claim my promise." Thereupon the messenger goeth his way; and forthright he issueth out of the city, for he feareth lest he be followed.[96]

The king was in his palace, and his barons were gathered about him: never before was he in so deep a study. He still held the horn by its ring, never had he seen one so fair; and he showeth it to Gawain and Iwain and Gillet; the eighty brethren looked at it, and so likewise did all the barons there gathered. Again the king took the horn, and on it he saw letters in the gold, enameled with silver, and saith to his chamberlain: "Take this horn, and show it to my chaplain, that he may read this writing, for I would know what it saith." The chamberlain taketh it, and gave it to the chaplain who read the writing. When he saw it he laughed, and saith to the king: "Sir, give heed, and anon I will tell you privately such a marvel that its like was never heard in England or any other realm; but here and now it may not be spoken." None the less the king will not so suffer it, rather he swore and declared that the chaplain should speak out before them all, and that his barons should hear it. "Nor shall a thing so desired be kept from the dames and demoiselles and gentle maidens here [97] assembled from many a far land," so saith the king.

One and all rejoiced when they heard from the king that they should know what the writing said; but many a one made merry who thereafter repented him, many a one was glad who thereafter was sorry. Now the chaplain, who was neither fool nor churl, saith: "If I had been heeded what is here written would not be read out in this place; but since it is your will, hear it now openly: 'Thus saith to you Mangon of Moraine, the Fair: this horn was wrought by an evil fay and a spiteful, who laid such a spell upon it that no man, howsoever wise and valiant, shall drink therefrom if he be either jealous or deceived, or if he hath a wife who has ever in folly turned her thoughts towards any man save him only; never will the horn suffer such a one to drink from it, rather will it spill out upon him what it may contain; howsoever valiant he be, and howsoever high, yet will it bespatter him and his garments, though they be worth a thousand marks. For whoso would drink from this horn must have a wife who has never [98] thought, whether from disloyalty, or love of power, or desire of fortune, that she would fain have another, better than her lord; if his wife be wholly true, then

only may he drink from it.' But I do not believe that any knight
from here to Montpelier who hath taken to him a wife will ever
drink any whit therefrom, if it so be that the writing speaketh
truth."

God! then was many a happy dame made sorrowful. Not one
was there so true but she bowed her head; even the queen sat with
bent brow, and so did all the barons around and about who had
wives that they doubted. The maidens talked and jested among
themselves, and looked at their lovers, and smiled courteously, saying: "Now will we see the jealous brought to the test; now will we
learn who is shamed and deceived."

Arthur was in great wrath, but made semblance of gladness,
and he calleth to Kay: "Now fill for me this rich horn, for I would
make assay, and know if I may drink therefrom." And Kay the
seneschal straightway filled it with a spiced wine, and offered it to
the emperor. King Ar- [99] thur took it and set his lips to it, for he
thought to drink, but the wine poured out upon him, down even to
his feet. Then was the king in sore wrath. "This is the worst,"
crieth he, and he seized a knife, and would have struck the queen
in the heart below the breast, had not Gawain and Iwain and
Cadain wrung it from him; they three and Giflet between them
took the knife from his hand, and bitterly blamed him. "Lord,"
then saith Iwain, "be not so churlish, for there is no woman born
who, if she be brought to the test, hath not sometime thought folly.
No marvel is it that the horn spilled its wine. All here that have
wives shall try it, to know if they can drink from it—thereafter may
ye blame the queen of the fair face. Ye are of great valiance, and
my lady is true; none ever spoke blame of her." "Iwain," saith the
queen, "now may my lord let kindle a fire of thorns, and cast me
into it, and if one hair of my head burneth, or any of my garments,
then may he let me be dragged to death by horses. No man have I
loved, and none will I ever love, save my lord only. This horn is
too [100] veracious, it has attacked me for a small cause. In years
past I gave a ring to a damoiseau, a young boy who had slain a
giant, a hateful felon who here in the court accused Gawain of sore
treason. The boy, Gawain's cousin germain, gave him the lie, and
did battle with him, and cut off his head with his sword: and as
soon as the giant was slain the boy asked leave of us. I granted him
my favour, and gave him a ring, for I hoped to retain him to

strengthen the court, but even had he remained here, he had never been loved by me. Certes," saith the queen, "since I was a maid and was given to thee—blessed was that hour—no other evil have I done on any day of my life. On all the earth is no man so mighty—no, not though he were king of Rome—that I would love him, even for all the gold of Pavia, no, nor any count or amiral. Great shame hath he done me who sent this horn; never did he love lady. And until I be revenged, I shall never know gladness."

Then said Arthur, "Speak no more of this. Were any mighty neighbor, or cousin or kinsman, to make war upon Man- [101] gon, never more would my heart love him; for I made the king a covenant before all my folk, and by all that is true, that I would hate him no hate for his gift. It is not meet to gainsay my word,—that were great villany; I like not the king who swiftly belies himself." "Lord," saith the queen, "blessed was I when as a maiden I was given to you. When a lady of high parentry who hath a good lord seeketh another friend, she doth great wrong. He who seeketh a better wine than that of the grape, or better bread than that of the wheat, such a one should be hung and his ashes given to the winds. I have the best one of the three who were ever king under God, why then should I go seeking a fairer or a braver? I promise you, lord, that wrongfully are you angry with me. Never should a noble knight be offered this horn to the shaming of his lady." But the king saith, "Let them do it. All shall try it, kings and counts and dukes; I alone will not have shame herein."

So Arthur giveth it to the king of Sinadone, but so soon as he took it, the wine spilled out upon him; then King Nuz [102] taketh it, and it spilled out upon him; and Angus of Scotland would fain drink from it by force, but the wine all poured out upon him, at which he was sore angered. The king of Cornwall thought certes to drink from it, but it splashed all over him that he was in great wrath; and the horn splashed over King Gahor, and spilled great plenty upon King Glovien, and it spilled out upon King Cadain as soon as he took it in his hands. Then King Lot taketh it, and looketh on himself as a fool; and it splashed the beard of Caraton; and of the two kings of Ireland there was not one it did not bespatter; and it splashed all the thirty counts, who had great shame thereof; nor of all the barons present who tried the horn was there one who might take a drop therefrom. It poured out over each king, and each was in great wrath; they passed it on and were in great sorrow by reason of it; and they all said, may the horn, and he who brought it and he who sent it, be given over to the devils, for whoso believeth this horn shameth his wife.

Now when King Arthur saw it spilled [103] out upon all, he forgot his sorrow and wrath, and began to laugh and made great joy. "Lords," he saith to his barons, "now hear me. I am not the only one bemocked. He who sent me this horn gave me a good gift: by the faith I owe all those here gathered, I will never part with it for all the gold of Pavia; no man shall have it save he who shall drink from it." The queen grew bright red because of the marvel whereof she dared not speak; fairer than the rose was she. The king looked on her and found her most fair; he drew her to him and three times he kissed her: "Gladly, dame, I forget my ill will." "Lord, gramercy," saith she.

Then all, high and low, tried the ivory horn. A knight took it and laughed across at his wife; he was the most joyous of all the court, and the most courteous; none boasted less, yet when he was armed none was more feared; for in Arthur's court there was no better warrior, none mightier of his hands, save only my lord Gawain. Fair was his hair, his beard russet, his eyes gray-blue and laughing, his body comely, his feet straight and well arched; [104] Caradoc was his name, a well skilled knight, and of full good renown. His wife sat at his left; she was sister to King Galahal and was born at Cirencester. Full true was she, and thereto comely and gracious, featly fashioned and like unto a fay; her hair was long and golden; fairer woman was there none, save the queen only. She looked upon Caradoc, nor changed colour, but bespoke him, saying: "Fair friend, fear not to drink from the horn at this high feast; lift up your head and do me honour. I would not take any man for lord however mighty; no, though he were amiral, I would not have him for my husband and leave you, friend; rather would I become a nun and wear the veil. For every woman should be as the turtle dove, who after she has had one mate will never take another: thus should a lady do if she be of good lineage."

Full glad was Caradoc, and he sprang to his feet; fair he was, a well skilled and a courteous knight. When they had filled the horn it held a *lot* and a half; full to the brim it was of red wine; "Wassail," he saith to the king. He was tall and strong,[105] and he set the horn to his lips, and I tell you truly that he tasted the wine and drank it all down. Right glad was he thereof, but all the table started in wonder. Straightway he goeth before Arthur, and as he goeth he saith to him, nor did he speak low-voiced: "Lord, I have emptied the horn, be ye certain thereof." "Caradoc," saith the king, "brave and courteous are you; of a sooth ye have drunk it, as was seen of more than a hundred. Keep you Cirencester; two years is it since I gave it in charge to you, and never will I take it from you, I give it to you for life and to your children; and for your wife—who is of great worth—I will give you this horn which is prized at a hundred pounds of gold." "Lord, I give you good thanks," Caradoc made answer, and sat down again at the board beside his wife of the fair face. Now when they had eaten, each man took leave and went back to his own domain whence he had come, taking with him the woman he best loved.

Lords, this lay was first sung by Caradoc, who wrought its adventure. And [106] whoso goeth to a high feast at Cirencester, will, of a sooth, see there the horn: so say I, Robert Biquet, who have learned much concerning the matter from an abbot, and do now, by his bidding, tell the tale,—how in this wise the horn was tested at Carlion.[107]

WACE

Roman de Brut (1155)

From *Arthurian Chronicles Represented by Wace and Layamon,*
trans. Eugene Mason, Everyman's Library (London: J. M. Dent
& Sons Ltd., [1912]).

. . . The king [Vortigern] seated himself upon the bank
of the pool. He prayed Merlin to show him the interpretation of
these dragons which met together so furiously. Merlin told the
king what these matters betokened, as you have oft-times heard.
These dragons prophesied of kings to come, who would yet hold
the realm in their charge. I say no more, for I fear to translate
Merlin's Prophecies,* when I cannot be sure of the interpretation
thereof. It is good to keep my lips from speech, since the issue of
events may make my gloss a lie.

The king praised Merlin greatly, and esteemed him for a true
prophet. He inquired of the youth in what hour he should die, and
by what means he would come to his end. For this king was marvellously fearful of death. "Beware," said Merlin, "beware of the sons
of Constantine. By them you shall taste of death. . . . If you yet
may flee, escape quickly; for the brethren approach, and that speedily. Of these brethren Aurelius shall first be king, but shall also
die the first, by poison. Uther Pendragon, his brother, will sit within
his chair. He will hold the realm in [19] peace; but he, too, will fall
sick before his time, and die, by reason of the brewage of his friends.
Then Arthur of Cornwall, his son, like to a boar grim in battle, will
utterly devour these false traitors, and destroy thy kinsfolk from the
land. A right valiant knight, and a courteous, shall he be, and all
his enemies shall he set beneath his feet." [20]

.   .   .   .   .   .

* **Merlin's Prophecies,** in Geoffrey of Monmouth's *Historia,* Book VII.
Editor's note.

After Uther had brought his business in the north to an end, he set forth to London, where he purposed to take the crown on Easter Day. Uther desired the feast to be very rich and great. He summoned therefore dukes, earls, and wardens, yea, all his baronage from near and far, by brief and message, to come with their wedded dames and privy households to London for his feast. So all the lords came at the king's commandment, bringing their wives as they were bidden. Very richly the feast was holden. After the Mass was sung, that fair company went in hall to meat. The king sat at the head of his hall, upon a dais. The lords of his realm were ranged about him, each in his order and degree. The Earl of Cornwall was near the king's person, so that one looked upon the other's face. By the earl's side was seated Igerne, his wife. There was no lady so fair in all the land. Right courteous was the dame, noble of peerage, and good as she was fair.

The king had heard much talk of this lady, and never aught but praise. His eyes were ravished with her beauty. He loved her dearly, and coveted her hotly in his heart, for certainly she was marvellously praised. He might not refrain from looking upon her at table, and his hope and desire turned to her more and more. Whether he ate or drank, spoke or was silent, she was ever in his thought. He glanced aside at the lady, and smiled if she met his eye. All that he dared of love he showed. He saluted her by his privy page, and bestowed upon her a gift. He jested gaily with the dame, looking nicely upon her, and made a great semblance of friendship. Igerne was modest and discreet. She neither granted Uther's hope, nor denied. The earl marked well these lookings and laughings, these salutations and gifts. He needed no other assurance that the king had set his love upon his wife. Gorlois deemed that he owed no faith to a lord who would supplant him in her heart. The earl rose from his seat at table; he took his dame by the hand, and went straight from the hall. He called the folk of his household about him, and going to the stables, got him to horse. Uther sent after Gorlois by his chamberlain, telling him that he did shame and wrong in departing from the court without taking leave of his king. He bade him to do the right, and not to treat his lord so despitefully, lest a worse thing should befall him. He could have but little trust in his king, if he would not return for a space. Gorlois rode proudly from the court without leave or farewell. The king men-

aced him very grievously, but [36] the earl gave small heed to his
threats, for he recked nothing of what might chance. He went into
Cornwall, and arrayed his two castles, making them ready against
the war. His wife he put in his castle of Tintagel, for this was the
home of his father and of his race. It was a strong keep, easily holden
of a few sergeants, since none could climb or throw down the walls.
The castle stood on a tall cliff, near by the sea. Men might not win
to enter by the gate, and saving the gate, there was no door to enter
in the tower.

The earl shut his lady fast in the tower. He dared hide his
treasure in no other place, lest thieves broke through, and stole her
from him. Therefore he sealed her close in Tintagel. For himself
he took the rest of his men-at-arms, and the larger part of his
knights, and rode swiftly to the other strong fortress that was his.
The king heard that Gorlois had garnished and made ready his
castle, purposing to defend himself even against his lord. Partly to
avenge himself upon the earl, and partly to be near his vassal's
wife, the king arrayed a great host. He crossed the Severn, and coming before the castle where the earl lay, he sought to take it by
storm. Finding that he might not speed, he sat down before the
tower, and laid siege to those within. The host invested the castle
closely for full seven days, but could not breach the walls. The earl
stubbornly refused to yield, for he awaited succour from the king
of Ireland, whom he had entreated to his aid. King Uther's heart
was in another place. He was wearied beyond measure of Gorlois
and his castle. His love for Igerne urged and called him thence, for
the lady was sweeter to his mind than any other in the world. At
the end he bade to him a baron of his household, named Ulfin, who
was privy to his mind. Him he asked secretly of that which he
should do. "Ulfin," said the king, "my own familiar friend, counsel
me wisely, for my hope is in thee. My love for Igerne hath utterly
cast me down. I am altogether broken and undone. I cannot go or
come about my business; I cannot wake nor sleep; I cannot rise
from my bed nor lay my head on the pillow; neither can I eat or
drink, except that this lady is ever in my mind. How to gain her to
my wish I cannot tell. But this I know, that I am a dead man if you
may not counsel me to my hope." "Oh my king," answered Ulfin,
"I marvel at your words. You have tormented the earl grievously
with your war, and have burned his lands. Do you think to win a

wife's heart by shutting her husband close in his tower? You show your love for the dame by harassing the lord! No, the [37] matter is too high for me, and I have one only counsel to give you. Merlin is with us in the host. Send after him, for he is a wise clerk, and the best counsellor of any man living. If Merlin may not tell you what to do, there is none by whom you may win to your desire."

King Uther, by the counsel of Ulfin, commanded Merlin to be brought before him. The king opened out his bitter need. He prayed that for pity's sake Merlin would find him a way to his hope, so he were able; since die he must if of Igerne he got no comfort. But let the clerk seek and buy so that the king had his will. Money and wealth would be granted plenteously, if gold were needed; for great as was the king's evil, so large would be his delight. "Sire," answered Merlin, "have her you shall. Never let it be said that you died for a woman's love. Right swiftly will I bring you to your wish, or evil be the bounty that I receive of the king's hand. Hearken to me. Igerne is guarded very closely in Tintagel. The castle is shut fast, and plenteously supplied with all manner of store. The walls are strong and high, so that it may not be taken by might; and it is victualled so well, that none may win there by siege. The castle also is held of loyal castellans; but for all their vigils, I know well how to enter therein at my pleasure, by reason of my potions. By craft I can change a man's countenance to the fashion of his neighbour, and of two men each shall take on his fellow's semblance. In body and visage, in speech and seeming, without doubt I can shape you to the likeness of the Earl of Cornwall. Why waste time with many words! You, sire, shall be fashioned as the earl. I, who purpose to go with you on this adventure, will wear the semblance of Bertel. Ulfin, here, shall come in the guise of Jordan. These two knights are the earl's chosen friends, and are very close to his mind and heart. In this manner we may enter boldly in his castle of Tintagel, and you shall have your will of the lady. We shall be known of none, for not a man will doubt us other than we seem." The king had faith in Merlin's word, and held his counsel good. He gave over the governance of the host, privily, to a lord whom he much loved. Merlin put forth his arts, and transfigured their faces and vesture into the likeness of the earl and his people. That very night the king and his companions entered in Tintagel. The porter in his lodge, and the steward within his office, deemed him with joy.

When meat was done the king had his delight of a lady who was much deceived.[38] Of that embrace Igerne conceived the good, the valiant, and the trusty king whom you have known as Arthur. Thus was Arthur begotten, who was so renowned and chivalrous a lord.

Now the king's men learned very speedily that Uther had departed from the host. The captains were wearied of sitting before the castle. To return the more quickly to their homes, they got into their harness and seized their arms. They did not tarry to order the battle, or make ready ladders for the wall, but they approached the tower in their disarray. The king's men assaulted the castle from every side, and the earl defended himself manfully; but at the last he himself was slain, and the castle was swiftly taken. . . .

Igerne praised the counsel of him she deemed her lord. The king embraced her by reason of her tenderness, and kissed her as he bade farewell. He departed straightway from the castle, and his familiars with him. When they had ridden for a while upon the road, Merlin again put forth his enchantments, so that he, the king, and Ulfin took their own shapes, and became as they had been before. They hastened to the host without drawing rein; for the king was with child to know how the castle was so swiftly taken, and in what manner the earl was [39] slain. He commanded before him his captains, and from this man and that sought to arrive at the truth. Uther considered the adventure, and took his lords to witness that whoever had done the earl to death, had done not according to his will. He called to mind Earl Gorlois' noble deeds, and made complaint of his servants, looking upon the barons very evilly. He wore the semblance of a man in sore trouble, but there were few who were so simple as to believe him. Uther returned with his host before Tintagel. He cried to those who stood upon the wall asking why they purposed to defend the tower, since their lord was dead and his castle taken, neither could they look for succour in the realm, or from across the sea. The castellans knew that the king spake sooth, and that for them there was no hope of aid. They therefore set open the gates of the castle, and gave the fortress and its keys into the king's hand. Uther, whose love was passing hot, spoused Igerne forthwith, and made her his queen. She was with child, and when her time was come to be delivered, she brought forth a son. This son was named Arthur, with the rumour of whose praise the whole world has been filled. After the birth of Arthur, Uther got upon

Igerne a daughter cleped Anna. When this maiden came of age she
was bestowed upon a right courteous lord, called Lot of Lyones. Of
this marriage was born Gawain, the stout knight and noble champion.[40]

. . . . . .

Uther the king having fallen asleep, his body was borne to Stonehenge, and laid to rest close by Aurelius, his brother; the brethren
lying side by side. The bishops and barons of the realm gathered
themselves together, and sent messages to Arthur, Uther's son, bidding him to Cirencester to be made their king. Arthur at the time
of his coronation was a damoiseau of some fifteen years, but tall and
strong for his age. His faults and virtues I will show you alike, for
I have no desire to lead you astray with words. He was a very virtuous knight, right worthy of praise, whose fame was much in the
mouths of men. To the haughty he was proud; but tender and pitiful to the simple. He was a stout knight and a bold: a passing crafty
captain, as indeed was but just, for skill and courage were his servants at need: and large of his giving. He was one of Love's lovers;
a lover also of glory; and his famous deeds are right fit to be kept
in remembrance. He ordained the courtesies of courts, and observed
high state in a very splendid fashion. When this Arthur was freshly
crowned king, of his own free will he swore an oath that never
should the Saxons have peace or rest so long as they tarried in his
realm. This he did by reason that for a great while they had
troubled the land, and had done his father and his uncle to their
deaths.[43]

. . . . . .

When Arthur had settled his realm in peace, righted all wrongs,
and restored the kingdom to its ancient borders, he took to wife a
certain fresh and noble maiden, named Guenevere, making her his
queen. This damsel was passing fair of face and courteous, very
gracious of manner, and come of a noble [53] Roman house. Cador
had nourished this lady long and richly in his earldom of Cornwall.
The maiden was the earl's near cousin, for by his mother he, too,
was of Roman blood. Marvellously dainty was the maiden in person
and vesture; right queenly of bearing; passing sweet and ready of
tongue. Arthur cherished her dearly, for his love was wonderfully

set upon the damsel, yet never had they a child together, nor betwixt them might get an heir.[54]

.   .   .   .   .   .

Arthur held high state in a very splendid fashion. He ordained the courtesies of courts, and bore himself with so rich and noble a bearing, that neither the emperor's court at Rome, nor any other bragged of by any man, was accounted as aught besides that of the king. Arthur never heard speak of a knight in praise, but he caused him to be numbered of his household. So that he might he took him to himself, for help in time of need. Because of these noble lords about his hall, of whom each knight pained himself to be the hardiest champion, and none would count him the least praiseworthy, Arthur made the Round Table, so reputed of the Britons. This Round Table was ordained of Arthur that when his fair fellowship sat to meat their chairs should be high alike, their service equal, and none before or after his comrade. Thus no man could boast that he was exalted above his fellow, for all alike were gathered round the board, and none was alien at the breaking of Arthur's bread. At this table sat Britons, Frenchmen, Normans, Angevins, Fremings, Burgundians, and Loherins.[55] . . . From all the lands there voyaged to this court such knights as were in quest either of gain or worship. Of these lords some drew near to tell of Arthur's courtesies; others to marvel at the pride of his state; these to have speech with the knights of his chivalry; and some to receive of his largeness costly gifts. For this Arthur in his day was loved right well of the poor, and honoured meetly by the rich. Only the kings of the world bore him malice and envy, since they doubted and feared exceedingly lest he should set his foot upon them every one, and spoil them of their heritage.[56]

.   .   .   .   .   .

Having delivered Norway from itself Arthur granted the kingdom to Lot, so only that he did Arthur homage as his lord. Amongst the barons who rode in this adventure was Gawain, the hardy and famous knight, who had freshly come from St. Sulpicius the Apostle, whose soul may God give rest and glory. The knight wore harness bestowed on him by the Apostle, and wondrously was he praised. This Gawain was a courteous champion, circumspect in word and deed, having no pride nor blemish in him. He did more than his boast, and gave more largely than he promised. His father had sent him to Rome, that he might be schooled the more meetly. Gawain was dubbed knight in the same day as Wavain, and counted himself of Arthur's household. Mightily he strove to do his devoir in the field, for the fairer service and honour of his lord.[57]

. . . . . .

Now in Arthur's day the land of France was known as Gaul. The realm had neither king nor master, for the Romans held it strongly as a province. This province was committed to the charge of Frollo, and the tribune had governed the country for a great space. He took rent and tribute of the people, and in due season caused the treasure to be delivered to the emperor at Rome. Thus had it been since the time of Caesar, that mighty emperor, who brought into subjection France and Germany, and all the land of Britain. Frollo was a very worthy lord, come of a noble Roman race, fearful of none, however hardy. He knew well, by divers letters, the loss and the mischief done by Arthur and his host. Frollo had no mind tamely to watch the Romans lose their heritage. The tribune summoned to his aid all the men abiding in the province who carried arms and owned fealty to Rome. He assembled these together, ordaining a great company, clad in harness and plenteously supplied with stores. With these he went out to battle against Arthur, but he prospered less than his merit deserved. . . . This was no great marvel, since the count of Arthur's host was more than Frollo might endure. From every [58] land he had subdued to himself, from every city that was taken, Arthur saw to it that not a spearman nor knight of fitting years and strength of body, but was numbered in the host, and commanded to serve Arthur as his lord. Of these outland folk, Arthur chose a fair company of the hardiest knights and most proven champions to be of his private household. The very French began to regard him as their king, so only that they had the courage of their minds. . . . Now Frollo, after his discomfiture by the king, fled to Paris with all the speed he might, making no stop upon the road. The tribune feared Arthur and his power very sorely, and since he sought a fortress to defend his person, he would not trust his fortune to any other city. . . .

Arthur learned that Frollo was making strong his towers, and filling the barns with victuals. He drew to Paris, and sat down without the city. He lodged his men in the suburbs beyond the walls, holding the town so close that food might not enter whether by the river or the gates. Arthur shut the city fast for more than a month, since the French defended them well and manfully. A mighty multitude was crowded within the walls, and there was a plentiful lack of meat. All the provand bought and gathered together in so short a space was quickly eaten and consumed, and the folk were afterwards anhungered. . . . Frollo perceived [59] that of a surety the end of all was come. The tribune chose to put his own body in peril—yea, rather to taste of death, than to abandon Paris to her leaguers. Frollo had full assurance of Arthur's rectitude. In the simplicity of his heart he sent urgent messages to the king, praying him to enter in the Island, that body to body they might bring their quarrel to an end. He who prevailed over his fellow, and came living from the battle, should take the whole realm as his own and receive all France for his guerdon. Thus the land would not perish, nor the folk be utterly destroyed. Arthur hearkened willingly to the heralds, for very greatly was their message to his mind. He accorded that the battle should be between the two captains, even as Frollo desired. Gauntlets were taken from one and the other, and hostages given on behalf of Paris and on the part of the besiegers for better assurance of the covenant that was made.

On the morrow the two champions arrayed them in harness, and coming to the Island, entered boldly in the lists. The banks were filled with a mighty concourse of people, making great tumult. Not a man or woman remained that day in his chamber. They climbed upon the walls, and thronged the roofs of the houses, crying upon God, and adjuring Him by His holy Name to give victory to him who would guard the realm in peace, and preserve the poor from war. Arthur's meinie, for their part, awaited the judgment of God, in praying the King of Glory to bestow the prize and honour on their lord. The two champions were set over against the other, laced each in his mail, and seated on his warhorse. The strong destriers were held with bit and bridle, so eager were they for the battle. The riders bestrode the steeds with lifted shields, brandishing great lances in their hands. It was no easy matter to perceive—however curiously men looked—which was the stouter knight, or to judge who would be victor in the joust. Certainly each was a very worthy lord and a right courageous champion. When all was made

ready the knights struck spurs to their steeds, and loosing the rein
upon the horses' necks, hurtled together with raised buckler and
lance in rest. They smote together with marvellous fierceness.
Whether by reason of the swerving of his destrier, I cannot tell,
but Frollo failed of his stroke. Arthur, on his side, smote the boss
of his adversary's shield so fairly, that he bore him over his horse's
buttock, as long as the ash staff held. Arthur drew forth his sword,
and hastened to Frollo to bring the battle to an end. Frollo
climbed [60] stoutly on his feet. He held his lance before him like a
rod, and the king's steed ran upon the spear, so that it pierced
deeply in his body. Of this thrust the destrier and his rider alike
came tumbling to the ground. When the Britons saw this thing, they
might not contain themselves for grief. They cried aloud, and seizing
their weapons, for a little would have violated the love-day. They
made ready to cross the river to the Island, and to avenge their lord
upon the Gauls. Arthur cried loudly to his Britons to observe their
covenant, commanding that not a man should move to his help
that day. He gripped Excalibur sternly in his hand, resolving that
Frollo should pay dearly for his triumph. Arthur dressed his shield
above his head, and handselling his sword, rushed upon Frollo.
Frollo was a passing good knight, hardy and strong, in no whit dismayed by the anger of his adversary. He raised his own glaive on
high, striking fiercely at Arthur's brow. Frollo was strong beyond
the strength of man. His brand was great and sharp, and the buffet
was struck with all his power. The blade sheared through helm and
coif alike, so that King Arthur was wounded in his forehead, and
the blood ran down his face.

When Arthur felt the dolour of his hurt, and looked upon his
blood, he desired nothing, save to wreak evil on the man who had
wrought this mischief. He pressed the more closely upon Frollo.
Lifting Excalibur, his good sword, in both hands, he smote so lustily
that Frollo's head was cloven down to his very shoulders. No helmet
nor hauberk, whatever the armourer's craft, could have given surety
from so mighty a blow. Blood and brains gushed from the wound.
Frollo fell upon the ground, and beating the earth a little with his
chausses of steel, presently died, and was still.[61]

.   .   .   .

When this letter [from the emperor of Rome] was read in the
hearing of those who were come to Arthur's solemnity, a great

tumult arose, for they were angered beyond measure. Many of the Britons took God to witness that they would do such things and more also to those ambassadors who had dared deliver the message. They pressed about those twelve ancient men, with many wild and mocking words. Arthur rose hastily to his feet, bidding the brawlers to keep silence. He cried that none should do the Romans a mischief, for they were an embassy, and carried the letters of their lord. Since they were but another's mouthpiece, he commanded that none should work them harm. After the noise was at an end, and Arthur was assured that the elders were no longer in peril, he called his privy council and the lords of his household together, in a certain stone keep, that was named the Giant's Tower. The king would be advised by his barons—so ran the summons—what answer he should give to the messengers of Rome. Now as they mounted the stairs, earl and prince, pell-mell, together, Cador, who was a merry man, saw the king before him. "Fair king," said the earl gaily, "for a great while the thought has disturbed me, that peace and soft living are rotting away the British bone. Idleness is the stepdame of virtue, as our preachers have often told us. Soft living makes a sluggard of the hardiest knight, and steals away his strength.[72] She cradles him with dreams of woman, and is the mother of chambering and wantonness. Folded hands and idleness cause our young damoiseaux to waste their days over merry tales, and dice, raiment to catch a lady's fancy and things that are worse. Rest and assurance of safety will in the end do Britain more harm than force or guile. May the Lord God be praised Who has jogged our elbow. To my mind He has persuaded these Romans to challenge our country that we may get us from sleep. If the Romans trust so greatly in their might that they do according to their letters, be assured the Briton has not yet lost his birthright of courage and hardness. I am a soldier, and have never loved a peace that lasts over long, since there are uglier things than war." Gawain overheard these words. "Lord earl," said he, "by my faith be not fearful because of the young men. Peace is very grateful after war. The grass grows greener, and the harvest is more plenteous. Merry tales, and songs, and ladies' love are delectable to youth. By reason of the bright eyes and the worship of his friend, the bachelor becomes knight and learns chivalry." [73]

. . . . . .

When Arthur was certified of the greatness of his power, and of the harness of his men, he wrote letters to each of his captains, commanding him that on an appointed day he should come in ships to Barfleur in Normandy. The lords of his baronage, who had repaired from the court to their fiefs, hastened to make ready with those whom they should bring across the sea. In like manner Arthur pushed on with his business, that nothing should hinder or delay.

Arthur committed the care of his realm, and of Dame Guenevere, his wife, to his nephew, Mordred, a marvellously hardy knight, whom Arthur loved passing well. Mordred was a man of high birth, and of many noble virtues, but he was not true. He had set his heart on Guenevere, his kinswoman, but such a love brought little honour to the queen. Mordred had kept this love close, for easy enough it was to hide, since who would be so bold as to deem that he loved his uncle's dame? The lady on her side had given her love to a lord of whom much good was spoken; but Mordred was of her husband's kin! This made the shame more shameworthy. Ah, God, the deep wrong done in this season by Mordred and the queen.[79]

Now it came to pass that whilst the host voyaged in great content with a fair wind towards Barfleur, that Arthur slept, for he was passing heavy, and it was night. As the king slumbered he beheld a vision, and, lo, a bear flying high in air towards the east. Right huge and hideous of body was the bear, and marvellously horrible to see. Also the king saw a dragon flying over against him towards the west. The brightness of his eyes was such, that the whole land and sea were filled with the radiance of his glory. When these two beasts came together, the dragon fell upon the bear, and the bear defended himself valiantly against his adversary. But the dragon put his enemy beneath him, and tumbling him to the earth, crushed him utterly in the dust. When Arthur had slept for awhile, his spirit came to him again, and he awoke and remembered his dream. The king called therefore for his wise clerks, and related to them and his household the vision that he had seen of the bear and of the dragon. Then certain of these clerks expounded to the [80] king his dream, and the interpretation thereof. The dragon that was beholden of the king signified himself. By the bear was shown forth a certain horrible giant, come from a far land, whom he should slay. The giant desired greatly that the adventure should end in another fashion; nevertheless all would be to the king's profit. But Arthur replied, "My interpretation of the dream is other than yours. To me it typifies rather the issue of the war between myself and the emperor. But let the Creator's will be done." [81]

.   .   .   .   .   .

Arthur stood a little apart, and gazed upon his adversary. He laughed aloud in his mirth; for his anger was well-nigh gone. He commanded Bedevere, his cupbearer, to strike off the giant's head, and deliver it to the squires, that they might bear it to the host, for the greater marvel. Bedevere did after his lord's behest. He drew his sword, and divided the head from the shoulders. Wonderfully huge and hideous to sight was the head of this giant. Never, said Arthur, had he known such fear; neither had met so perilous a giant, save only that Riton, who had grieved so many fair kings. This Riton in his day made war upon divers kings. Of these some were slain in battle, and others remained captive in his hand. Alive or dead, Riton used them despitefully; for it was his wont to shave the beards of these kings, and purfle therewith a cloak of furs that he wore, very rich. Vainglorious beyond measure was Riton of his broidered cloak. Now by reason of folly and lightness, Riton sent messages to Arthur, bidding him shave his beard, and commend it forthwith to the giant, in all good will. Since Arthur was a mightier lord and a more virtuous prince than his fellows, Riton made covenant to prefer his beard before theirs, and hold it in honour as the most silken fringe of his mantle. Should [85] Arthur refuse to grant Riton the trophy, then nought was there to do, but that body to body they must fight out their quarrel, in single combat, alone. He who might slay his adversary, or force him to own himself vanquished, should have the beard for his guerdon, together with the mantle of furs, fringes and garniture and all. Arthur accorded with the giant that this should be so. They met in battle on a high place, called Mount Aravius, in the far east, and there the king slew Riton with the sword, spoiling him of that rich garment of furs, with its border of dead kings' beards. Therefore, said Arthur, that never since that day had he striven with so perilous a giant, nor with one of whom he was so sorely frighted. Nevertheless Dinabuc was bigger and mightier than was Riton, even in the prime of his youth and strength. For a monster more loathly and horrible, a giant so hideous and misshapen, was never slain by man, than the devil Arthur killed to himself that day, in Mont St. Michel, over against the sea.[86]

.   .   .   .   .   .

The Romans and their fellows from the east fled before the [108] pursuers, but the Britons following after did them sore mischief. They waxed weary of slaying, so that they trod the Romans underfoot. Blood ran in runnels, and the slain they lay in heaps. Fair palfreys and destriers ran masterless about the field, for the rider was dead, and had neither joy nor delight in the sun. Arthur rejoiced and made merry over so noble a triumph, which had brought the pride of Rome to the dust. He gave thanks to the King of Glory, who alone had granted him the victory. Arthur commanded search to be made about the country for the bodies of the slain, whether they were friend or foe. Many he buried in the self-same place, but for the others he carried them to certain fair abbeys, and laid them together to rest. As for the body of Lucius, the emperor, Arthur bade it to be held in all honour, and tended with every high observance. He sealed it in a bier, and sent it worshipfully to Rome. At the same time he wrote letters to the senate that no other truage would he pay them for Britain, which he guarded as his realm. If truage they yet required, then truage they should receive coined in the very mint. Kay, who was wounded to death in the battle, was carried to Chinon, the castle he had builded, and called after his own name. There he was interred in a holy hermitage, standing in a little grove, near by the city. Bedevere was brought to Bayeux in Normandy, a town of his lordship. He was lain in the ground beyond the gate, looking over towards the south. Holdin was borne to Flanders, and buried at Tervanna. Ligier was buried at Boulogne.

Arthur, for his part, sojourned all through the winter in Burgundy, giving peace and assurance to the land. He purposed when summer was come to pass the mountains, and get him to Rome. He was hindered in his hope by Mordred, of whose shame and vileness you shall now hear. This Mordred was the king's kin, his sister's very son, and had Britain in his charge. Arthur had given the whole realm to his care, and committed all to his keeping. Mordred did whatever was good in his own eyes, and would have seized the land to his use. He took homage and fealty from Arthur's

men, demanding of every castle a hostage. Not content with this
great sin he wrought yet fouler villainy. Against the Christian law
he took to himself the wife of the king. His uncle's queen, the dame
of his lord, he took as wife, and made of her his spouse.

These tidings were carried to Arthur. He was persuaded that
Mordred observed no faith towards him, but had betrayed the
queen, stolen his wife, and done him no fair service. The king [109]
gave half his host to Hoel, committing Burgundy and France to his
hand. He prayed him to keep the land shut from its foes till he
came again in peace. For himself he would return to Britain, to
bring the kingdom back to its allegiance, and to avenge himself on
Mordred, who had served his wife and honour so despitefully. Britain, at any cost, must be regained, for if that were lost all the rest
would quickly fall a prey. Better to defer for a season the conquest
of Rome, than to be spoiled of his own realm. . . .

Mordred learned of Arthur's purpose. He cared not though he
came, for peace was not in his heart. . . . Mordred numbered
his army with a quiet mind. He considered he was so strong as
to drive Arthur from any haven. Let come what might he would
never abandon his spoil. For him there was no place for repentance;
yea, so black was his sin that to proffer peace would be but a jest.
Arthur saw to the harness of his men. He got them on the ships, a
multitude whom none could number, and set forth to Romney,
where he purposed to cast anchor. Arthur and his people had
scarcely issued from the galleys, when Mordred hastened against
him with his own men, and those folk from beyond the sea who had
sworn to fight in his quarrel. The men in the boats strove to get
them to shore; whilst those on the land contended to thrust them
deeper in the water. Arrows flew and spears were flung from one
to the other, piercing heart and bowels and breast of those to whom
they were addressed. The mariners pained themselves mightily to
run their boats aground. They could neither defend themselves, nor
climb from the ships; so that those were swiftly slain who struggled
to land. Often they staggered and fell,[110] crying aloud; and in
their rage they taunted as traitors who hindered them from coming
on shore. Ere the ships could be unladen in that port, Arthur suffered wondrous loss. Many a bold sergeant paid the price with his
head. There, too, was Gawain, his nephew, slain; and Arthur made
over him marvellous sorrow; for the knight was dearer to his heart

than any other man. . . . So long as Mordred kept the shipmen
from the sand, he wrought them much mischief. But when Arthur's
sergeants won forth from the boats, and arrayed them in the open
country, Mordred's meinie might not endure against them. Mordred
and his men had fared richly and lain softly overlong. They were
sickly with peace. They knew not how to order the battle, neither
to seek shelter nor to wield arms, as these things were known to
Arthur's host, which was cradled and nourished in war. Arthur and
his own ravened amongst them, smiting and slaying with the sword.
They slew them by scores and by hundreds, killing many and taking captive many more. . . .

   Arthur might find no rest by reason of the hatred he bore to
Mordred. Great grief was his for Aguisel and Gawain, the friends
whom he had lost. He sorrowed heavily above his nephew, and offered him seemly burial, though in what place I cannot tell. The
chronicles are silent, and meseems there is not a man who knows
where Gawain was laid, nor the name of him who slew him with
the sword. When Arthur had performed these fitting rites he gave
himself over to his wrath, considering [111] only in what way he
could destroy Mordred. He followed after the traitor to Winchester,
calling from every part his vassals as he went. Arthur drew near the
city, and lodged his host without the walls. Mordred regarded the
host which shut him fast. Fight he must, and fight he would, for the
army might never rise up till he was taken. Once Arthur had him
in his grip well he knew he was but a dead man. . . . Mordred was
persuaded that for him there was only one hope of safety; for his
trespass was beyond forgiveness, and much he feared the king. He
assembled privily the folk of his household, his familiar friends,
and those who cherished against Arthur the deepest grudge. With
these he fled over by-ways to Southampton, leaving the rest of his
people to endure as they could. At the port he sought pilots and
mariners. These he persuaded by gifts and fair promises straightway to put out to sea, that he might escape from his uncle. With a
favourable wind the shipmen carried him to Cornwall. Mordred
feared exceedingly for his life and rejoiced greatly to begone.

   King Arthur besieged Winchester strictly. At the end he took
burgesses and castle. To Yvain, son of Urian, a baron beloved of the
court, Arthur granted Scotland as a heritage. . . .

   That queen, who was Arthur's wife, knew and heard tell of

the war that was waged by Mordred in England. She learned also
that Mordred had fled from before the king, because he might
not endure against him, and durst not abidc him in the field. The
queen was lodged at York, in doubt and sadness. She called to mind
her sin, and remembered that for Mordred her name was a hissing.
Her lord she had shamed, and set her love on her husband's sister's
son. Moreover, she had wedded Mordred in defiance of right, since
she was wife already, and so must suffer reproach in earth and hell.
Better were the dead [112] than those who lived, in the eyes of
Arthur's queen. Passing heavy was the lady in her thought. The
queen fled to Caerleon. There she entered in a convent of nuns,
and took the veil. All her life's days were hidden in this abbey.
Never again was this fair lady heard or seen; never again was she
found or known of men. This she did by reason of her exceeding
sorrow for her trespass, and for the sin that she had wrought.

Mordred held Cornwall in his keeping, but for the rest the
realm had returned to its allegiance. . . . Mordred had no desire
to shrink from battle. He preferred to stake all on the cast, yea,
though the throw meant death—rather than be harried from place
to place. The battle was arrayed on the Camel, over against the entrance to Cornwall. A bitter hatred had drawn the hosts together,
so that they strove to do each other sore mischief. Their malice was
wondrous great, and the murder passing grim. I cannot say who
had the better part. I neither know who lost, nor who gained that
day. No man wists the name of overthrower or of overthrown. All
are alike forgotten, the victor with him who died. . . . There perished the brave and comely youth Arthur had nourished and gathered from so many and far lands. There also the knights of his
Table Round, whose praise was bruited about the whole world.
There, too, was Mordred slain in the press, together with the greater
part of his folk; and in the self-same day were destroyed the flower
of Arthur's host, the best and hardiest of his men. So the chronicle
speaks sooth, Arthur himself was wounded in his body to the death.
He caused him [113] to be borne to Avalon for the searching of his
hurts. He is yet in Avalon, awaited of the Britons; for as they say
and deem he will return from whence he went and live again.
Master Wace, the writer of this book, cannot add more to this
matter of his end than was spoken by Merlin the prophet. Merlin
said of Arthur—if I read aright—that his end should be hidden in

doubtfulness. The prophet spoke truly. Men have ever doubted, and—as I am persuaded—will always doubt whether he liveth or is dead. Arthur bade that he should be carried to Avalon in this hope in the year 642 of the Incarnation. The sorer sorrow that he was a childless man. To Constantine, Cador's son, Earl of Cornwall, and his near kin, Arthur committed the realm, commanding him to hold it as king until he returned to his own. The earl took the land to his keeping. He held it as bidden, but nevertheless Arthur came never again.[114]

LAYAMON

Brut (c. 1205)

From Roger Sherman Loomis and Rudolph Willard, *Medieval English Verse and Prose* (New York: Appleton-Century-Crofts, Inc., 1948).

(vss. 1-67)

There was a priest in the land;   Layamon was he called.
He was Leovenath's son;   the Lord be gracious to him;
He dwelt at Earnley,   at a noble church,
Upon Severn shore,—good there he thought it,—
Quite near to Redstone;   he read there his service book.
    It came to his mind   and into his serious thought,
To relate of the English   their noble deeds,
What they were called,   and whence they had come,
Who first did possess   the land of the English,
After the flood,   which came from the Lord,

And did destroy all things   that it found alive,
Except Noah and Shem,   Japhet and Ham,
And their four wives   who were with them in the ark.
Layamon did travel   widely among the people,
And got him those noble books   that he set as his pattern.
He took that English book   that Saint Bede had made;
Another he took, in Latin,   that Saint Albin had made
And the fair Augustine,   who brought baptism hither;
A third book he took,   and laid it alongside,
Which a French cleric had made,   well learned in lore;
Wace was his name,   he knew well how to write,
And he then did give it   to the noble Eleanor,
Who was Henry's queen,   that high king's.[3]
Layamon laid these books out,   and he turned the leaves;
With love he searched them,   the Lord be to him gracious.
He took feathers in his fingers,   and he composed on parchment;
And these three books   he condensed into one.
        Now Layamon prayeth   each noble man,
For the love of Almighty God   and of his gracious heart,
Who will read these books   and learn these runes,
That some true words   he will say together
For his father's soul,   who did beget him,
And for his mother's soul,   who bore him as man,
And for his own soul,   that it be the better for them.   Amen.[4]

(vss. 19246- 69)

There Uther the king   took Ygerne for queen.
Ygerne was with child   by Uther the king,
All through Merlin's wiles,   ere she was wedded.
The time came that was chosen;   then was Arthur born.
As soon as he came on earth   fays took him.
They enchanted the child   with magic right strong:
They gave him the might   to be best of all knights;
They gave him another thing,   that he should be a mighty king;
They gave him a third,—his death would be long deferred.
They gave to that royal child   right good virtues,
That he was most liberal   of all living men.
This the fays gave him,   and thus the child thrived.[18]

(vss. 21111-456)

There came tidings   to Arthur the king,
That his kinsman Howell   lay sick at Clud.
Therefor he was sorry,   but there he left him.
With very great haste   he hied him forth
Until beside Bath   he came to a field.
There he alighted   and all his knights,
And the doughty warriors   donned their byrnies,
And he in five parts   divided his army.
When he had arrayed all,   and all seemed ready,
He did on his byrny,   made of linked steel,
Which an elvish smith made   with his noble craft;
It was called Wigar,   and a wizard wrought it.
He hid his shanks   in hose of steel.
Caliburn, his sword,   he swung at his side;
It was wrought in Avalon   with cunning craft.[18]
He set on his head   a high helm of steel;
Thereon was many a jewel   all adorned with gold.
It had been Uther's,   the noble king's;
It was called Goose-white;   'twas unlike any other.
He slung from his neck   a precious shield;
Its name in British   was called Pridwen.
Thereon was graven   in red-gold figures
A dear likeness   of the Lord's Mother.
He took in hand his spear,   which was called Ron.
When he had all his weeds,   he leapt on his steed.
Then might they behold   who stood there beside him
The fairest knight   who would ever lead host.
Never saw any man   a goodlier knight
Than Arthur was,   the noblest of ancestry.
    Then Arthur called   with a loud voice:
"Lo, here are before us   the heathen hounds
Who killed our chieftains   with their base crafts;
And they on this land   are loathest of all things.
Now let us attack them   and lay on them starkly,
And avenge wonderously   our kin and our kingdom,

And wreak the great shame   with which they have shamed us,
That they over the waves   have come to Dartmouth.
They are all forsworn   and they all shall be lorn;
They all are doomed   with the aid of the Lord.
Hasten we forward   fast together,
Even as softly   as if we thought no evil.
And when we come on them,   I myself will attack;
Foremost of all   I will begin the fight.
Now let us ride and pass over the land,
And let no man, on his life,   make any noise,
But fare firmly,   with the help of the Lord."
Then Arthur, the rich man,   to ride forth began,
Went over the weald   and would seek Bath.
         The tidings came to Childric,   the strong and the mighty,
That Arthur came with his army,   all ready to fight.
Childric and his brave men   leapt on their horses,
Gripped their weapons;   they knew themselves fey.
This saw Arthur,   noblest of kings.
He saw a heathen earl   hastening against him,
With seven hundred knights   all ready to fight.
The earl himself came   ahead of his troop,[19]
And Arthur himself galloped   before all his army.
Arthur, the fierce,   took Ron in his hand;
He couched the strong shaft,   that stern-minded king.
He let his horse run   so that the earth rumbled.
He laid shield to his breast;   the king was bursting with anger.
He smote Borel the earl   right through the breast,
So that his heart was split.   The king cried at once:
"The foremost hath met his fate!   Now the Lord help us
And the heavenly Queen,   who gave birth to the Lord!"
Then cried Arthur,   noblest of kings:
"Now at them, now at them!   The foremost is done for!"
The Britons laid on,   as men should do to the wicked.
They gave bitter strokes   with axes and swords.
There fell of Childric's men   fully two thousand,
But Arthur never lost   one of his men.
There were the Saxon men   most wretched of all folk,
And the men of Almain   most miserable of all peoples.
Arthur with his sword   executed doom;

All whom he smote   were soon destroyed.
The king was enraged   as is the wild boar
When he in the beechwood   meeteth many swine.
This Childric beheld   and began to turn back,
And bent his way over Avon   to save himself.
Arthur pursued him,   as if he were a lion,
And drove them to the flood;   many there were fey.
There sank to the bottom   five and twenty hundred.
Then was Avon's stream all   bridged over with steel.
Childric fled over the water   with fifteen hundred knights;
He thought to journey forth   and pass over sea.
Arthur saw Colgrim   climb to a mount,
Turn to a hill   that standeth over Bath;
And Baldulf followed after with seven thousand knights.
They thought on that hill   to make a stout stand,
To defend themselves with weapons   and work harm to Arthur.
     When Arthur saw,   noblest of kings,
Where Colgrim withstood   and made a stand,
Then cried the king   keenly and loud:
"My bold thanes,   make for that hill!
For yesterday was Colgrim   most daring of all men.
Now he is as sad as a goat,   where he guardeth the hill.
High on a hilltop   he fighteth with horns,
When the wild wolf cometh,   toward him stalking.[20]
Though the wolf be alone,   without any pack,
And there be in the fold   five hundred goats,
The wolf falleth on them   and biteth them all.
So will I now today   destroy Colgrim altogether.
I am a wolf and he is a goat.   The man shall be fey!"
Then still shouted Arthur,   noblest of kings:
"Yesterday was Baldulf   of all knights boldest.
Now he standeth on the hill   and beholdeth the Avon,
How there lie in the stream   steel fishes!
Ready with sword,   their health is broken!
Their scales float   like gold-colored shields;
There float their fins   as if they were spears.
These are marvelous things   come to this land,
Such beasts on the hill,   such fish in the stream!
Yesterday was the kaiser   boldest of all kings;

Now hath he become a hunter,   and horns follow him;
He flieth over the broad weald;   his hounds bark.
But beside Bath   he hath abandoned his hunting;
He fleeth from his deer   and we shall bring it down,
And bring to naught   his bold threats;
And so we shall revel   in our rights again."
　　　Even with the words   that the king said,
He raised high his shield   before his breast,
He gripped his long spear   and set spurs to his horse.
Nearly as swiftly   as the bird flieth,
There followed the king   five and twenty thousand
Valorous men,   raging under their arms,
Held their way to the hill   with high courage,
And smote at Colgrim   with full smart strokes.
There Colgrim received them   and felled the Britons to earth.
In the foremost attack   there fell five hundred.
Arthur saw that,   noblest of kings,
And wroth he was   with wondrous great wrath,
And Arthur the noble man   to shout thus began:
"Where be ye, Britons,   my warriors bold?
Here stand before us   our foes all chosen.
My warriors good,   let us beat them to the ground."
Arthur gripped his sword aright   and smote a Saxon knight,
So that the good sword   stopped at the teeth.
Then he smote another   who was that knight's brother,
So that his helm and his head   fell to the ground.
Soon a third dint he gave   and in two a knight clave.[21]
Then were the Britons   much emboldened
And laid on the Saxons   right sore strokes
With spears that were long   and swords that were strong.
There Saxons fell,   met their fated hour,
By hundreds and hundreds   sank to the earth,
By thousands and thousands   dropped there to the ground.
When Colgrim saw   where Arthur came toward him,
He could not, for the slaughter,   flee to any side.
There fought Baldulf   beside his brother.
Then called Arthur   with a loud voice:
"Here I come, Colgrim!   we will gain us a country.
We will so share this land   as will be least to thy liking."

Even with the words, that the king uttered,
He heaved up his broad sword   and brought it down hard,
And smote Colgrim's helm   and clove it in the middle,
And the hood of the byrny;   the blade stopped at the breast.
He struck at Baldulf   with his left hand,
And smote off the head   and the helm also.
    Then laughed Arthur,   the noble king,
And began to speak   with gamesome words:
"Lie now there, Colgrim!   Thou didst climb too high!
And Baldulf thy brother   lieth by thy side.
Now all this good land   I place in your hand,
Dales and downs   and all my doughty folk.
Thou didst climb on this hill   wondrously high,
As if thou soughtest heaven;   now thou shalt to hell!
There thou mayst ken   many of thy kin!
Greet thou there Hengest,   who of knights was fairest,
Ebissa and Ossa,   Octa and more of thy kin;
And bid them dwell there,   winters and summers.
And we on this land   will live in bliss,
And pray for your souls   that they may never be blessed,
And here shall your bones   lie beside Bath." [22]

(vss. 22737-996)

    It was on a Yule Day   that Arthur in London lay.
Then were come to him   from out his whole kingdom,
From Britain, from Scotland,   from Ireland, from Iceland,
And from out every land   that Arthur had in hand,
All the highest thanes   with horses and with swains.
There were seven kings' sons   come with seven hundred knights,
Besides that household   which followed Arthur.
Each one had in his heart   over-proud feelings,
And felt that he was better   than his fellow.
That folk was from many lands;   there was great envy:
When one held him high,   the other held him much higher.
    Then men blew upon trumpets   and spread the tables;
Water was brought on the floor   with golden bowls;

And then soft cloths, all of white silk.
Then Arthur sat him down, and by him Wenhaver;
After him sat the earls, and after them the nobles;
Afterwards the knights, even as it was ordained them.
Men of high birth then bore in the meats,
First to the head of the table, and then to the knights,
Then towards the thanes, after that to the swains,
Then to the bearers forth at the board.
The courtiers became angered; dints there were rife.
First they hurled the loaves the while that they lasted,
And then the silver bowls that were filled with wine;
And afterwards fists sped forth to necks.
Then there leapt forth a young man who came from Winetland;
He was given to Arthur to hold as a hostage;
He was the son of Rumaret, the king of Winet;
From the beginning to the ending, of Arthur the king,
"Lord Arthur, go quickly into thy bower,
And thy queen with thee, and thy native-born kinsmen,[23]
And we shall settle this fight with these foreign-born warriors."
With these very words he leapt to the board,
Where lay the knives before the land's king.
Three knives he seized, and with the one he smote
On the neck of that knight who first began that fight,
That his head on the floor fell to the ground.
At once he slew another, that same thane's brother;
Ere the swords came in, seven he had cut down.
There was then a great fight; each man smote the other;
There was much bloodshed; in the court was disaster.
   Then came the king hastening out from his bower,
With him a hundred warriors with helms and with byrnies;
Each bore in his hand a white steel brand.
Then called out Arthur, the noblest of kings:
"Sit down, sit down at once, each man on pain of his life!
And whoever will not do that, condemned shall he be.
Take me that same man who this fight first began,
And put a withy on his neck and drag him to a moor,
And throw him in a low-lying fen, where he shall lie.
And take all his next of kin, whom ye can find,
And smite off their heads with your broad swords;

And the women that ye can find   nearest him of kin,
Carve off their noses   and ruin their beauty;
And thus will I wholly destroy   that kin that he came from.
And if I evermore   shall hear afterwards
That any in my court,   be he high, be he low,
For this same assault   stir a quarrel later,
No ransom shall be given for him,   neither gold nor any treasure,
Tall horse nor armor,   that he shall not die
Or be drawn asunder with horses,   as beseemeth such traitors.
Bring ye holy relics,   and I will swear thereon;
And so shall ye, knights,   who were at this fight,
Both earls and warriors,   that ye will not break it."
First swore Arthur,   the noblest of kings;
Then swore the earls;   after swore the warriors;
Then swore the thanes,   and then swore the swains,
That they would nevermore   stir up that quarrel.
They took all the dead men   and to their grave bore them.
Afterwards they blew trumpets   with exceeding merry sounds.
Were him lief, were him loath,   each took water and cloth;
And they afterwards sat down   in peace at the board,
All in fear of Arthur,   the noblest of kings.[24]
Cup bearers then thronged in;   minstrels sang there,
Harps aroused melodies;   the court was in happiness.
Thus for a full seven nights   was that company maintained.
       Afterwards, it says in the tale,   the king went to Cornwall;
There came to him anon   one who was a skilled craftsman,
And went to meet the king,   and courteously greeted him:
"Hail to thee, Arthur,   noblest of kings.
I am thine own man;   I have traversed many a land.
I know in woodwork   wondrous many devices.
I heard beyond the sea   men telling new tidings,
How thine own knights   at thy board did fight
On midwinter's day;   many there fell;
For their mighty pride   they played the death-game,
And because of his high race   each would be on the inside.
Now I will make for thee   a work most skillful
That there may sit at it   sixteen hundred and more,
All in succession,   that none may sit at the end,
But without and within,   man beside man.

Whenever thou wilt ride,   with thee thou mayst take it,
And set it up where thou wilt   after thine own will;
And thou needest never dread   throughout the wide world
That ever any proud knight   at thy board stir a fight;
For there shall the high   be equal to the low.
Let me but have timber,   and begin that board."
In four weeks' time   that work was completed.
On a high day   the court was assembled;
And Arthur himself went   forthwith to that board,
And summoned every knight   to that table forthright.
When they were all set,   the knights at their meat,
Then spoke each with the other   as though it were his brother.
All of them sat round about;   none had an end seat;
A knight of every race   had there a good place;
They were all side by side,   the low and the high;
None might there boast   of a better beverage,
Than had his companions   who were at that table.

     This was the same board   that the Britons boast of,
And tell many kinds of lies   about Arthur the king.[25]
So doth every man   who loveth another;
If he is too dear to him,   then will he lie,
And say in his worship   more than he is worth;
Be he never so base,   his friends will wish him well.
Further, if among people   there arise hostility,
At any time so ever,   between two men,
Men can tell of the loathed one   many lies,
Though he were the best man   that ever ate at board.
The man who is loath to him   can find charges against him.
'Tis neither all truth nor all lies   which the people's bards sing.
But this is the truth   about Arthur the king:
Was never ere such a king   so valiant in everything,
For the truth stands in writings,   how it came to pass,
From the beginning to the ending   of Arthur the king,
Neither more nor less,   but as his traits were.
But the Britons loved him greatly,   and oft tell lies of him,
And say many things   about Arthur the king,
That took place never   in this earthly kingdom.
Enough can he say   who will relate the truth
Of wondrous things   about Arthur the king.

(vss. 27993-28200)

Then there came at that time   a valiant man riding,
And brought tidings   to Arthur the king
From Modred, his sister's son;   to Arthur he was welcome,
For he weened that he brought   exceeding good news.
Arthur lay all the long night   and spoke with that young knight;
But he never would tell him   the truth, how it fared.
When it was day, in the morning,   and the court began to stir,
Arthur then rose up   and stretched his arms;
He rose up, and down he sat,   as though he were very sick.
Then asked the young knight,   "Lord, how hast thou fared this
     night?"
Arthur then answered,   in mood he was uneasy,
"This night in my bed,   as I lay in my bower,
I dreamt a dream   for which I am most sorrowful.
I dreamt I was taken   high upon a hall;
That hall I did bestride   as though I would ride; [26]
All the lands that I owned,   all them I looked over;
And Walwain sat before me,   my sword he bore in hand.
Then came Modred faring thither   with numberless folk;
He bore in his hand   a strong battle-ax;
He began to hew   exceeding vigorously,
And all the posts he hewed down   that held up the hall.
There I saw Wenhaver also,   the woman dearest to me;
All that mighty hallroof   with her hands she pulled apart.
The hall began to fall,   and I fell to the ground,
So that my right arm broke.   Then said Modred, 'Take that.'
Down fell that hall,   and Walwain began to fall,
And fell to the earth;   both his arms broke.
And I gripped my beloved sword   with my left hand,
And smote off Modred's head   that it rolled to the field.
And the queen I cut to pieces   with my dear sword,
And I then put her down   in a dark pit.
And all my royal folk   betook them to flight,
So that I knew not under Christ   where they had gone.
But myself, I did stand   upon a wooded land.

And there I did wander   widely over the moors.
There saw I griffins   and grisly fowl;
Then came a golden lic.1ess   moving over the down,
Of all beasts the most gracious   that our Lord hath made;
The lioness ran towards me,   and by the middle seized me,
And forth she betook her,   and turned towards the sea;
And I saw the waves   driving in the sea,
And the lioness into the flood   went bearing me.
When we two were in the sea,   the waves took me from her;
There came a fish gliding,   and ferried me to land;
Then was I all wet and weary,   and sick from sorrow.
When I did awake,   I began greatly to quake,
And I began to quiver   as though I were all afire.
And so I have thought   all the night of my dream,
For I know in certain   that gone is all my bliss;
Forever in my life   I must suffer sorrow;
Woe is me I have not here   Wenhaver my queen!"
        Then answered the knight,   "Lord, thou art not right;
Never should a dream   with sorrow distress me.
Thou art the mightiest man   that reigneth on earth,
And the wisest of all   that dwell under heaven.
If it hath befallen—may the Lord forbid it—[27]
That Modred, thy sister's son,   have taken thy queen,
And all thy royal land   have set in his own hand,
Which thou didst entrust him   when thou didst set out for Rome,
And he have done all this   in his treachery,
Even yet thou mightest avenge thee   honorably with weapons,
And hold again thy land   and rule thy people,
And fell thy foes   who wish thee evil,
And slay them all wholly,   that none should survive."
        Arthur then answered,   the noblest of kings:
"So long as is ever,   I have weened never
That Modred, my kinsman,   who of men is dearest to me,
Would betray me   for all of my riches,
Or Wenhaver, my queen,   weaken in her thoughts;
She will never begin it   for any man on earth!"
        With those words straightway   then answered the knight:
"I tell thee the truth, dear king,   for I am thine underling,
Thus hath Modred now done: thy queen he hath taken,

And thy beautiful land   he hath set in his own hand.
He is king, she is queen;   of thy coming they no longer ween,
For they believe never   that thou wilt return from Rome ever.
I am thine own man,   and I saw this betrayal;
And I am come to thee myself   the truth to tell thee;
I will stake my head,   it is true what I have said,
The truth without lies,   of thy beloved queen,
And of Modred, thy sister's son,   how he hath taken Britain from
      thee!"
Still sat they all   in Arthur's hall;
Then was there great sorrow   for that blessed king.
Then were the British men   much disheartened therefor.
Then after a while   there stirred a sound;
Widely might one hear   the Britons' outcries,
And they began to tell   in various speeches
How they would condemn   Modred and the queen,
And punish all those men   who held with Modred.
'   Then called out Arthur,   most gracious of all Britons:
"Sit you down still,   knights in this hall,
And I will tell you   news unheard of.
Now tomorrow when it is day,   if the Lord send it,
Forth will I turn me   on towards Britain;
And Modred I will slay   and burn the queen,
And I will destroy all   who favored that treachery.
And here will I leave   the man dearest to me,
Howell, my dear kinsman,   the highest of my race,[28]
And half of my army   I leave in this country,
To hold all this royal land   that I have in my hand.
And when these things are all done   I will go on to Rome,
And entrust my beloved land   to Walwain my kinsman,
And perform my promise afterwards   with my bare life;
All of my enemies   shall make a doomed journey."

(vss. 28486-651)

Modred was in Cornwall,   and summoned many knights;
To Ireland he sent   his messenger in haste;
To Saxonland he sent   his messenger in haste;

To Scotland he sent   his messenger in haste;
He bade all come at once,   those who would have land,
Either silver or gold,   either goods or lands;
He in every wise   looked out for himself,
As doth wise man   when need cometh upon him.
       Arthur heard that,   the most wrathful of kings,
That Modred was in Cornwall   with a very great host,
And would there abide   till Arthur thither should ride.
Arthur sent messengers   throughout all his kingdom,
And commanded all to come   who were alive in the land,
Who were able to fight,   and could bear weapons;
And whoso should neglect   what the king ordered,
The king would to the ground   burn him alive wholly.
There moved towards the court   countless folk,
Riding and marching,   as the rain falleth down.
Arthur went to Cornwall   with immeasurable army.
Modred heard that,   and held against him
With countless folk—there were many fated.
Upon the Tamar   they met together;
The place called Camelford,   forever will that name endure;
And at Camelford were assembled   sixty thousand,
And more thousands besides;   Modred was their leader.
       Now thitherwards did ride   Arthur the royal,
With countless folk,   fated though they were;
Upon the Tamar   they met together,
Raised their battle-standards,   advanced together; [29]
Drew their long swords,   laid on upon helms;
Fire sprang out there;   and spears did shiver;
Shields began to break,   shafts to shatter;
There fought together   folk uncounted.
The Tamar was in flood   with immeasurable blood;
No man there in that fight   could know any knight,
Who did worse, or who better,   so closely joined was the conflict.
For each one struck downright,   were he swain, were he knight.
There was Modred slain   and taken from his lifeday,
And all his knights   were slain in that fight.
There too were slain   all the swift men,
Arthur's retainers,   the high and the low,
And all of the Britons   of Arthur's board,

And all his fosterchildren   from many kingdoms.
And Arthur was wounded   with a broad battle-spear;
Fifteen had he,   all ghastly wounds:
Into the least could one   thrust two gloves.
There were none more   left in that fight,
Of two hundred thousand,   who lay hewn in pieces,
Save Arthur the king only,   and two of his knights.
    Arthur was wounded   wondrously sore.
There came to him a boy   who was of his kin;
He was the son of Cador,   the earl of Cornwall;
Constantine was the boy called;   he was dear to the king.
Arthur looked at him   as he lay on the ground,
And these words spoke he   with sorrowful heart:
"Constantine, thou art welcome;   thou wert Cador's son;
Here I commit to thee   all of my kingdom;
Defend my Britons ever   to thy life's end,
And keep all the laws   that have stood in my days,
And all the good laws   that stood in Uther's days.
And I will fare to Avalon,   to the fairest of all maidens,
To Argante the queen,   a fay most fair,
And she will make sound   all my wounds,
And make me all whole   with healing potions;
And afterwards I shall come   again to my kingdom,
And dwell with the Britons   in very great joy."
    At these very words   there came from out the sea
A short boat gliding,   driven by the waves,
And two women therein,   wondrously clad; [30]
And they took Arthur anon   and in haste bore him,
And softly laid him down,   and then forth did glide.
Then was it come to pass   what Merlin once said,
There would be very great sorrow   at Arthur's departure;
The Britons believe yet   that he is alive,
And dwelleth in Avalon   with the fairest of fays;
And the Britons still look ever   for Arthur to come.
There was never man born,   of any maiden chosen,
Who knoweth of the truth   more to say of Arthur.
But there was once a prophet,   Merlin by name;
He foretold in words,—his sayings were true,—
That an Arthur must still come   to help the Britons. [31]

"THE MABINOGION"

"The Dream of Rhonabwy" (c. 1220)

Translated by Gwyn Jones and Thomas Jones, Everyman's Library (London: J. M. Dent & Sons, Ltd., 1949).

Madawg son of Maredudd held Powys from end to end, that is, from Porffordd unto Gwafan in the uplands of Arwystli. And at that time he had a brother. He was not a man of rank equal with himself: he was Iorwoerth son of Maredudd. And he felt great heaviness and sorrow at seeing the honour and power that were his brother's, whereas he had naught. And he sought out his comrades and foster-brothers and took counsel of them what he should do about it. They decided by their counsel to send some from amongst them to demand provision for him. The offer Madawg made him was the captaincy of his war-band, and equal standing with himself, and steeds and arms and honour. And Iorwoerth rejected that, and went harrying into Lloegyr. And Iorwoerth made slaughter and burned houses and carried off prisoners.

And Madawg took counsel, and the men of Powys with him. They decided by their counsel to place a hundred men in every three commots in Powys, to seek him out. And they reckoned Rhychdir Powys, from Aber Ceirawg in Hallictwn as far as the Ford of Wilfre on Efyrnwy, as equal to the three best commots that were in Powys. And the man would not prosper with a war-band in Powys who would not prosper in that cultivated land. And as far as Didlystwn, a hamlet in that cultivated land, those men took their quarters.

And there was a man on that quest, his name was Rhonabwy. And Rhonabwy and Cynwrig Frychgoch, a man from Mawddwy, and Cadwgawn Fras, a man from Moelfre in Cynlleith, came to the house of Heilyn Goch son of Cadwgawn son of Iddon for lodgings. And as they came towards the house, they could see a black old hall with a straight gable end, and smoke a-plenty from it. And when [137] they came inside, they could see a floor full of holes and uneven. Where there was a bump upon it, it was with difficulty a man might stand thereon, so exceeding slippery was the floor with cows' urine and their dung. Where there was a hole, a man would go over the ankle, what with the mixture of water and cow-dung; and branches of holly a-plenty on the floor after the cattle had eaten off their tips. And when they came to the main floor of the house they could see bare dusty dais boards, and a crone feeding a fire on the one dais, and when cold came upon her she would throw a lapful of husks on to the fire, so that it was not easy for any man alive to endure that smoke entering his nostrils. And on the other dais they could see a yellow ox skin. And good luck would it be for the one of them whose lot it would be to go on that skin.

And after they had sat down they asked the crone where were the people of the house. But the crone spoke nothing to them save incivility. And thereupon, lo, the people coming: a red-headed, exceeding bald and wizened man, with a bundle of sticks on his back, and a little skinny livid woman, and with her too a bundle under the arm. And a cold welcome they had for the men. And the woman lit a fire of sticks for them and went to cook, and brought them their food, barley-bread and cheese and watered milk.

And thereupon, lo, a storm of wind and rain, so that it was not easy for any to go to relieve himself. And so exceeding weary were they from their journey that they drowsed and went to sleep.

And when their resting-place was examined there was nothing on it save dusty flea-ridden straw-ends, and branch butts a-plenty throughout it, after the oxen had eaten all the straw that was on it above their heads and below their feet. A greyish-red, threadbare, flea-infested blanket was spread thereon, and over the blanket a coarse broken sheet in tatters, and a half-empty pillow and filthy pillow-case thereon, on top of the sheet. And they went to sleep. And [138] sleep came heavily upon Rhonabwy's two companions after the fleas and the discomfort had fretted them. And Rhonabwy, since he could neither sleep nor rest, thought it would be less of a

torture for him to go on the yellow ox skin on the dais, to sleep.
And there he slept.

And the moment sleep came upon his eyes he was granted a
vision, how he and his companions were traversing the plain of
Argyngroeg; and his mind and purpose, it seemed to him, were
towards Rhyd-y-Groes on the Severn. And as he journeyed he heard
a commotion, and the like of that commotion he had never heard.
And he looked behind him.

He could see a youth with yellow curly hair and his beard new
trimmed, upon a yellow horse, and from the top of his two legs
and the caps of his knees downwards green. And a tunic of yellow
brocaded silk about the rider, sewn with green thread, and a gold-
hilted sword on his thigh, and a scabbard of new cordwain for it,
and a deerskin thong and a clasp of gold thereon. And over and
above those a mantle of yellow brocaded silk sewn with green silk,
and the fringes of the mantle green. And what was green of the
rider's and his horse's apparel was green as the fronds of the fir
trees, and what was yellow of it was yellow as the flowers of the
broom. And so awe-inspiring did they see the rider that they were
frightened and made to flee. And the rider pursued them, and when
the horse breathed forth his breath the men grew distant from him,
and when he drew it in they were drawn near to him, right to the
horse's chest. And when he caught up with them they asked him
for quarter. 'You shall have it gladly, and let there be no fear upon
you.' 'Ah, chieftain, since thou hast granted us quarter, wilt thou
tell us who thou art?' said Rhonabwy. 'I will not hide my identity
from thee: Iddawg son of Mynio. But for the most part it is not
by my name I am spoken of, but by my nickname.' 'Wilt thou tell
us what thy nickname [139] is?' 'I will. Iddawg the Embroiler of
Britain am I called.' 'Chieftain,' said Rhonabwy, 'for what reason
then art thou so called?' 'I will tell thee the reason. I was one of the
envoys at the battle of Camlan, between Arthur and Medrawd his
nephew. And a spirited young man was I then! And I so craved for
battle that I kindled strife between them. This was the kind of
strife I kindled: when the emperor Arthur would send me to remind Medrawd that he was his foster-father and uncle, and ask for
peace lest the kings' sons of the Island of Britain and their noblemen should be slain, and when Arthur would speak to me the

fairest words he could, I would speak those words the ugliest way I knew how to Medrawd. And because of that the name Iddawg the Embroiler of Britain was set on me. And because of that was woven the battle of Camlan. But even so, three nights before the end of the battle of Camlan I parted from them, and I went to Y Llech Las in Prydein to do penance. And I was there seven years doing penance, and I won pardon.'

Thereupon, lo, they could hear a commotion which was greater by far than the former commotion. And when they looked in the direction of the commotion, lo, a young man with yellow-red hair, without beard and without moustache, and a nobleman's bearing upon him, on a great charger. And from the top of his shoulders and the caps of his knees downwards the horse was yellow, and a garment about the man of red brocaded silk, sewn with yellow silk, and the fringes of the mantle yellow. And what was yellow of his and his horse's apparel was yellow as the flowers of the broom, and what of them was red was red as the reddest blood in the world. And then, lo, the rider overtaking them and asking Iddawg if he might have a share of those little fellows from him. 'The share it is proper for me to give, I will give: to be a comrade to them even as I myself have been.' And so the rider did, and went away.[140] 'Iddawg,' said Rhonabwy, 'who was this horseman?' 'Rhwawn Bebyr son of Deorthach Wledig.'

And then they traversed the great plain of Argyngroeg as far as Rhyd-y-Groes on the Severn. And a mile from the ford, on either side the road, they could see the tents and the pavilions and the mustering of a great host. And they came to the bank of the ford. They could see Arthur seated on a flat island below the ford, and on one side of him Bedwin the bishop, and on the other side Gwarthegydd son of Caw, and a big auburn-haired youth standing before them, with his sword in its sheath in his hand, and a tunic and surcoat of pure black brocaded silk about him, and his face as white as ivory and his eyebrows black as jet; and where a man might see aught of his wrist between his gloves and his sleeves, it was whiter than the water-lily, and thicker it was than the small of a warrior's leg.

And then Iddawg and they too along with him came before Arthur and greeted him. 'God prosper thee,' said Arthur. 'Where, Iddawg, didst thou find those little fellows?' 'I found them, lord,

away up on the road.' The emperor smiled wrily. 'Lord,' said
Iddawg, 'at what art thou laughing?' 'Iddawg,' said Arthur, 'I am
not laughing; but rather how sad I feel that men as mean as these
keep this Island, after men as fine as those that kept it of yore.'

And then Iddawg said, 'Rhonabwy, dost see the ring with the
stone in it on the emperor's hand?' 'I do,' said he. 'It is one of the
virtues of the stone that thou shalt remember what thou hast seen
here to-night. And hadst thou not seen the stone, thou shouldst
remember not a whit of this adventure.'

And after that he saw a troop coming towards the ford. 'Iddawg,' said Rhonabwy, 'whose is the troop yonder?' 'The comrades
of Rhwawn Bebyr son of Deorthach Wledig; and yonder men have
mead and bragget in honour, and they have the wooing of the
kings' daughters of the Island of Britain, without let; and they
have a right thereto, for in [141] every strait they come in his van
and in his rear.' And no other colour could he see upon horse or
man of that troop save that they were red as blood. And if one of
the riders parted from that troop, like to a pillar of fire would he
be, mounting into the sky. And that troop pitching its tents above
the ford.

And thereupon they could see another troop coming towards
the ford, and from the front saddlebows of the horses upwards as
white as the water-lily, and thence downwards as black as jet. They
could see a rider coming on ahead and spurring his horse into the
ford till the water splashed over Arthur and the bishop and those
who held counsel along with them, until they were as wet as if they
had been dragged out of the river. And as he was turning his horse's
head, the youth who was standing in front of Arthur struck the
horse on its nostrils with the sword in its scabbard, so that it would
be a marvel were it struck upon iron that it were not broken, let
alone flesh or bone. And the rider drew his sword the length of half
his scabbard and asked him, 'Why didst thou strike my horse, by
way of insult, or by way of counsel to me?' 'Thou hadst need of
counsel. What madness could make thee ride so recklessly that the
water of the ford was splashed over Arthur and the holy bishop
and their counsellors, till they were as wet as if they had been
dragged out of the river?' 'Then I shall take it as counsel.' And he
turned his horse's head back towards his troop.

'Iddawg,' said Rhonabwy, 'who was the rider just now?' 'He

who is reckoned the most accomplished and wisest young man in this kingdom, Addaon son of Teliesin.' 'And who was the man who struck his horse?' 'A cross-grained froward youth, Elphin son of Gwyddno.'

And then a proud handsome man, with bold eloquent speech, said that it was a marvel how a host so big as this was contained within a place so exceeding strait as this; and that it was to him a greater marvel how there should [142] be here at this very hour those who promised to be in the battle of Baddon by mid-day, fighting against Osla Big-knife. 'And choose thou, whether thou go or go not. I shall go.' 'Thou speakest true,' said Arthur, 'and let us go together.' 'Iddawg,' said Rhonabwy, 'who is the man who spoke so forwardly to Arthur as he spoke just now?' 'A man who had a right to speak to him as bluntly as he wished, Caradawg Stout-arm son of Llŷr Marini, chief counsellor and his first cousin.'

And after that Iddawg took Rhonabwy up behind him, and they set out, that great host, each troop in its place, in the direction of Cefyn Digoll. And when they had come to the middle of the ford on the Severn, Iddawg turned his horse's head around, and Rhonabwy looked upon the valley of the Severn. He could see two most leisurely troops coming towards the ford on the Severn; and a brilliant white troop coming, and a mantle of white brocaded silk about each man of them, and the fringes of each one pure black, and the knee-caps and the tops of the horses' two legs black, and the horses pale white all over save for that; and their standards pure white, and the tip of each one of them pure black.

'Iddawg,' said Rhonabwy, 'what is the pure white troop yonder?' 'Those are the men of Llychlyn, and March son of Meirchawn at their head. A first cousin of Arthur is he.'

And then he could see a troop, and a pure black garment about each one of them, and the fringes of each mantle pure white, and from the top of the horses' two legs and the caps of their knees pure white; and their standards pure black, and the tip of each one of them pure white.

'Iddawg,' said Rhonabwy, 'what is the pure black troop yonder?' 'The men of Denmark, and Edern son of Nudd at their head.'

And when they overtook the host, Arthur and his host of the Mighty had descended below Caer Faddon, and the [143] way that Arthur was going he could see that he and Iddawg were going too.

And when they had descended, he could hear great and dreadful
commotion amongst the host, and the man who would be now on
the flank of the host would be back in their centre, and he who
would be in their centre would be on the flank. And thereupon, lo,
he could see a rider coming with mail upon him and his horse, and
its rings as white as the whitest water-lily, and its rivets red as the
reddest blood. And he riding in amongst the host.

'Iddawg,' said Rhonabwy, 'is the host fleeing before me?' 'The
emperor Arthur never fled. And hadst thou been overheard making
that remark thou wert a doomed man. But the rider thou seest
yonder, that is Cei. The fairest man who rides in Arthur's court is
Cei. And the man on the flank of the host is hurrying back to the
centre to look on Cei riding, and the man in the centre is fleeing
to the flank lest he be hurt by the horse. And that is the meaning
of the commotion amongst the host.'

Thereupon they could hear Cadwr earl of Cornwall called for.
Lo, he arising, and Arthur's sword in his hand, and the image of
two serpents on the sword in gold; and when the sword was drawn
from its sheath as it were two flames of fire might be seen from the
mouths of the serpents, and so exceeding dreadful was it that it
was not easy for any to look thereon. Thereupon, lo, the host settling down and the commotion ceasing. And the earl returned to
the tent.

'Iddawg,' said Rhonabwy, 'who was the man who brought the
sword to Arthur?' 'Cadwr earl of Cornwall, the man whose duty
it is to array the king in arms on the day of battle and combat.'

And thereupon they could hear Arthur's servitor, Eiryn Wych
son of Peibyn, called for, a rough red-headed ugly man, with a red
moustache, and bristling hair therein. Lo, he coming on a big red
horse, with its mane parted on both sides of its neck, and with him
a large handsome pack. And [144] the big red servitor dismounted
in Arthur's presence and drew forth a golden chair from the pack,
and a mantle of ribbed brocaded silk. And he spread the mantle
in front of Arthur, and an apple of red gold at each of its corners,
and he set the chair on the mantle, and so big was the chair that
three warriors armed might sit therein. Gwen was the name of the
mantle. And one of the properties of the mantle was that the man
around whom it might be wrapped, no one would see him, whereas

he would see every one. And no colour would ever abide on it save its own colour.

And Arthur seated himself upon the mantle, with Owein son of Urien standing before him. 'Owein,' said Arthur, 'wilt play gwyddbwyll?' 'I will, lord,' said Owein. And the red-headed servitor brought the gwyddbwyll to Arthur and Owein: gold pieces and a board of silver. And they began to play.

And when they were in this wise most engrossed in play over the gwyddbwyll, lo, they could see coming from a white red-topped pavilion, with the image of a pure black serpent on top of the pavilion, and bright red venomous eyes in the serpent's head, and its tongue flame-red, a young, curly yellow-haired, blue-eyed squire, with a beard starting, and a tunic and surcoat of yellow brocaded silk about him, and a pair of hose of thin greenish-yellow cloth upon his feet, and over the hose two buskins of speckled cordwain, and buckles of gold across his insteps fastening them, and a heavy gold-hilted triple-grooved sword and a scabbard of black cordwain to it, and a tip of refined red gold to the scabbard, coming towards the place where the emperor and Owein were playing gwyddbwyll.

And the squire greeted Owein. And Owein marvelled that the squire greeted him and did not greet the emperor Arthur. And Arthur knew it was of that Owein was thinking, and he said to Owein, 'Marvel not that the squire greeted thee just now. He greeted me a while back. And it [145] is to thee that his message is.' And then the squire said to Owein, 'Lord, is it with thy leave that the emperor's bachelors and his squires are contending with and harassing and molesting thy ravens? And if it is not with thy leave, have the emperor call them off.' 'Lord,' said Owein, 'thou hearest what the squire says? If it please thee, call them off my little ravens.' 'Play thy game,' said he. And then the squire returned towards his pavilion.

They finished that game and started another. And when they were towards the middle of the game, lo, a young ruddy curly-headed, auburn-haired, keen-eyed, well-built attendant, with his beard shaved, coming from a bright yellow pavilion, with the image of a bright red lion on top of the pavilion, and a tunic of yellow brocaded silk about him reaching to the small of his leg, sewn with threads of red silk, and a pair of hose on his feet of fine white

buckram, and over and above the hose two buskins of black cordwain on his feet, and clasps of red gold upon them, and a huge
heavy triple-grooved sword in his hand, and a sheath of red deerskin to it, and a gold tip to the scabbard, coming towards the place
where Arthur and Owein were playing gwyddbwyll.

And he greeted him. And Owein was put out at being greeted,
but Arthur was no more taken aback than before. The squire said
to Owein, 'Is it against thy will that the emperor's squires are
wounding thy ravens, killing some and molesting others? And if it
is against thy will, beseech him to call them off.' 'Lord,' said Owein,
'call off thy men, if it please thee.' 'Play thy game,' said the emperor.
And then the squire returned towards his pavilion.

That game was ended and another begun. And as they were
beginning the first move in the game, they could see some distance
away from them a spotted yellow pavilion, the largest that any one
had seen, and the image of a golden eagle thereon, and a precious
stone in the eagle's head. Coming from the pavilion they could see
a squire with [146] crisp yellow hair upon his head, fair and graceful,
and a mantle of green brocaded silk about him, and a gold brooch
in the mantle on his right shoulder as thick as a warrior's third
finger, and a pair of hose upon his feet of fine totnes, and a pair of
shoes of speckled cordwain upon his feet, and gold clasps thereto;
the youth noble of countenance, with white face and ruddy cheeks,
and great hawk-like eyes. In the squire's hand there was a thick
speckled yellow spear, and a newly sharpened head on it, and upon
the spear a conspicuous standard.

The squire came with rage and passion at a quick canter
to the place where Arthur was playing with Owein over the
gwyddbwyll. And they saw how he was in a rage. But even so he
greeted Owein and told him how the most notable ravens among
them had been slain. 'And those of them that are not slain have
been wounded and hurt to that extent that not one of them can
lift its wings one fathom from the ground.' 'Lord,' said Owein, 'call
off thy men.' 'Play,' said he, 'if thou wilt.' And then Owein said to
the squire, 'Away with thee, and in the place where thou seest the
battle hardest raise on high the standard, and let it be as God will.'

And then the squire went on his way to the place where the
battle was hardest on the ravens, and raised on high the standard.
And even as it was raised, they too rose into the air in passion, rage

and exultation, to let wind into their wings and to throw off their weariness. And having recovered their strength and their magic powers, in rage and exultation they straightway swooped down to earth upon the men who had earlier inflicted hurt and injury and loss upon them. Of some they were carrying off the heads, of others the eyes, of others the ears, and of others the arms; and they were raising them up into the air, and there was a great commotion in the air, what with the fluttering of the exultant ravens and their croaking, and another great commotion what with the cries of the men being gashed and wounded and others being slain. And Arthur's amazement [147] was as great as Owein's over the gwyddbwyll, hearing that commotion.

And as they looked they could hear a rider coming towards them upon a dapple-grey horse. An exceeding strange colour was upon his horse, dapple-grey and his right leg bright red, and from the top of his legs to the middle of his hoof-horn bright yellow; the rider and his horse arrayed in heavy foreign armour. The housing of his horse from his front saddlebow upwards pure red sendal, and from the saddlebow downwards pure yellow sendal. A huge gold-hilted one-edged sword on the youth's thigh, and a new bright green scabbard to it, and a tip to the scabbard of laton of Spain; his sword belt of black fleecy cordwain, and gilt crossbars upon it, and a clasp of ivory thereon. And a pure black tongue to the clasp. A gold helm upon the rider's head, and precious stones of great virtue therein, and on top of the helm the image of a yellow-red leopard with two bright red stones in its head, so that it was dreadful for a warrior, however stout his heart might be, to look on the face of the leopard, let alone on the face of the rider. A long heavy green-shafted spear in his hand, and from its hand-grip upwards bright red; the head of the spear red with the blood of the ravens and their plumage.

The rider came to the place where Arthur and Owein were over the gwyddbwyll, and they could see how he was weary and ill-tempered coming towards them. The squire greeted Arthur and said that Owein's ravens were slaying his bachelors and squires. And Arthur looked at Owein and said, 'Call off thy ravens.' 'Lord,' said Owein, 'play thy game.' And they played. The rider returned towards the battle, and the ravens were no more called off than before.

And when they had played awhile they could hear a great commotion, and the shrieking of men and the croaking of ravens in their strength bearing the men into the air and rending them betwixt them and letting them fall in pieces to the ground.[148]

And out of the commotion they could see a horseman coming on a pale white horse, and the left leg of the horse pure black down to the middle of his hoof; the rider arrayed, he and his horse, in great heavy green armour, a surcoat about him of yellow ribbed brocaded silk, and the fringes of his cloak green. The housing of his horse pure black, and its fringes pure yellow. On the squire's thigh was a long heavy triple-grooved sword, and a sheath of red embossed leather to it, and the belt of fresh red deerskin, with many gold cross-bars thereon, and a clasp of walrus-ivory with a pure black tongue thereto. A gold helm on the rider's head, and magic sapphires in it, and on top of the helm the image of a yellow-red lion, and his tongue flame-red a foot-length out of his mouth, and bright red venomous eyes in his head. The rider coming with a stout ashen spear-shaft in his hand, and a new blood-stained head to it, and silver rivets therein. And the squire greeted the emperor. 'Lord,' said he, 'thy squires and thy bachelors have been slain, and the noblemen's sons of the Island of Britain, so that it will not be easy to defend this Island from this day forth for ever.' 'Owein,' said Arthur, 'call off thy ravens.' 'Lord,' said Owein, 'play this game.'

That game was ended and another begun. And when they were at the end of that game, lo, they could hear a great commotion and a shrieking of armed men and the croaking of ravens and their flapping their wings in the air and dropping the armour unshattered to the ground and dropping the men and the horses in pieces to the ground.

And then they could see a rider on a handsome black high-headed horse, and the top of the horse's left leg pure red, and his right leg to the middle of his hoof pure white; the rider and his horse arrayed in spotted yellow armour speckled with laton of Spain, and a cloak about him and about his horse, in two halves, white and pure black, and the fringes of his cloak of golden purple, and over his cloak a gold-hilted gleaming triple-grooved sword, the sword [149] belt of yellow cloth of gold, and a clasp upon it of the eyelid of a pure black whale, and a tongue of yellow gold on the clasp. A gleaming helm of yellow laton on the rider's head, and gleaming crystal stones therein, and on top of the helm the image of a griffin, and a magic stone in his head; an ashen spear with rounded shaft in his hand, coloured with blue-azure; a new blood-stained point upon the shaft, riveted with refined silver. And the rider came in a rage to the place where Arthur was, and said how the ravens had slain his war-band and the noblemen's sons of this Island, and bade him have Owein call off his ravens. Then Arthur bade Owein call off his ravens. And then Arthur crushed the golden pieces that were on the board till they were all dust. And Owein bade Gwres son of Rheged lower his banner. And therewith it was lowered and all was peace.

Then Rhonabwy asked Iddawg who were the first three men who came to Owein to tell him how his ravens were being slain, and Iddawg said: 'Men who grieved that Owein should suffer loss, fellow chieftains and comrades of his, Selyf son of Cynan White-shank from Powys, and Gwgawn Red-sword, and Gwres son of Rheged, the man who bears his banner on the day of battle and combat.' 'Who,' asked Rhonabwy, 'are the last three men who came to Arthur to tell him how the ravens were slaying his men?' 'The best of men,' said Iddawg, 'and the bravest, and those to whom it is most hateful that Arthur should suffer loss in aught, Blathaon son of Mwrheth, and Rhwawn Bebyr son of Deorthach Wledig, and Hyfeidd One-cloak.'

And thereupon, lo, four-and-twenty horsemen coming from Osla Big-knife to ask a truce of Arthur till the end of a fortnight and a month. Arthur arose and went to take counsel. He went to the place where some way from him was a big curly-headed auburn man, and his counsellors were brought to him there: Bedwin the bishop, and Gwarthegydd son of Caw, and March son of Meir-chawn,[150] and Caradawg Stout-arm, and Gwalchmei son of Gwyar, and Edern son of Nudd, and Rhwawn Bebyr son of Deorthach Wledig, and Rhiogan son of the king of Ireland, and Gwenwynwyn son of Naf, Howel son of Emyr Llydaw, Gwilym son of the ruler of France, and Daned son of Oth, and Goreu son of Custennin, and Mabon son of Modron, and Peredur Longspear and Hyfeidd One-cloak, and Twrch son of Peryf, Nerth son of Cadarn, and Gobrw son of Echel Big-hip, Gweir son of Gwestel, and Adwy son of Gereint, Dyrstan son of Tallwch, Morien Manawg, Granwen son of Llŷr, and Llacheu son of Arthur, and Llawfrodedd the Bearded, and Cadwr the earl of Cornwall, Morfran son of Tegid, and Rhyawdd son of Morgant, and Dyfyr son of Alun Dyfed, Gwryr Interpreter of Tongues, Addaon son of Teliesin, and Llara son of Casnar Wledig, and Fflewdwr Fflam, and Greidiawl Gallddofydd, Gilbert son of Cadgyffro, Menw son of Teirgwaedd, Gyrthmwl Wledig, Cawrda son of Caradawg Stout-arm, Gildas son of Caw, Cadyrieith son of Saidi, and many a man of Norway and Denmark, and many a man of Greece along with them; and sufficient of a host came to that counsel.

'Iddawg,' said Rhonabwy, 'who is the auburn-haired man to whom they came just now?' 'Rhun son of Maelgwn Gwynedd, a man whose authority is such that all men shall come and take counsel of him.' 'For what reason was so young a youth as Cadyrieith son of Saidi brought into the counsel of men of such high rank as those yonder?' 'Because there was not in Britain a man more mighty in counsel than he.'

And thereupon, lo, bards coming to chant a song to Arthur. But never a man was there might understand that song save Cadyrieith himself, except that it was in praise of Arthur. And thereupon, lo, four-and-twenty asses coming with their burdens of gold and silver, and a weary worn man with each of them, bringing tribute to Arthur from the Isles of Greece. Then Cadyrieith son of Saidi asked that [151] a truce be granted to Osla Big-knife till the end of a fortnight and a month, and that the asses which had brought the tribute be given to the bards, and what was upon them, as an earnest of reward, and that during the truce they should be given payment for their song. And they determined upon that. 'Rhonabwy,' said Iddawg, 'were it not wrong to forbid the young man who gave such munificent counsel as this from going to his lord's counsel?'

And then Cei arose and said, 'Whoever wishes to follow Arthur, let him be with him to-night in Cornwall; and as for him who does not wish that, let him come to meet with Arthur by the end of the truce.'

And with the magnitude of that commotion Rhonabwy awoke, and when he awoke he was on the yellow ox skin, having slept three nights and three days.

And this story is called the Dream of Rhonabwy. And here is the reason why no one, neither bard nor story-teller, knows the Dream without a book—by reason of the number of colours that were on the horses, and all that variety of rare colours both on the arms and their trappings, and on the precious mantles, and the magic stones.[152]

"ARTHUR AND MERLIN" (*c.* 1265)

"The Choosing of Arthur"

From *The Chief Middle English Poets*, trans. Jessie L. Weston (Boston: Houghton Mifflin Company, 1914).

At Yule the Bishop Bricius, he
Gave proof that he no fool should be,
There stood he forth amid them all,
In this wise did upon them call:
"Lordings, since ye may not accord
To choose unto ye here a lord,
I pray, for love of Christ so dear,
Ye work by wile and wisdom here;
For such a choice the time is right—
Now go we all to church to-night   10
And pray to Christ, so good and free,
A king to send us, who shall be
Strong for the right against the wrong,
Whom He shall choose our ranks among;

Pray that to us He token send
When the morn's Mass be brought to end."
That in such wise it might be done,
To this, they say, *"Amen,"* each one.
Thus they betake them, more or less,
That night to church, with morn to Mass,   20
In prayer their cause to God commend
That He a rightful king should send.
And thus, when at the end of Mass,
From out the church the folk would pass,
Before the church door, there they found
A great stone standing on the ground,
'T was long and high, the sooth to say,
Therein a right fair sword, it lay.
Then king and duke, baron, and knight,
Were filled with wonder at that sight;   30
The Bishop, he beheld with eye,
And rendered thanks to Christ on high,
And here I rede ye all to wit
That on the pommel fair 't was writ:
"Excalibur, the name I bear,
For a king's treasure fashioned fair."
In English writing there displayed,
In steel 't was graven on the blade.
The Bishop quoth to them anon:
'Who draws this sword from out the stone   40
That same shall be our king indeed,
By God's Will, and by this, our rede."
Thereto they give consent alway,—
King Lot, his hand to hilt did lay,
Thinking to draw it out forthright,
But stirred it not, for all his might;
King Nanters, nor King Clarion,
Might not withdraw it from the stone,
Nor gentle man, whoe'er he be,
Was there might stir it, verily.   50
Thither came all of noble blood,
And there till Candlemas it stood;
All who were born in English land

Each to this stone he set his hand,
For life or death, I trow, was none
Might stir that sword from out the stone.
There did it stand till Easter-tide;
Thither came men from far and wide,
From this shore, from beyond the sea,
But prospered not 't was God's decree!   60
The stone stood there till Pentecost;
And thither came a goodly host,
For tournament at that same tide
E'en as it were the stone beside.
Sir Antour did his son then, Kay,
With honour make a knight, that day,
This Kay was ta'en, so saith the Geste,
Away from this, his mother's breast,
For Arthur's sake, she nursed that child
Who grew up courteous, meek, and mild.   70
Kay was a noble knight, I trow,
Save that he stammered somewhat now,
Thro' nurture did he win that same,
They say that from his nurse it came;
And Arthur, he had served King Lot
For this long time, so do I wot.

When thus, Sir Kay, he was made knight,
Sir Antour counselled him forthright [119]
Arthur to fetch to him again
And there to make of him his swain,   80
For he was hardy, true to test,
Thro' all the land of youths the best.
Therewith Kay, he was right well paid—
Then all was done as Antour said,
Arthur came home, and was with Kay,
To tourney went with him alway;
There Kay, he shewed himself in fight
To be a very valiant knight,
O'er all the field, at end, by side,
Full many did he fell that tide.   90

Then, as he came amid the throng,
He laid about with strokes so strong
That this, his sword, asunder brake—
Anon, to Arthur thus he spake:
"Now to my lady swiftly wend,
Pray her another sword to send."
And so he did, nor thought to bide,
But swiftly home again did ride,
His lady found he not that day
So turned him back upon his way.   100

Then to that sword within the stone
I trow me, he hath swiftly gone,
(And never man was there to see
Since all should at the Tourney be,)
Arthur, he took the hilt in hand
Towards himself he drew the brand,
Light from the stone it came away—
He took it in his hand straightway
And leapt upon his horse anon,
Back to the Tourney hath he gone   110
And said: "Have here this sword, Sir Kay,
Thy lady found I not to-day."
Right well Kay knew the sword, I wis,
To Arthur spake "Whence had'st thou this?"
"Certes" quoth Arthur, "that same brand
There, in a stone, I saw it stand."
(Arthur, he saw it ne'er before
Nor wist the meaning that it bore.)
With that, to Arthur spake Sir Kay,
"*Par amour*, now to no man say   120
Whence thou didst take this sword, I trow,
And riches shalt thou have enow."
Arthur he answered, "Certes, nay!"
With that he gat him forth, Sir Kay,
And led his father, Sir Antour
Straight to the church of Saint Saviour,
And saith: "The sword I forth did draw,
Now am I king, by right and law!"

Sir Antour, he beheld that sword,
Answered again with ready word   130
" 'T is but a boast, by God above!
An sooth it be, that must thou prove
Before these nobles everyone,
Must thrust this sword back in the stone;
Save thou again canst draw it free
Then shame upon thy head shall be!"

With that, they get them to the stone,
And Kay thrust back the sword anon,
But tho' a knight both stiff and stout
He had no strength to draw it out.   140
With that besought him Sir Antour,
"Now tell me son, here, *par amour,*
Who was it drew this sword so good?"
Sir Kay, he laughed as there he stood,
And sware: "By God, as here I stand,
Arthur, he brought it in his hand!"
Antour, he calléd Arthur there
And to the stone he bade him fare
And there, I trow me, swift and soft,
Both in and out he drew it oft.   150
Antour was blithe and glad that day,
Arthur he took to church straightway
And saith to him full secretly,
"Arthur, I prithee, hearken me,
Since thou wast born, 't is true, I ween,
In my house nourished hast thou been."
With that he told him all that morn
How he begotten was, and born;
How that King Uther was his sire,
And how, at that same king's desire,   160
"A nurse I took for my son Kay,
And thee at my wife's breast did lay."
Then Antour quoth: "Now list to me,
Thro' nurture thou my son shalt be,[120]
It were not right didst thou gainsay
A boon that I should rightful pray,

So I beseech, grant me a boon
Which I will ask of thee full soon,
And Arthur, son, I will thee aid
That king with honour thou be made."   170
Then Arthur answered, fair and free:
"Now Christ in Heaven forbid it me
That I deny thee anything
When thou to me a prayer dost bring."
Quoth Antour: "God thee well repay;
Now I for love this boon will pray,
To Kay my son the stewardship give
For all the years that thou mayst live;
In weal, in woe, I pray thee fair,
In every stead, protection swear,   180
And I shall aid, in this, thy need,
That thro' God's Help thou surely speed."

With that Sir Arthur spake full soon;
"Sir Antour, take thou this, thy boon,
Kay shall be steward in my land,
For weal or woe I'll by him stand,
And if I ever fail Sir Kay
Then Christ forget me, that same day!"
With that Sir Antour, he forthright
Took Arthur, and hath dubbed him knight,   190
First gave him cloth and fitting weed,
Then found him harness for his steed,
Helmet, and byrnie, coat of mail,
Nor plate for arm or thigh did fail;
With collar, shield, and sword to smite,
And shaft with blade that well could bite.
Anon, of knights he gave him there
Forty, to do him service fair.
With morn to tournament they go,
And so they dealt, I'ld have ye know,   200
That here Sir Arthur, day by day,
Honour and praise he bare away.
At morn Sir Antour, who should be
No fool, to Bishop Brice went he,

And saith to him, a knight he knew
Both fair and noble, good and true,
"Who shall be king, by this our law,
For that the sword he forth may draw."
With that, the Bishop, well content,
After Sir Arthur straightway sent,   210
Before the nobles of that land
Arthur, he took the sword in hand,
He drew it out, he thrust it in—
Then many a man must wonder win,
For none might stir it from that stone
I plight my word, save he alone!
Then kings and earls, without a doubt,
They crowded there, the lad about,
Thinking to prove his knowledge here—
Ever he was of gracious cheer,   220
Nor better could a man devise
Than this, his speech, in every wise.
With that, Sir Antour help did bring
So that he there was chosen king,
And to his crowning there withal
Full many a prince and king they call,
And who would come, they pray them well
To gather, as Saint John's-tide fell.

.   .   .   .

'T is merry in the June-tide fair
When fennel hangeth everywhere,   230
And violets and rose in flower
Be found in every maiden's bower;
The sun is hot, the day is long,
And merry sounds the birdling's song;
Then first King Arthur bare the crown
Within Cardoil, that noble town.
King Lot, who wedded Belisent,
He to the coronation went,
The King of Lyoneis was he,
A strong man, of great courtesie.   240
Five hundred knights were in his train,
Hardy and strong, for fighting fain.

King Nanters came, as I am told,
Who did the land of Garlot hold,
A noble man, a valiant wight,
Strong to defend himself in fight.
The same had wedded with Blasine,
King Arthur's sister, fair and fine,
Full seven hundred knights, the king
Did with him, as his mesnie, bring,   250
And many a charger, many a steed,
That should be found right good at need.[121]
And thither too, King Urien sped,
Who did with the third sister wed,
'T was from the land of Gorre he came,
A young man he, of noble fame,
With twenty thousand men, and five,
No better knights were there alive.

King Carados, he too, was there,
The crown of Strangore did he bear,   260
A mighty man, and well renowned,
Knight was he of the Table Round,
From far, unto Cardoil he sought,
Six hundred knights with him he brought,
Who well knew how to joust in field,
With stiff lance, 'neath the sheltering shield.
Thither came Ider in that hour,
King of the Marches, of great power,
And with him brought full thirty score
Of knights who rode his face before.   270

King Anguisant did thither ride,
The King of Scotland at that tide,
The richest he, among them all,
Youngest, and of great power withal,
Five hundred knights he brought, I wot,
Both stout and strong, each man a Scot;
And many more, from South and East,
Thither have come, to that high feast.
Then king and baron, as I tell,

Nobly they welcomed them, and well,   280
And Bishop Brice, the court among,
Crowned Arthur, and the office sung.
And when the service came to end,
Unto the feast their way they wend;
They found all ready, cloth and board,
And first hath gone the highest lord;
Men serve them then with plenteous fare,
With meat and drink, and dainties rare,
With venison of hart and boar,
Swan, peacock, bustard, to them bore;   290
Of pheasant, partridge, crane, that day
Great plenty and no lack had they.
Piment and claret served they free
To high lords, and their companie,
Serving them in such noble wise
As any man might well devise.
And when the guests had eaten all,
Both high and low, within that hall,
His gifts to give did Arthur rise,
To noble men, of high emprise,   300
Their homage they should straightway plight
E'en as the custom was, and right.
But, e'en as this he did, I trow,
King Lot, King Nanters, men enow,
Of these his gifts they had despite,
And to the crown denied his right.

Up from the board they spring with boast,
Each king of them, with all his host,
Swearing that ne'er for anything
They'ld own a bastard for their king,   310
Thus, with dishonour great they fare,
Thinking to slay King Arthur there.
But Arthur's men, they came between,
And Merlin, in that strife, I ween,
Stood forth, and spake, no bastard he,
But nobler than them all should be,
And there he told them all that morn

How Arthur was begat, and born.
The wise men of that country, they
Gave thanks to Jesu Christ, alway,   320
In that their king, thro' this, His Grace,
Was come of royal Pendragon's race.
The barons, they to Merlin say:
"Thy witchcraft wrought his birth alway,
Thou traitor, know that verily,
For all enchantments known to thee,
No child born in adultery
The king and lord o'er us shall be,
But he shall starve here, now anon—"
Towards King Arthur have they gone,   330
The king was armed, from head to heel,
And all his friends, in iron and steel,
Resistance made they, strong, and stout,
And of a surety, drave them out,
With swords and knives full speedily,
From hall, who Arthur's foes should be.[122]
Those same six kings, they were right wroth,
And all their barons sware an oath,
That never they two meals should eat
Till they had taken vengeance meet;   340
With that they pitch their tents that day
Without the town, a little way.[123]

"MORTE ARTHURE" (c. 1360)

"The Alliterative Version"

From Roger Sherman Loomis and Rudolph Willard, *Medieval English Verse and Prose* (New York: Appleton-Century-Crofts, 1948).

Arthur turns into Tuscany   when the time is favorable,
Takes towns very quickly,   with towers of height;
Walls he cast down,   and knights he wounded;
Made many fair widows   woefully sing,
Be weary often, and weep,   and wring their hands.
He wastes all with war   wherever he rides past;
Their wealth and their dwellings   he turns to destruction.
Thus they spring forth and spread far,   and spare but little,
They spoil without pity,   and lay waste their vines;
Spend without sparing   what long was saved up;   3160
Speed then to Spoleto,   with spears in plenty.
From Spain into Spruysland   the report of him springs,
The tale of his destruction;   despair is full huge.
    Towards Viterbo this valiant man   turns his reins.
Wisely in that vale   he victuals his warriors,
With vernage and other wines,   and venison baked.
And with the viscount of that land   he decides to tarry.
Quickly the vanguard   dismount from their horses,
In the vale of Vertennon   among the vineyards;
There sojourns this sovereign   with solace of heart,   3170
To see when the senators   should send any word;
He revels with rich wine,   rejoices himself,
This king with his royal men   of the Round Table,
With mirth and melody,   and manifold games;

Were never merrier men   made on this earth.
    But on a Saturday, at noon,   a seven-night thereafter,
The cunningest cardinal   that to the court belonged,
Kneels to the conqueror   and utters these words:
Prays him for peace   and proffers full largely,
To have pity on the pope,   who thus was put down;   3180
Besought him assurance,   for the sake of our Lord,[128]
But a seven-night's day,   when they would all be assembled,
And they would surely see him   the Sunday thereafter
In the city of Rome   as sovereign and lord,
And crown him properly   with chrismed hands,
With his scepter and his sword,   as sovereign and lord.
For this undertaking   hostages are come thither,
Of heirs most comely   eight score children,
In togas of Tars   most richly attired,
And commit themselves to the king   and his renowned
        knights.   3190
    When they had treated their truce,   with trumpet blasts after,
They turn unto a tent   where tables are set up;
The king himself is seated   and certain lords
Under a ceiling of silk,   in peace at the table;
All the senators are set   apart by themselves,
And are solemnly served   with seldom-known dishes.
The king, mighty of mirth,   with his mild words
Heartens the Romans   at his rich table,
Comforts the cardinal   in knightly wise himself;
And this royal ruler,   as the romance tells us,   3200
The Romans did reverence   at his rich table.
The trained men and knowing,   when time it seemed them,
Took their leave of the king,   and turned them again;
To the city that night   they made way the quickest.
And thus the hostage of Rome   is left with Arthur.
    Then this royal king   rehearses these words:
"Now may we revel and rest,   for Rome is our own;
Make our hostages at ease,   these comely young nobles,
And look ye hold them all,   who linger in my host;
The Emperor of Almain   and all these east marches,   3210
We shall be overlord of all   that dwell upon earth.
We will by Holy Cross Day   acquire these lands,

And at Christmas Day   be crowned accordingly;
Reign in my royalty   and hold my Round Table
With the rents from Rome,   as it right pleases me.
Then go over the Great Sea   with good men of arms,
To avenge that Warrior   that died on the Rood."
    Then this comely king,   as chronicles tell us,
Turns bravely to bed   with a blithe heart;
He slings off with sleight   and slackens his girdle,   3220
And for sloth of slumber   falls then asleep.[129]
But at one after midnight   all his mood changed;
He dreamt in the morning hour   most marvelous dreams.
And when his dreadful dream   was driven to its end,
The king stares in dismay,   as though he should die,
Sends after philosophers,   and his affright tells them.
    "Since I was formed in faith,   so frightened was I never!
Wherefore ransack readily   and reveal me my dreams,
And I shall fully and rightly   rehearse the truth.
Me thought I was in a wood   at mine own will,   3230
Since I knew no way,   whither I should wend,
Because of wolves and wild swine   and wicked beasts.
I walked in that wasteland   to seek out dangers.
There lions full loathly   licked their tushes,
As they lapped up the blood   of my loyal knights.
Through that forest I fled,   where flowers grew tall,
For the great fear that I had   of those foul creatures.
I made way to a meadow,   with mountains closed in,
The merriest of middle-earth   that men might behold.
The enclosure was encompassed   and closed all about,   3240
With clover and with cleve-wort   clad evenly all over;
The vale was environed   with vines of silver,
All with grapes of gold—   greater grew never,
Surrounded with shrubs   and all kinds of trees,
Arbors most handsome   and herdsmen thereunder.
All fruits were produced   that flourished on earth,
Fairly sheltered in hedges   upon the tree boughs.
There was no dankness of dew   that could harm aught;
With the drying of daytime   wholly dry were the flowers.
    "There descends in the dale,   down from the clouds,   3250
A duchess preciously dight   in diapered garments,

In a surcoat of silk   most rarely hued,
Wholly with ermine overlaid   low to the hems,
And with lady-like lappets   the length of a yard,
And all readily reversed   with ribbons of gold,
With brooches and bezants   and other bright stones
Her back and her breast   were bedecked all over;
With a caul and a coronal   she was neatly arrayed,
And that so comely of color   none was known ever.
    "About she whirled a wheel   with her white hands,   3260
Turned most skilfully   the wheel as she would.[130]
The rim was of red gold   with royal stones,
Arrayed in richness   and rubies in plenty;
The spokes were resplendent   with splinters of silver,
The space of a spear-length   springing most fairly;
Thereon was a chair   of chalk-white silver,
And checkered with carbuncle,   changing in hues;
To the circumference there clung   kings in a row,
With crowns of clear gold   that were cracked asunder;
Six from that seat   were suddenly fallen,   3270
Each man by himself,   and said these words:
    " 'That ever I reigned on this wheel,   it rues me ever.
Was never king so rich,   that reigned upon earth!
When I rode on my route,   I wrought nothing else
But hawk and revel   and tax the people.
And thus I drive forth my days,   while I can endure it;
And therefore in agony   am I condemned forever.'
    "The last was a little man   that was laid beneath,
His loins lay very lean   and loathly to look on,
The locks gray and long   the length of a yard,   3280
His flesh and his body   were lamed quite sorely;
The one eye of the man   was brighter than silver,
The other was yellower   than the yolk of an egg.
'I was lord,' quoth the man,   'of lands aplenty,
And all people louted to me,   who lived upon earth;
And now is left me no flap   to cover my body,
But lightly am I lost;   let all men believe it.'
    "The second sir, forsooth,   that followed him after,
Was surer in my sight,   and more serious in arms;
Oft he sighed heavily,   and spoke these words: 3290

'On yonder seat have I sat   as sovereign and lord,
And ladies loved me,   to embrace in their arms:
And now is my lordship lost   and laid by forever!'
   "'The third man was massive   and thick in the shoulders,
A stout man to threaten   where thirty were gathered;
His diadem had dropped down,   bedecked with stones,
Indented all with diamonds,   and richly adorned.
'I was dreaded in my days,' he said,   'in divers realms,
And now am damned among the dead,   and my dole is the more.'
   "The fourth was a fair man   and forceful in arms,[131]   3300
The fairest in figure   that ever was formed.
'I was fierce in my faith,' he said,   'whilst I on earth reigned,
Famous in far lands,   and flower of all kings;
Now my face is faded,   and foul hap has befallen me,
For I am fallen from afar,   and friendless am left.'
   "The fifth was a fairer man   than many of these others,
A forceful man and fierce,   with foaming lips;
He hung fast to the felly   and clasped his arms,
But still he failed and fell   a full fifty feet;
But still he sprang up and leapt   and spread his arms,   3310
And on the spear-length spokes   he speaks these words:
'I was a sire in Syria,   and set by myself
As sovereign and seigneur   of several kings' lands;
Now from my solace am I   full suddenly fallen,
And for sake of my sin   yonder throne is lost to me.'
   "The sixth had a psalter   most seemly bound,
And a surplice of silk,   sewn very fairly,
A harp and a hand-sling,   with hard flint stones;
What harms he has had   he declares straightway:
'I was deemed in my days,' he said,   'for deeds of arms   3320
One of the doughtiest   that dwelt upon earth;
But I was marred upon earth   in my greatest strength,
By this maiden so mild   that moves us all.'
   "Two kings were climbing   and clambering on high,
The crest of the compass   they covet most eagerly.
'This chair of carbuncle,' they said,   'we claim hereafter,
As two of the chiefest   chosen upon earth.'
The young nobles were chalk-white,   both cheeks and faces,
But the chair above them   achieved they never.

The furthermost was handsome, with a broad forehead,   3330
The fairest of physiognomy   that ever was formed;
And he was clad in a coat   of noble blue,
With fleurs-de-lys of gold   flourished all over;
The other was clad in a coat   all of pure silver,
With a comely cross   carved out of fine gold;
Four skillful crosslets   by that cross rest them,
And thereby I knew the king,   that christened he seemed.
    "Then went I to that fair one,   and affectionately greeted her,
And she said, 'Welcome, in truth,   well art thou found now;
Thou oughtest worship my will,   and thou well knowest,   3340
Of all the valiant men   that were ever in the world; [132]
For, all thy worship in war,   by me hast thou won it;
I have been friendly, man,   and helped against others;
That hast thou found in faith,   and many of thy warriors,
For I felled down Sir Frolle   with froward knights,
Wherefore the fruits of France   are freely thine own.
Thou shalt achieve the chair,   I choose thee myself,
Before all the chieftains   chosen in this earth.'
    "She lifted me up lightly   with her slim hands,
And set me softly in that seat;   the scepter she reached me;   3350
Carefully with a comb   she combed my head,
That the crisping curl   reached my crown;
Dressed me in a diadem   beauteously bedecked;
Then she proffers me an apple   set full of fair stones,
Enameled with azure,   the earth thereon painted,
Encircled with the salt sea   upon every side,
In sign that I surely   was sovereign on earth.
Then she brought me a brand   with very bright hilts,
And bade me brandish the blade: 'The brand is mine own;
Many a swain with the swing   has left his blood;   3360
For, while thou didst work with the sword,   it failed thee never.'
    "Then she departed in peace,   and in quiet, when it pleased
        her,
To the trees of the forest,   a richer was never;
No orchard is so ordained   by princes on earth,
No appointments so proud,   but paradise only.
She bade the boughs bend down   and bring to my hands
Of the best that they bore   on branches so high;

Then they inclined to her command   all wholly at once,
The highest of every holt: I tell thee the truth.
She bade me spare not the fruit,   but take whilst it pleased
    me: 3370
'Take of the finest,   thou noble warrior,
And reach towards the ripest,   and refresh thyself;
Rest, thou royal king,   for Rome is thine own,
And I shall readily bring thee   rest most quickly,
And reach thee the rich wine   in well-rinsed cups.'
    Then she went to the well   by the wood-border,
That bubbled up with wine   and wondrously runs,
Caught up a cupful,   and covered it carefully;
She bade me deeply draw   and drink to herself,
And thus she led me about   the length of an hour,   3380
With all the liking and love   that any man should have.
    "But just at midday exactly   all her mood changed,[183]
And she made me great menace   with marvelous words.
When I cried upon her,   she lowered her brows:
'King, thou speakest for naught,   by Christ that made me!
For thou shalt lose this game   and thy life after;
Thou hast lived in delight   and lordship enough.'
    "About she whirls the wheel,   and whirls me under,
Till all my quarters that time   were crushed all to pieces,
And my backbone with that chair   was chopped asunder;   3390
And I have shivered with chill   since this chance happened.
Then I awakened, indeed,   all weary and dreamt out,
And now thou knowest my woe;   word it as it please thee."
    "Friend," said the philosopher,   "thy fortune has passed,
For thou shalt find her thy foe,   ask when thou likest.
Thou art at the highest,   I declare to thee truly;
Complain now when thou wilt,   thou achievest no more.
Thou hast shed much blood   and fighters destroyed
Guiltless, in thy pride,   in many kings' lands;
Shrive thee of thy shame,   and shape thee for thine end.   3400
Thou hast a foreshadowing, Sir King,   take keep it thou like.
For fiercely shalt thou fall   within five winters.
Found abbeys in France,   the fruits are thine own,
For Frolle and for Feraunt,   and for their fierce knights,
Whom thou hostilely in France   didst leave as dead.

Take thought now of the other kings,   and cast in thy heart,
Who were conquerors renowned,   and crowned upon earth.
   "The eldest was Alexander,   that all the earth louted to;
The second was Hector of Troy,   the chivalrous man;
The third was Julius Caesar,   who held was a giant,   3410
On each famous campaign,   accompanied with lords.
The fourth was Sir Judas,   a jouster most noble,
The masterful Maccabee,   the mightiest in strength;
The fifth was Joshua,   that jolly man of arms,
To whom in a Jerusalem inn   great joy befell once;
The sixth was David the valiant,   deemed among kings
One of the doughtiest   that dubbed was ever,
For he slew with a sling,   by the sleight of his hands,
Goliath the great giant,   grimmest on earth.[134]
He endited in his days   all the dear psalms,   3420
That in the psalter are set forth   in peerless words.
   "The one climbing king,   I know it in truth,
Shall Charles be called,   the king's son of France;
He shall be cruel and keen   and held a conqueror,
Recover by conquests   countries many;
He shall acquire the crown   that Christ Himself bore;
And that beloved lance   that leapt to His heart,
When He was crucified on the cross,   and all the keen nails
As a knight he shall conquer   for Christian men's hands.
   "The second shall be Godfrey,   who God shall revenge   3430
For that Good Friday,   with gallant knights;
He shall be lord of Lorraine   by leave of his father;
And after in Jerusalem   much joy shall befall him,
For he shall recover the cross   by craft of arms,
And then be crowned king   with chrism anointed.
   "There shall no duke in his day   attain such destiny,
Nor suffer so great misfortune,   when truth shall be measured.
For thy fortune will fetch thee   to fill up the number
As ninth of the noblest   named upon earth;
This shall be read in romances   by noble knights,   3440
Be reckoned and renowned   by reveling kings,
And deemed on Doomsday,   for deeds of arms,
As the doughtiest ever   that dwelt upon earth.
Thus, many clerks and kings   shall proclaim your deeds,

And keep your conquests   in chronicles for ever.
But the wolves in the wood,   and the wild beasts,
Are certain wicked men   that war on thy realms,
Are entered in thine absence   to attack thy people,
And aliens and hosts   from barbarous lands.
Thou gettest tidings, I trow,   within ten days,   3450
That some trouble is betid   since thou didst turn from home;
I urge thee recall and reckon   unreasonable deeds,
Or repent thee most quickly   of all thy wrongful works.
Man, amend thy heart   ere mishap befall thee,
And meekly ask mercy   for meed of thy soul."
    Then rises the king,   and arrayed him in clothing,[135]
A red jacket of rose,   the richest of flowers,
A pisan and a paunch-cover,   and a precious girdle;
And he slips on a hood   of very rich hue,
A shield-like pillion-hat,   that set was most richly   3460
With pearls of Orient   and precious stones;
His gloves gaily gilt   and embroidered at the hems,
Sprinkled with rubies,   full seemly to look on;
His greedy greyhound and his brand,   and no man with him,
He walks over a broad meadow   with woe at his heart;
He stalks over a path   by the still wood-edge,
Stops at a high street,   in his deep study.
At the rising of the sun   he sees there coming,
Hastening Rome-wards,   by the shortest way,
A man in a round cloak   with right full clothes.   3470
With hat and high shoes,   homely and round;
With flat farthings the man   was flourished all over;
Many shreds and tatters   at his skirts hang,
With scrip and with mantle,   and scallops aplenty,
With pike and with palm,   such as pilgrims should have.
    The man hastily greeted him,   and bade him good-morning;
The king himself, lordly,   in the language of Rome,
In Latin quite corrupt,   speaks to him courteously:
"Whither wilt thou, wight,   walking by thyself?
Whilst this world is at war,   a peril I hold it;   3480
Here is an enemy with a host   under yon vines;
If they see thee, in truth,   sorrow betides thee,
Unless thou hast conduct   from the king himself,

Knaves will kill thee, and keep what thou hast;
And if thou holdest the highway, they will seize thee also,
Unless thou hastily have help from his friendly knights."
   Then replies Sir Craddock to the king himself:
"I shall forgive him my death, so God help me,
Any groom under God, that walks on this ground
Let the keenest one come, that to the king belongs   3490
I shall encounter him as a knight, so Christ have my soul!
For thou canst not reach me nor arrest me thyself,
Though thou be richly arrayed in very rich weeds;
I shall not shrink for any war, to wend where it please me,
Nor for any wight of this world that is wrought on earth.[136]
But I shall pass in pilgrimage this path unto Rome,
To procure me pardon of the pope himself,
And from the pains of Purgatory be plenarily absolved.
Then shall I seek surely my sovereign lord,
Sir Arthur of England, that adventurous warrior.   3500
For he is in this empire, as valiant men tell me,
Campaigning in this Orient with awesome knights."
   "From whence comest thou, keen man," quoth the king then,
"Who knowest King Arthur, and his knights also?
Wast thou ever in his court whilst he dwelt at home?
Thou speakest so familiarly it comforts my heart;
Full well hast thou come, and wisely thou seekest,
For thou art a British warrior, by thy broad speech."
   "I ought to know the king, he is my avowed lord,
And I was called in his court a knight of his chamber;   3510
Sir Craddock was I called in his royal court,
Keeper of Caerleon under the king himself.
Now am I chased out of the country with care at my heart,
And that castle is captured by uncouth people."
   Then the comely king caught him in his arms,
Cast off his kettle-hat, and kissed him at once;
Said, "Welcome, Sir Craddock, so may Christ help me!
Dear cousin in kin, thou makest cold my heart.
How fares it in Britain with all my bold men?
Are they beat down or burnt or brought out of life?   3520
Make me know quickly what chance has befallen;
I need crave no assurance, I know thee a true man."

"Sir, thy warden is wicked and wild of his deeds,
For he has caused sorrow since thou wentest away.
He has captured castles and crowned himself,
Taken in all the rent of the Round Table;
He has divided the realm, and dealt as it pleased him;
Dubbed them of Denmark dukes and earls,
Sent them out diversely, and destroyed cities;
Of Saracens and Saxons, upon many sides,   3530
He has assembled an army of strange warriors,
Sovereigns of Surgenale, and mercenaries many,
Of Picts and of Paynims, and proved knights
Of Ireland and of Argyle, outlawed fighters;
All those lads are knights who belong to the mountains,[137]
And lead and have lordship as it pleases them.
And there is Sir Childeric held as a chieftain;
That same chivalrous man, he afflicts thy people.
They rob thy religious and ravish thy nuns;
And he rides ready with his rout to ransack the poor.   3540
From Humber to Hawick he holds as his own,
And all the country of Kent, by covenant entailed,
The comely castles that belonged to the crown,
The holts and hoar-wood and the hard banks,
All that Hengist and Horsa held in their time.
At Southampton on the sea are sevenscore ships,
Freighted full of fierce folk out of far lands,
To fight with thy forces, when thou assailest them.
But yet a word, truly; thou knowest not the worst:
He has wedded Waynor and as wife holds her,   3550
And dwells in the wild bounds of the west marches,
And has got her with child, as witnesses tell us.
Of all men of this world, may woe befall him,
As the warden unworthy to look after women!
Thus has Sir Modred marred us all!
Wherefore I marched over these mountains to report thee the
      truth."
      Then the burly king, for anger at his heart,
And for this bootless bale, quite changed all his hue.
"By the Rood," said the king, "I shall revenge it;
He shall repent full quickly all his wicked works!"   3560

Weeping deeply for woe   he went to his tents;
Without joy this wise king   awakens his warriors,
Called in by a clarion   kings and others,
Calls them to council,   and tells of this case:
"I am betrayed through treason   for all my true deeds!
And all my labor is lost;   it befalls me no better;
Woe shall betide him   who wrought this treason,
If I can surely take him,   and I am a true lord!
This is Modred, the man,   whom I most trusted;
He has captured my castles,   and crowned himself   3570
With the rents and riches   of the Round Table.
He has made his whole retinue   of renegade wretches,
And dealt out my kingdom   to divers lords,
To soldiers and to Saracens   out of several lands.[138]
He has wedded Waynor,   and holds her as wife;
And a child is begotten,   the luck is no better.
They have assembled on the sea   sevenscore ships,
Full of fierce folk   to fight with mine own.
Wherefore, to Britain the Broad   to return it behoves us,
To break down the warrior   that has begun all this injury.   3580
No fierce man shall fare thither   except on fresh horses,
That are tested in fight,   and flower of my knights.
Sir Howell and Sir Hardolf   here shall remain
To be lords of these people   that belong here to me;
They shall look into Lombardy,   that there no man change,
And tenderly to Tuscany   take charge as I bid them;
Receive the rents of Rome,   when they are reckoned;
Take seizin the same day   that last was assigned,
Or else all the hostages,   without the walls,
Shall be hanged high aloft   all wholly at once."   3590
Now prepares the bold king   with his best knights,
Bids sound trumpet and truss,   and goes forth after;
Turns through Tuscany,   tarries but little,
Alights not in Lombardy,   except when the light failed;
Marches over the mountains   many marvelous ways.
Journeys through Germany   even at the quickest;
Fares into Flanders   with his fierce knights.
Within fifteen days   his fleet is assembled,
And then he shaped him to ship,   and shuns no longer;

Steers with the sharp wind   over the sheer waters;   3600
By the rocks with ropes   he rides at anchor.
    There the false men floated   and on the flood lingered,
With strong cargo chains   linked together,
Charged even cheekful   with chivalrous knights;
And in the hind part on high   were helms and crests,
Hatches with heathen men   covered were thereunder.
Proudly portrayed   upon painted cloths,
Each, piece by piece,   fastened to the other,
Dubbed with dagswain,   they seemed to be doubled;
And thus had the sharp Danes   dressed all their ships,   3610
That no dint from any dart   might damage them ever.[139]
    Then the king and the knights   of the Round Table
All royally in red   array his ships.
That day he dealt out duchies   and dubbed knights;
Dressed dromons and drags,   and they draw up stones;
The top-castles he stuffed   with tools as it pleased him,
Bent bows with screws   swiftly afterwards;
Toolmen attentively   their tackle do righten,
Brazen heads very broad   they mount upon arrows;
Make ready to defend them,   draw up their men,   3620
With grim gads of steel,   gyves of iron;
Station strong men on the stern,   with stiff men of arms;
Many a fair lance   stands up aloft;
Men upon lee-board,   lords and others,
Place pavises on the port,   painted shields;
On the hinder hurdace on high   stood helmed knights.
Thus they make way with their shots   toward those sheer strands,
Each man in his mantle,   resplendent were their weeds.
    The bold king is in a barge,   and he rows about,
Quite bareheaded and busy,   with beaver-brown locks—   3630
And a warrior bears his brand   and an inlaid helmet,
Attached to a mantle   of silver mail—
Crowned with a coronet,   and covered very richly,
He keeps his way to each cog,   to comfort his knights.
To Cleges and to Cleremond   he cries aloud:
"O Gawain! O Galyron!   these good men's bodies!"
To Lot and to Lionel   he lovingly calls out,
And to Sir Launcelot of the Lake,   in lordly words:

"Let us recover the country,   the coast is our own,
And make them hastily blench,   all yonder bloodhounds.   3640
Break them down aboard,   and burn them afterwards;
Hew down heartily   yonder heathen tikes:
They are on the rascal's side,   I wager my hand."
    Then regains he his cog,   and catches an anchor,
Caught up his comely helm   with the shining mail;
Runs up banners abroad,   embroidered with gules,
With crowns of clear gold   carefully arrayed.
But there was seen in the top   a chalk-white Maiden,
And a Child in her arms,   that is Chief of heaven;
Without change thereafter,   these were the chief arms [140]   3650
Of Arthur the adventurous   whilst he lingered on earth.
    Then the mariners call forth,   and masters of ships,
Merrily each mate   shouts to the other;
In their jargon they jangle,   how it befell them:
They tow trussel on treats,   and truss up sails,
Beat bonnets abroad,   battened down hatches;
Brandished brown steel,   bragged on trumpets;
Stand stiffly on the stem,   and steer thereafter;
Streak over the stream,   where the striving begins
From the time the raging wind   out of the west rises,   3660
And fiercely sweeps with the blast   into the warriors' sails;
With her bring on board   the heavy cogs,
Whilst the bilge and the beam   burst asunder;
So stoutly the fore-stern   on the stem hits,
The stocks of the steerboard   strike in pieces.
At that, cog upon cog,   one craft and another,
Cast creepers across,   as to the craft is fitting.
Then were the head-ropes hewn,   that held up the masts;
There was conflict most keen,   and crashing of ships;
Great ships of battle   dashed asunder;   3670
Many a cabin was cleaved,   cables destroyed;
Knights and keen men   killed the fighters,
Splendid castles were carved   with all their keen weapons,
Castles most comely,   beautifully painted.
With upward glances   they cut in afterwards,
With the swinge of the sword   the mast sways;
At the first moment fall over   fighters and others,

Many a bold man in the foreship is found to be fated.
Then sternly they turn about with savage tackle;
There brush boldly aboard byrnied knights;   3680
Out of boats on decks they attack with stones,
Beat down the best ones, burst the hatches;
Some men are gored through with gads of iron.
Men gaily clad bebloody the weapons.
Archers of Ireland shoot full eagerly,
They hit through the hard steel many mortal dints.
Soon stagger in the hull the heathen knights,[141]
Hurt through the hard steel; heal will they never.
Then they fall to the fight, foin with spears,
All the fiercest of front, as befits that fighting;   3690
And each one freshly puts forth his strength,
To fight the war in the fleet with their fell weapons.
Thus they dealt that day, these dubbed knights,
Till all the Danes were dead and into the deep thrown.
    Then Britons breathing wrath hew with their brands,
There leap up aloft lordly fighters;
When men from foreign lands lept into the waters,
All our lords aloud laughed together.
At that spears were sprung, ships splintered,
Spaniards speedily sprinted overboard;   3700
All the keen men of war, knights and others,
Are killed cold dead, and cast overboard.
Their squires swiftly shed their life-blood,
Heave up hence on the hatches, arise on the hedged place,
Sinking into the salt sea seven hundred at once.
Then Sir Gawain the good has gained his desire,
And all the great cogs he gave to his knights.
Sir Geryn and Sir Griswold, and other great lords,
Caused Galuth, a good knight, to strike off their heads.
Thus to the false fleet it befell on the flood,   3710
And thus the foreign folk are left there as fated.
    Yet is the traitor on land with his trusted knights,
And with trumpets they trip on their trapped steeds,
Show themselves under shields upon the sheer banks.
He shuns not for any shame, but shows himself on high.
Sir Arthur and Gawain made way, both of them,

To sixty thousand men   that in their sight hovered.
But when the folk was felled,   then was the tide out;
It was much like a mire   in mud-banks most huge,
That hindered the king from landing   in the low water;   3720
Wherefore he lingered a while,   lest he lose his horses,
To look over his liegemen   and his loyal knights.
If any were lamed or lost,   and whether they should live.
    Then Sir Gawain the good,   a galley he takes him,
And glides up an inlet   with good men of arms;
When he grounded, in grief   he springs into the water,
That to the girdle he goes,   in all his gilt weeds;
He shoots up upon the sand   in sight of the lords,
Singly with his band—   my sorrow is the greater! [142]
With banners of his emblems,   the best of his arms,   3730
He twists up upon the bank   in his bright clothing.
He bids his banner-man,   "Betake thee quickly
To yonder broad battalion   that stands on yon bank;
And I assure you, truly,   I shall follow after you.
Look that ye blench for no brand,   nor for any bright weapon,
But bear down on the best,   and bring them out of day.
Be not abashed of their boast;   abide on the earth;
Ye have borne my banners   in very great battles;
We shall fell yon false ones—   the fiend have their souls!
Fight fast with that phalanx,   the field shall be ours.   3740
If I overtake that traitor,   misfortune betide him,
Who has timbered this treason   against my true lord;
Of such an engendrure   full little joy happens,
And that shall this day   be judged most justly."
    Now they seek over the sand   this band at the best point,
Meet with the soldiers,   and deal them their dints;
Through the shields so radiant   the men they touch,
With the short-shivered shafts   of those bright lances;
Dreadful dints they dealt   with dagging spears;
In the dank of the dew   many a dead man lies;   3750
Dukes and douzepers,   and dubbed knights.
The doughtiest of Denmark   are undone for ever.
Thus these men in misery   rip their byrnies,
And receive from the strongest   unreckoned blows;
There they throng in the thick   and thrust to the earth

Of the sturdiest men   three hundred at once.
    But Sir Gawain in grief   could not resist:
He grips him a spear   and runs toward a man,
Who bore gules most gay   with gouts of silver;
He thrusts him in at the throat   with his grim lance,   3760
So that the ground glaive   breaks asunder;
With that massive blow   he puts him to death.
The king of Gothland it was,   a good man of arms.
Their advance guard then   all retreat after this,
As vanquished verily   by valiant warriors;
They meet with the middle guard   that Modred is leading.
Our men make towards them,   as it misfalls them;
For had Sir Gawain had grace   the green hill to hold,[143]
He had won him indeed   worship for ever.
    But Sir Gawain in truth   watches full well   3770
To avenge him on this traitor   who this war had started;
And makes way to Sir Modred   among all his fighters,
With the Montagues lightly,   and other great lords.
    Then Sir Gawain was grieved,   and with a great will
Fixes a fair spear   and freshly challenges:
"False fostered fellow,   the fiend have thy bones!
Fie on thee, felon,   and thy false works!
Thou shalt be dead and undone   for thy deeds so violent,
Or I shall die this day,   if it be my destiny."
    Then his enemy with a host   of outlawed barons   3780
Wholly engulfs   our excellent knights,
As the traitor in his treason   had devised himself;
Dukes of Denmark   he draws up most quickly,
And leaders of Lettow   with legions in plenty,
Surrounded our men   with very keen lances.
Mercenaries and Saracens   out of many lands,
Sixty thousand men,   seemlily arrayed.
Surely there assail   seven score knights
Suddenly by stratagem   near those salt strands.
    Then Sir Gawain wept   with his gray eyes   3790
For grief of his good men,   whom he must guide;
For he knew they were wounded,   weary and fought out;
And what for wonder and woe,   all his wit failed him.
Then said he sighing,   with sliding tears,

"We are with Saracens beset   upon several sides!
I sigh not for myself,   so save me our Lord;
But to see us surprised,   my sorrow is the more.
Be doughty today,   yon dukes shall be yours!
For our dear Lord today,   dread no weapons.
We shall end this day   as peerless knights,   3800
Go to endless joy   with the spotless angels.
Though we have unwittingly   wasted ourselves,
We shall work all well   in the worship of Christ.
We shall for yon Saracens,   I plight you my troth,
Sup with our Savior   solemnly in heaven,
In the presence of that precious One,   Prince of all others,
With prophets and patriarchs,   and apostles most noble,
Before His gracious face,   who formed us all!
Now to yon jades' sons,   he who yields him ever,
Whilst he is quick and in health,   unkilled by hands,[144]   3810
Be he never more saved,   nor succored by Christ,
But may Satan his soul   sink into hell!"
        Then grimly Sir Gawain   grips his weapon,
Against that great battalion   he addresses him forthwith;
Hastily rightens the chains   of his rich sword;
He brandishes his shield;   he holds back no longer,
But quite unwisely and madly   the quickest way charges.
The wounds of those adversaries,   for the vengeful dints,
All well full of blood   where he passes by;
And though he were in great woe,   he wanders but little,   3820
But wreaks, to his worship,   the wrath of his lord.
He strikes steeds in the onset   and stern-faced knights,
That strong men in their stirrups   stone-dead lie there.
He rives the stout steel,   he rips the coats of mail,
There can no man stop him,   his reason was gone.
He fell in a frenzy   through fierceness of heart;
He fights and fells down   him who stands before him.
There befell never a doomed man   such fortune on earth.
In the whole battle   headlong he runs him,
And hurts the hardiest of men   that move upon earth;   3830
Raging like a lion   he lunges throughout them,
These lords and leaders   who wait on the land.
Still Sir Gawain in his woe   wavers but little,

But wounds his opponents   with wonderful dints,
As one who wilfully   would waste himself;
And through his pain and his will   all his wits failed him,
That mad as a wild beast   he charged at the nearest;
All wallowed in blood   where he had passed by;
Each man could be wary   at the vengeance on the others.
    Then he moved towards Sir Modred   among all his
       knights,   3840
And met him in the midshield,   and hammers him through it;
But the man at the sharpness   shunts him a little,
He shore him in the shortribs   about a hand-breadth wide.
The shaft shuddered and shot   onto the bright warrior,
That the blood as it shed   over his shanks ran down,
And showed on the shin-plates,   that were brightly burnished.
And as they shifted and shoved,   he shot to the earth;
With the lunge of the lance   he lighted on his shoulders,
Full length on the lawn,   with loathly wounds.
Then Gawain struck at the man,   and fell groveling;   3850
Although his anger was roused,   his luck was no better.[145]
He pulled out a short knife,   sheathed with silver,
And would have stuck his throat,   but no slit followed;
His hand slipped and slid   aslant on the mail,
And the other man slyly   slipped him under;
With a trenchant knife   the traitor hit him
Through the helm and the head   high up in the brain;
And thus Sir Gawain is gone,   the good man of arms,
Unrescued by any man,   and more is the pity;
Thus Sir Gawain is gone,   that guided many others!   3860
From Gower to Guernsey   all the great lords
Of Glamorgan and of Wales,   these gallant knights,
From assaults of sadness   they may never be glad.
    King Frederick of Friesland   carefully after that
Asks of the false man   about our fierce knight:
"Knewest thou ever this knight   in thy rich kingdom?
Of what kind was he come,   reveal now the truth.
What man was he,   this with the gay arms,
With his griffon of gold,   who is fallen face downward?
He has greatly grieved us,   so may God help me!   3870
Struck down our good men,   and grieved us sorely.

He was the sternest in stress   that ever wore steel,
For he has stunned our host,   and destroyed it for ever!"
    Then Sir Modred with his mouth   speaks most fairly:
"He was matchless on earth,   man, by my truth;
This was Sir Gawain the good,   the gladdest of others,
The graciousest man   that under God lived,
A man the hardiest of hand,   happiest in arms,
And most courteous in the court   under heaven's kingdom;
The lordliest of leaders,   whilst he might live.   3880
For he was renowned as a lion   in many lands;
Hadst thou known him, Sir King,   in the land he belonged to,
His knowledge, his knighthood,   and his kindly works,
His doings, his doughtiness,   his deeds of arms,
Thou wouldst have dole for his death   the days of thy life."
    Yet that traitor as quickly   tears does let fall,
Turns him forth quickly,   and talks no more,
Went weeping away,   and curses the hour
That his wierd was wrought   to work such destruction;
When he thought on this thing,   it pierced his heart.   3890
For the sake of his kinsman's blood,   sighing he rides off;
When that renegade wretch   remembered within him [146]
The reverence and revelry   of the Round Table,
He cried out and repented him   of all his cruel works,
Rode away with his rout,   rests there no longer,
For fear of our rich king,   who should arrive.
Then turns he to Cornwall,   full of care at heart,
Because of his kinsman   who lies on the coast;
He tarries trembling ever   to harken after tidings.
    Then the traitor crept forth   the Tuesday after that,   3900
Went with a trick   treason to work,
And by the Tamar that time   his tents he raises,
And then in a short time   a messenger he sends,
And wrote unto Waynor   how the world was changed,
And at what convenient coast   the king had arrived,
On the flood fought with his fleet,   and felled them alive;
Bade her go far away,   and flee with her children.
Whilst he might slip away,   and get to speak with her,
Withdraw into Ireland,   into those outer mountains,
And live there in the wilderness   within the waste lands.   3910

Then she weeps and she cries   at York in her chamber,
Groans most grievously   with dropping tears,
Passes out of the palace   with all her peerless maidens;
Towards Chester in a chariot   they choose their way,
Made her ready to die   for dole at her heart.
She goes to Caerleon,   and caught her a veil,
Asks there for a habit   in the honor of Christ,
And all for falsehood and fraud,   and for fear of her lord.
   But when the wise king knew   that Gawain had landed,
He quite writhes for woe,   and, wringing his hands,   3920
Has them launch his boats   upon the low water,
Lands like a lion   with lordly knights,
Slips into the sloppy water   aslant to the girdle,
Sweeps up swiftly   with his sword drawn,
Makes ready his battalion   and his banners displays,
Moves over the broad sands   with anger at his heart.
Fares fiercely afield,   where the dead men lie.
Of the traitor's men   on trapped steeds,
Ten thousand were lost,   the truth to declare,
And certain on our side,   sevenscore knights,   3930
In suit with their sovereign   unsound are left there.
   The king glanced proudly   over knights and others,
Earls of Africa   and Austrian warriors,[147]
From Argyle and from Orkney,   the Irish kings,
The noblest of Norway,   numbers full huge,
Dukes of Denmark   and dubbed knights;
And the king of Gothland   in the gay armor
Lies groaning on the ground,   pierced through and through.
The rich king searches about   with sorrow at heart,
And seeks out the men   of all the Round Table;   3940
Sees them all in a band   together by themselves,
With the Saracens unsound   encircled about,
And Sir Gawain the good,   in his gay armor,
Clutching the grass,   and fallen face downward,
His banners cast down,   adorned with gules,
His brand and his broad shield   with blood overrun.
Was never our fair king   so sorrowful in heart,
Nor did aught touch him so sadly   as that sight alone.
   Then stares the good king   and grieves in his heart,

Groans most grievously   with falling tears,   3950
Kneels down by the corpse,   and caught him in his arms,
Casts up his visor,   and kisses him forthwith,
Looks upon his eyelids,   that closely were shut,
His lips like to lead,   and his cheeks now fallowed.
   Then the crowned king   cries out aloud,
"Dear cousin in kinship,   in care am I left here,
For now my worship has turned   and my war ended;
Here is the health of my welfare,   my success in arms;
My heart and my hardiness   lay wholly in him,
My counsel, my comfort,   that kept up my heart!   3960
Of all knights the king,   who lived under Christ,
Thou wert worthy to be king,   though I wore the crown.
My weal and my worship   in this rich world
Were won through Sir Gawain,   and through his wisdom only.
Alas!" said Sir Arthur,   "now my sorrow increases!
I am utterly undone   within mine own lands;
O, doubtful dread death,   thou dwellest too long!
Why drawest thou on so slowly?   thou drownest my heart!"
   Then faints the sweet king,   and aswoon falls down,
Staggers up swiftly,   and lovingly kisses him,   3970
Until his burly beard   was berun with blood,
As though beasts he had quartered   and brought out of life.
Had not Sir Ewain come,   and other great lords,
His bold heart had burst   for sorrow at that moment.
"Cease," said this bold man,   'thou harmest thyself; [148]
This is bootless bale,   for better it grows never.
This is no worship, truly,   to wring thy hands;
To weep like a woman   is held to be no wit.
Be knightly of countenance,   as a king should be,
And leave off such clamor,   for Christ's love of heaven!"   3980
"For blood," said the bold king,   "cease will I never,
Ere my brain burst in two,   or my breast either;
Was never sorrow so soft   that sank to my heart,
He is close kin to myself,   my sorrow is the more;
So sorrowful a sight   was never seen with mine eyes.
In his innocence was he surprised   for a sin of mine own."
   Down kneels the king,   and cries out aloud;
With sorrowful countenance   he utters these words:

"O righteous, almighty God, behold Thou this sorrow!
This royal red blood   run upon earth,   3990
It were worthy to be taken up   and enshrined in gold,
For it is guiltless of sin,   so save me our Lord!"
Down knelt the king,   with care at his heart,
Caught it up reverently   with his clean hands,
Stored it in a kettle-hat,   and covered it fairly,
And went forth with the corpse   toward the land where he dwells.
"Here make I mine avow,"   quoth the king then,
"To Messiah and to Mary,   the mild Queen of heaven,
I shall never go hunting   or hunting dogs uncouple,
At roe or at reindeer,   that run upon earth,   4000
Never greyhound let glide,   or goshawk let fly,
And never see fowl felled   that flies upon wing;
Falcon nor formel   upon my fist handle,
Nor yet with gerfalcon   rejoice me on earth;
Nor reign in my royalty,   nor hold my Round Table,
Till thy death, my dear one,   be duly revenged;
But ever droop and mourn,   while my day lasts out,
Till the Lord and grim death   have done what pleases them."

·   ·   ·   ·   ·   ·

Then draws he to Dorset   and delays no longer,   4052
Doleful, dreadless,   with dropping tears;
Comes into Cornwall   with care at his heart.
The trace of the traitor   he tracks ever steadily,
And turns in by the Treyntis   to seek the betrayer,
Finds him in a forest   the Friday thereafter.[149]
The King alights on foot   and freshly observes,
And with his bold folk   he has taken the field.
Now issues the enemy   from under the wood-eaves,   4060
With hosts of aliens,   most horrible to look at.
Sir Modred the Malebranch,   with his many people,
Advances from the forest   upon many sides,
In seven great battalions   seemlily arrayed,
Sixty thousand men;   the sight was full huge.
All fighting folk   from faraway lands,
They formed one front   by those fresh strands.
And all Arthur's host   was made up of knights

But eighteen hundred in all,   entered in the rolls.
This was a match unmeet,   but for the might of Christ,   4070
To meddle with that multitude   in those main lands.

. . . . . .

Sir Ewain and Sir Errake,   these excellent warriors,   4161
Enter against the host   and eagerly strike;
The giants of Orkney   and Irish kings
They hack in grimmest wise   with their ground swords;
They hew on those hulks   with their hard weapons,
Laid down those men   with loathly dints;
Shoulders and shields   they shred to the haunches,
And their middles through mail-coats   they strike asunder.
Such honor had never   any earthly kings
At their ending day,   save Arthur himself.   4170
The drought of the day so dried up their hearts
That drinkless they die,   the more was the pity!
Now moves in our main force,   and mingles in with them.
Sir Modred the Malebranch,   with his many people,
Had hid himself behind   within the wood-eaves,
With a whole battalion on the heath,   the harm was the greater.
He had seen all the conflict   clean to the end,
How our chivalry had achieved   through chances of arms;
He knew our folk were fought out,   who fated were left there;
To encounter with the king   he decides promptly.   4180
But the churlish chicken   had changed his arms;
He had indeed forsaken   the saltire engrailed,
And caught up three lions   all of light silver,
Passant on purple,   with rich precious stones,[150]
That the king should not know   the crafty wretch.
Because of his cowardice   he cast off his attire,
But the comely king   knew him right well,
Calls to Sir Cador   these keen words:
"I see the traitor come yonder   moving most eagerly;
Yon lad with the lions   is like to himself.   4190
Misfortune shall betide him,   if I may once touch him,
For all his treason and treachery,   as I am true lord!
Today Clarent and Caliburn   shall contest together,
Which is keener in carving   or harder of edge;

We shall test fine steel   upon fair weeds.
It was my dainty darling,   and held most dear,
Kept for the coronation   of kings anointed;
On days when I dubbed   dukes and earls,
It was gravely borne   by the bright hilts.
I durst never draw it   in deeds of arms,   4200
But ever kept it clean   for mine own cause.
Since I see Clarent unclad,   that is crown of swords,
My wardrobe at Wallingford   I know is destroyed;
There knew no man of its place   but Waynor herself;
She had the keeping herself   of that choice weapon,
Of coffers enclosed,   that belonged to the crown,
With rings and relics   and the regalia of France,
That was found on Sir Frolle,   when he was left dead."
      Then Sir Marroke in melancholy   meets with Sir Modred,
With a hammered mace   mightily strikes him;   4210
The border of his basinet   he bursts asunder,
That the sheer red blood   runs over the byrnie.
The man blenches for pain,   and all his hue changes,
But still he waits like a boar,   and savagely strikes back.
He brings out a brand,   bright as ever any silver,
Which was Sir Arthur's own,   and Uther's, his father's;
In the wardrobe at Wallingford   it was wont to be kept;
Therewith the doughty dog   dealt him such blows,
That the other withdrew aside,   and durst do no other,
For Sir Marroke was a man   marred by old age,   4220
And Sir Modred was mighty   and in his greatest strength;
Came none within the compass,   knight or other man,
Within the swing of that sword,   who lost not his life.
      That perceives our prince,   and presses fast towards him,
Strikes into the struggle   by strength of his hands,[151]
Meets with Sir Modred,   cries out sternly,
"Turn, traitor untrue,   it betides thee no better;
By great God, thou shalt die   with dint of my hands,
No man shall rescue thee,   nor reach thee on earth!"
      The king with Caliburn   like a knight strikes him,   4230
The cantle of the bright shield   he carves asunder,
In the shoulder of the man,   a hand's-breadth large,
That the sheer red blood   showed on his mail.

He shudders and flinches   and shrinks a little,
But shoves in sharply   in his fair weeds;
The felon with the fine sword   fiercely strikes at him,
The flesh on the far side   he flashes asunder,
Through jupon and jesseraunt   of noble mail.
The man cut out in the flesh   a half-foot in breadth,
That the grievous blow was his death,   and the dole was the
          greater   4240
That ever the doughty one should die,   but at the Lord's will!
Yet with Caliburn his sword   in knightly wise he strikes,
Casts up his shining shield,   and covers himself well;
Swaps off the sword hand,   as he glances by,
An inch from the elbow   he hacked it asunder,
That he swoons down on the sward   and falls in a faint,
Through bracer of brown steel   and the bright mail,
That the hilt and the hand   lie upon the heath.
Then fiercely that man   raises up the shield,
Bears him in with the brand   to the bright hilts,   4250
So that he cries out at the sword,   and droops to die.
      "In faith," said the fey king,   "much it grieves me,
That such a false thief   have so fair an end."
      When they had finished this fight,   then was the field won,
And the false folk in the field   are left as fated.
To a forest they fled,   and fall in the tangle,
And the fierce fighting folk   follow after them;
They hunt out and hew down   the heathen tikes,
Murder in the mountains   Sir Modred's knights;
There escaped never noble youth,   chieftain or other,   4260
But they chopped them down in the chase,   it cost them but little.
      But when Sir Arthur forthwith   does find Sir Ewain,
And Errake the affable,   and other great lords,
He caught up Sir Cador   with care at his heart,[152]
Sir Cleges, Sir Cleremonde,   these famed men of arms,
Sir Loth and Sir Lionel,   Sir Launcelot and Lowes,
Marroke and Meneduke,   who mighty were ever;
With pain on the heath   he lays them together;
Looked on their bodies,   and with a loud voice,
As man that might not live   and had lost his mirth;   4270
Then he staggers like one mad,   and all his strength fails him,

He looks up aloft, and his whole face changes;
Down he sways heavily, and falls in a swoon,
Recovers him up on his knees, and cries very often:
"O King, comely with crown, in care am I left here;
All my lordship is laid low on the land,
They who gave me guerdons of their own grace,
Maintained my manhood by might of their hands,
Made me manly in the world, and master on earth.
In a sorrowful time this misfortune has arisen,   4280
Which has lost through a traitor all my true lords.
Here rests the rich blood of the Round Table,
Struck down by a scoundrel, the more is the pity!
I must, helpless on the heath, house by myself.
Like a woeful widow, that wants her lord,
I must be weary and weep, and wring my hands,
For my wit and my worship are gone from me for ever.
Of all lordship I take leave now at my ending.
Here is the Britons' blood brought out of life,
And now in this day's work all my joy ends!"   4290
    Then rally the men of all the Round Table;
To that lordly king they all ride up together;
There assemble straightway seven score knights.
In the sight of their sovereign, who was left wounded.
    Then kneels the crowned king, and cries out aloud:
"I thank Thee, God, for Thy grace, with a good will,
That gavest us virtue and wit to vanquish these warriors,
And hast granted us the victory over these great lords!
He sent us never any shame, or disgrace upon earth,
But ever yet the upper hand of all other kings!   4300
We have no leisure now those lords to seek out,
For yon loathly lad has lamed me so sorely.
Let us make our way to Glastonbury, nought else will avail us;
There may we rest us in peace, and ransack our wounds.
For this dear day's work the Lord be praised,
Who has destined and adjudged us to die among our own." [153]
    Then they hold to his behest wholly at once,
And go towards Glastonbury by the quickest way;
They enter the Isle of Avalon, and Arthur alights,
Makes way there to a manor, for he might go no further.   4310

A surgeon from Salerno   searches his wounds;
The king sees by testing   that he will never be sound,
And at once to his faithful men   he utters these words:
     "Call me a confessor,   with Christ in his arms;
I shall be houseled in haste,   whatso may betide me.
Constantine my cousin   shall bear the crown,
As becomes him by nature,   if Christ will permit him.
Man, for my blessing,   do thou bury yon lords,
Who in battle with brands   are brought out of life;
And after make thy way manfully   to Modred's children,   4320
That they be duly slain   and slung into the waters;
Let no wicked weed wax   or bloom on this earth;
I warn thee, for thy worship;   do as I bid thee!
I forgive all the grief,   for God's love of heaven,
If Waynor have wrought well,   well may it betide her!"
     He said *"In manus tuas"*   on the earth where he lies,
And thus passes his spirit,   and he speaks no more.
The baronage of Britain then,   bishops and others,
Go to Glastonbury   with grieving hearts,
To bury their bold king,   and bring him to earth,   4330
With all honor and richness   that any man should have.
Sadly they toll the bells,   and sing requiem,
Say masses and matins,   with mourning notes;
The religious vest them   in their rich copes,
Pontiffs and prelates   in precious vestments;
Dukes and douzepers   in their coats of mourning;
Countesses kneeling,   and clasping their hands,
Ladies languishing,   and sorrowful in appearance.
All were clad in black,   brides and others,
Who were seen at the burial   with streaming tears.   4340
Was never so sorrowful a sight   seen in their time!
     Thus ends King Arthur,   as authors declare it,[154]
Who was of Hector's kin,   the king's son of Troy,
And of Sir Priam the prince,   praised upon earth;
From thence brought the Britons   all their bold elders,
Into Britain the broad,   as the *Brut* tells us.[155]

"LE MORTE ARTHUR"
(c. 1400)

"The Stanzaic Version"

Rendered into prose by Richard L. Brengle from *Le Morte Arthur*, ed. J. Douglas Bruce, Early English Text Society, Extra Series, No. LXXXVII (London: Kegan Paul, Trench, Trübner & Co., Ltd., 1903).

[vv. 1-136] Sirs, who are beloved and dear, listen and I shall tell you what adventures befell our ancestors in olden days—in the days of Arthur, that noble King, wonderfully many adventures befell—and I shall tell the ending there of those who knew much of sorrow and joy.

When the knights of the Table Round had sought the Holy Grail and had finished and brought to an end the adventures they found before them, they beat and bound their enemies, not leaving them alive even for gold. And when they had wrought these deeds they lived well for four years, until one day it happened that as the King lay in bed beside the Queen they began to talk about the many events which had occurred in that land.

"Sir," she said, "if it is your will, I would tell you about a strange thing, of how your court begins to empty of valiant knights altogether. Sir, your honor begins to decline, which was once spread wide in the world [1] by Lancelot and all the others who were so doughty in deed."

"Madame, on account of this I ask your counsel: what is best for such peril?"

"If you want to keep your honor, it is best to proclaim a tournament, through which adventure shall begin and be spoken of everywhere, and knights shall win fame there riding in deeds of arms. Sir, in this way allow your court no decline, but life in honor and in pride."

"Certainly, Madame," the King said then, "this wasting away shall no longer continue."

The King proclaimed a tournament to be held at Winchester, in which young Galehod was to be the leader, with knights who were bold horsemen, so that ladies and maidens might see who were best in deeds, through bravery to win the prize. The knights armed themselves together to ride to the tournament, with broad shields and bright helmets, to win great honor and glory.

Lancelot lay sick at that same time, and remained behind with the Queen; because of the love between them, he made an excuse for staying. The King mounted his steed and went forth upon his way, but Sir Agravaine also tarried at home—for, to tell the truth,[2] men in many a country said that Lancelot lay by the Queen, and Agravaine watched both night and day to catch them in the act.

Lancelot went forth to the Queen's chamber, bent upon his knee, and saluted there that shining lady.

"Lancelot, what are you doing here with me? The King has gone and the court altogether. I fear that the love between us shall be discovered. Sir Agravaine is at home and watches us night and day."

"Nay, my noble lady," he said. "I come to take my leave of you before I go out of the court."

"Yea, arm yourself quickly, for your staying fills me with woe."

Lancelot went to his chamber where rich attire lay before him. He dressed himself in noble apparel—armor, sword, and shield—and mounted a grey steed King Arthur had given him. He, the brave and valiant knight, did not take the main road, but night and day hastened towards that rich city,[3] called Winchester, where the tournament was truly held.

King Arthur abode in a castle, full of sport and joy; and because he would see Lancelot, who did not want to be recognized, the knight bent his shoulders and hung his head full low as if he could not control his limbs. He heeded no bugle blast, appearing as if he were old so that no one could know who he was.

The King stood above on a tower and called Sir Ywain: "Sir, do you know the knight who rides down below?"

Sir Ywain spoke full courteously, "Sir, it is some old knight who is coming to see the young knights ride."

They both looked at him just as his horse stumbled on a stone and all his body began to tremble; but the knight reacted with such agility as he took up the bridle that they both thereby knew at once that it was Lancelot of the Lake.

King Arthur then said these words to Sir Ywain: "Well may Lancelot be held in all the world the best knight,[4] of beauty and bounty; and since there is no one of such might and good deeds, since he wants no one to know it, Sir Ywain, we will stop him. He thinks we do not recognize him."

"Sir, it is better to let him ride and do what he wants to do. He will be nearby, for he has come hither this far. We shall know him by his deeds and by the horse that he has brought." [5]

[vv. 1672-1863] A time befell, to tell the truth, when the knights stood in a chamber and spoke together, Gareth, Sir Gawain, and Mordred who came to such great trouble.

"Alas!" said Sir Agravaine, "what false men we make of ourselves! How long shall we conceal the treason of Lancelot of the Lake? Well we know, beyond question, that King Arthur is our uncle and that Lancelot lies by the Queen, a traitor to the King. We know that every day all the court hears and sees it. If you want my advice, we should tell the King."

"Well we know," said Sir Gawain, "that we are the King's kin, and that Lancelot is so very strong that such words were better stopped.[49] Brother Agravaine, you well know that by doing this we will only come to harm. It is better to conceal it than thus to begin war and ruin. Well you know, brother Agravaine, Lancelot is a hardy and bold knight: King and court had often been slain had he not been better than we. And since I cannot describe the love that has been between us two, I shall never betray Lancelot nor be his foe behind his back. Lancelot is the King's faithful follower, besides being a hardy and bold knight, who will stand by him and hold many a land. Much blood would be shed were this story told. Sir Agravaine, he who starts such a thing is full mad."

Then, as Gawain and all the other knights of the company talked this way, the King came in quietly.

Gawain said, "Comrades, peace!"

The King became nearly crazed with anger to know what it

was all about. Agravaine swore by the Cross, "I shall tell you without falsehood."

Gawain went to his chamber so that he might hear none of this tale; Gareth and Gaheris with his consent went there with their brother.[50] Well they knew that all was lost.

Sir Gawain then swore by God: "Here now is the beginning of something which will not be ended for many a year."

Sir Agravaine told the King everything in a straightforward manner, how Lancelot lay by the Queen. "He has done so full many a year; all the court knows it, and sees and hears it each day. We have been false traitors never to have disclosed it to you."

"Alas!" said the King. "That is indeed a great pity. No man ever had more beauty and bounty; no man in the world ever before was so noble. Alas! great sorrow it is that any treason should be in him. But since it is so without a doubt, Sir Agravaine, what now is your best advice in order to catch him in the act? He is a man of such accomplishment in arms that I fear him greatly. All the court would not assail him if he were armed upon his steed."

"Sir, you and all the court together go hunting tomorrow, and then send word to the Queen that you will be gone all night.[51] I and the other twelve bold knights will prepare ourselves full secretly. Beyond question we will catch him tomorrow or some time soon."

So the next day with all the court together the King rode out hunting, and afterwards he sent word to the Queen that he would abide out all night. At the same time, Agravaine remained at home with twelve bold knights; all day long they were not seen, so carefully did they hide themselves.

Then was the Queen wonderfully glad that the King would stay in the forest overnight. Swiftly she sent word to Lancelot, bidding him come to her. Sir Bors overheard, and his heart was uneasy.

"Sir," he said, "I would have a word with you, if it be your will. Sir, I advise you to stay here tonight. I fear there has been some treason undertaken by Agravaine, something deadly which awaits you both day and night; of all the times that you have gone to her, never before has it grieved me so strongly nor given my heart such uneasiness as it does tonight."

"Bors," he said, "hold your peace. It is not for you to speak such words. I will go to my lady, some new tidings to hear; [52] I shall not better know her will. Look, be happy and blithe: certainly I will not stay there—I shall return to you quickly."

Thus he departed, intending to come back soon; and for this reason he wore an uniquely-made robe rather than armor. He took a sword in his hand, not fearing treason at all, for there was no man under the moon would have dared try to harm him.

When he came to the beautiful lady, he kissed and embraced that sweet person. In truth, they never thought that any treason was being prepared against him; the love between them was so great that they could not part. He went to bed with the Queen and there he intended to stay all night.

Lancelot had not been in bed long in the Queen's private room when Agravaine and Sir Mordred came with twelve battlewise knights. They accused Lancelot of treason, called him false and the King's betrayer. He was very strongly endangered because he had no armor.

"Alas!" then said the Queen, "Lancelot, what shall become of us both? That the love which has been between us should come to such an ending! [53] Bold Agravaine has ever been our foe. Now I know, without a doubt, that all our happiness is turned to woe."

"Lady," he said, "you must stop. I know your words are the natural ones, but is there any armor about that I could use to save my life?"

"Indeed, not," she said then. "This event is so unexpected that no armor, helmet, hauberk, sword, or knife is to be had."

Agravaine and Sir Mordred continued to call him a cowardly, false knight, bidding him rise out of his bed to fight with them. He clad himself in his robe, for he could get no armor. Angrily he drew out his sword and opened up the chamber door. An armed knight dashed in, hoping to slay Lancelot, but Lancelot gave him such a blow that he fell dead to the ground. All the others then stopped, no one daring to follow after him. He sprang to the chamber door and bolted it with two bars.

Lancelot found the armor of the knight he had slain both fair and bright: hastily he drew it off and dressed himself in it.[54]

"Now, know you well, Sir Agravaine, you can imprison me no more tonight." Then out he sprang with great strength to fight against all of them alone. Lancelot smote with good heart, know you well, without falsehood. Sir Agravaine went to his death, and then all the rest of the company. There was none so strong who withstood him when he made even a small attack. But Mordred fled as if he were deranged, full eager to save his life.[55]

.   .   .   .   .   .

[vv. 1904-2029] Mordred then took the straightest way to the forest and related what events had happened that same night.

"Mordred, have you slain that traitor, and how have you disposed of him?"

"Nay, Sir, but dead is Agravaine, and so are all our other knights."

When the hardy and bold knight Sir Gawain heard this, he said, "Alas! is my brother slain?" His heart began to grow dreadfully cold.[56] "I warned Sir Agravaine some time ago that Lancelot is so strong that it would be very difficult to combat him."

In a short time the King and all his bold knights then took counsel what was best to do with the Queen. It was quickly decided that she should be put to death by burning. They made a fire in the field and brought that noble lady there; all those who could wield weapons stood armed about her. Gawain, who was powerful in arms, as well as Gareth and Gaheris, refused to be witnesses; they kept to their chambers because they had great pity for the Queen.

King Arthur sent for Gawain and Gareth. Their answers were open: they could not be of his opinion. Gawain would never be present where any woman should be burned. But Gareth and Gaheris with little pride went thither all unarmed.

A squire Lancelot had sent to court heard these tidings. He went quickly to the forest where Lancelot and his men stayed,[57] and bade them hasten with all speed to where the Queen was to be burned. They armed themselves quickly, sprang to their horses, and dashed off.

The Queen stood near the fire, smoke already about her. Nearby, truly, were many good and powerful lords. Lancelot rushed up as if he were unhinged; very quickly he dispersed the throng: there was no one bold enough to stand up against him when he had made a small attack. There was no steel stood against him. Though they fought but a little while, many good and strong lords were brought to the ground. Gareth and Gaheris were both slain, with many a doleful death's wound. The Queen was seized without concealment and taken back to the forest.

The tidings were brought to the King of how Lancelot bore away the Queen. "Such woe as there is wrought! Slain are all our bold knights!" Down he fell and swooned often—it was a great pity to hear and see—the sorrow smote so near his heart, no man doubted it nearly took his life. "O Christ Jesus, what can I say? There was never so woeful a man on earth. Such knights as are slain there are no more in all this world.[58] Let no man tell Sir Gawain that Gareth his brother is dead. Alas, for the sad kingdom that ever Lancelot was my foe!"

Gawain had taken himself to his chamber and would not leave it all day long. A squire then told him the tidings—no wonder that his heart was broken! "Alas!" he said, "is then my bold brother Gareth dead and gone?" His heart began to ache so that he almost slew himself.

The squire tried to comfort Sir Gawain: "Gareth is not badly hurt; he will soon be all right."

But Gawain dashed madly to the room where his brothers lay slain. The chamber floor was covered with blood, and cloths of gold were drawn over them. Then he lifted up a cloth: what wonder that his heart was sore, to see them so sadly reduced that once were such valiant knights! When he caught sight of his brother, he could speak no more words: he lost there his strength and might and fell into a deep swoon. But when this hardy knight, Sir Gawain, recovered his senses, like the powerful man he was he swore by God and spoke loudly: [59] "Between myself and Lancelot of the Lake there is truly no man on earth shall set a truce and make peace before one of us has slain the other."

A squire Lancelot had sent to court heard these tidings. He went quickly to the forest and told Lancelot how many good, wealthy knights had lost their lives, among them Gareth and Gaheris.

Then did Lancelot grieve. "Lord," he said, "how can this be? By Jesus Christ, what can I say? That ever Gareth was against me, after the love that has been between us! Now I know well that Sir Gawain is a sorrowful man, and that there will never be a reconciliation until one of us has slain the other." [60]

    .   .   .   .   .

[vv. 2086-2451] Arthur would wait no longer, but hastened with all his might. He sent messengers to ride both day and night throughout all parts of England to bid earl, baron, and knight come at once with strong horse and bright armor. Though their great trouble began with those who were dead, three hundred more knights came out of their castles, the best men in England, Ireland, Wales, and Scotland, to slay Lancelot and his forces with hearts fierce as any boar's.

When this host was all prepared, they could wait no longer. They raised their spears and banners like men of great pride; [62] with helmet and shield and brown hauberk, Gawain himself rode at the head of them to Joyous Gard, that rich town, and started to besiege it on all sides.

They stayed around Joyous Gard for seventeen weeks and more, until it happened one day Lancelot bade them go home: "Break your siege! Go away! It would be a great pity to slay you." He said, "Alas and woe, that this sore sorrow ever began!"

But the King and Sir Gawain still called him a false, recreant knight, and said he had slain his brothers and was a traitor by day and by night. They bade him come and prove his strength by fighting with them in the field. Lancelot sighed, for it was truly a sad thing to see. So loudly they called upon Lancelot with voice and terrible clamor of horns that Bors of Gawnes came sorrowfully to him.

"Sir," he said, "why should we have to listen to these proud words? I think it is cowardly for none of us to answer their challenge. Let us dress ourselves in rich array, both with spear and shield, as quickly as we possibly can, and ride out into the field.[63] While my life may last, I shall never yield my weapons this day. Therefore, I dare wager well my life that we two shall make them all yield."

"Alas!" said Lancelot, "woe is me, that I should ever see the time when I am against my lord—the noble King who made me a knight! Sir Gawain, I beseech you, as you are a man of great might, let not my lord come into that field nor yourself fight with me."

But he could wait no longer and hastened to prepare himself. When they were ready to ride, they raised their spears and pennons; and when these hosts began to come together, with shouts and the sound of loud horns, so many good men were struck down on both sides that it was a great pity. Sir Lionel began to advance powerfully with a spear before him; Sir Gawain rode against him, forcing both horse and rider to the ground, and everyone thought that he had been slain, such a wound had Sir Lionel. He was drawn from the field, badly wounded.

In all the battle that day no man could stand up against Lancelot. Neither could any man ride so fast as he to see that no one should be killed.[64] The King was always near him and attacked him with all his strength, but he was so courteous he would not return a single blow. At last Sir Bors saw the King, rode against him, and struck him so hard that he nearly lost all his grandeur: his steed's back broke under him, so that he fell to the ground. Bors spoke loud words in rebuke of Sir Lancelot: "Sir, will you allow the King to assault you all day? Since his heart is so hardened, your courtesy will not avail you. There will be no more battles if you will take my advice. Give us leave to slay them all, for in this battle you have vanquished."

"Alas!" said Lancelot, "woe is me that I should ever see unhorsed before me the noble King who made me a knight!" He was then so courteous and generous that from his steed he alighted, helped the King back on his horse, and bade him escape if he could.

When the King was in the saddle, he looked upon Lancelot as the most chivalrous of all men.[65] As he thought how things had formerly been, tears ran down from his eyes. With a deep sigh he said, "Alas! that ever this war began!"

The two sides, their ranks grown thin of knights, withdrew from one another. Tomorrow the battle would begin again. They dressed themselves in rich array and parted their hosts in two. He who began this wretched encounter, no wonder he felt so guilty!

But Sir Bors, fierce as any boar, rode out to Sir Gawain to avenge his brother Lionel who was sore wounded. Sir Gawain bore down on Bors like a man of great strength. Each one severely wounded the other, so that they were nearly slain; they both fell to the ground, making many people full sad. The King's party was ready to carry them both away, but Lancelot himself rode up and rescued Bors from them. The men who carried him from the field were also wounded. One can well understand how in this battle knights were struck from their saddles and came down with sad hearts,[66] and that bold and quick steeds waded in the blood among them. But by the time of the evening bell, Lancelot's party fared the better.

The forces fought this battle no more that day but thus departed. Men led their friends home and bore the slain who lay in the field. The battle over with, Lancelot went to his castle. Truly there was grief and sore weeping: among them there was no child's play.

Word of this war sprang into every land both north and south. At Rome it was well known what great sorrow England had; for this the Pope had full compassion. A letter he sealed with his hand, saying that unless the warring sides were reconciled he would lay the land under an interdict. The Bishop of Rochester was then at Rome; he came with this message to England, to Carlisle where the King was. In the palace, before the dais, he took out the Pope's letter and bade them follow the Pope's command to keep England in rest and peace. The Pope's letter was read before all together, ordering the King to take the Queen back again and come to accord with Lancelot of the Lake,[67] to make peace and an everlasting truce between them, or else England would be interdicted and brought to sorrow on account of them.

The King was gladly willing to follow the Pope's commandment to take the Queen back again, but Gawain was so hard of heart that he would never agree to make peace with Lancelot as long as any life was in him. With the consent of everyone else the King wrote a letter, delivered by the Bishop to Lancelot of the Lake, asking if he would courteously return the Queen to him, or else all England would be interdicted and brought to sorrow for their sake.

Lancelot, as a knight who was hardy and bold, answered with great submission: "Sir, I have been in many a battle, both for the King and for the Queen; his best tower would have been very cold had it not been for me. He repays me with small honor, even though I have served him so completely."

The Bishop answered directly and totally unafraid, "Sir, remember that you have been victorious in many a battle through the grace that God has given you.[68] You will follow now my counsel: think of him to whom you have brought harm. Women are frail of character. Sir, let not England come to naught."

"Sir Bishop, you well know I have no need to acquire castles. If I chose, I might be king of all Bayonne, that rich country; I might ride boldly over my lands with my well-mounted knights. If I yielded to my foes I would have great fear for the Queen's life."

"Sir, by Mary the Flower of maidens and God Who directs and rights all, I plight you my troth she shall come to no dishonor, but be brought directly to her private chamber, to her ladies and bright maidens, and held in greater honor than she ever was before."

"Now, if I grant such a thing as to deliver the Queen, Sir Bishop, promise that my lord the King, Sir Gawain, and all with them, will guarantee that the truce between us will hold."

Then was the Bishop wonderfully happy that Lancelot gave him this answer. He went quickly to his palfrey and rode to Carlisle.[69] There tidings of Lancelot's words soon were heard: the King and the court were very glad, and set and confirmed an armistice at once. Through the assent of all together a safe truce they made there. Though Gawain was bold of heart, he was not against having a respite between them while Lancelot brought home the Queen; but he never thought of reconciliation, nor did either man seek out the other's heart.

Having made a safe truce and binding it with their seals, they next sent three of the wisest bishops in all the land to Lancelot of the Lake. These men found him at Joyous Gard; they presented him with the peace letters and Lancelot set his hand to these documents. The bishops then went on their way to Carlisle where the King was. Lancelot was to come the next day proudly in company with the lady. He dressed himself in rich array, know you well, without falsehood; and he chose a hundred knights, the best truly of all his host.

Lancelot and the Queen were clad in rich apparel, robes of white samite, with cut silver, ivory saddle and white steed,[70] housings of the same thread that was made in heathen country. Lancelot held her bridle, as we read in the romance. Every one of the other knights wore green samite from heathen lands, and in their kirtles rode alone. Each knight wore a green garland; the saddles were set with rich stones, and each man bore a branch of olive in his hand. All the fields about them shone, through which the knights rode singing lustily.

They alighted in the palace when they came to the castle. Lancelot took the Queen from her palfrey (they said it was a beautiful sight); he saluted the King at once, as a man who had great might. There were few fair words, but many a knight stood there weeping.

Lancelot spoke to the mighty King: "Sir, I have brought you your Queen, and rightly saved her as a lady who is beautiful and bright and is always true. If any man says she is not pure, I offer to fight him."

King Arthur answered with bold, hard words: "Lancelot, I never thought that you would create this sorrow for me; [71] that though we were so dear to one another you should become my foe. But nothing makes me more sad than that there ever was war between us two."

Lancelot, when he had listened long, then replied, "Sir, you blame me for your woe, yet you know you do so wrongly. I was never far away from you when you had any strong sorrow. But you have listened to liars lie, from whom all these words spring up."

Then spoke the hardy and noble knight Sir Gawain: "Lancelot, you cannot deny that you have slain my three brothers. On account of this we shall prove by our might in the field who shall have the supremacy. Until one of us shall slay the other, I will never be happy."

Though he was not afraid, Lancelot answered with a sore heart: "Gawain," he said, "although I was there, I did not slay your brothers myself. Many other knights were there who paid then for the harm of this war." Lancelot sighed deeply and wept.

Then Lancelot spoke, as I will tell you, to the King and Sir Gawain: "Sir, shall I never think of reconciliation, that we might be friends again?" [72]

Gawain spoke with a bold heart, as a man who has great strength: "Nay, you need never think of reconciliation till one of us has slain the other."

"Since it never can happen that peace will come between us, may I ride safely into my lands with my bold knights? Then will I no longer stay here, but take leave of you altogether; wherever I go in the wide world, I shall never see England again."

King Arthur answered there, the tears running from his eyes, "By Jesus Christ!" he swore, "Who created and won all this world, when you go you shall allow no living man in your land."

He said, "Alas!" with some sighing, "that ever yet this war began! Since I shall go away and dwell in my own lands, may I live there safely and not have you wage war on me?"

Sir Gawain then said, "Nay. By Him Who made the sun and

moon, get ready as best you can, for we shall follow after you full soon." [73]

.   .   .   .   .   .

[vv. 2500-2539] Arthur would wait no longer, for his heart was sore both night and day. He sent messengers riding throughout England to earls and barons on every side, bidding them hasten and make ready to attack Lancelot's lands, to burn and kill and make all bare.

The King took counsel with all his knights together: he bade them decide among themselves who would make the best steward to keep and take care of the realm and be best for Britain's sake. They were all greatly fearful that aliens would capture the land. The knights answered, without hesitation, and said truly that they thought Sir Mordred was the most trustworthy, though men searched throughout the realm,[75] to keep the land in safety and in peace. A book was brought before him, and many who afterwards paid for it chose Sir Mordred to be steward.

There was no further delay: everything was hastily prepared. When they were ready to ride, they raised their spears and pennons and went forth with great pride to a port called Caerleon. There they equipped great galleys of many kinds. Then they shipped out on the sea and went over the wide water. When they could see Bayonne they landed in great numbers; neither tree nor stone withstood them, but they burned and slew on every side. Lancelot waited in his best city for battle.[76]

.   .   .   .   .   .

[vv. 2938-3573] Afterwards it was two months, as noble people understand it, before Gawain recovered enough to get around by foot or by horseback. A third time he was bold enough to do Lancelot battle with heart and hand, but then word came to them that they must go home to England. The message brought to them was one which no man thought good. The King himself thought that he must needs sail quickly over the sea (full greatly mourned he in his mind that such treason should be wrought in England). They broke the siege and made homeward, and afterwards they were greatly angry.

For that false traitor, Sir Mordred—the King's sister's son he was, and also his own son, as I read (thus men chose him to be steward)—so falsely had he led England, know you well in truth, he desired to wed his uncle's wife, so that many a man rued Arthur's expedition. Mordred held a great many feasts and gave large gifts also, so that people said he brought joy and prosperity while in Arthur's time there was sorrow and need.[89] And thus right began to go wrong, and, not to conceal anything, all the counsel was to keep Mordred in the land with joy.

He had false letters made, and caused messengers to bring them, saying that Arthur was brought to the ground and that they must choose another king. All said what they thought: "Arthur loved nothing but warring and such things as he sought for himself. It is right he came to his end."

Mordred proclaimed a parliament; the people came thither and wholly through their assent crowned Mordred the king. He held a feast for a fortnight at Canterbury, in Kent, and after that he went to Winchester. There he prepared a rich wedding: in the summer, when it was fair and bright, he planned to wed his father's wife and keep her with might and main, and so bring her as a bride to bed. But she begged him to delay a fortnight—the lady was much oppressed—so that she might go to London to clothe herself and her maidens. Then the Queen, white as the lily flower, went to the Tower of London and shut the gates and lived therein.[90] Mordred was exceedingly angry. He went there and would not cease; he made many attacks on the Tower, but he could not enter it.

The Archbishop of Canterbury went thither, bearing his cross before him. He said, "Sir, By Christ on the Rood, what have you in your thoughts? It is insanity for you to wish now to wed your father's wife. Though you may be bold, Arthur will come over the sea to take revenge."

"You foolish cleric," Mordred said. "Do you think you can prevent my will? By Him Who suffered pain for us, you shall greatly rue these words. You shall be drawn by wild horses and hanged high upon a hill."

The Bishop then was eager to flee and allow him to carry out his follies. At Canterbury, in faraway Kent, he then cursed him with book and bell. Soon after Mordred heard tell of this, he sent men to seek out the Bishop. The Bishop dared stay there no longer, but took his gold and silver and went into the wilderness. There he forsook the world's wealth and attended to joy no longer, but had a chapel built between two tall, ancient groves; [91] therein he wore black clothes as if he were a hermit in the woods. Often he wept and kept vigils for England, which had such sore sorrows.

Mordred then remained there a long time, but he could not capture the Tower, not by strength, nor great struggle, nor with any other kind of stratagem. All the while he feared his father; thus he did not cease his sorrow. He went forth to mislead the kingdom in which he was crowned. He rode then to Dover, knowing well all the coasts; he gave great gifts and sent letters to earls and to barons on one side, and guarded the sea on the other side with bold men with bent bows. He wanted to defend England, which is broad and wide, from his own father.

Arthur, who was great of strength, came with his forces over the sea: a hundred galleys that were well filled with bold and high-spirited barons. He intended to land at Dover, the usual and most advantageous place, but he found that many a hardy, battlewise knight prevented him. So he soon went ashore where it was easier to land. The many enemies that he found there he thought before that time were his friends.[92] The King was furious—well nigh unhinged—and with his men began to attack. So great a struggle took place on that strand that many a man met his end there.

Sir Gawain armed himself at that moment, but, alas, too long was his head bare (he was sick and very unsound, his hurt grieved him full sore): someone struck him on the old wound with the handle of an oar, forcing him to the ground, and he never spoke again.

Brave men, with bows bent, came boldly up in boats, and they pierced and tore rich hauberks so that the red blood burst out. Sharpened spears went through them—they thought nothing good of those games—and by the time that this savage conflict was over the broad streams all ran with blood.

Arthur was so great in strength there was none who could withstand him. He hewed on their bright helmets so that the blood ran down their breasts. By the time that the fight was ended the false ones had fallen; some fled to Canterbury all that night to warn their master, Sir Mordred.

Mordred then made himself ready and boldly went forth to do battle with helmet, shield, and brown hauberk. So all his company began to ride out; [93] they met him at Barham Down early the following morning. With great spears and pennons grimly they began to ride together.

Arthur of rich array blew his horn loudly from the heights, and Mordred the false traitor came glad and gay. They fought all that day long until night was nearly nigh. Whoever saw it might well say he never witnessed such a struggle. Arthur fought with good heart—there never was a nobler knight; he struck through helmets and slew knights both left and right.

Mordred was nearly out of his mind with wrath. He called to his forces and said to them, "Onward! Recover yourselves, by the Cross! Alas, this day is so soon gone!"

Many men lay on the bare banks, with bright torches all through burning; many a brave man died and many a lord lost his life. Mordred was full of sorrow and care. He came to Canterbury in the morning. And Arthur stayed there all night: proudly his noble men lodged with him. Early the next day Arthur bade his horns blow, calling his followers from every side, and buried many a dead man in a row,[94] in wide and deep pits. Over each they made a small mound so that all men who passed might know them by their marks.

Arthur then went to his repast—his noble men quickly followed him—but when he found Sir Gawain lying dead in a ship by a mast, before he could recover his might or strength his heart nearly burst a hundred times.

They laid Sir Gawain upon a bier, bore him to the castle, and in the chancel of a chapel there buried that bold baron. Arthur then changed all his manner. No wonder his heart was breaking: he should never again hear of his sister's son who was so dear to him.

Sir Arthur could rest no longer until he had put an end to all manner of evil. He traveled out of the south side of England and went west toward Wales. He thought it would be best to stay then at Salisbury, and at Whitsuntide he called to him bold barons eager for battle. Unto him came many a doughty knight, for the word had gone out over the world that Sir Arthur was in the right and Mordred wrongly warred on him.[95] It was a terrible thing to see: Arthur's host was vast; and the mighty Mordred was made strong through great gifts.

Soon after the feast of the Trinity a battle between them was set: it would be a fierce battle, for no man could stop it. Sir Arthur was exceedingly glad that they should meet. Sir Mordred came to the country with many men who had been brought from afar.

At night when Arthur went to bed—he was to do battle on the morrow—it came to him in strange dreams that on that day many a man should have sorrow. He thought he sat all clad in gold, a handsome crowned king, upon a wheel which spread full wide, and all his knights bowed to him. The wheel was wonderfully rich and round, in the world none half so high; thereon he sat richly crowned with many a bezant, brooch, and ring. He looked down upon the ground, and saw black water under him with many dragons lying there unbound, so that no man dared come near them. He was greatly fearful of falling among the fiends who fought there, but the wheel completely overturned and every one of them caught him by a limb.[96] The King raised a hue and cry, like a bewildered man of disturbed mind. His chamberlain awakened him and he started wildly out of his sleep. He stayed awake all night and wept, with saddened heart and sorrowful voice, but towards daybreak he fell asleep.

He dreamed that seven tapers were set about him. He thought Sir Gawain guarded him with more men than anyone can name by a river that was broad and deep. It seemed that angels came from heaven. The King had never been so happy as when he saw his sister's son. "Welcome, Sir Gawain," he said. "If you could stay, I should be well again. Now, dear friend, without concealing anything, who are those people who follow you?"

"Sir," Gawain answered, "they live in bliss where I am permitted to be. They were lords and gentle ladies who have lost the life of this world. When I was a man alive I fought for them against their foes. Now I find them my best friends: they bless the time that I was born. They asked to come with me to meet you this morning. You must take a month of truce and then you will be ready for battle. Lancelot of the Lake will come to help you at that time with many a man of great strength.[97] Tomorrow you must refuse to do battle, or else you assuredly will be slain."

The King began to weep woefully and mourn, and said, "Alas, this sad kingdom!" He hastily put on his clothes, and said to his lords, "I have been warned in strange dreams that I may not be gladdened by the delights of battle. We must send unto Sir Mordred and try to offer another day, or truly on this day I must be disgraced, a fact I learned as I lay in bed. Go, Sir Lucan the Butler, so that wise words gain control, and see that you take with you many bishops and bold barons."

They went forth all in a company, as it is told in true books, to where Sir Mordred and his lords were, and a hundred knights all uncounted. The most valorous knights stood before Sir Mordred and greeted him with great courtesy: "King Arthur sends his best greetings, and with open heart asks you to stop this struggle for a month, for the love of Him Who died on the Cross."

Mordred, who was both brave and bold, turned fierce as any boar at bay and swore by Judas who sold Jesus, "Such words are hardly in order now.[98] What he has promised he shall have: one of us will die this day. And tell him truly what I said—I shall mar him if I can."

"Sir," they said, "though you and he are prepared for battle, many a mighty one shall rue that attack before all is decided on this field. It is better to cease and let him be king and bear the crown; and after his days doubtless you will rule all of England, tower and town."

Then Mordred stood still awhile and his eyes turned up angrily. "I know that it is his will to give me Cornwall and Kent. Let us meet together on yonder hill and talk together with good intent. I shall soon assent to fulfill such agreements. And if we succeed with our talks to hold to the promise that we as noblemen proclaim—to give me Kent and Cornwall—true love shall long exist between us. But certainly if we fail to come to an agreement, Arthur must spring upon his steed ready to do battle."

"Sir, what manner will you come in, with twelve knights or fourteen, or else with all your strength in company, with bright helmets and shining hauberks?" [99]

"Certainly not," he said. "Other things you need not question; both our hosts shall approach near and we shall talk in between them."

They took their leave and quickly went on their way to King Arthur, to where he sat within his tent.

"Sir, we have proffered peace, if you will assent to it: give him the crown after your days and during your lifetime give him Cornwall and Kent. If you will hold to his offer and plight your troth to it truly, make all ready your bold men with helmet, sword, and bright hauberk. You shall meet upon yonder ground, which each host can see, and if your agreement fails to hold there is nothing left to do but fight."

When Arthur heard of this, he swore to it and arrayed himself with seven battalions bearing broad banners before him. They shone bright as any lightning when they met in the morning. No man living under heaven has seen a fairer sight before.

But Mordred had many more men, and was thus mighty of strength. Arthur had against him twelve bold barons ready for battle to every one of his own.[100] Arthur and Mordred—both were fierce—were to meet each other on a plain; the leaders could truly come to and fro to reach accord. Arthur had searched his heart, and said to his lords, "I have no trust in yonder traitor. He will betray us falsely if we do not make fast our agreements. If you see any weapon drawn, press forward as eager princes to slay him and all his host."

Mordred, who was bold and fierce, said before his noble men, "I know that Arthur is full sad that he has thus lost his lands. With fourteen knights and no more we shall meet at yonder thorn-tree. If any treason comes between us, let broad banners be carried forth."

Arthur with his fourteen knights advanced to that thorn-tree on foot, with helmet, shield, and shining hauberk. Straightway they all came together at that place; but as they were reaching accord an adder slithered out over the ground and stung a knight, so that one could see he was sick and unsound. He drew out his bright sword suddenly, thinking to kill the adder. When Arthur's host saw that, nobly they pressed forward together; [101] there was nothing which could withstand them, since they thought that treason had been done. That day many a doughty knight died and many a bold man was brought to destruction.

Arthur sprang to his steed, seeing that nothing could stop his men. Mordred nearly went out of his mind, and angrily he leaped into his saddle. Of the accord nothing remained: spears were brought out, and the forces dashed at one another. Full many a man of deeds was soon laid out on the field of battle.

Mordred marred many a man, and boldly endured his battle. So sternly his steed ran out that he rode through many a company of men. Arthur never stopped dealing severe, deep wounds in battle. From the morning that it began until it was nearly nightfall there was many a spear spent and many a hard word spoken; many a firebrand was bowed and bent and many a knight's helmet broken; rich helmets were split and rent. The mighty companies began to rush together, a hundred thousand on the field of battle where even the boldest was made right meek.

Since Brutus left Troy to seek Britain, and made his own dwelling in England, such wonders were never wrought before, never yet under the sun.[102] By evening there were none left alive but Arthur and two men he brought thither, and Mordred who was left alone. One of them was Lucan the Butler, who bled from many a terrible wound; and his brother, Sir Bedivere, was very sick and sore unsound.

Then spoke Arthur these words there: "Shall we not bring this thief to the ground?" He gripped a spear fiercely and savagely they attacked each other. He hit Mordred in the center of the chest, his blow cleaving through the backbone; there Mordred lost his life, and spoke no more. But boldly he thrust up his arm and gave Arthur a sore wound through the helmet and crest into the head, so that he swooned three times.

Between them Sir Lucan and Sir Bedivere held up the King, and the three of them together left the field where everyone else was slain. The brave King who was so dear to them could not bear himself up. They went to a chapel: they saw no better remedy or comfort. All night they lay in the chapel by the seaside, as I tell you, ever crying mercy to Mary with sad heart and sorrowful voice.[103] And to her dear Son they prayed: "Jesus, for Thy seven names, direct his soul the right way, so that he will not lose the bliss of heaven."

As Sir Lucan the Butler stood, he saw people on the high plains robbing the bold dead barons of bezants, brooches, and rings. He went to the King to warn him with well-chosen words, speaking as calmly as he then could: "Sir, I have been at yon hill, to the field where many people are drawn. I do not know whether they wish us good or ill. I suggest that we hasten, if you so wish, to get ready and go to some town."

"Now, Sir Lucan, as you counsel, lift me up while I am still alive." Both his arms he put around him to hold fast with all his strength. The King was wounded and weakened by loss of blood;

and, swooning, he cast his eyes upon him. Sir Lucan was hard pressed: he held the King to his own burst heart.

When the King had swooned there, Sir Bedivere stood up by an altar. Sir Lucan, who was dear to him, lay dead foaming in blood.[104] Bedivere greatly mourned in his heart; he could not for sorrow come near him, but kept weeping as if he were mad.

The King turned to where he stood, and said with sharp words, "Here is Excalibur, my good sword—never was a better brand seen. Go, cast it in the salt flood and I think you shall see a wonderful thing. Go quickly, by the Cross, and tell me what you have seen there."

The knight was both courteous and noble. He was full happy to take care of that sword, thinking, It is better that no one have it after me, but if I cast it into the sea there is no more insane man on earth. He hid the sword under a tree, and said, "Sir, I did as you bade me do."

"What did you see there?" asked the King then. "Tell me now, if you can."

"Certainly, Sir," he said, "nothing but deep waters and dark waves."

"Ah, now you have failed to do my bidding! Why have you done so, false man? You must bring me another report."

Then the knight ran forth with care, thinking now he would hide the sword but cast the scabbard in the waters. If anything is to happen, he thought, I shall see it by good tokens.[105] He let the scabbard pass into the sea. He stood there awhile on the land; then he went to the King and said, "Sir, by the Rood, it is done."

"Did you see any more wonders?"

"No, Sir, I saw none."

"Ah, false traitor," he said. "Twice you have betrayed me. This you shall very sorely rue; and, since you are so bold, it shall be repaid."

The knight then cried, "Lord, have mercy!" Quickly he went to the sword. Sir Bedivere saw that amends were best. He took up the good sword and cast it into the sea. A hand without the rest of the body came out of the water, caught it easily, brandished it as if to break it, and afterwards, as it gleamed, glided away with it.

To the King he went and said, "Dear Sir, I saw a hand come all bare out of the water, and thrice it brandished that rich sword."

"Help me so that I can soon be there."

He led his lord to that strand, to where they found a rich ship, with mast and oars, full of ladies. These ladies, who were fair and noble, courteously received the King; the one with the brightest face wept sorely and wrung her hands.[106]

"Brother," she said, "woe is me! You have waited too long for medical treatment, and I am greatly grieved because your pains are so great."

The knight uttered a rueful speech as he stood there both sore and unsound: "Lord, whither are you bound? Alas, whither are you going from me?"

The King spoke in a sad voice: "I will go for a little while into the vale of Avalon to be healed of my wound."

When the ship left the land, Sir Bedivere saw them no more. He went through the forest over hills and through ancient woods. He cared nothing for his life; all night he went weeping bitterly. At daybreak he found there a chapel built between two old groves. He took his way to the chapel, and there he saw a wondrous sight: he saw where a hermit lay before a newly-prepared tomb. It was covered with grey marble and adorned aright with rich lettering; thereon was a framework holding one hundred lit candles in it.

He went to the hermit and asked who was buried there. The hermit answered very quickly, "I can tell you no more than this: [107] about midnight some ladies were here—I do not know who in the world they were. They brought this sore-wounded body on a bier and buried it. They offered bright bezants here, I think a hundred pounds and more, and bade me pray both day and night for him who lies buried in this ancient ground, pray to our Lady both day and night to help his soul."

The knight read the letters correctly, and sorrowfully fell to the ground. "Hermit," he said, "without falsehood, here lies the lord I have lost, bold Arthur, the best king who was ever born in Britain. Give me some of your clothing, for Him Who bore the crown of thorns, and permit me to stay with you, while I may live, and pray for him."

The holy hermit did not hesitate—he was once the Archbishop Mordred banished from the land, and chose his dwelling in the woods—he thanked Jesus for His message that Sir Bedivere was come in peace. He received him with heart and hand to dwell truly together with him.

When Queen Guinevere, the King's wife, knew that all had come to ruin, she went away with five ladies to Amesbury to become a nun.[108] There she lived a holy life, weeping and waking in prayers. Never afterwards could she be happy; there she wore white and black clothes.[109]

THE PROSE "MERLIN"
(c. 1450)

"The Early History of King Arthur"

Rendered into modern English by Richard L. Brengle from *Merlin, or the Early History of King Arthur: a Prose Romance,* ed. Henry B. Wheatley, Early English Text Society, Second Edition, Revised, Volumes X, XXI, XXXVI (London: N. Trübner & Co., 1875-1879).

[X(1875)] From PART I, CHAPTER 5:

Then Merlin [87] said, "There is in this country a good man, one of the most loyal in all the realm, and he has a good and wise wife who is faithful and unblemished inwardly. She is now in childbed with a male infant, and her husband is not a very rich man; therefore, I want you to send for him and reward him so that he and his good wife will swear on a book to keep a child who shall be brought to them, that she will nurse it herself, giving her own son to another woman to be suckled, and that she and her husband will nourish and keep the new child."

"I shall do what you say," said the king.

Then Merlin took his leave and went to Blase.

Uther Pendragon sent for this noble knight, and when he came the king greeted him warmly. The man wondered why this was so.

"Dear friend," said the king, "I must reveal to you a marvelous thing which has happened to me. You are my faithful subject, and thus I ask you by the loyalty you owe to help me after I have told you what it is—and that you do all in your power to keep it a secret."

"Sir," the knight answered, "there is nothing that you command me to do that I will not try with all my might. But if it is something I cannot do, I shall keep it a secret."

The king said, "A wondrous thing has happened to me in a dream: a man came before me and told me that you are the worthiest and most loyal person in all my realm. He also said that you and your wife had begotten a child. He bade me ask you to give your infant to another woman to nurse, and that your wife suckle, keep, and nourish another one which will be brought to her."

When the good man heard this, he answered, "Sir, this is an extraordinary thing you ask of me, that I should take my child away from his mother to be nursed by another woman. When, I pray, will this second one be born and brought to me?"

The king said, "God [88] help me, I do not know."

To which the knight responded, "Sir, there is nothing in this world you command that I will not do."

Then the king gave him so many gifts he was amazed, and he went home to his wife and told her what the king had said. When she heard it, she thought it a strange thing, and said, "Sir, how can I give up my own son for another person's?"

"There is nothing for us but to do it for him who is our sovereign lord," the good man said. "He has favored us and promised so much more that we must consent to his wish, and I truly hope you will grant it."

"I am yours and the child is yours," she answered; "therefore, do what you want to with me and with him. I grant it completely, for I ought in no way to go against your will."

Then he bade her pick another woman to nourish their son, and he waited for the hour when the second child should be brought: thus the good man took his son away from his wife.

Meanwhile, the king saw that the queen was ready to give birth. The day before, Merlin came secretly to the court and said to Ulfyn, "I am well pleased with the king, for he has done exactly what I told him. Now, bid him go to the queen, and bid him tell her that she shall have a child tomorrow after midnight, and order her to give the infant to the first man who arrives at the doorway of the hall."

When Ulfyn heard that, he asked, "Will you not speak with the king?"

"No," said Merlin.

Then Ulfyn went to the king and repeated what Merlin had commanded. When the king heard this, he was overjoyed, and said, "Shall I not speak with Merlin before he goes?"

"No," said Ulfyn, "but do what he has told you."

So the king went to the queen. "I am going to tell you something which you shall find true," he said, "and do as I command you."

"Sir, I will," she said.

"Tomorrow after midnight," said the king, "with the grace of God, you shall be delivered of the child in your [80] womb. I command you to take it to one of your most trustworthy women as soon as it is born and bid her deliver it to the first man she finds at the doorway of the hall, and that you tell those who are present at the birth of the child never to speak about it or disclose that you had a child—for many people will say then that it is not or cannot be mine."

The lady answered, "Sir, what I have told you is true. I do not know who begat it: I shall do what you bid, as one who has great shame of her misadventure. But I marvel that you know so well the time of my delivery."

Thus ended the conversation of the king and queen. The following evening she began her pain of labor, until the hour that the king had told her, and a short time after midnight she was delivered. Then she called a woman that she trusted most and said, "Take this child and carry it to the hall door, and if you find there a man who asks for it give it to him—and be careful what man it is."

The woman did as the queen commanded. She took the child, wrapped it in the best clothes she had, and carried it to the hall door. When she came there, she found a man who seemed very old and wrinkled.

"What are you waiting for?" she asked.

"For that which you bring," he said.

"Who are you?" she answered. "To whom shall I tell my lady I have given her child?"

"You are not to know that, but do as you are commanded," said he, and took the child. As soon as he had it he left instantly, she knew not where.

She went to the lady and told her that she had given the child to a very old man. "But I know not what else he is, for when I delivered it to him he vanished so quickly that I know not where he went."

The queen wept as one who had great sorrow, and he who had her child [90] proceeded as fast as he could to Antor, finding him as he was going to early Mass. He had taken the appearance of a very old man, and he called to him and said, "Antor, I would speak with you."

"And I with you," said Antor gladly.

"I have brought you a child," the old man said, "and I ask you to nourish it as fully as you would your own. For, know it well, if you do this great God shall bless you and your heirs. If any man told you this, you would not believe it."

Antor answered, "This is the child that the king asked me to have my wife nurse, and to give mine away for him."

"It is without fail the same one," the old man said. "The king and all worthy men and women ought to pray for you. I myself pray for you, and, know it well, my prayer is worth as much as a rich man's."

Antor took the child and saw that it was right fair. When he asked if it were christened, the old man said, "No, but baptize it immediately in this church."

Antor was very glad. "What shall be his name?"

"My counsel is that you call him Arthur. You will find that he shall come into great wealth before you have kept him a long while. And neither you nor your wife will know whether you love him or your own child better."

"What person shall I say has given me this child?" Antor said. "Who are you?"

"At this time you shall know no more about me," said the old man.

And thus they parted. Antor had the child baptized, naming him Arthur. He bore him to his wife and said, "Lo, here is the child for which I have asked you to do so much."

"He is welcome," she said. She took him and asked if he were baptized.

"Yes," said Antor. "His name is Arthur."

Then the woman nursed it, and nourished it, and gave her own son to another woman.[91]

. . . . . .

Merlin turned the king to the other side of the couch and whispered to him, "You have come to a fair end, if your conscience is such as it appears to be. I tell you that your son Arthur shall be the next king of your realm after you, by the grace of Jesus Christ, and he shall fulfill the Round Table which you have begun."

When Uther heard that, he drew close to Merlin and said, "For God's love, ask him to pray to our Lord Jesus Christ for me."

"Now you have heard the last word that the king has spoken to me," said Merlin to those who were there, "and you thought he would never speak." Then they left, Merlin and all the others who greatly marveled that he had made the king speak; but there was no one who knew what the king had said save Merlin.

In this way King Uther died. The princes, barons, bishops, and archbishops did him the greatest honor and fairest religious service that they could. And so the land was left without a ruler. The morning after the king was buried the barons and the prelates of the Church assembled, taking counsel how the realm should be governed. But they could come to no agreement. Then they decided, by common consent, to confer with Merlin, who had great wisdom; they said they had never heard him give anything but true and good advice. Thus they agreed, and sent to find Merlin.

CHAPTER 6:

When he came before them, they said, "Merlin, we know well you are wise and have always loved well the kings of this realm. You know that this land is left without a ruler, and a land without a lord prospers [95] little. Therefore, we ask and require you to help us choose such a man, one who might govern the realm to the benefit of the people and the salvation of the Holy Church."

"I am not one to meddle in such matters," said Merlin, "nor should I choose a man to be governor. Yet if you will allow me, I will tell you; but you do not have to agree with my choice."

"Our Lord send grace to the welfare and profit of us all!" they said.

"I have loved this realm and its people greatly," Merlin said, "and if I should tell you whom you should make your king I ought to be well believed, as is right. If you want to know, a lucky thing has happened to you. The king has been dead since Martinmas, and from then till Christmas is but a short time. If you accept my counsel, I shall make it good and true both towards God and the world."

They declared all at once, "Say what you will, and we shall esteem it."

"You well know that now comes the holiday when our Lord was born," said Merlin, "and He is Lord of all lords. I will undertake it, if you and all the people pray together to our Lord in His great mercy that He send you a rightful ruler, as He through His great humility at this time called Christmas came to be born of a Virgin, King of all kings; that He at Christmas choose such a man to be your king and lord who will rule and govern the people according to His will; and that He give such a sign that the people may see and know that he is His choice alone. Know well, that if you do so, you shall see the choice of our Lord Jesus Christ."

They all answered with one assent, "We accord with this counsel; there is no man on earth who should not do so." Then they all prayed, bishops and archbishops, and commanded throughout the Church that the people pray also. All the lords swore to one another to hold to the decision of the Holy Church, which God would reveal to them. In this manner they agreed to Merlin's counsel. Merlin took his leave of them, and they begged him to be with them at Christmas to see if what he had told them were [96] true or not.

"I shall not be there, for you shall not see me until the choice is made," he said. Then Merlin went to Blase and told him all these things.

All the worthy men of the realm came to Logres at Yuletide, and waited for Christmas. Antor had nourished the child until he was grown to his fifteenth year; the young man was fair and large, having been nursed by no other woman than Antor's wife. Antor knew not whether he loved his own son better than this one. He never called the youth anything but son, so that Arthur thought that Antor was his father. At Hallowmas Antor made him a knight and at Yule he came to Logres, as did the other knights of the land, bringing his two sons with him.

On Christmas Eve all the clergy of the realm assembled, as well as the valorous barons, doing just as Merlin had said. When they all arrived, they led a simple and honest life. Thus they remained all Christmas Eve, went to midnight Mass, and meekly said their prayers to our Lord, that He of His grace send them such a man who might profitably maintain them and the Christain faith. They remained for the Mass of the day also, and so there were many who said they were fools to think our Lord would deign to choose their king. And as they were talking this way, there was a ringing for the Mass of the day, so they went to the service. When they were all assembled, they found there one of the holiest men in the land dressed to sing the Mass. But before he began, he spoke to the people.

"You are gathered for three things to your benefit," he said, "and I shall tell you what they are: first of all, for the salvation of your souls and for the worship of God; second, for the miracle and great power that He this day shall show us, if it be His will to give us a king and leader who may save and maintain the Holy Church, the sustenance of all true Christian people; third, we are come to choose one of us, but we are not so wise [97] as to know who is the most worthy of all our people—and since we do not know we ought to pray mightily to the King of kings, Jesus Christ our Saviour, born on this day, that He show us a true sign of His pleasure."

So they did as the good man advised them. He went on with the Mass, preached the Gospel, and conducted the offertory. Some of the people went out of the church to where there was an empty

place. They saw that it began to dawn and clear, and they saw
before the church a great stone four feet square. No one knew what
kind of stone it was, but some said it was marble. On top, in the
middle of the stone, there stood an iron anvil over half a foot high,
and through this anvil was a sword fixed into the stone.

When those who first came out of the church saw this they
marveled greatly, and went back in the church and told the archbishop. When the good man who sang the Mass heard about it he
took holy water and sprinkled it on the anvil. The archbishop bent
over the sword, saw letters of gold in the steel, and read them:

"Whoever takes this sword out of this stone shall be king by
the election of Jesus Christ."

When he read this, he told the people what it meant. Then
the stone was given to ten worthy men and two clerics to keep. The
people said that our Lord had shown them a fair miracle, and they
went back into the church to hear out the Mass and to give thanks
to our Lord. They sang, "We praise Thee, O God."

When the good man came to the altar he turned to the people
and said, "Fair lords, now may you see that some of you are good
men, when through your prayers and orisons our Lord has shown
this great miracle. Wherefore, I pray and require you above all
virtues on this earth, for neither highness nor earthly riches that
God has given in this world, that no one be against this election
which God has shown by sign. The surplice He shall show us at
His pleasure." [98]

Then the good man sang forth the Mass. When it was finished,
they gathered about the stone to see who might take the sword out
first. Then they all agreed that they should try it as the ministers
of the Holy Church should assign. To this there was great discord
among the highest and most powerful men: they that had might
said they would try first. So there were many words that ought not
to be repeated.

The archbishop spoke so that all could hear: "Sirs, you are
not so wise nor well advised men as I thought. I well know that
you all understand our Lord has chosen one, but I know not whom.
This much I say to you, that neither gentility nor riches shall have
power against the will of Jesus Christ; but trust so much in Him
that if he who is thereby chosen is yet unborn the sword shall never

be taken out of the stone until he comes to whom the honor is ordained."

Then the noble and wise men all agreed, saying the archbishop had spoken the truth. And the wise men and mighty barons spoke to one another and agreed to follow the ordinance of the archbishop. This they said within hearing of all the people. Then the bishop was overjoyed and wept for pity, and said, "This humility in your hearts is of God. I want you to know my endeavor shall be for God's will and the furthering of the Christian faith, so that I shall be blameless before God."

After this conversation and the High Mass for the trying of the sword, the archbishop spoke to the people and showed them the great miracle that God had done for them at this election. "And when our Lord sent Justice to earth," he said, "He put it in the anvil and in the sword; and the Justice over the laity ought to be the sword, for the sword in the beginning was given to the three orders to defend the Holy Church and maintain righteousness. Our Lord has now put the election in the sword—know it well, all of you who have seen and beheld, to whom He will give Justice. Let no man be too hasty to try, for it shall never be drawn out because of riches, nor for pride. Let not [99] poor people be displeased, though the lords and high-born try before them, because it is right and reasonable that the lords attempt it first. There is not one of you but ought to have as his king and lord the best and most worthy man he can."

Thus they agreed with the archbishop with glad heart, and without evil intent, that he should choose those who would try first. Then the archbishop singled out one hundred and fifty of the highest and most worthy lords and directed them to make the attempt. When they had all tried, he commanded all others to do the same. And so everyone tried who wanted to, one after the other, but there was no one who could take it out. Thus it was ordered to be kept with ten noble men, and they were charged to take good heed who came to try it and if there were anyone who might draw it out of the stone. In this way was the sword tested for full eight days.

All the barons were at High Mass, where the archbishop preached to them as it seemed best to him. "I told you well that everyone far and wide, high and low, could come to try the sword. Now may you truly know that none ever, save the one our Lord wills, shall take it out."

To that they all said they would not leave the town till they knew to whom God would grant that honor. In this manner they remained at Mass, and afterwards went to their hostelries to eat. Then, as men used to at that time, the barons and the knights went to tourney on a broad plain, and the ten men who were ordained to watch over the sword went also to see this sport. When the knights had jousted a while, they gave their shields to their squires so that the people of the town came out to arm them.

Antor had made his eldest son a knight at the Hallowtide before Yule, and when the tourney began Kay called his brother Arthur and said, "Go fast to our lodging and fetch my sword."

Arthur was good and ready to serve. "With glad heart," he said, and then smote his horse with the [100] spurs, riding forth to his hostelry to get his brother's sword, or else some other one if he could not find any. He found none, for the hostess had put it in her chamber; so he turned back again, and when he saw he could not find one he began to weep in his great dismay. As he came before the church where the stone was, he saw the sword which he had never tried, and thought he might get it to take to his brother. He approached close by on horseback, took the sword by the hilt, and drew it out, covering it with his coat.

His brother who waited for him outside the town saw him coming, rode up, and asked for his sword.

Arthur said he might not have it. "But I have brought here another one," he said, drew it out from under his coat, and gave it to his brother.

As Kay saw this sword, immediately he knew well that it was the one from the stone and that he would be king. He sought his father until he found him. "Sir, I shall be king," he said. "Lo, here is the sword of the stone."

When the father saw it, he marveled how he got it. Kay said he took it out of the stone. Antor heard him, but did not believe it and said that he lied. Then they went to the square where the stone was, and Arthur followed. When Antor saw the stone, and the sword not therein, he said, "Fair son, how did you get this sword? Look, do not lie. If you do lie I shall know it well and nevermore will love you."

Kay answered, sore ashamed, "I shall not lie to you, for my brother Arthur brought it to me when I bade him go fetch mine. But I do not know how he got it."

When Antor heard this, he said, "Son, give it to me, for you have no right to it." Kay gave it to his father, who looked behind him and saw Arthur. He called him, and said, "Come hither, fair son. Take this sword back from whence you got it."

Arthur took the sword and put it back in the anvil. It held as well or better than it did before. Next, Antor commanded his son Kay to take it out: he tried, but it would not be. Then [101] Antor called them both to him, saying to Kay, "I knew well that you had not taken the sword out." He clasped Arthur in his arms. "Fair, dear son, if I can contrive that you be king, what good should I have therefrom?"

"Father," said Arthur, "I want no other honor nor good than that you be my lord and father."

"Sir," Antor said, "I am the father who nurtured you, but I certainly never did engender you, nor do I know who did."

When Arthur heard Antor deny he was his real father, he wept tenderly and was greatly sad. "Fair sir," he asked, "how is it that I should receive this honor, or any other, when I have failed to have a father?"

"You must have had a father," said Antor. "But, fair, dear sir, if our Lord wills it that you have His grace, and I help you to bring it about, tell me how I may benefit therefrom."

"Sir, you may have whatever you want."

Then Antor told Arthur what good he had done him and how he had nourished him, giving his son Kay to another woman to be nursed by a strange woman. "Therefore, you ought to give my son and me a reward, for there was never a man more tenderly nourished than you were by us. Thus, I pray you, if God gives you this honor, and I help you, that you reward me and my son."

Arthur said, "I beg you not to deny being my father, for then I should not know where to go. If you help me achieve this honor, and God wills that I shall have it, there is nothing which you say or command but that I shall do it."

"I will not ask for your land," Antor said. "But this much I do ask of you: if you become king you will make my son Kay your steward in such a way that, no matter what offence he may do to you or any of your subjects, he will not lose his office. If he be foolish or cruel or shameful, you ought to put up with him better than with any other man. Therefore, I ask you to grant him that which I demand."

Arthur said he would do it with good will. Then he went before the altar and swore that he would truly perform what he had said. When he had made this vow, he went outside in front of the church. The tournament having ended, the barons came to hear vespers.[102]

Antor called all his friends, went to the archbishop, and said, "Sir, lo, here is a child of mine who is no knight but who has asked my help that he might try the test of the sword, and that you please call the barons."

And so he did, and they assembled about the stone. Antor bade Arthur take out the sword and deliver it to the archbishop. Arthur grasped the sword by the hilt and without more tarrying gave it to the archbishop. At once he enfolded Arthur in his arms, saying, "We praise Thee, O God," and brought him into the church. The barons and high men who saw and heard this were angry and sorrowful; they said it might not be that such a simple man of so low degree should be lord of them all.

With this the archbishop was displeased. "Sirs," he said, "our Lord knows best what every man is."

Antor and his friends remained by Arthur, as well as the common people. But all the barons were against them and against Arthur.

Then the archbishop spoke out with great boldness. "I want you to know that though all men in the world were against this election, it is our Lord's will that this man be king, and he shall be it without fail. I shall show you how, and what trust I have in our Lord Jesus Christ. Now, fair brother Arthur, go put the sword again in the same place you took it from."

Arthur put the sword in the same place, and it held as fast as before. Said the archbishop, "So fair an election was never seen. Now go, you rich barons and lords, and try if you may take out the sword."

They all tried, but none could remove it from the place it was in.

Then the archbishop said, "Greatly foolish are you who are against our Lord's will, for now you see well what it is."

"Sir," they said, "we are not against our Lord's will, but it is a grievous thing to us to have a stripling to be lord over us all."

"He Who has chosen him knows best what he is," said the archbishop.

Then the barons begged the bishop to let the sword remain in the stone until Candlemas; by that time men of more distant countries [103] could come to try the test. The archbishop granted their wish. Then whoever wanted to came from every country. When they had tried it, the archbishop said, "Arthur, if it is pleasing to our Lord Jesus Christ that you be king, go forth and bring that sword."

And Arthur went to the sword. He took it out as lightly as if nothing had held it. When the prelates and the common people saw this they began to weep for joy and sorrow, and said, "Sirs, is there yet any man who speaks against this election?"

The barons said, "Sir, we pray you that the sword be allowed to remain in the stone until Easter, but any man who comes before that time may try it. Then we will abide by this. If you will not allow so long a time, every man do the best he can."

"If he waits until Easter," the archbishop asked, "and no one else comes who can perform this feat, will you then agree to this election?"

"Yes," they all said.

The archbishop then spoke to Arthur. "Set the sword in the stone again, for if God wills you shall not fail of the honor which He has promised you."

Arthur did as he commanded. Ten men and five clerics were ordered to watch over the stone, and in this manner they waited for Easter. The archbishop who had taken Arthur into his keeping said, "Know right well you shall be king and lord of this people. Now look that you be a good man, and from henceforth choose such men as shall be of your counsel and officers for your household even as if you were now king—for so you shall be with the help of God."

"I put myself wholly in God, in the Holy Church, and in your good counsel," Arthur said. "Therefore, you choose as seems to be most to the pleasure of Jesus Christ. And I pray you call to you my lord and father."

Then the archbishop called Antor and told him of Arthur's answer. They chose such counselors as they wanted to: by the advice of the archbishop and certain of the barons Kay was made steward. Above all, they waited for Easter, and then they all assembled at Logres.[104]

When they all came together on Easter Eve, the archbishop drew them all to his palace and enumerated to them the great wisdom and the good inner character that he found in Arthur.

"We will not be against God's ordinance," the barons said, "but it is to us a marvelous thing that so young a man, and of such low lineage, should be lord and governor of us all."

"You do not as Christian men thus to be against Christ's election," said the archbishop.

"We are not against that," they said; "but you have determined his character and we have not done so. Therefore, we ask you to allow us to know it, and what manner of governor he will be hereafter."

The archbishop said, "Will you thus delay his coronation?"

"We wish that his consecration and coronation be delayed until Pentecost. Thus we all hope and pray."

The archbishop granted it, and all the council departed. The next day, when High Mass was said, Arthur went to the sword and took it out as lightly as he had done before. Then they all said that they would have him as their lord and governor, and they begged him to put the sword back again. Arthur answered the barons full courteously, saying he would fulfill their request or anything they wanted him to do. They led him into the church to speak with him, and to test his character.

"Sir," they said, "we see well that God wills that you be our king and lord over us, wherefore we will do you our homage and keep our honors for you. We beseech you to put off your consecration until Pentecost, then nothing shall interfere with your being our lord and our king. But to this we pray you to tell us what is your desire."

Said Arthur, "You say you will do homage to me and uphold your honors for me, but I cannot allow these things, and ought not to, for I cannot give honors to you or anyone else until I have received mine. You say that you want me to be lord of you and the realm; but that cannot be before I am consecrated and receive the honor of the empire. But the delay that you desire I grant you with [105] good will, for I will not be consecrated, nor anything which pertains thereto, and I may not be so without God's will and your pleasure."

Then the barons said among themselves, "If this child lives he shall be right wise, and well has he answered us. Sir," they said to him, "we concur with your advice that you be crowned and consecrated at Pentecost, and by that time we shall obey you as the archbishop has commanded."

Then they brought jewels and all other riches and gave them to him to see whether he would be covetous and grasping. When he had received all these gifts, the book says he bestowed them thus: to knights the steeds, coursers, and fresh robes; to those who were pleasant and lively, he gave the jewels; to those who were propertied, gold and silver; to solemn wise men he gave such things as he thought would please them; and with those of his company, he enquired about what might please them best.

Thus he gave away the gifts presented to him by those who wanted to know about his character. When they saw the way he conducted himself, there was no one who did not praise him in his heart. They said that he should be of high renown, and that they could see in him no trace of covetousness: as soon as he received the great gifts, he distributed them so that everyone said no man of whatever estate or degree could have done better. In this way they tested Arthur and could find nothing in him but high virtue and great discretion.

So they waited till Whitsuntide. Then all the baronage assembled at Logres, and there they who wanted to tried the sword again, but no man was found who could remove it from the stone. The archbishop had ordained the crown, sceptre, and all that belonged to the consecrating to be ready. On Whitsunday Eve, by common counsel of all the barons, the archbishop made Arthur a knight. All night he remained in the great church, until morning. When it was day, all the barons came to the church. The archbishop said, "Sirs, here is the man whom God has chosen to be your king, as you have seen and know.[106] And here is the crown and the royal vestments, ordained by your counsel and all the common consent. If there be any of you who will not assent to this election, let him now say so."

They answered and said, "We agree that in God's name he be consecrated and anointed with this: if there be any of us with whom he is displeased because we have been against his coronation, that he pardon us all on this day." And therewith they all kneeled at once to Arthur, asking his mercy.

Arthur, for pity, began to weep, and said to them, "The Lord Who has granted me this honor must pardon you, and as much as is in me I acquit you."

Therewith they rose up, took him by the arms, and led him to the royal vestments. When he was arrayed, the archbishop made ready to sing Mass, and said to Arthur, "Now go bring the sword, wherewith you shall keep Justice to defend the Holy Church and maintain right and the Christian faith to your power."

So they went in procession to the stone. Then said the archbishop to Arthur, "If you will swear to God, to our Lady Saint Mary, to our Mother Holy Church, to Saint Peter, and to all the saints to save and to keep truth and peace in the land, and to your power to maintain true Justice, come forth and take this sword, whereby God has put the election upon you."

When Arthur heard this, he began to weep for pity, and so did many others. "As truly as God is Lord over all things," he said, "so He in His great mercy grant me grace and power to uphold this as you have said and I have well understood." Then he kneeled down, holding up his hands, took out the sword lightly without difficulty, and so bore it upright. They led him to the altar and there he laid the sword. Then they consecrated and anointed him, and performed what belonged to a king. And after all the service was ended, they went out of the church and came to the place where the stone was. But no man knew what became of it. Thus was Arthur chosen king, and held the realm of Logres long in peace.[107]

·   ·   ·   ·   ·   ·

[XXI (1877)] From PART II, CHAPTER 12:

This is the truth, the wife of King Lot was Arthur's sister on his mother's side, in the same manner as was the wife of

King Uentres. From the wife of King Lot came Gawein, Agravain, Geheret, and Gaheries: these four were sons to King Lot. And from her also came Mordred, the youngest, whom King Arthur begat. I will [179] tell you in what manner. . . . It happened at the time that the barons of the realm of Logres were gathered at Cardoel in Wales to choose a king after the death of Uther Pendragon. King Lot brought thither his wife, as did many another baron. It chanced that he was lodged in a fair hall, he and his company, and in the same lodging was Antor and his sons Kay and Arthur, in the most private way that he could. When the king knew that Antor was a knight, he made him sit at his table, as well as Kay, who was a young knight. King Lot had a couch provided in his chamber where his wife slept. Antor slept in the middle of the same chamber, and Kay and Arthur made their beds at King Lot's chamber door, in a corner, as squires should.

Arthur was a fair young squire. He took great notice of the lady and of those who were around her. He saw that she was fair and full of great beauty, and in his heart he coveted her greatly and loved her; but the lady knew it not, nor took any heed of it, for she was very good and right true to her lord.

It happened that the barons had to take counsel to speak together at the black cross. Why it was called the black cross you shall hear later, and the names of the knights of the Round Table, but the time has not come to speak more thereof. So it befell that on the night before King Lot went to this council, he ordered secretly that his horse be saddled about midnight and his arms be made all ready. And they carried out his commandment so secretly no one saw it, not even the lady herself. Thus the king arose about midnight, unknown and unperceived. He went to the gathering of the black cross, leaving the lady abed by herself in her chamber. Arthur, who took careful notice of all this, saw well that the king was gone. He arose as quietly as he could, and went to bed [180] with the lady. He lay turning and tossing, fearing to do anything else lest the lady recognize him. It happened that the lady awoke, turned herself towards him, and took him in her arms as a woman sleeping who thought it was her lord. And that night Mordred was begotten, as you have heard. When Arthur had had his pleasure of the queen, she immediately fell asleep. Arthur arose slyly so that

he was not seen. But the next day he told her himself at dinner
when he served her at the table, kneeling.

"Sir squire, rise up," she said, "for you have been kneeling
long enough."

He answered softly, saying that he might never deserve the
favors she had done him. She asked him what bounty it was that
she had given him. He replied that he could never tell her unless
she assured him she would in no way reveal it to any person, nor
bring about harm or blame to him. She said that it would not
grieve her, and promised him she would not mind this thing. Then
he told her how he had lain by her that night. The lady felt great
shame and blushed deeply, but no one knew the cause. She lost her
appetite completely.

Thus Arthur lay by his sister, the wife of King Lot, but it never
after happened to her again. And so the lady found that she was
with child by him, and the child she had at that time was his without a doubt. When it was born, and also the tidings were spread
abroad that the father was the son of Uther Pendragon, she loved
her child so much in her heart that no man could guess it. But she
dared not reveal it, for King Lot was her lord; and she was sorry
for the war between him and the barons of the realm.[181]

.   .   .   .   .   .

[XXXVI (1879)] From PART III, CHAPTER 26:

. . . then spoke King Arthur so loudly that all who
were in the hall might hear it, and he said, "Now, lords, all you
who have come here into my court for me to gladden and comfort, I
give you graces and thanks for the honor and joy that you have
done me and that you came in order to do. I want you to know
that I will establish in my court these customs all the time I wear
the crown: that never from henceforth shall I eat before I hear
some strange tiding or else some adventure. From now on if there
is some need I shall have it redressed by the knights of my court,
who for hazardous undertaking and honor return here and are my
friends, my fellows, and my peers.

When the knights of the Round Table heard this vow that the

king had made, they spoke together and said, "Seeing that the king has made avowal in his court, it behooves us to make our vow . . . 'that if any maiden has any need or comes to your court to seek help or succor, it may be achieved by the body of one knight or another: they will with right go into whatever country she leads them to rescue her and redress all the wrongs that have been done to her.' " [481]

SIR THOMAS MALORY

Le Morte D'Arthur (c. 1469, 1485)

From *Le Morte D'Arthur*, Everyman's Library, Two Volumes (London: J. M. Dent & Sons Ltd., 1906).

[I] BOOK I, CHAPTER 1:

HOW UTHER PENDRAGON SENT FOR THE DUKE OF CORNWALL AND IGRAINE HIS WIFE, AND OF THEIR DEPARTING SUDDENLY AGAIN

It befell in the days of Uther Pendragon, when he was king of all England, and so reigned, that there was a mighty duke in Cornwall that held war against him long time. And the duke was called the duke of Tintagil. And so by means King Uther sent for this duke, charging him to bring his wife with him, for she was called a fair lady, and a passing wise, and her name was called Igraine. So when the duke and his wife were come unto the king, by the means of great lords they were accorded both: the king liked and loved this lady well, and he made them great cheer out of measure, and desired to have lain by her. But she was a passing good woman, and would not assent unto the king. And then she told the duke her husband, and said, I suppose that we were sent for that I should be dishonoured, wherefore, husband, I counsel you, that we depart from hence suddenly, that we may ride all night unto our own castle. And in like wise as she said so they departed, that neither the king nor none of his council were ware of their departing. All so soon as King Uther knew of their departing so suddenly, he was wonderly wroth. Then he called to him his privy council, and told them of the sudden departing of the duke and his wife. Then they asked the king to send for the duke and his wife by a great charge; And if he will not come at your summons, then may ye do your best, then have ye cause to make mighty war upon him. So that was done, and the messengers had their answers, and that was this shortly, that neither he nor his wife would not come at him. Then was the king wonderly wroth. And then the king sent him plain word again, and bade him be ready and [5] stuff him and garnish him, for within forty days he would fetch him out of the biggest castle that he had. When the duke had this warning, anon he went and furnished and garnished two strong castles of his, of the which the one hight Tintagil, and the other castle hight Terrabil. So his wife Dame Igraine he put in the castle of Tintagil, and himself he put in the castle of Terrabil, the which had many issues and posterns out. Then in all haste came Uther with a great host, and laid a siege about the castle of Terrabil. And there he pyght many pavilions, and there was great war made on both parties, and much people slain. Then for pure anger and for great love of fair Igraine the King Uther fell sick. So came to the King Uther, Sir Ulfius a noble knight, and asked the king why he was sick. I shall tell thee, said the king, I am sick for anger and for love of fair Igraine that I may not be hool. Well, my lord, said Sir Ulfius, I shall seek Merlin, and he shall do you remedy, that your heart shall be pleased. So Ulfius departed, and by adventure he met Merlin in a beggar's array, and then Merlin asked Ulfius whom he sought. And he said he had little ado to tell him. Well, said Merlin, I know whom thou seekest, for thou seekest Merlin; therefore seek no farther, for I am he, and if King Uther will well reward me, and be sworn unto me to fulfil my desire, that shall be his honour and profit more than mine, for I shall cause him to have all his desire. All this will I undertake, said Ulfius, that there shall be nothing reasonable but thou shalt have thy desire. Well, said Merlin, he shall have his entente and desire. And therefore, said Merlin, ride on your way, for I will not be long behind.

CHAPTER 2:

HOW UTHER PENDRAGON MADE WAR ON THE DUKE OF CORNWALL, AND HOW BY THE MEANS OF MERLIN HE LAY BY THE DUCHESS AND GAT ARTHUR

Then Ulfius was glad, and rode on more than a paas till that he came to King Uther Pendragon, and told him he had met with Merlin. Where is he? said the king. Sir, said Ulfius, he will not dwell long; therewithal Ulfius was ware where Merlin stood at the porch of the pavilion's door.[6] And then Merlin was bound to come to the king. When King Uther saw him, he said he was welcome. Sir, said Merlin, I know all your heart every deal; so ye will be sworn unto me as ye be a true king anointed, to fulfil my desire, ye shall have your desire. Then the king was sworn upon the four Evangelists. Sir, said Merlin, this is my desire: the first night that ye shall lie by Igraine ye shall get a child on her, and when that is born, that it shall be delivered to me for to nourish there as I will have it; for it shall be your worship, and the child's avail as mickle as the child is worth. I will well, said the king, as thou wilt have it. Now make you ready, said Merlin, this night ye shall lie with Igraine in the castle of Tintagil, and ye shall be like the duke her husband, Ulfius shall be like Sir Brastias, a knight of the duke's, and I will be like a knight that hight Sir Jordans, a knight of the duke's. But wayte ye make not many questions with her nor her men, but say ye are diseased, and so hie you to bed, and rise not on the morn till I come to you, for the castle of Tintagil is but ten miles hence; so this was done as they devised. But the duke of Tintagil espied how the king rode from the siege of Terrabil, and therefore that night he issued out of the castle at a postern for to have distressed the king's host. And so, through his own issue, the duke himself was slain or-ever the king came at the castle of Tintagil. So after the death of the duke, King Uther lay with Igraine more than three hours after his death, and begat on her that night Arthur, and or day came Merlin came to the king, and bade him make him ready, and so he kissed the lady Igraine and departed in all haste. But when the lady heard tell of the duke her husband, and by all record he was dead or-ever King Uther came to her; then she marvelled who that might be that lay with her in likeness of her lord; so she mourned privily and held her peace. Then all the barons by one assent prayed the king of accord betwixt the lady Igraine and him; the king gave them leave, for fain would he have been accorded with her. So the king put all the trust in Ulfius to entreat between them, so by the entreaty at the last the king and she met together. Now will we do well, said Ulfius, our king is a lusty knight and wifeless, and my lady Igraine is a passing fair lady; it were great joy unto us all, an it might please the king to make her his queen. Unto that they all well accorded and moved it to the king.[7] And anon, like a lusty knight, he assented thereto with good will, and so in all haste they were married in a morning with great mirth and joy. And King Lot of Lothian and of Orkney then wedded Margawse that was Gawaine's mother, and King Nentres of the land of Garlot wedded Elaine. All this was done at the request of King Uther. And the third sister Morgan le Fay was put to school in a nunnery, and there she learned so much that she was a great clerk of necromancy, and after she was wedded to King Uriens of the land of Gore, that was Sir Ewain's le Blanchemain's father.

CHAPTER 3:

OF THE BIRTH OF KING ARTHUR AND OF HIS NURTURE

Then Queen Igraine waxed daily greater and greater, so it befell after within half a year, as King Uther lay by his queen, he asked her, by the faith she owed to him, whose was the child within her body; then was she sore abashed to give answer. Dismay you not, said the king, but tell me the truth, and I shall love you the better, by the faith of my body. Sir, said she, I shall tell you the truth. The same night that my lord was dead, the hour of his death, as his knights record, there came into my castle of Tintagil a man like my lord in speech and in countenance, and two knights with him in likeness of his two knights Brastias and Jordans, and so I went unto bed with him as I ought to do with my lord, and the same night, as I shall answer unto God, this child was begotten upon me. That is truth, said the king, as ye say; for it was I myself that came in the likeness, and therefore dismay you not, for I am father of the child; and there he told her all the cause, how it was by Merlin's counsel. Then the queen made great joy when she knew who was the father of her child. Soon came Merlin unto the king, and said, Sir, ye must purvey you for the nourishing of your child. As thou wilt, said the king, be it. Well, said Merlin, I know a lord of yours in this land, that is a passing true man and a faithful, and he shall have the nourishing of your child, and his name is Sir Ector, and he is a lord of fair livelihood in many parts in England and Wales; and this lord, Sir Ector, let him be sent for, for to come and speak with you, and desire him yourself [8] as he loveth you, that he will put his own child to nourishing to another woman, and that his wife nourish yours. And when the child is born let it be delivered to me at yonder privy postern unchristened. So like as Merlin devised it was done. And when Sir Ector was come he made fyaunce to the king for to nourish the child like as the king desired; and there the king granted Sir Ector great rewards. Then when the lady was delivered, the king commanded two knights and two ladies to take the child, bound in a cloth of gold, and that ye deliver him to what poor man ye meet at the postern gate of the castle. So the child was delivered unto Merlin, and so he bare it forth unto Sir Ector, and made an holy man to christen him, and named him Arthur; and so Sir Ector's wife nourished him with her own pap.

CHAPTER 4:

OF THE DEATH OF KING UTHER PENDRAGON

Then within two years King Uther fell sick of a great malady. And in the meanwhile his enemies usurped upon him, and did a great battle upon his men, and slew many of his people. Sir, said Merlin, ye may not lie so as ye do, for ye must to the field though ye ride on an horse-litter: for ye shall never have the better of your enemies but if your person be there, and then shall ye have the victory. So it was done as Merlin had devised, and they carried the king forth in an horse-litter with a great host towards his enemies. And at St. Albans there met with the king a great host of the North. And that day Sir Ulfius and Sir Brastias did great deeds of arms, and King Uther's men overcame the Northern battle and slew many people, and put the remnant to flight. And then the king returned unto London, and made great joy of his victory. And then he fell passing sore sick, so that three days and three nights he was speechless: wherefore all the barons made great sorrow, and asked Merlin what counsel were best. There is none other remedy, said Merlin, but God will have his will. But look ye, all barons, be before King Uther to-morn, and God and I shall make him to speak. So on the morn all the barons with Merlin came before the king; then Merlin said aloud unto King Uther, Sir, shall your [9] son Arthur be king after your days, of this realm with all the appurtenance? Then Uther Pendragon turned him, and said in hearing of them all, I give him God's blessing and mine, and bid him pray for my soul, and righteously and worshipfully that he claim the crown upon forfeiture of my blessing; and therewith he yielded up the ghost, and then was he interred as longed to a king. Wherefore the queen, fair Igraine, made great sorrow, and all the barons.

CHAPTER 5:

HOW ARTHUR WAS CHOSEN KING, AND OF WONDERS AND MARVELS OF A SWORD TAKEN OUT OF A STONE BY THE SAID ARTHUR

Then stood the realm in great jeopardy long while, for every lord that was mighty of men made him strong, and many weened to have been king. Then Merlin went to the Archbishop of Canterbury, and counselled him for to send for all the lords of the realm, and all the gentlemen of arms, that they should to London come by Christmas, upon pain of cursing; and for this cause, that Jesus, that was born on that night, that he would of his great mercy show some miracle, as he was come to be king of mankind, for to show some miracle who should be rightways king of this realm. So the Archbishop, by the advice of Merlin, sent for all the lords and gentlemen of arms that they should come by Christmas even unto London. And many of them made them clean of their life, that their prayer might be the more acceptable unto God. So in the greatest church of London, whether it were Paul's or not the French book maketh no mention, all the estates were long or day in the church for to pray. And when matins and the first mass was done, there was seen in the churchyard, against the high altar, a great stone four square, like unto a marble stone, and in midst thereof was like an anvil of steel a foot on high, and therein stuck a fair sword naked by the point, and letters there were written in gold about the sword that said thus:—Whoso pulleth out this sword of this stone and anvil, is rightwise king born of all England. Then the people marvelled, and told it to the Archbishop. I command, said the Archbishop, that ye keep you within your church, and pray unto God still; that no man touch the sword till [10] the high mass be all done. So when all masses were done all the lords went to behold the stone and the sword. And when they saw the scripture, some assayed; such as would have been king. But none might stir the sword nor move it. He is not here, said the Archbishop, that shall achieve the sword, but doubt not God will make him known. But this is my counsel, said the Archbishop, that we let purvey ten knights, men of good fame, and they to keep this sword. So it was ordained, and then there was made a cry, that every man should essay that would, for to win the sword. And upon New Year's Day the barons let make a jousts and a tournament, that all knights that would joust or tourney there might play, and all this was ordained for to keep the lords and the commons together, for the Archbishop trusted that God would make him known that should win the sword. So upon New Year's Day, when the service was done, the barons rode unto the field, some to joust and some to tourney, and so it happened that Sir Ector, that had great livelihood about London, rode unto the jousts, and with him rode Sir Kay his son, and young Arthur that was his nourished brother; and Sir Kay was made knight at All Hallowmass afore. So as they rode to the joustsward, Sir Kay had lost his sword, for he had left it at his father's lodging, and so he prayed young Arthur for to ride for his sword. I will well, said Arthur, and rode fast after the sword, and when he came home, the lady and all were out to see the jousting. Then was Arthur wroth, and said to himself, I will ride to the churchyard, and take the sword with me that sticketh in the stone, for my brother Sir Kay shall not be without a sword this day. So when he came to the churchyard, Sir Arthur alit and tied his horse to the stile, and so he went to the tent, and found no knights there, for they were at jousting; and so he handled the sword by the handles, and lightly and fiercely pulled it out of the stone, and took his horse and rode his way until he came to his brother Sir Kay, and delivered him the sword. And as soon as Sir Kay saw the sword, he wist well it was the sword of the stone, and so he rode to his father Sir Ector, and said: Sir, lo here is the sword of the stone, wherefore I must be king of this land. When Sir Ector beheld the sword, he returned again and came to the church, and there they alit all three, and went into the church. And anon he made Sir Kay to swear upon a [11] book how he came to that sword. Sir, said Sir Kay, by my brother Arthur, for he brought it to me. How gat ye this sword? said Sir Ector to Arthur. Sir, I will tell you. When I came home for my brother's sword, I found nobody at home to deliver me his sword, and so I thought my brother Sir Kay should not be swordless, and so I came hither eagerly and pulled it out of the stone without any pain. Found ye any knights about this sword? said Sir Ector. Nay, said Arthur. Now, said Sir Ector to Arthur, I understand ye must be king of this land. Wherefore I, said Arthur, and for what cause? Sir, said Ector, for God will have it so, for there should never man have drawn out this sword, but he that shall be rightways king of this land. Now let me see whether ye can put the sword there as it was, and pull it out again. That is no mastery, said Arthur, and so he put it in the stone, therewithal Sir Ector essayed to pull out the sword and failed.

CHAPTER 6:

HOW KING ARTHUR PULLED OUT THE SWORD DIVERS TIMES

Now assay, said Sir Ector unto Sir Kay. And anon he pulled at the sword with all his might, but it would not be. Now shall ye essay, said Sir Ector to Arthur. I will well, said Arthur,

and pulled it out easily.   And therewithal Sir Ector knelt down to
the earth, and Sir Kay.   Alas, said Arthur, my own dear father and
brother, why kneel ye to me?   Nay, nay, my lord Arthur, it is not
so, I was never your father nor of your blood, but I wot well ye are
of an higher blood than I weened ye were.   And then Sir Ector
told him all, how he was bitaken him for to nourish him, and by
whose commandment, and by Merlin's deliverance.   Then Arthur
made great doole when he understood that Sir Ector was not his
father.   Sir, said Ector unto Arthur, will ye be my good and gracious lord when ye are king?   Else were I to blame, said Arthur,
for ye are the man in the world that I am most beholden to, and my
good lady and mother your wife, that as well as her own hath
fostered me and kept.   And if ever it be God's will that I be king
as ye say, ye shall desire of me what I may do, and I shall not fail
you, God forbid I should fail you.   Sir, said Sir [12] Ector, I will ask
no more of you, but that ye will make my son, your foster brother,
Sir Kay, seneschal of all your lands.   That shall be done, said Arthur, and more, by the faith of my body, that never man shall have
that office but he, while he and I live.   Therewithal they went
unto the Archbishop, and told him how the sword was achieved,
and by whom; and on Twelfth-day all the barons came thither,
and to essay to take the sword, who that would essay.   But there
afore them all, there might none take it out but Arthur; wherefore
there were many lords wroth, and said it was great shame unto
them all and the realm, to be overgoverned with a boy of no high
blood born, and so they fell out at that time that it was put off till
Candlemas, and then all the barons should meet there again; but
always the ten knights were ordained to watch the sword day and
night, and so they set a pavilion over the stone and the sword, and
five always watched.   So at Candlemas many more great lords came
thither for to have won the sword, but there might none prevail.
And right as Arthur did at Christmas, he did at Candlemas, and
pulled out the sword easily, whereof the barons were sore agrieved
and put it off in delay till the high feast of Easter.   And as Arthur
sped before, so did he at Easter, yet there were some of the great
lords had indignation that Arthur should be king, and put it off
in a delay till the feast of Pentecost.   Then the Archbishop of
Canterbury by Merlyn's providence let purvey then of the best
knights that they might get, and such knights as Uther Pendragon

loved best and most trusted in his days. And such knights were
put about Arthur as Sir Baudwin of Britain, Sir Kay, Sir Ulfius,
Sir Brastias. All these with many other, were always about Arthur,
day and night, till the feast of Pentecost.

CHAPTER 7:

HOW KING ARTHUR WAS CROWNED, AND HOW HE MADE OFFICERS

And at the feast of Pentecost all manner of men essayed to pull at the sword that would essay, but none might prevail
but Arthur, and pulled it out afore all the lords and commons that
were there, wherefore all the commons cried at once, We will have
Arthur unto our king, we will put him [13] no more in delay, for
we all see that it is God's will that he shall be our king, and who
that holdeth against it, we will slay him. And therewith they all
kneeled at once, both rich and poor, and cried Arthur mercy because they had delayed him so long, and Arthur forgave them, and
took the sword between both his hands, and offered it upon the
altar where the Archbishop was, and so was he made knight of the
best man that was there. And so anon was the coronation made.
And there was he sworn unto his lords and the commons for to be
a true king, to stand with true justice from thenceforth the days of
this life. Also then he made all lords that held of the crown to
come in, and to do service as they ought to do. And many complaints were made unto Sir Arthur of great wrongs that were done
since the death of King Uther, of many lands that were bereaved
lords, knights, ladies, and gentlemen. Wherefore King Arthur
made the lands to be given again unto them that owned them.
When this was done, that the king had stablished all the countries
about London, then he let make Sir Kay seneschal of England; and
Sir Baudwin of Britain was made constable; and Sir Ulfius was
made chamberlain; and Sir Brastias was made warden to wait upon
the north from Trent forwards, for it was that time the most part
the king's enemies. But within few years after, Arthur won all the
north, Scotland, and all that were under their obeissance. Also
Wales, a part of it held against Arthur, but he overcame them all,

as he did the remnant, through the noble prowess of himself and his knights of the Round Table.

CHAPTER 8:

HOW KING ARTHUR HELD IN WALES, AT A PENTECOST, A GREAT FEAST, AND
WHAT KINGS AND LORDS CAME TO HIS FEAST

Then the king removed into Wales, and let cry a great feast that it should be holden at Pentecost after the incoronation of him at the city of Carlion. Unto the feast came King Lot of Lothian and of Orkney, with five hundred knights with him. Also there came to the feast King Uriens of Gore with four hundred knights with him. Also there came to that feast King Nentres of Garlot, with seven [14] hundred knights with him. Also there came to the feast the king of Scotland with six hundred knights with him, and he was but a young man. Also there came to the feast a king that was called the king with the hundred knights, but he and his men were passing well bisene at all points. Also there came the king of Carados with five hundred knights. And King Arthur was glad of their coming, for he weened that all the kings and knights had come for great love, and to have done him worship at his feast, wherefore the king made great joy, and sent the kings and knights great presents. But the kings would none receive, but rebuked the messengers shamefully, and said they had no joy to receive no gifts of a beardless boy that was come of low blood, and sent him word they would none of his gifts, but that they were come to give him gifts with hard swords betwixt the neck and the shoulders: and therefore they came thither, so they told to the messengers plainly, for it was great shame to all them to see such a boy to have a rule of so noble a realm as this land was. With this answer the messengers departed and told to King Arthur this answer. Wherefore, by the advice of his barons, he took him to a strong tower with five hundred good men with him: and all the kings aforesaid in a manner laid a siege tofore him, but King Arthur was well victualed. And within fifteen days there came Merlin among them into the city of Carlion. Then all the kings were passing glad of Merlin, and asked him, For what cause is that boy Arthur made your king? Sirs, said Merlin, I shall tell you the cause, for he is King Uther Pendragon's son, born in wedlock, gotten on Igraine, the duke's wife of Tintagil. Then is he a bastard, they said all. Nay, said Merlin, after the death of the duke, more than three hours, was Arthur begotten, and thirteen days after King Uther wedded Igraine; and therefore I prove him he is no bastard, and who saith nay, he shall be king and overcome all his enemies; and, or he die, he shall be long king of all England, and have under his obeissance Wales, Ireland, and Scotland, and more realms than I will now rehearse. Some of the kings had marvel of Merlin's words, and deemed well that it should be as he said; and some of them laughed him to scorn, as King Lot; and more other called him a witch. But then were they accorded with Merlin, that King Arthur should come out and speak with the kings, and to come [15] safe and to go safe, such assurance there was made. So Merlin went unto King Arthur, and told him how he had done, and bade him fear not, but come out boldly and speak with them, and spare them not, but answer them as their king and chieftain, for ye shall overcome them all, whether they will or nill.

CHAPTER 9:

OF THE FIRST WAR THAT KING ARTHUR HAD, AND HOW HE WON THE FIELD

Then King Arthur came out of his tower, and had under his gown a jesseraunte of double mail, and there went with him the Archbishop of Canterbury, and Sir Baudwin of Britain, and Sir Kay, and Sir Brastias: these were the men of most worship that were with him. And when they were met there was no meekness, but stout words on both sides; but always King Arthur answered them, and said he would make them to bow an he lived. Wherefore they departed with wrath, and King Arthur bade keep them well, and they bade the king keep him well. So the king returned him to the tower again and armed him and all his knights. What will ye do? said Merlin to the kings; ye were better for to stynte, for ye shall not here prevail though ye were ten times so many. Be we well advised to be afeard of a dream-reader? said

King Lot. With that Merlin vanished away, and came to King Arthur, and bade him set on them fiercely; and in the meanwhile there were three hundred good men of the best that were with the kings, that went straight unto King Arthur and that comforted him greatly. Sir, said Merlin to Arthur, fight not with the sword that ye had by miracle, till that ye see ye go unto the worse, then draw it out and do your best. So forthwithal King Arthur set upon them in their lodging. And Sir Baudwin, Sir Kay, and Sir Brastias slew on the right hand and on the left hand that it was marvel; and always King Arthur on horseback laid on with a sword, and did marvelous deeds of arms that many of the kings had great joy of his deeds and hardiness. Then King Lot brake out on the back side, and the king with the hundred knights, and King Carados, and set on Arthur fiercely behind him. With that [16] Sir Arthur turned with his knights, and smote behind and before, and ever Sir Arthur was in the foremost press till his horse was slain underneath him. And therewith King Lot smote down King Arthur. With that his four knights received him and set him on horseback. Then he drew his sword Excalibur, but it was so bright in his enemies' eyes, that it gave light like thirty torches. And therewith he put them on back, and slew much people. And then the commons of Carlion arose with clubs and staves and slew many knights; but all the kings held them together with their knights that were left alive, and so fled and departed. And Merlin came unto Arthur, and counselled him to follow them no further. [17]

CHAPTER 19:

HOW KING ARTHUR RODE TO CARLION, AND OF HIS DREAM, AND HOW HE SAW THE QUESTING BEAST

Then after the departure of King Ban and of King Bors, King Arthur rode unto Carlion. And thither came to him, King Lot's wife, of Orkney, in manner of a message, but she was sent thither to espy the court of King Arthur; and she came richly bisene, with her four sons [84] Gawaine, Gaheris, Agravine, and Gareth, with many other knights and ladies. For she was a passing fair lady, therefore the king cast great love unto her, and desired to lie by her; so they were agreed, and he begat upon her Mordred, and she was his sister, on his mother's side, Igraine. So there she rested her a month, and at the last departed. Then the king dreamed a marvellous dream whereof he was sore adread. But all this time King Arthur knew not that King Lot's wife was his sister. Thus was the dream of Arthur: Him thought there was come into this land griffins and serpents, and him thought they burnt and slew all the people in the land, and then him thought he fought with them, and they did him passing great harm, and wounded him full sore, but at the last he slew them. When the king awaked, he was passing heavy of his dream, and so to put it out of thoughts, he made him ready with many knights to ride a-hunting. As soon as he was in the forest the king saw a great hart afore him. This hart will I chase, said King Arthur, and so he spurred the horse, and rode after long, and so by fine force oft he was like to have smitten the hart; whereas the king had chased the hart so long, that his horse lost his breath, and fell down dead; then a yeoman fetched the king another horse. So the king saw the hart embushed, and his horse dead; he set him down by a fountain, and there he fell in great thoughts. And as he sat so, him thought he heard a noise of hounds, to the sum of thirty. And with that the king saw coming toward him the strangest beast that ever he saw or heard of; so the beast went to the well and drank, and the noise was in the beast's belly like unto the questyng of thirty couple hounds; but all the while the beast drank there was no noise in the beast's belly: and therewith the beast departed with a great noise, whereof the king had great marvel. And so he was in a great thought, and therewith he fell asleep. Right so there came a knight afoot unto Arthur and said, Knight full of thought and sleepy, tell me if thou sawest a strange beast pass this way. Such one saw I, said King Arthur, that is past two mile; what would ye with the beast? said Arthur. Sir, I have followed that beast long time, and killed mine horse, so would God I had another to follow my quest. Right so came one with the king's horse, and when the knight saw the horse, he prayed the king to give him the horse: for I have followed [35] this quest this twelvemonth, and either I shall achieve him, or bleed of the best blood of my body. Pellinore, that time king, followed the questing beast, and after his death Sir Palamides followed it.

Chapter 20:

HOW KING PELLINORE TOOK ARTHUR'S HORSE AND FOLLOWED THE QUESTING BEAST, AND HOW MERLIN MET WITH ARTHUR

Sir knight, said the king, leave that quest, and suffer me to have it, and I will follow it another twelvemonth. Ah, fool, said the knight unto Arthur, it is in vain thy desire, for it shall never be achieved but by me, or my next kin. Therewith he started unto the king's horse and mounted into the saddle, and said, Gramercy, this horse is my own. Well, said the king, thou mayst take my horse by force, but an I might prove thee whether thou were better on horseback or I. Well, said the knight, seek me here when thou wilt, and here nigh this well thou shalt find me, and so passed on his way. Then the king sat in a study, and bade his men fetch his horse as fast as ever they might. Right so came by him Merlin like a child of fourteen year of age, and saluted the king, and asked him why he was so pensive. I may well be pensive said the king, for I have seen the marvellest sight that ever I saw. That know I well, said Merlin, as well as thyself, and of all thy thoughts, but thou art but a fool to take thought, for it will not amend thee. Also I know what thou art, and who was thy father, and of whom thou wert begotten; King Uther Pendragon was thy father, and begat thee on Igraine. That is false, said King Arthur, how shouldest thou know it, for thou are not so old of years to know my father? Yes, said Merlin, I know it better than ye or any man living. I will not believe thee, said Arthur, and was wroth with the child. So departed Merlin, and came again in the likeness of an old man of fourscore year of age, whereof the king was right glad, for he seemed to be right wise. Then said the old man, Why are ye so sad? I may well be heavy, said Arthur, for many things. Also here was a child, and told me many things that meseemeth he should not know, for he was not of age to know my father. Yes, said the old man, the child told [36] you truth, and more would he have told you an ye would have suffered him; but ye have done a thing late that God is displeased with you, for ye have lain by your sister, and on her ye have gotten a child that shall destroy you and all the knights of your realm. What are ye, said Arthur, that tell me these tidings? I am Merlin, and I was he in the child's likeness. Ah, said King Arthur, ye are a marvellous man, but I marvel much of thy words that I must die in battle. Marvel not, said Merlin, for it is God's will your body to be punished for your foul deeds; but I may well be sorry, said Merlin, for I shall die a shameful death to be put in the earth quick, and ye shall die a worshipful death. And as they talked this, came one with the king's horse, and so the king mounted on his horse, and Merlin on another, and so rode unto Carlion. And anon the king asked Ector and Ulfius how he was begotten, and they told him Uther Pendragon was his father and Queen Igraine his mother. Then he said to Merlin, I will that my mother be sent for, that I may speak with her; and if she say so herself, then will I believe it. In all haste, the queen was sent for, and she came and brought with her Morgan le Fay, her daughter, that was as fair a lady as any might be, and the king welcomed Igraine in the best manner.

CHAPTER 21:

HOW ULFIUS IMPEACHED QUEEN IGRAINE, ARTHUR'S MOTHER, OF TREASON; AND HOW A KNIGHT CAME AND DESIRED TO HAVE THE DEATH OF HIS MASTER REVENGED

Right so came Ulfius, and said openly that the king and all might hear that were feasted that day, Ye are the falsest lady of the world, and the most traitress unto the king's person. Beware, said Arthur, what thou sayest; thou speakest a great word. I am well ware, said Ulfius, what I speak, and here is my glove to prove it upon any man that will say the contrary, that this Queen Igraine is causer of your great damage, and of your great war. For, an she would have uttered it in the life of King Uther Pendragon, of the birth of you, and how ye were begotten, ye had never had the mortal wars that ye have had; for the most part of your barons of your realm knew never whose son ye were, nor of whom ye were begotten; and she that bare you of her [37] body should have made it known openly in excusing of her worship and yours, and in likewise to all the realm, wherefore I prove her false to God and to you and to all your realm, and who will say the contrary I will prove it on his body. Then spake Igraine and said, I am a woman and I may not fight, but rather than I should be dishonoured, there would some good man take my quarrel. More, she said, Merlin knoweth well, and ye Sir Ulfius, how King Uther came to me in the Castle of Tintagel in the likeness of my lord, that was dead three hours tofore, and thereby gat a child that night upon me. And after the thirteenth day King Uther wedded me, and by his commandment when the child was born it was delivered unto Merlin and nourished by him, and so I saw the child never after, nor wot not what is his name, for I knew him never yet. And there Ulfius said to the queen, Merlin is more to blame than ye. Well I wot, said the queen, I bare a child by my lord King Uther, but I wot not where he is become. Then Merlin took the king by the hand, saying, This is your mother. And therewith Sir Ector bare witness how he nourished him by Uther's commandment. And therewith King Arthur took his mother, Queen Igraine, in his arms and kissed her, and either wept upon other. And then the king let make a feast that lasted eight days.[38]

CHAPTER 23:

HOW TWELVE KNIGHTS CAME FROM ROME AND ASKED TRUAGE FOR THIS LAND OF ARTHUR, AND HOW ARTHUR FOUGHT WITH A KNIGHT [39]

. . . Right so came into the court twelve knights, and were aged men, and they came from the Emperor of Rome, and they asked of Arthur truage for this realm, other-else the emperor would destroy him and his land. Well, said King Arthur, ye are messengers, therefore ye may say what ye will, other-else ye should die therefore. But this is mine answer: I owe the emperor no truage, nor none will I hold him, but on a fair field I shall give him my truage that shall be with a sharp spear, or else with a sharp sword, and that shall not be long, by my father's soul, Uther Pendragon. And therewith the messengers departed passingly wroth, and King Arthur was wroth, for in evil time came they then; for the king was passingly wroth for the hurt of Sir Griflet. And so he commanded a privy man of his chamber that or it be day his best horse and armour, with all that longeth unto his person, be without the city or to-morrow day. Right so or to-morrow day he met with his man and his horse, and so mounted up and dressed his shield and took his spear, and bade his chamberlain tarry there till he came again. And so Arthur rode a soft pace till it was day, and then was he ware of three churls chasing Merlin, and would have slain him. Then the king rode unto them, and bade them: Flee, churls! then were they afeard when they saw a knight, and fled. O Merlin, said Arthur, here hadst thou been slain for all thy crafts had I not been. Nay, said Merlin, not so, for I could save myself an I would; and thou art more near thy death than I am, for thou goest to the deathward, an God be not thy friend. So as they went thus talking they came to the fountain, and the rich pavilion there by it. Then King Arthur was ware where sat a knight armed in a chair. Sir knight, said Arthur, for what cause abidest thou here, that there may no knight ride this way but if he joust with thee? said the king. I rede thee leave that custom, said Arthur. This custom, said the knight, have I used and will use maugre who saith nay, and who is grieved with my custom let him amend it that will. I will amend it, said Arthur. I shall defend thee, said the knight. Anon he took his horse and dressed his shield and took a spear, and they met so hard either in other's shields, that all to-shivered their spears. Therewith anon Arthur pulled out his sword. Nay, not so,[40] said the knight; it is fairer, said the knight, that we twain run more together with sharp spears. I will well, said Arthur, an I had any more spears. I have enow, said the knight; so there came a squire and brought two good spears, and Arthur chose one and he another; so they spurred their horses and came together with all their mights, that either brake their spears to their hands. Then Arthur set hand on his sword. Nay, said the knight, ye shall do better, ye are a passing good jouster as ever I met withal, and once for the love of the high order of knighthood let us joust once again. I assent me, said Arthur. Anon there were brought two great spears, and every knight gat a spear, and therewith they ran together that Arthur's spear all to-shivered. But the other knight hit him so hard in midst of the shield, that horse and man fell to the earth, and therewith Arthur was eager, and pulled out his sword, and said, I will assay thee, sir knight, on foot, for I have lost the honour on horseback. I will be on horseback, said the knight. Then was

Arthur wroth, and dressed his shield toward him with his sword drawn. When the knight saw that, he alit, for him thought no worship to have a knight at such avail, he to be on horseback and he on foot, and so he alit and dressed his shield unto Arthur. And there began a strong battle with many great strokes, and so hewed with their swords that the cantels flew in the fields, and much blood they bled both, that all the place there as they fought was overbled with blood, and thus they fought long and rested them, and then they went to the battle again, and so hurtled together like two rams that either fell to the earth. So at the last they smote together that both their swords met even together. But the sword of the knight smote King Arthur's sword in two pieces, wherefore he was heavy. Then said the knight unto Arthur, Thou art in my daunger whether me list to save thee or slay thee, and but thou yield thee as overcome and recreant, thou shalt die. As for death, said King Arthur, welcome be it when it cometh, but to yield me unto thee as recreant I had liefer die than to be so shamed. And therewithal the king leapt unto Pellinore, and took him by the middle and threw him down, and rased off his helm. When the knight felt that he was adread, for he was a passing big man of might, and anon he brought Arthur under him, and rased off his helm and would have smitten off his head.[41]

CHAPTER 24:

HOW MERLIN SAVED ARTHUR'S LIFE, AND THREW AN ENCHANTMENT ON KING PELLINORE AND MADE HIM TO SLEEP

Therewithal came Merlin and said, Knight, hold thy hand, for an thou slay that knight thou puttest this realm in the greatest damage that ever was realm: for this knight is a man of more worship than thou wotest of. Why, who is he? said the knight. It is King Arthur. Then would he have slain him for dread of his wrath, and heaved up his sword, and therewith Merlin cast an enchantment to the knight, that he fell to the earth in a great sleep. Then Merlin took up King Arthur, and rode forth on the knight's horse. Alas! said Arthur, what hast thou done, Merlin? hast thou slain this good knight by thy crafts? There liveth not so

worshipful a knight as he was; I had liefer than the stint of my land
a year that he were alive. Care ye not, said Merlin, for he is
wholer than ye; for he is but a-sleep, and will awake within three
hours. I told you, said Merlin, what a knight he was; here had ye
been slain had I not been. Also there liveth not a bigger knight
than he is one, and he shall hereafter do you right good service;
and his name is Pellinore, and he shall have two sons that shall be
passing good men; save one they shall have no fellow of prowess
and of good living, and their names shall be Percivale of Wales and
Lamerake of Wales, and he shall tell you the name of your own son
begotten of your sister that shall be the destruction of all this realm.

CHAPTER 25:

HOW ARTHUR BY THE MEAN OF MERLIN GAT EXCALIBUR HIS SWORD OF THE LADY OF THE LAKE

Right so the king and he departed, and went unto an
hermit that was a good man and a great leech. So the hermit
searched all his wounds and gave him good salves; so the king was
there three days, and then were his wounds well amended that he
might ride and go, and so departed. And as they rode, Arthur
said, I have no sword. No force, said Merlin, hereby is a sword
that shall be yours, an I [42] may. So they rode till they came to a
lake, the which was a fair water and broad, and in the midst of the
lake Arthur was ware of an arm clothed in white samite, that held
a fair sword in that hand. Lo! said Merlin, yonder is that sword
that I spake of. With that they saw a damosel going upon the lake.
What damosel is that? said Arthur. That is the Lady of the Lake,
said Merlin; and within that lake is a rock, and therein is as fair
a place as any on earth, and richly beseen; and this damosel will
come to you anon, and then speak ye fair to her that she will give
you that sword. Anon withal came the damosel unto Arthur, and
saluted him, and he her again. Damosel, said Arthur, what sword
is that, that yonder the arm holdeth above the water? I would
it were mine, for I have no sword. Sir Arthur, king, said the
damosel, that sword is mine, and if ye will give me a gift when I
ask it you, ye shall have it. By my faith, said Arthur, I will give

you what gift ye will ask. Well! said the damosel, go ye into
yonder barge, and row yourself to the sword, and take it and the
scabbard with you, and I will ask my gift when I see my time. So
Sir Arthur and Merlin alit and tied their horses to two trees, and so
they went into the ship, and when they came to the sword that the
hand held, Sir Arthur took it up by the handles, and took it with
him, and the arm and the hand went under the water. And so
they came unto the land and rode forth, and then Sir Arthur saw
a rich pavilion. What significth yonder pavilion? It is the
knight's pavilion, said Merlin, that ye fought with last, Sir Pellinore; but he is out, he is not there. He hath ado with a knight of
yours that hight Egglame, and they have foughten together, but at
the last Egglame fled, and else he had been dead, and he hath
chased him even to Carlion, and we shall meet with him anon in
the highway. That is well said, said Arthur, now have I a sword,
now will I wage battle with him, and be avenged on him. Sir, you
shall not so, said Merlin, for the knight is weary of fighting and
chasing, so that ye shall have no worship to have ado with him;
also he will not be lightly matched of one knight living, and therefore it is my counsel, let him pass, for he shall do you good service
in short time, and his sons after his days. Also ye shall see that
day in short space, you shall be right glad to give him your sister
to wed. When I see him, I will do as ye advise me, said Arthur.
Then Sir Arthur looked on the sword, and liked [43] it passing well.
Whether liketh you better, said Merlin, the sword or the scabbard?
Me liketh better the sword, said Arthur. Ye are more unwise, said
Merlin, for the scabbard is worth ten of the swords, for whiles ye
have the scabbard upon you, ye shall never lose no blood be ye
never so sore wounded, therefore keep well the scabbard always
with you. So they rode unto Carlion, and by the way they met
with Sir Pellinore; but Merlin had done such a craft, that Pellinore
saw not Arthur, and he passed by without any words. I marvel,
said Arthur, that the knight would not speak. Sir, said Merlin, he
saw you not, for an he had seen you, ye had not lightly departed.
So they came unto Carlion, whereof his knights were passing glad.
And when they heard of his adventures, they marvelled that he
would jeopard his person so, alone. But all men of worship said
it was merry to be under such a chieftain, that would put his person in adventure as other poor knights did.

CHAPTER 26:

HOW TIDINGS CAME TO ARTHUR THAT KING RIENCE HAD OVERCOME ELEVEN
KINGS, AND HOW HE DESIRED ARTHUR'S BEARD TO TRIM HIS MANTLE

This meanwhile came a messenger from King Rience
of North Wales, and king he was of all Ireland, and of many isles.
And this was his message, greeting well King Arthur in this manner
wise, saying that King Rience had discomfited and overcome eleven
kings, and every each of them did him homage, and that was this,
they gave him their beards clean flayed off, as much as there was;
wherefore the messenger came for King Arthur's beard. For King
Rience had purfled a mantle with kings' beards, and there lacked
one place of the mantle; wherefore he sent for his beard, or else he
would enter into his lands, and burn and slay, and never leave till
he have the head and the beard. Well, said Arthur, thou hast said
thy message, the which is the most villainous and lewdest message
that ever man heard sent unto a king; also thou mayest see my beard
is full young yet to make a purfle of it. But tell thou thy king
this: I owe him none homage, nor none of mine elders, but or it
be long to, he shall do me homage on both his knees, or else he
shall lose his head, by the faith of my body, for this [44] is the most
shamefulest message that ever I heard speak of. I have espied thy
king met never yet with worshipful man, but tell him, I will have
his head without he do me homage. Then the messenger departed. Now is there any here, said Arthur, that knoweth King
Rience? Then answered a knight that hight Naram, Sir, I know
the king well; he is a passing good man of his body, as few be living,
and a passing proud man, and Sir, doubt ye not he will make war
on you with a mighty puissance. Well, said Arthur, I shall ordain
for him in short time.

CHAPTER 27:

HOW ALL THE CHILDREN WERE SENT FOR THAT WERE BORN ON MAY-DAY, AND
HOW MORDRED WAS SAVED

Then King Arthur let send for all the children born
on May-day, begotten of lords and born of ladies; for Merlin told

King Arthur that he that should destroy him should be born on May-day, wherefore he sent for them all, upon pain of death; and so there were found many lords' sons, and all were sent unto the king, and so was Mordred sent by King Lot's wife, and all were put in a ship to the sea, and some were four weeks old, and some less. And so by fortune the ship drave unto a castle, and was all to-riven, and destroyed the most part, save that Mordred was cast up, and a good man found him, and nourished him till he was fourteen year old, and then he brought him to the court, as it rehearseth afterward, toward the end of the Death of Arthur. So many lords and barons of this realm were displeased, for their children were so lost, and many put the wyte on Merlin more than on Arthur; so what for dread and for love, they held their peace.[45]

Book III, Chapter 1:

HOW KING ARTHUR TOOK A WIFE, AND WEDDED GUENEVER, DAUGHTER TO
LEODEGRANCE, KING OF THE LAND OF CAMELIARD, WITH WHOM
HE HAD THE ROUND TABLE

In the beginning of Arthur, after he was chosen king by adventure and by grace; for the most part of the barons knew not that he was Uther Pendragon's son, but as Merlin made it openly known. But yet many kings and lords held great war against him for that cause, but well Arthur overcame them all, for the most part the days of his life he was ruled much by the counsel of Merlin. So it fell on a time King Arthur said unto Merlin, My barons will let me have no rest, but needs I must take a wife, and I will none take but by thy counsel and by thine advice. It is well done, said Merlin, that ye take a wife, for a man of your bounty and noblesse should not be without a wife. Now is there any that ye love more than another? Yea, said King Arthur, I love Guenever the king's daughter, Leodegrance of the land of Cameliard, the which holdeth in his house the Table Round that ye told he had of my father Uther. And this damosel is the most valiant and fairest lady that I know living, or yet that ever I could find. Sir, said Merlin, as of her beauty and fairness she is one of the fairest on live, but, an ye loved her not so well as ye do, I should find you a

damosel of beauty and of goodness that should like you and please
you, an your heart were not set; but there as a man's heart is set,
he will be loth to return. That is truth, said King Arthur. But
Merlin warned the king covertly that Guenever was not wholesome
for him to take to wife, for he warned him that Launcelot should
love her, and she him again; and so he turned his tale to the adventures of Sangreal. Then Merlin desired of the king for to have
men with him that should enquire of Guenever, and so the king
granted him, and Merlin went forth unto King Leodegrance of
Cameliard, and told him of the desire of the king that he would
have unto his wife Guenever his daughter. That is to me, said
King Leodegrance, the best [71] tidings that ever I heard, that so
worthy a king of prowess and noblesse will wed my daughter. And
as for my lands, I will give him, wist I it might please him, but he
hath lands enow, him needeth none, but I shall send him a gift shall
please him much more, for I shall give him the Table Round, the
which Uther Pendragon gave me, and when it is full complete, there
is an hundred knights and fifty. And as for an hundred good
knights I have myself, but I fawte fifty, for so many have been slain
in my days. And so Leodegrance delivered his daughter Guenever
unto Merlin, and the Table Round with the hundred knights, and
so they rode freshly, with great royalty, what by water and what by
land, till that they came nigh unto London.

CHAPTER 2:

HOW THE KNIGHTS OF THE ROUND TABLE WERE ORDAINED AND THEIR SIEGES BLESSED BY THE BISHOP OF CANTERBURY

When King Arthur heard of the coming of Guenever
and the hundred knights with the Table Round, then King Arthur
made great joy for her coming, and that rich present, and said
openly, This fair lady is passing welcome unto me, for I have loved
her long, and therefore there is nothing so lief to me. And these
knights with the Round Table please me more than right great
riches. And in all haste the king let ordain for the marriage and

the coronation in the most honourable wise that could be devised. Now, Merlin, said King Arthur, go thou and espy me in all this land fifty knights which be of most prowess and worship. Within short time Merlin had found such knights that should fulfil twenty and eight knights, but no more he could find. Then the Bishop of Canterbury was fetched, and he blessed the sieges with great royalty and devotion, and there set the eight and twenty knights in their sieges. And when this was done Merlin said, Fair sirs, you must all arise and come to King Arthur for to do him homage; he will have the better will to maintain you. And so they arose and did their homage, and when they were gone Merlin found in every sieges letters of gold that told the knights' names that had sitten therein. But two sieges were void. And so anon came young Gawaine and asked the king a [72] gift. Ask, said the king, and I shall grant it you. Sir, I ask that ye will make me knight that same day ye shall wed fair Guenever. I will do it with a good will, said King Arthur, and do unto you all the worship that I may, for I must by reason ye are my nephew, my sister's son.[73]

BOOK IV, CHAPTER 10:

Then Sir Accolon began with words of treason, and said, Knight, thou art overcome, and mayst not endure, and also thou art weaponless, and thou hast lost much of thy blood,[102] and I am full loath to slay thee, therefore yield thee to me as recreant. Nay, said Sir Arthur, I may not so, for I have promised to do the battle to the uttermost, by the faith of my body, while me lasteth the life, and therefore I had lever to die with honour than to live with shame; and if it were possible for me to die an hundred times, I had lever to die so oft than yield me to thee; for though I lack weapon, I shall lack no worship, and if thou slay me weaponless that shall be thy shame. Well, said Accolon, as for the shame I will not spare, now keep thee from me, for thou art but a dead man. And therewith Accolon gave him such a stroke that he fell nigh to the earth, and would have had Arthur to have cried him mercy. But Sir Arthur pressed unto Accolon with his shield, and gave him with the pommel in his hand such a buffet that he went three strides aback. When the damosel of the lake beheld Arthur, how full of prowess his body was, and the false treason that was wrought for him to have had him slain; she had great pity that so good a knight and such a man of worship should so be destroyed. And at the next stroke Sir Accolon struck him such a stroke that by the damosel's enchantment the sword Excalibur fell out of Accolon's hand to the earth. And therewithal Sir Arthur lightly leapt to it, and gat it in his hand, and forthwithal he knew that it was his sword Excalibur, and said, Thou hast been from me all too long, and much damage hast thou done me; and therewith he espied the scabbard hanging by his side, and suddenly he sterte to him and pulled the scabbard from him, and threw it from him as far as he might throw it. O knight, said Arthur, this day hast thou done me great damage with this sword; now are ye come unto your death, for I shall not warrant you but ye shall as well be rewarded with this sword or ever we depart as thou hast rewarded me, for much pain have ye made me to endure, and much blood have I lost. And therewith Sir Arthur rushed on him with all his might and pulled him to the earth, and then rushed off his helm, and gave him such a buffet on the head that the blood came out at his ears, his nose, and his mouth. Now will I slay thee, said Arthur. Slay me ye may well, said Accolon, an it please you, for ye are the best knight that ever I found, and I see well that God is with you. But for I promised to do this battle, said Accolon, to the uttermost, and never to be recreant while I lived, therefore shall I never yield me with my mouth, but God do with my body what he [103] will. Then Sir Arthur remembered him, and thought he should have seen this knight. Now tell me, said Arthur, or I will slay thee, of what country art thou, and of what court? Sir knight, said Sir Accolon, I am of the court of King Arthur, and my name is Accolon of Gaul. Then was Arthur more dismayed than he was before-hand; for then he remembered him of his sister Morgan le Fay, and of the enchantment of the ship. O sir knight, said he, I pray you tell me who gave you this sword, and by whom ye had it.

CHAPTER 11:

HOW ACCOLON CONFESSED THE TREASON OF MORGAN LE FAY, KING ARTHUR'S
SISTER, AND HOW SHE WOULD HAVE DONE SLAY HIM

Then Sir Accolon bethought him, and said, Woe
worth this sword, for by it have I gotten my death. It may well
be, said the king. Now, sir, said Accolon, I will tell you; this
sword hath been in my keeping the most part of this twelvemonth;
and Morgan le Fay, King Uriens' wife, sent it me yesterday by a
dwarf, to this intent, that I should slay King Arthur, her brother.
For ye shall understand King Arthur is the man in the world that
she most hateth, because he is most of worship and of prowess of
any of her blood; also she loveth me out of measure as paramour,
and I her again; and if she might bring about to slay Arthur by
her crafts, she would slay her husband King Uriens lightly, and then
had she me devised to be king in this land, and so to reign, and
she to be my queen; but that is now done, said Accolon, for I am
sure of my death. Well, said Sir Arthur, I feel by you ye would
have been king in this land. It had been great damage to have destroyed your lord, said Arthur. It is truth, said Accolon, but now
I have told you truth, wherefore I pray you tell me of whence ye
are, and of what court? O Accolon, said King Arthur, now I let
thee wit that I am King Arthur, to whom thou hast done great
damage. When Accolon heard that he cried aloud, Fair, sweet
lord, have mercy on me, for I knew not you. O Sir Accolon, said
King Arthur, mercy shalt thou have, because I feel by thy words
at this time thou knewest not my person; but I understand well by
thy [104] words that thou hast agreed to the death of my person, and
therefore thou art a traitor; but I wyte thee the less, for my sister
Morgan le Fay by her false crafts made thee to agree and consent
to her false lusts, but I shall be sore avenged upon her an I live,
that all Christendom shall speak of it; God knoweth I have honoured her and worshipped her more than all my kin, and more
have I trusted her than mine own wife and all my kin after. Then
Sir Arthur called the keepers of the field, and said, Sirs, come hither,
for here are we two knights that have fought unto a great damage
unto us both, and like each one of us to have slain other, if it had

happed so; and had any of us known other, here had been no battle, nor stroke stricken. Then all aloud cried Accolon unto all the knights and men that were then there gathered together, and said to them in this manner, O lords, this noble knight that I have fought withal, the which me sore repenteth, is the most man of prowess, of manhood, and of worship in the world, for it is himself King Arthur, our alther liege lord, and with mishap and with misadventure have I done this battle with the king and lord that I am holden withall.[105]

BOOK V, CHAPTER 1:

HOW TWELVE AGED AMBASSADORS OF ROME CAME TO KING ARTHUR TO DEMAND TRUAGE FOR BRITAIN

When King Arthur had after long war rested, and held a royal feast and Table Round with his allies of kings, princes, and noble knights all of the Round Table, there came into his hall, he sitting in his throne royal, twelve ancient men, bearing each of them a branch of olive, in token that they came as ambassadors and messengers from the Emperor Lucius, which was called at that time, Dictator or Procuror of the Public Weal of Rome; which said messengers, after their entering and coming into the presence of King Arthur, did to him their obeisance in making to him reverence, and said to him in this wise: The high and mighty Emperor Lucius sendeth to the King of Britain greeting, commanding thee to acknowledge him for thy lord, and to send him the truage due of this realm unto the Empire, which thy father and other tofore thy precessors have paid as is of record, and thou as rebel not knowing him as thy sovereign, withholdest and retainest contrary to the statutes and decrees made by the noble and worthy Julius Cesar, conqueror of this realm, and first Emperor of Rome. And if thou refuse his demand and commandment, know thou for certain that he shall make strong war against thee, thy realms and lands, and shall chastise thee and thy subjects, that it shall be ensample perpetual unto all kings and princes, for to deny their truage unto that noble empire which domineth upon [130] the universal world. Then when they had showed the effect of their message, the king commanded them to withdraw them, and said he should take advice of council and give to them an answer. Then some of the young knights, hearing this their message, would have run on them to have slain them, saying that it was a rebuke to all the knights there being present to suffer them to say so to the king. And anon the king commanded that none of them, upon pain of death, to myssaye them nor do them any harm, and commanded a knight to bring them to their lodging, and see that they have all that is necessary and requisite for them, with the best cheer, and that no dainty be spared, for the Romans be great lords, and though their message please me not nor my court, yet I must remember mine honour. After this the king let call all his lords and knights of the Round Table to counsel upon this matter, and desired them to say their advice. Then Sir Cador of Cornwall spake first and said, Sir, this message liketh me well, for we have many days rested us and have been idle, and now I hope ye shall make sharp war on the Romans, where I doubt not we shall get honour. I believe well, said Arthur, that this matter pleaseth thee well, but these answers may not be answered, for the demand grieveth me sore, for truly I will never pay truage to Rome, wherefore I pray you to counsel me. I have understood that Belinus and Brenius, kings of Britain, have had the empire in their hands many days, and also Constantine the son of Heleine, which is an open evidence that we owe no tribute to Rome, but of right we that be descended of them have right to claim the title of the empire.

CHAPTER 2:

HOW THE KINGS AND LORDS PROMISED TO KING ARTHUR AID AND HELP AGAINST THE ROMANS

Then answered King Anguish of Scotland, Sir, ye ought of right to be above all other kings, for unto you is none like nor pareylle in Christendom, of knighthood nor of dignity, and I counsel you never to obey the Romans, for when they reigned on us they distressed our elders, and put this land to great extortions and taylles, wherefore I make here mine avow to avenge me on them; and for to [131] strengthen your quarrel I shall furnish twenty thousand good men of war, and wage them on my costs, which shall await on you with myself when it shall please you. And the king of Little Britain granted him to the same thirty thousand; wherefore King Arthur thanked them. And then every man agreed to make war, and to aid after their power; that is to wit, the lord of West Wales promised to bring thirty thousand men, and Sir Uwaine, Sir Ider his son, with their cousins, promised to bring thirty thousand. Then Sir Launcelot with all other promised in likewise every man a great multitude. And when King Arthur understood their courages and good wills he thanked them heartily, and after let call the ambassadors to hear their answer. And in the presence of all his lords and knights he said to them in this wise: I will that ye return unto your lord and Procuror of the Common Weal for the Romans, and say ye to him, Of his demand and commandment I set nothing, and that I know of no truage nor tribute that I owe to him, nor to none earthly prince, Christian nor heathen; but I pretend to have and occupy the sovereignty of the empire, wherein I am entitled by the right of my predecessors, sometime kings of this land; and say to him that I am delibered and fully concluded, to go with mine army with strength and power unto Rome, by the grace of God, to take possession in the empire and subdue them that be rebel. Wherefore I command him and all them of Rome, that incontinent they make to me their homage, and to acknowledge me for their Emperor and Governor, upon pain that shall ensue. And then he commanded his treasurer to give to them great and large gifts, and to pay all their dispenses, and assigned Sir Cador to convey them out of the land. And so they took their leave and departed, and took their shipping at Sandwich, and passed forth by Flanders, Almaine, the mountains, and all Italy, until they came unto Lucius. And after the reverence made, they made relation of their answer, like as ye tofore have heard. When the Emperor Lucius had well understood their credence, he was sore moved as he had been all araged, and said, I had supposed that Arthur would have obeyed to my commandment, and have served you himself, as him well beseemed or any other king to do. O Sir, said one of the senators, let be such vain words, for we let you wit that I and my fellows were full sore afeared to behold his [132] countenance; I fear me ye have made a rod for yourself, for he intendeth to be lord of this empire, which sore is to be doubted if he come, for he is all another man than ye ween, and holdeth the most noble court of the world, all other kings nor princes may not compare unto his noble maintenance. On New Year's Day we saw him in his estate, which was the royalest that ever we saw, for he was served at his table with nine kings, and the noblest fellowship of other princes, lords, and knights that be in the world, and every knight approved and like a lord, and man that liveth, and is like to conquer all the world, for unto his courage it is too little: wherefore I advise you to keep well your marches and straits in the mountains; for certainly he is a lord to be doubted. Well, said Lucius, before Easter I suppose to pass the mountains, and so forth into France, and there bereave him his lands with Genoese and other mighty warriors of Tuscany and Lombardy. And I shall send for them all that be subjects and allied to the empire of Rome to come to mine aid. And forthwith sent old wise knights unto these countries following: first to Ambage and Arrage, to Alexandria, to India, to Armenia, whereas the river of Euphrates runneth into Asia, to Africa, and Europe the Large, to Ertayne and Elamye, to Araby, Egypt, and to Damascus, to Damietta and Cayer, to Cappadocia, to Tarsus, Turkey, Pontus and Pamphylia, to Syria and Galatia. And all these were subject to Rome and many more, as Greece, Cyprus, Macedonia, Calabria, Cateland, Portugal, with many thousands of Spaniards. Thus all these kings, dukes, and admirals, assembled about Rome, with sixteen kings at once, with great multitude of people. When the emperor understood their coming he made ready his Romans and all the people between him and Flanders. Also he had gotten with him fifty giants which had been engendered of fiends; and they were ordained to guard his person, and to break the front of the battle of King Arthur. And thus departed from Rome, and came down the mountains for to destroy the lands that Arthur had conquered, and came unto Cologne, and besieged a castle thereby, and won it soon, and stuffed it with two hundred Saracens or Infidels, and after destroyed many fair countries which Arthur had won of King Claudas. And thus Lucius came with all his host [133] which were disperplyd sixty mile in breadth, and commanded them to meet with him in Burgoyne, for he purposed to destroy the realm of Little Britain.

CHAPTER 3:

HOW KING ARTHUR HELD A PARLIAMENT AT YORK, AND HOW HE ORDAINED THE
REALM SHOULD BE GOVERNED IN HIS ABSENCE

Now leave we of Lucius the Emperor and speak we of
King Arthur, that commanded all them of his retinue to be ready
at the utas of Hilary for to hold a Parliament at York. And at
that Parliament was concluded to arrest all the navy of the land,
and to be ready within fifteen days at Sandwich, and there he
showed to his army how he purposed to conquer the empire which
he ought to have of right. And there he ordained two governors
of this realm, that is to say, Sir Bawdwin of Britain, for to counsel
to the best, and Sir Constantine, son to Sir Cador of Cornwall,
which after the death of Arthur was king of this realm. And in
the presence of all his lords he resigned the rule of the realm and
Gwenever his queen to them, wherefore Sir Launcelot was wroth,
for he left Sir Tristram with King Mark for the love of Beale Isoud.
Then the Queen Gwenever made great sorrow for the departing of
her lord and other, and swooned in such wise that the ladies bare
her into her chamber. Thus the king with his great army departed,
leaving the queen and realm in the governance of Sir Bawdwin and
Constantine. And when he was on his horse he,said with an high
voice, If I die in this journey I will that Sir Constantine be mine
heir and king crowned of this realm as next of my blood. And
after departed and entered into the sea at Sandwich with all his
army, with a great multitude of ships, galleys, cogges, and dro-
moundes, sailing on the sea.

CHAPTER 4:

HOW KING ARTHUR BEING SHIPPED AND LYING IN HIS CABIN HAD A MARVELLOUS
DREAM AND OF THE EXPOSITION THEREOF

And as the king lay in his cabin in the ship, he fell in
a slumbering and dreamed a marvellous dream: him seemed that
a dreadful dragon did drown much of his people, and he came flying out of the west, and his head was enamelled [134] with azure,

and his shoulders shone as gold, his belly like mails of a marvellous hue, his tail full of tatters, his feet full of fine sable, and his claws like fine gold; and an hideous flame of fire flew out of his mouth, like as the land and water had flamed all of fire. After, him seemed there came out of the orient, a grimly boar all black in a cloud, and his paws as big as a post; he was rugged looking roughly, he was the foulest beast that ever man saw, he roared and romed so hideously that it were marvel to hear. Then the dreadful dragon advanced him and came in the wind like a falcon giving great strokes on the boar, and the boar hit him again with his grizzly tusks that his breast was all bloody, and that the hot blood made all the sea red of his blood. Then the dragon flew away all on an hight, and came down with such a swough, and smote the boar on the ridge, which was ten foot large from the head to the tail, and smote the boar all to powder both flesh and bones, that it flittered all abroad on the sea. And therewith the king awoke anon, and was sore abashed of this dream, and sent anon for a wise philosopher, commanding to tell him the signification of his dream. Sir, said the philosopher, the dragon that thou dreamedst of betokeneth thine own person that sailest here, and the colours of his wings be thy realms that thou hast won, and his tail which is all to-tattered signifieth the noble knights of the Round Table; and the boar that the dragon slew coming from the clouds betokeneth some tyrant that tormenteth the people, or else thou art like to fight with some giant thyself, being horrible and abominable, whose peer ye saw never in your days, wherefore of this dreadful dream doubt thee nothing, but as a conqueror come forth thyself. Then after this soon they had sight of land and sailed till they arrived at Barflete in Flanders, and when they were there he found many of his great lords ready, as they had been commanded to wait upon him.

Chapter 5:

HOW A MAN OF THE COUNTRY TOLD TO HIM OF A MARVELLOUS GIANT, AND HOW HE FOUGHT AND CONQUERED HIM

Then came to him an husbandman of the country, and told him how there was in the country of Constantine, beside

Brittany, a great giant which had slain, murdered [135] and de-
voured much people of the country, and had been sustained seven
year with the children of the commons of that land, insomuch that
all the children be all slain and destroyed; and now late he hath
taken the Duchess of Brittany as she rode with her meyne, and hath
led her to his lodging which is in a mountain, for to ravish and lie
by her to her life's end, and many people followed her, more than
five hundred, but all they might not rescue her, but they left
her shrieking and crying lamentably, wherefore I suppose that he
hath slain her in fulfilling his foul lust of lechery. She was wife
unto thy cousin Sir Howell, whom we call full nigh of thy blood.
Now, as thou art a rightful king, have pity on this lady, and revenge
us all as thou art a noble conqueror. Alas, said King Arthur, this
is a great mischief, I had lever than the best realm that I have that
I had been a furlong way tofore him for to have rescued that lady.
Now, fellow, said King Arthur, canst thou bring me thereas this
giant haunteth? Yea, Sir, said the good man, look yonder whereas
thou seest those two great fires, there shalt thou find him, and more
treasure than I suppose is in all France. When the king had understood this piteous case, he returned into his tent. Then he
called to him Sir Kay and Sir Bedivere, and commanded them
secretly to make ready horse and harness for himself and them
twain; for after evensong he would ride on pilgrimage with them
two only unto Saint Michael's mount. And then anon he made
him ready, and armed him at all points, and took his horse and his
shield. And so they three departed thence and rode forth as fast
as ever they might till that they came to the forbond of that mount.
And there they alighted, and the king commanded them to tarry
there, for he would himself go up into that mount. And so he
ascended up into that hill till he came to a great fire, and there he
found a careful widow wringing her hands and making great sorrow, sitting by a grave new made. And then King Arthur saluted
her, and demanded of her wherefore she made such lamentation,
to whom she answered and said, Sir knight, speak soft, for yonder
is a devil, if he hear thee speak he will come and destroy thee; I
hold thee unhappy; what dost thou here in this mountain? for if
ye were such fifty as ye be, ye were not able to make resistance
against this devil: here lieth a duchess dead, the which was the
fairest of all the world, wife to Sir Howell, Duke of Brittany,[136]

he hath murdered her in forcing her, and hath slit her unto the navel. Dame, said the king, I come from the noble conqueror King Arthur, for to treat with that tyrant for his liege people. Fie on such treaties, said she, he setteth not by the king nor by no man else; but an if thou have brought Arthur's wife, dame Gwenever, he shall be gladder than thou hadst given to him half France. Beware, approach him not too nigh, for he hath vanquished fifteen kings, and hath made him a coat full of precious stones enbroidered with their beards, which they sent him to have his love for salvation of their people at this last Christmas. And if thou wilt, speak with him at yonder great fire at supper. Well, said Arthur, I will accomplish my message for all your fearful words; and went forth by the crest of that hill, and saw where he sat at supper gnawing on a limb of a man, baking his broad limbs by the fire, and breechless, and three fair damosels turning three broaches whereon were broached twelve young children late born, like young birds. When King Arthur beheld that piteous sight he had great compassion on them, so that his heart bled for sorrow, and hailed him saying in this wise: He that all the world wieldeth give thee short life and shameful death; and the devil have thy soul; why hast thou murdered these young innocent children, and murdered this duchess? Therefore, arise and dress thee, thou glutton, for this day shalt thou die of my hand. Then the glutton anon started up, and took a great club in his hand, and smote at the king that his coronal fell to the earth. And the king hit him again that he carve his belly and cut off his genytours, that his guts and his entrails fell down to the ground. Then the giant threw away his club, and caught the king in his arms that he crushed his ribs. Then the three maidens kneeled down and called to Christ for help and comfort of Arthur. And then Arthur weltered and wrung, that he was other while under and another time above. And so weltering and wallowing they rolled down the hill till they came to the sea mark, and ever as they so weltered Arthur smote him with his dagger. And it fortuned they came to the place whereas the two knights were and kept Arthur's horse; then when they saw the king fast in the giant's arms they came and loosed him. And then the king commanded Sir Kay to smite off the giant's head, and to set it upon a truncheon of a spear, and bear it to Sir Howell, and tell him that his [137] enemy was slain; and after let this head be bounden to a barbican that all the people may see and behold it; and go ye two up to the mountain, and fetch me my shield, my sword, and the club of iron; and as for the treasure, take ye it, for ye shall find there goods out of number; so I have the kirtle and the club I desire no more. This was the fiercest giant that ever I met with, save one in the mount of Araby, which I overcame, but this was greater and fiercer. Then the knights fetched the club and the kirtle, and some of the treasure they took to themselves, and returned again to the host. And anon this was known through all the country, wherefore the people came and thanked the king. And he said again, Give the thanks to God, and depart the goods among you. And after that King Arthur said and commanded his cousin Howell, that he should ordain for a church to be builded on the same hill in the worship of Saint Michael. And on the morn the king removed with his great battle, and came into Champayne and in a valley, and there they pyght their tents; and the king being set at his dinner, there came in two messengers, of whom that one was Marshal of France, and said to the king that the emperor was entered into France, and had destroyed a great part, and was in Burgoyne, and had destroyed and made great slaughter of people, and burnt towns and boroughs; wherefore, if thou come not hastily, they must yield up their bodies and goods.

CHAPTER 6:

HOW KING ARTHUR SENT SIR GAWAINE AND OTHER TO LUCIUS, AND HOW THEY WERE ASSAILED AND ESCAPED WITH WORSHIP

Then the king did do call Sir Gawaine, Sir Bors, Sir Lionel, and Sir Bedivere, and commanded them to go straight to Sir Lucius, and say ye to him that hastily he remove out of my land; and if he will not, bid him make him ready to battle and not distress the poor people. Then anon these noble knights dressed themselves to horseback, and when they came to the green wood, they saw many pavilions set in a meadow, of silk of divers colours, beside a river, and the emperor's pavilion was in the middle with an eagle displayed above. To the which tent our knights rode toward, and ordained Sir Gawaine and Sir Bors to do the message,[138] and left in a bushment Sir Lionel and Sir Bedivere. And then Sir Gawaine and Sir Bors did their message, and commanded Lucius, in Arthur's name to avoid his land, or shortly to address him to battle. To whom Lucius answered and said, Ye shall return to your lord, and say ye to him that I shall subdue him and all his lands. Then Sir Gawaine was wroth and said, I had lever than all France fight against thee; and so had I, said Sir Bors, lever than all Brittany or Burgoyne. Then a knight named Sir Gainus, nigh cousin to the emperor, said, Lo, how these Britons be full of pride and boast, and they brag as though they bare up all the world. Then Sir Gawaine was sore grieved with these words, and pulled out his sword and smote off his head. And therewith turned their horses and rode over waters and through woods till they came to their bushment, whereas Sir Lionel and Sir Bedivere were hovyng. The Romans followed fast after, on horseback and on foot, over a champaign unto a wood; then Sir Bors turned his horse and saw a knight come fast on, whom he smote through the body with a spear that he fell dead down to the earth; then came Caliburn one of the strongest of Pavie, and smote down many of Arthur's knights. And when Sir Bors saw him do so much harm, he addressed toward him, and smote him through the breast, that he fell down dead to the earth. Then Sir Feldenak thought to revenge the death of Gainus upon Sir Gawaine, but Sir Gawaine was ware thereof, and smote him on the head, which stroke stinted not till it came to his breast. And then he returned and came to his fellows in the bushment. And there was a recounter, for the bushment brake on the Romans, and slew and hew down the Romans, and forced the Romans to flee and return, whom the noble knights chased unto their tents. Then the Romans gathered more people, and also foot-men came on, and there was a new battle, and so much people that Sir Bors and Sir Berel were taken. But when Sir Gawaine saw that, he took with him Sir Idrus the good knight, and said he would never see King Arthur but if he rescued them, and pulled out Galatine his good sword, and followed them that led those two knights away; and he smote him that led Sir Bors, and took Sir Bors from him and delivered him to his fellows. And Sir Idrus in likewise rescued Sir Berel. Then began the battle to be great, that our knights were in great jeopardy, wherefore Sir Gawaine [139] sent to King Arthur for succour, and that he hie him, for I am sore wounded, and that our prisoners may pay goods out of number. And the messenger came to the king and told him his message. And anon the king did do assemble his army, but anon, or he departed the prisoners were come, and Sir Gawaine and his fellows gat the field and put the Romans to flight, and after returned and came with their fellowship in such wise that no man of worship was lost of them, save that Sir Gawaine was sore hurt. Then the king did do ransake his wounds and comforted him. And thus was the beginning of the first journey of the Britons and Romans, and there were slain of the Romans more than ten thousand, and great joy and mirth was made that night in the host of King Arthur. And on the morn he sent all the prisoners into Parish under the guard of Sir Launcelot, with many knights, and of Sir Cador.

CHAPTER 7:

HOW LUCIUS SENT CERTAIN SPIES IN A BUSHMENT FOR TO HAVE TAKEN HIS KNIGHTS BEING PRISONERS, AND HOW THEY WERE LETTED

Now turn we to the Emperor of Rome, which espied that these prisoners should be sent to Paris, and anon he sent to lie in a bushment certain knights and princes with sixty thousand men, for to rescue his knights and lords that were prisoners. And so on the morn as Launcelot and Sir Cador, chieftains and governors of all them that conveyed the prisoners, as they should pass through a wood, Sir Launcelot sent certain knights to espy if any were in the woods to let them. And when the said knights came into the wood, anon they espied and saw the great embushment, and returned and told Sir Launcelot that there lay in await for them three score thousand Romans. And then Sir Launcelot with such knights as he had, and men of war to the number of ten thousand, put them in array, and met with them and fought with them manly, and slew and dretenchid many of the Romans, and slew many knights and admirals of the party of the Romans and Saracens; there was slain the king of Lyly and three great lords, Aladuke, Herawd, and Heringdale. But Sir Launcelot fought so nobly that no man might endure a stroke of his [140] hand, but where he came he shewed his prowess and might, for he slew down right on every side; and the Romans and Saracens fled from him as the sheep from the wolf or from the lion, and put them all that abode alive to flight. And so long they fought that tidings came to King Arthur, and anon he graythed him and came to the battle, and saw his knights how they had vanquished the battle, he embraced them knight by knight in his arms, and said, Ye be worthy to wield all your honour and worship; there was never king save myself that had so noble knights. Sir, said Cador, there was none of us failed other, but of the prowess and manhood of Sir Launcelot were more than wonder to tell, and also of his cousins which did that day many noble feats of war. And also Sir Cador told who of his knights were slain, as Sir Beriel, and other Sir Moris and Sir Maurel, two good knights. Then the king wept, and dried his eyes with a kerchef, and said, Your courage had near hand destroyed you, for though ye had returned again, ye had lost no worship; for I call it folly, knights to abide when they be overmatched. Nay, said Launcelot and the other, for once shamed may never be recovered.

CHAPTER 8:

HOW A SENATOR TOLD TO LUCIUS OF THEIR DISCOMFITURE, AND ALSO OF THE GREAT BATTLE BETWEEN ARTHUR AND LUCIUS

Now leave we King Arthur and his noble knights which had won the field, and had brought their prisoners to Paris, and speak we of a senator which escaped from the battle, and came to Lucius the emperor, and said to him, Sir emperor, I advise thee for to withdraw thee; what dost thou here? thou shalt win nothing in these marches but great strokes out of all measure, for this day one of Arthur's knights was worth in the battle an hundred of ours. Fie on thee, said Lucius, thou speakest cowardly; for thy words grieve me more than all the loss that I had this day. And anon he sent forth a king, which hight Sir Leomie, with a great army, and bad him hie him fast tofore, and he would follow hastily after. King Arthur was warned privily, and sent his people to Sessoine, and took up the towns and castles from the Romans. Then the king commanded Sir [141] Cador to take the rearward, and to take ʷⁱᵗʰ him certain knights of the Round Table,—And Sir Launcelot,

Sir Bors, Sir Kay, Sir Marrok, with Sir Marhaus, shall await on our person. Thus the King Arthur disperplyd his host in divers parties, to the end that his enemies should not escape. When the emperor was entered into the vale of Sessoine, he might see where King Arthur was embattled and his banner displayed; and he was beset round about with his enemies, that needs he must fight or yield him, for he might not flee, but said openly unto the Romans, Sirs, I admonish you that this day ye fight and acquit you as men, and remember how Rome domineth and is chief and head over all the earth and universal world, and suffer not these Britons this day to abide against us; and therewith he did command his trumpets to blow the bloody sounds, in such wise that the ground trembled and dyndled. Then the battles approached and shove and shouted on both sides, and great strokes were smitten on both sides, many men overthrown, hurt, and slain; and great valiances, prowesses and appertyces of war were that day showed, which were over long to recount the noble feats of every man, for they should contain an whole volume. But in especial, King Arthur rode in the battle exhorting his knights to do well, and himself did as nobly with his hands as was possible a man to do; he drew out Excalibur his sword, and awaited ever whereas the Romans were thickest and most grieved his people, and anon he addressed him on that part, and hew and slew down right, and rescued his people; and he slew a great giant named Galapas, which was a man of an huge quantity and height, he shorted him and smote off both his legs by the knees, saying, Now art thou better of a size to deal with than thou were, and after smote off his head. There Sir Gawaine fought nobly and slew three admirals in that battle. And so did all the knights of the Round Table. Thus the battle between King Arthur and Lucius the Emperor endured long. Lucius had on his side many Saracens which were slain. And thus the battle was great, and oftsydes that one party was at a fordele and anon at an afterdele, which endured so long till at the last King Arthur espied where Lucius the Emperor fought, and did wonder with his own hands. And anon he rode to him. And either smote other fiercely, and at last Lucius smote Arthur thwart the visage, and gave him a large wound. And when King [142] Arthur felt himself hurt, anon he smote him again with Excalibur that it cleft his head, from the summit of his head, and stinted not till it came to his breast. And then the emperor fell down dead and there ended his life. And when it was known that the emperor was slain, anon all the Romans with all their host put them to flight, and King Arthur with all his knights followed the chase, and slew down right all them that they might attain. And thus was the victory given to King Arthur, and the triumph; and there were slain on the part of Lucius more than an hundred thousand. And after King Arthur did do ransack the dead bodies, and did do bury them that were slain of his retinue, every man according to the estate and degree that he was of. And them that were hurt he let the surgeons do search their hurts and wounds, and commanded to spare no salves nor medicines till they were whole. Then the king rode straight to the place where the Emperor Lucius lay dead, and with him he found slain the Sultan of Syria, the King of Egypt and of Ethiopia, which were two noble kings, with seventeen other kings of divers regions, and also sixty senators of Rome, all noble men, whom the king did do bawme and gum with many good gums aromatic, and after did do cere them in sixty fold of cered cloth of Sendal, and laid them in chests of lead, by cause they should not chafe nor savour, and upon all these bodies their shields with their arms and banners were set, to the end they should be known of what country they were. And after he found three senators which were on live, to whom he said, For to save your lives I will that ye take these dead bodies, and carry them with you unto great Rome, and present them to the Potestate on my behalf, shewing him my letters, and tell them that I in my person shall hastily be at Rome. And I suppose the Romans shall beware how they shall demand any tribute of me. And I command you to say when ye shall come to Rome, to the Potestate and all the Council and Senate, that I send to them these dead bodies for the tribute that they have demanded. And if they be not content with these, I shall pay more at my coming, for other tribute owe I none, nor none other will I pay. And methinketh this sufficeth for Britain, Ireland and all Almaine with Germany. And furthermore, I charge you to say to them, that I command them upon pain of their heads never to demand tribute nor tax of me nor of my lands.[143] Then with this charge and commandment, the three senators aforesaid departed with all the said dead bodies, laying the body of Lucius in a car covered with the arms of the Empire all alone; and after alway two

bodies of kings in a chariot, and then the bodies of the senators
after them, and so went toward Rome, and showed their legation
and message to the Potestate and Senate, recounting the battle done
in France, and how the field was lost and much people and innumerable slain.   Wherefore they advised them in no wise to move
no more war against that noble conqueror Arthur, for his might
and prowess is most to be doubted, seeing the noble kings and great
multitude of knights of the Round Table, to whom none earthly
prince may compare.

CHAPTER 9:

HOW ARTHUR, AFTER HE HAD ACHIEVED THE BATTLE AGAINST THE ROMANS, ENTERED INTO ALMAINE, AND SO INTO ITALY

Now turn we unto King Arthur and his noble knights,
which, after the great battle achieved against the Romans, entered
into Loraine, Brabant and Flanders, and sythen returned into Haut
Almaine, and so over the mountains into Lombardy, and after, into
Tuscany wherein was a city which in no wise would yield themself
nor obey, wherefore King Arthur besieged it, and lay long about
it, and gave many assaults to the city; and they within defended
them valiantly.[144]

CHAPTER 12:

. . . HOW THE KING WON A CITY, AND HOW HE WAS CROWNED EMPEROR

. . . And then anon the king let do cry assault to the
city, and there was rearing of ladders, breaking of walls, and the
ditch filled, that men with little pain might enter into the city.
Then came out a duchess, and Clarisin the countess, with many
ladies and damosels, and kneeling before King Arthur, required
him for the love of God to receive the city, and not to take it by
assault, for then should many guiltless be slain.   Then the king
avalyd his visor with a meek and noble countenance, and said,

Madam, there shall none of my subjects misdo you nor your maidens, nor to none that to you belong, but the duke shall abide my judgment. Then anon the king commanded to leave the assault, and anon the duke's oldest son brought out the keys, and kneeling [149] delivered them to the king, and besought him of grace; and the king seized the town by assent of his lords, and took the duke and sent him to Dover, there for to abide prisoner term of his life, and assigned certain rents for the dower of the duchess and for her children. Then he made lords to rule those lands, and laws as a lord ought to do in his own country; and after he took his journey toward Rome, and sent Sir Floris and Sir Floridas tofore, with five hundred men of arms, and they came to the city of Urbino and laid there a bushment, thereas them seemed most best for them, and rode tofore the town, where anon issued out much people and skirmished with the fore-riders. Then brake out the bushment and won the bridge, and after the town, and set upon the walls the king's banner. Then came the king upon an hill, and saw the city and his banner on the walls, by which he knew that the city was won. And anon he sent and commanded that none of his liege men should defoul nor lie by no lady, wife, nor maiden; and when he came into the city, he passed to the castle, and comforted them that were in sorrow, and ordained there a captain, a knight of his own country. And when they of Milan heard that thilk city was won, they sent to King Arthur great sums of money, and besought him as their lord to have pity on them, promising to be his subjects for ever, and yield to him homage and fealty for the lands of Pleasance and Pavia, Petersaint, and the Port of Tremble, and to give him yearly a million of gold all his lifetime. Then he rideth into Tuscany, and winneth towns and castles, and wasted all in his way that to him will not obey, and so to Spolute and Viterbe, and from thence he rode into the Vale of Vicecount among the vines. And from thence he sent to the senators, to wit whether they would know him for their lord. But soon after on a Saturday came unto King Arthur all the senators that were left on live, and the noblest cardinals that then dwelt in Rome, and prayed him of peace, and proferred him full large, and besought him as governor to give licence for six weeks for to assemble all the Romans, and then to crown him emperor with chrism as it belongeth to so high estate.   I assent, said the king, like as ye have devised, and at Christmas there to be crowned, and to hold my Round Table with my knights as me liketh.   And then the senators made ready for his enthronization.   And at the day appointed, as the romance telleth, he came into Rome, and [150] was crowned emperor by the pope's hand, with all the royalty that could be made, and sojourned there a time, and established all his lands from Rome into France, and gave lands and realms unto his servants and knights, to every each after his desert, in such wise that none complained, rich nor poor.   And he gave to Sir Priamus the duchy of Lorraine; and he thanked him, and said he would serve him the days of his life; and after made dukes and earls, and made every man rich.   Then after this all his knights and lords assembled them afore him, and said: Blessed be God, your war is finished and your conquest achieved, in so much that we know none so great nor mighty that dare make war against you: wherefore we beseech you to return homeward, and give us licence to go home to our wives, from whom we have been long, and to rest us, for your journey is finished with honour and worship.   Then said the king, Ye say truth, and for to tempt God it is no wisdom, and therefore make you ready and return we into England.   Then there was trussing of harness and baggage and great carriage.   And after licence given, he returned and commanded that no man in pain of death should not rob nor take victual, nor other thing by the way but that he should pay therefor. And thus he came over the sea and landed at Sandwich, against whom Queen Gwenever his wife came and met him, and he was nobly received of all his commons in every city and burgh, and great gifts presented to him at his home-coming to welcome him with.[151]

[II] BOOK XX, CHAPTER 1:

HOW SIR AGRAVAINE AND SIR MORDRED WERE BUSY UPON SIR GAWAINE FOR
TO DISCLOSE THE LOVE BETWEEN SIR LAUNCELOT AND QUEEN GUENEVER

In May when every lusty heart flourisheth and bourgeoneth, for as the season is lusty to behold and comfortable, so man and woman rejoice and gladden of summer coming with his fresh flowers: for winter with his rough winds and blasts causeth a lusty man and woman to cower, and sit fast by the fire. So in this season, as in the month of May, it befell a great anger and unhap that stinted not till the flower of chivalry of all the world was destroyed and slain; and all was long upon two unhappy knights, the which were named Agravaine and Sir Mordred, that were brethren unto Sir Gawaine. For this Sir Agravaine and Sir Mordred had ever a privy hate unto the queen Dame Guenever and to Sir Launcelot, and daily and nightly they ever watched upon Sir Launcelot. So it mishapped, Sir Gawaine and all his brethren were in King Arthur's chamber; and then Sir Agravaine said thus openly, and not in no counsel, that many knights might hear it: I marvel that we all be not ashamed both to see and to know how Sir Launcelot lieth daily and nightly by the queen, and all we know it so; and it is shamefully suffered of us all, that we all should suffer so noble a king as King Arthur is so to be shamed. Then spake Sir Gawaine, and said: Brother Sir Agravaine, I pray you and charge you move no such matters no more afore me, for wit you well, said Sir Gawaine, I will not be of your counsel. So God me help, said Sir Gaheris and Sir Gareth, we will not be knowing, brother Agravaine, of your deeds. Then will I, said Sir Mordred. I leave well that, said Sir Gawaine, for ever unto all unhappiness, brother Sir Mordred, thereto will ye grant; and I would that ye left all this, and made you not so busy, for I know, said Sir Gawaine, what will fall of it. Fall of it what fall may, said Sir Agravaine, I will disclose it to the king. Not [339] by my counsel, said Sir Gawaine, for an there rise war and wrake betwixt Sir Launcelot and us, wit you well brother, there will many kings and great lords hold with Sir Launcelot. Also, brother Sir Agravaine, said Sir Gawaine, ye must remember how ofttimes Sir Launcelot hath rescued the king and the queen; and the best of us all had been full cold at the heart root had not Sir Launcelot been better than we, and that hath he proved himself full oft. And as for my part, said Sir Gawaine, I will never be against Sir Launcelot for one day's deed, when he rescued me from King Carados of the Dolorous Tower, and slew him, and saved my life. Also, brother Sir Agravaine and Sir Mordred, in like wise Sir Launcelot rescued you both, and threescore and two, from Sir Turquin. Methinketh brother, such kind deeds and kindness should be remembered. Do as ye list, said Sir Agravaine, for I will layne it no longer. With these words came to them King Arthur. Now brother, stint your noise, said Sir Gawaine. We will not, said Sir Agravaine and Sir Mordred. Will ye so? said Sir Gawaine; then God speed you, for I will not hear your tales ne be of your counsel. No more will I, said Sir Gareth and Sir Gaheris, for we will never say evil by that man; for by cause, said Sir Gareth, Sir Launcelot made me knight, by no manner owe I to say ill of him: and therewithal they three departed, making great dole. Alas, said Sir Gawaine and Sir Gareth, now is this realm wholly mischieved, and the noble fellowship of the Round Table shall be disparply: so they departed.

CHAPTER 2:

HOW SIR AGRAVAINE DISCLOSED THEIR LOVE TO KING ARTHUR, AND HOW KING
ARTHUR GAVE THEM LICENCE TO TAKE HIM

And then Sir Arthur asked them what noise they made. My lord, said Agravaine, I shall tell you that I may keep no longer. Here is I, and my brother Sir Mordred, brake unto my brothers Sir Gawaine, Sir Gaheris, and to Sir Gareth, how this we know all, that Sir Launcelot holdest your queen, and hath done long; and we be your sister's sons, and we may suffer it no longer, and all we wot that ye should be above Sir Launcelot; and ye are the king that made him knight, and therefore we will prove it, that he is [340] a traitor to your person. If it be so, said Sir Arthur, wit you well he is none other, but I would be loath to begin such a thing but I might have proofs upon it; for Sir Launcelot is an hardy knight, and all ye know he is the best knight among us all; and but if he be taken with the deed, he will fight with him that bringeth up the noise, and I know no knight that is able to match him. Therefore an it be sooth as ye say, I would he were taken with the deed. For as the French book saith, the king was full loath thereto, that any noise should be upon Sir Launcelot and his queen; for the king had a deeming, but he would not hear of it, for Sir Launcelot

had done so much for him and the queen so many times, that wit
ye well the king loved him passingly well. My lord, said Sir Agravaine, ye shall ride to-morn on hunting, and doubt ye not Sir
Launcelot will not go with you. Then when it draweth toward
night, ye may send the queen word that ye will lie out all that
night, and so may ye send for your cooks, and then upon pain of
death we shall take him that night with the queen, and outher we
shall bring him to you dead or quick. I will well, said the king;
then I counsel you, said the king, take with you sure fellowship.
Sir, said Agravaine, my brother, Sir Mordred, and I, will take with
us twelve knights of the Round Table. Beware, said King Arthur,
for I warn you ye shall find him wight. Let us deal, said Sir Agravaine and Sir Mordred. So on the morn King Arthur rode on
hunting, and sent word to the queen that he would be out all that
night. Then Sir Agravaine and Sir Mordred gat to them twelve
knights, and hid themself in a chamber in the Castle of Carlisle,
and these were their names: Sir Colgrevance, Sir Mador de la Porte,
Sir Gingaline, Sir Meliot de Logris, Sir Petipase of Winchelsea,
Sir Galleron of Galway, Sir Melion of the mountain, Sir Asta-
more, Sir Gromore Somir Joure, Sir Curselaine, Sir Florence, Sir
Lovel. So these twelve knights were with Sir Mordred and Sir
Agravaine, and all they were of Scotland, outher of Sir Gawaine's
kin, either well-willers to his brethren. So when the night came,
Sir Launcelot told Sir Bors how he would go that night and
speak with the queen. Sir, said Sir Bors, ye shall not go this
night by my counsel. Why? said Sir Launcelot. Sir, said Sir
Bors, I dread me ever of Sir Agravaine, that waiteth you daily to
do you shame and us all; and never gave my heart against no going,
that ever ye went to the queen, so much as now; for [341] I mistrust
that the king is out this night from the queen by cause peradventure he hath lain some watch for you and the queen, and therefore
I dread me sore of treason. Have ye no dread, said Sir Launcelot,
for I shall go and come again, and make no tarrying. Sir, said Sir
Bors, that me repenteth, for I dread me sore that your going out
this night shall wrath us all. Fair nephew, said Sir Launcelot, I
marvel much why ye say thus, sithen the queen hath sent for me;
and wit ye well I will not be so much a coward, but she shall understand I will see her good grace. God speed you well, said Sir Bors,
and send you sound and safe again.

CHAPTER 3:

HOW SIR LAUNCELOT WAS ESPIED IN THE QUEEN'S CHAMBER, AND HOW SIR
AGRAVAINE AND SIR MORDRED CAME WITH TWELVE KNIGHTS TO SLAY HIM

So Sir Launcelot departed, and took his sword under
his arm, and so in his mantle that noble knight put himself in great
jeopardy; and so he passed till he came to the queen's chamber, and
then Sir Launcelot was lightly put into the chamber. And then,
as the French book saith, the queen and Launcelot were together.
And whether they were abed or at other manner of disports, me
list not hereof make no mention, for love that time was not as is
nowadays. But thus as they were together, there came Sir Agravaine and Sir Mordred, with twelve knights with them of the
Round Table, and they said with crying voice: Traitor knight, Sir
Launcelot du Lake, now art thou taken. And thus they cried with
a loud voice, that all the court might hear it; and they all fourteen
were armed at all points as they should fight in a battle. Alas, said
Queen Guenever, now are we mischieved both. Madam, said Sir
Launcelot, is there here any armour within your chamber, that I
might cover my poor body withal? An if there be any give it me,
and I shall soon stint their malice, by the grace of God. Truly,
said the queen, I have none armour, shield, sword, nor spear; wherefore I dread me sore our long love is come to a mischievous end, for
I hear by their noise there be many noble knights, and well I wot
they be surely armed; against them ye may make no resistance.
Wherefore ye are likely to be slain, and then shall I be brent. For
an ye might escape [342] them, said the queen, I would not doubt
but that ye would rescue me in what danger that ever I stood in.
Alas, said Sir Launcelot, in all my life thus was I never bestad, that
I should be thus shamefully slain for lack of mine armour. But
ever in one Sir Agravaine and Sir Mordred cried: Traitor knight,
come out of the queen's chamber, for wit thou well thou art so beset
that thou shalt not escape. O Jesu mercy, said Sir Launcelot, this
shameful cry and noise I may not suffer, for better were death at
once than thus to endure this pain. Then he took the queen in
his arms, and kissed her, and said: Most noble Christian queen, I

beseech you as ye have been ever my special good lady, and I at all
times your true poor knight unto my power, and as I never failed
you in right nor in wrong sithen the first day King Arthur made
me knight, that ye will pray for my soul if that I here be slain; for
well I am assured that Sir Bors, my nephew, and all the remnant of
my kin, with Sir Lavaine and Sir Urre, that they will not fail you
to rescue you from the fire; and therefore, mine own lady, recom-
fort yourself, whatsomever come of me, that ye go with Sir Bors,
my nephew, and Sir Urre, and they all will do you all the pleasure
that they can or may, that ye shall live like a queen upon my lands.
Nay, Launcelot, said the queen, wit thou well I will never live
after thy days, but an thou be slain I will take my death as meekly
for Jesu Christ's sake as ever did any Christian queen. Well,
madam, said Launcelot, sith it is so that the day is come that our
love must depart, wit you well I shall sell my life as dear as I may;
and a thousandfold, said Sir Launcelot, I am more heavier for you
than for myself. And now I had lever than to be lord of all
Christendom, that I had sure armour upon me, that men might
speak of my deeds or ever I were slain. Truly, said the queen, I
would an it might please God that they would take me and slay
me, and suffer you to escape. That shall never be, said Sir Launcelot, God defend me from such a shame, but Jesu be thou my shield
and mine armour! [343]

CHAPTER 4:

HOW SIR LAUNCELOT SLEW SIR COLGREVANCE, AND ARMED HIM IN HIS HARNESS, AND AFTER SLEW SIR AGRAVAINE, AND TWELVE OF HIS FELLOWS

And therewith Sir Launcelot wrapped his mantle
about his arm well and surely; and by then they had gotten a great
form out of the hall, and therewithal they rashed at the door.
Fair lords, said Sir Launcelot, leave your noise and your rashing,
and I shall set open this door, and then may ye do with me what
it liketh you. Come off then, said they all, and do it, for it availeth
thee not to strive against us all; and therefore let us into this
chamber, and we shall save thy life until thou come to King Arthur.

Then Launcelot unbarred the door, and with his left hand he held it open a little, so that but one man might come in at once; and so there came striding a good knight, a much man and large, and his name was Colgrevance of Gore, and he with a sword struck at Sir Launcelot mightily; and he put aside the stroke and gave him such a buffet upon the helmet, that he fell grovelling dead within the chamber door. And then Sir Launcelot with great might drew that dead knight within the chamber door; and Sir Launcelot with help of the queen and her ladies was lightly armed in Sir Colgrevance's armour. And ever stood Sir Agravaine and Sir Mordred crying: Traitor knight, come out of the queen's chamber. Leave your noise, said Sir Launcelot unto Sir Agravaine, for wit you well, Sir Agravaine, ye shall not prison me this night; and therefore an ye do by my counsel, go ye all from this chamber door, and make not such crying and such manner of slander as ye do; for I promise you by my knighthood, an ye will depart and make no more noise, I shall as to-morn appear afore you all before the king, and then let it be seen which of you all, outher else ye all, that will accuse me of treason; and there I shall answer you as a knight should, that hither I came to the queen for no manner of mal engine, and that will I prove and make it good upon you with my hands. Fie on thee, traitor, said Sir Agravaine and Sir Mordred, we will have thee maugre thy head, and slay thee if we list; for we let thee wit we have the choice of King Arthur to save [344] thee or to slay thee. Ah sirs, said Sir Launcelot, is there none other grace with you? then keep yourself. So then Sir Launcelot set all open the chamber door, and mightily and knightly he strode in amongst them; and anon at the first buffet he slew Sir Agravaine. And twelve of his fellows after, within a little while after, he laid them cold to the earth, for there was none of the twelve that might stand Sir Launcelot one buffet. Also Sir Launcelot wounded Sir Mordred, and he fled with all his might. And then Sir Launcelot returned again unto the queen, and said: Madam, now wit you well all our true love is brought to an end, for now will King Arthur ever be my foe; and therefore, madam, an it like you that I may have you with me, I shall save you from all manner adventures dangerous. That is not best, said the queen; meseemeth now ye have done so much harm, it will be best ye hold you still with this. And if ye see that as tomorn they will put me unto the death, then may ye rescue me as ye think best. I will well, said Sir Launcelot, for have ye no doubt, while I am living I shall rescue you. And then he kissed her, and either gave other a ring; and so there he left the queen, and went until his lodging.[345]

CHAPTER 7:

HOW SIR MORDRED RODE HASTILY TO THE KING, TO TELL HIM OF THE AFFRAY AND DEATH OF SIR AGRAVAINE AND THE OTHER KNIGHTS

Now turn we again unto Sir Mordred, that when he was escaped from the noble knight, Sir Launcelot, he anon gat his horse and mounted upon him, and rode unto King Arthur, sore wounded and smitten, and all forbled; and there he told the king all how it was, and how they were all slain save himself all only. Jesu mercy, how may this be? said the king; took ye him in the queen's chamber? Yea, so God me help, said Sir Mordred, there we found him unarmed, and there he slew Colgrevance, and armed him in his armour; and all this he told the king from the beginning to the ending. Jesu mercy, said the king, he is a marvellous knight of prowess. Alas, me sore repenteth, said the king, that ever Sir Launcelot should be against me. Now I am sure the noble fellowship of the Round Table is broken for ever, for with him will many a noble knight hold; and now it is fallen so, said the king, that I may not with my worship, but the queen must suffer the death. So then there was made great ordinance in this heat, that the queen must be judged to the death. And the law was such in those days that whatsomever they were, of what estate or degree, if they were found guilty of treason, there should be none other remedy but death; and either the men or the taking with the deed [349] should be causer of their hasty judgment. And right so was it ordained for Queen Guenever, by cause Sir Mordred was escaped sore wounded, and the death of thirteen knights of the Round Table. These proofs and experiences caused King Arthur to command the queen to the fire there to be brent. Then spake Sir Gawaine, and said: My lord Arthur, I would counsel you not to be over-hasty, but that ye would put it in respite, this judgment of my lady the queen, for many causes.   One it is, though it were so that Sir Launcelot were found in the queen's chamber, yet it might be so that he came thither for none evil; for ye know my lord, said Sir Gawaine, that the queen is much beholden unto Sir Launcelot, more than unto any other knight, for ofttimes he hath saved her life, and done battle for her when all the court refused the queen; and peradventure she sent for him for goodness and for none evil, to reward him for his good deeds that he had done to her in times past.   And peradventure my lady, the queen, sent for him to that intent that Sir Launcelot should come to her good grace privily and secretly, weening to her that it was best so to do, in eschewing and dreading of slander; for ofttimes we do many things that we ween it be for the best, and yet peradventure it turneth to the worst.   For I dare say, said Sir Gawaine, my lady, your queen, is to you both good and true; and as for Sir Launcelot, said Sir Gawaine, I dare say he will make it good upon any knight living that will put upon himself villainy or shame, and in like wise he will make good for my lady, Dame Guenever.   That I believe well, said King Arthur, but I will not that way with Sir Launcelot, for he trusteth so much upon his hands and his might that he doubteth no man; and therefore for my queen he shall never fight more, for she shall have the law. And if I may get Sir Launcelot, wit you well he shall have a shameful death.   Jesu defend, said Sir Gawaine, that I may never see it. Why say ye so? said King Arthur; forsooth ye have no cause to love Sir Launcelot, for this night last past he slew your brother, Sir Agravaine, a full good knight, and almost he had slain your other brother, Sir Mordred, and also there he slew thirteen noble knights; and also, Sir Gawaine, remember ye he slew two sons of yours, Sir Florence and Sir Lovel.   My lord, said Sir Gawaine, of all this I have knowledge, of whose deaths I repent me sore; but insomuch I gave them warning, and told my brethren and my sons [350] aforehand what would fall in the end, insomuch they would not do by my counsel, I will not meddle me thereof, nor revenge me nothing of their deaths; for I told them it was no boot to strive with Sir Launcelot.   Howbeit I am sorry of the death of my brethren and of my sons, for they are the causers of their own death; for ofttimes I warned my brother Sir Agravaine, and I told him the perils the which be now fallen.

CHAPTER 8:

HOW SIR LAUNCELOT AND HIS KINSMEN RESCUED THE QUEEN FROM THE FIRE,
AND HOW HE SLEW MANY KNIGHTS

Then said the noble King Arthur to Sir Gawaine: Dear nephew, I pray you make you ready in your best armour, with your brethren, Sir Gaheris and Sir Gareth, to bring my queen to the fire, there to have her judgment and receive the death. Nay, my most noble lord, said Sir Gawaine, that will I never do; for wit you well I will never be in that place where so noble a queen as is my lady, Dame Guencver, shall take a shameful end. For wit you well, said Sir Gawaine, my heart will never serve me to see her die; and it shall never be said that ever I was of your counsel of her death. Then said the king to Sir Gawaine: Suffer your brothers Sir Gaheris and Sir Gareth to be there. My lord, said Sir Gawaine, wit you well they will be loath to be there present, by cause of many adventures the which be like there to fall, but they are young and full unable to say you nay. Then spake Sir Gaheris, and the good knight Sir Gareth, unto Sir Arthur: Sir, ye may well command us to be there, but wit you well it shall be sore against our will; but an we be there by your straight commandment ye shall plainly hold us there excused: we will be there in peaceable wise, and bear none harness of war upon us. In the name of God, said the king, then make you ready, for she shall soon have her judgment anon. Alas, said Sir Gawaine, that ever I should endure to see this woful day. So Sir Gawaine turned him and wept heartily, and so he went into his chamber; and then the queen was led forth without Carlisle, and there she was despoiled into her smock. And so then her ghostly father was brought to her, to be shriven of her misdeeds. Then was there weeping, and wailing, and [351] wringing of hands, of many lords and ladies, but there were but few in comparison that would bear any armour for to strength the death of the queen. Then was there one that Sir Launcelot had sent unto that place for to espy what time the queen should go unto her death; and anon as he saw the queen despoiled into her smock, and so shriven, then he gave Sir Launcelot warning. Then was there but spurring and plucking up of horses, and right so they came to the fire. And who that stood against them, there were they slain; there might none withstand Sir Launcelot, so all that bare arms and withstood them, there were they slain, full many a noble knight. For there was slain Sir Belliance le Orgulous, Sir Segwarides, Sir Griflet, Sir Brandiles, Sir Aglovale, Sir Tor; Sir Gauter, Sir Gillimer, Sir Reynolds' three brethren; Sir Damas, Sir Priamus, Sir Kay the Stranger, Sir Driant, Sir Lambegus, Sir Herminde; Sir Pertilope, Sir Perimones, two brethren that were called the Green Knight and the Red Knight. And so in this rushing and hurling, as Sir Launcelot thrang here and there, it mishapped him to slay Gaheris and Sir Gareth, the noble knight, for they were unarmed and unware. For as the French book saith, Sir Launcelot smote Sir Gareth and Sir Gaheris upon the brainpans, wherethrough they were slain in the field; howbeit in very truth Sir Launcelot saw them not, and so were they found dead among the thickest of the press. Then when Sir Launcelot had thus done, and slain and put to flight all that would withstand him, then he rode straight unto Dame Guenever, and made a kirtle and a gown to be cast upon her; and then he made her to be set behind him, and prayed her to be of good cheer. Wit you well the queen was glad that she was escaped from the death. And then she thanked God and Sir Launcelot; and so he rode his way with the queen, as the French book saith, unto Joyous Gard, and there he kept her as a noble knight should do; and many great lords and some kings sent Sir Launcelot many good knights, and many noble knights drew unto Sir Launcelot. When this was known openly, that King Arthur and Sir Launcelot were at debate, many knights were glad of their debate, and many were full heavy of their debate.[352]

CHAPTER 9:

OF THE SORROW AND LAMENTATION OF KING ARTHUR FOR THE DEATH OF HIS
NEPHEWS AND OTHER GOOD KNIGHTS, AND ALSO FOR THE QUEEN, HIS WIFE

So turn we again unto King Arthur, that when it was told him how and in what manner of wise the queen was taken away from the fire, and when he heard of the death of his noble knights, and in especial of Sir Gaheris and Sir Gareth's death, then the king swooned for pure sorrow. And when he awoke of his swoon, then he said: Alas, that ever I bare crown upon my head! for now have I lost the fairest fellowship of noble knights that ever held Christian king together. Alas, my good knights be slain away from me: now within these two days I have lost forty knights, and also the noble fellowship of Sir Launcelot and his blood, for now I may never hold them together no more with my worship. Alas that ever this war began. Now fair fellows, said the king, I charge you that no man tell Sir Gawaine of the death of his two brethren; for I am sure, said the king, when Sir Gawaine heareth tell that Sir Gareth is dead he will go nigh out of his mind. Mercy Jesu, said the king, why slew he Sir Gareth and Sir Gaheris, for I dare say as for Sir Gareth he loved Sir Launcelot above all men earthly. That is truth, said some knights, but they were slain in the hurtling as Sir Launcelot thrang in the thick of the press; and as they were un-armed he smote them and wist not whom that he smote, and so unhappily they were slain. The death of them, said Arthur, will cause the greatest mortal war that ever was; I am sure, wist Sir Gawaine that Sir Gareth were slain, I should never have rest of him till I had destroyed Sir Launcelot's kin and himself both, outher else he to destroy me. And therefore, said the king, wit you well my heart was never so heavy as it is now, and much more I am sorrier for my good knights' loss than for the loss of my fair queen; for queens I might have enow, but such a fellowship of good knights shall never be together in no company. And now I dare say, said King Arthur, there was never Christian king held such a fellowship together; and alas that ever Sir Launcelot and [353] I should be at debate. Ah Agravaine, Agravaine, said the king, Jesu forgive it thy soul, for thine evil will that thou and thy brother Sir Mordred hadst unto Sir Launcelot hath caused all this sorrow: and ever among these complaints the king wept and swooned. Then there came one unto Sir Gawaine, and told him how the queen was led away with Sir Launcelot, and nigh a twenty-four knights slain. O Jesu defend my brethren, said Sir Gawaine, for full well wist I that Sir Launcelot would rescue her, outher else he would die in that field; and to say the truth he had not been a man of worship had he not rescued the queen that day, insomuch she should have been brent for his sake. And as in that, said Sir Gawaine, he hath done but knightly, and as I would have done myself an I had stood in

like case. But where are my brethren? said Sir Gawaine, I marvel
I hear not of them. Truly, said that man, Sir Gareth and Sir
Gaheris be slain. Jesu defend, said Sir Gawaine, for all the world
I would not that they were slain, and in especial my good brother,
Sir Gareth. Sir, said the man, he is slain, and that is great pity.
Who slew him? said Sir Gawaine. Sir, said the man, Launcelot
slew them both. That may I not believe, said Sir Gawaine, that
ever he slew my brother, Sir Gareth; for I dare say my brother
Gareth loved him better than me, and all his brethren, and the
king both. Also I dare say, an Sir Launcelot had desired my
brother, Sir Gareth, with him he would have been with him against
the king and us all, and therefore I may never believe that Sir
Launcelot slew my brother. Sir, said this man, it is noised that he
slew him.

CHAPTER 10:

HOW KING ARTHUR AT THE REQUEST OF SIR GAWAINE CONCLUDED TO MAKE WAR AGAINST SIR LAUNCELOT, AND LAID SIEGE TO HIS CASTLE CALLED JOYOUS GARD

Alas, said Sir Gawaine, now is my joy gone. And
then he fell down and swooned, and long he lay there as he had
been dead. And then, when he arose of his swoon, he cried out
sorrowfully, and said: Alas! And right so Sir Gawaine ran to the
king, crying and weeping: O King Arthur, mine uncle, my good
brother Sir Gareth is slain,[354] and so is my brother Sir Gaheris,
the which were two noble knights. Then the king wept, and he
both; and so they fell on swooning. And when they were revived
then spake Sir Gawaine: Sir, I will go see my brother, Sir Gareth.
Ye may not see him, said the king, for I caused him to be interred,
and Sir Gaheris both; for I well understood that ye would make
over-much sorrow, and the sight of Sir Gareth should have caused
your double sorrow. Alas, my lord, said Sir Gawaine, how slew he
my brother, Sir Gareth? Mine own good lord I pray you tell me.
Truly, said the king, I shall tell you how it is told me, Sir Launcelot
slew him and Sir Gaheris both. Alas, said Sir Gawaine, they bare

none arms against him, neither of them both. I wot not how it was, said the king, but as it is said, Sir Launcelot slew them both in the thickest of the press and knew them not; and therefore let us shape a remedy for to revenge their deaths. My king, my lord, and mine uncle, said Sir Gawaine, wit you well now I shall make you a promise that I shall hold by my knighthood, that from this day I shall never fail Sir Launcelot until the one of us have slain the other. And therefore I require you, my lord and king, dress you to the war, for wit you well I will be revenged upon Sir Launcelot; and therefore, as ye will have my service and my love, now haste you thereto, and essay your friends. For I promise unto God, said Sir Gawaine, for the death of my brother, Sir Gareth, I shall seek Sir Launcelot throughout seven kings' realms, but I shall slay him or else he shall slay me. Ye shall not need to seek him so far, said the king, for as I hearsay, Sir Launcelot will abide me and you in the Joyous Gard; and much people draweth unto him, as I hearsay. That may I believe, said Sir Gawaine; but my lord, he said, essay your friends, and I will essay mine. It shall be done, said the king, and as I suppose I shall be big enough to draw him out of the biggest tower of his castle. So then the king sent letters and writs throughout all England, both in the length and the breadth, for to summon all his knights. And so unto Arthur drew many knights, dukes, and earls, so that he had a great host. And when they were assembled, the king informed them how Sir Launcelot had bereft him his queen. Then the king and all his host made them ready to lay siege about Sir Launcelot, where he lay within Joyous Gard. Thereof heard Sir Launcelot, and purveyed [355] him of many good knights, for with him held many knights; and some for his own sake, and some for the queen's sake. Thus they were on both parties well furnished and garnished of all manner of thing that longed to the war. But King Arthur's host was so big that Sir Launcelot would not abide him in the field, for he was full loth to do battle against the king; but Sir Launcelot drew him to his strong castle with all manner of victual, and as many noble men as he might suffice within the town and the castle. Then came King Arthur with Sir Gawaine with an huge host, and laid a siege all about Joyous Gard, both at the town and at the castle, and there they made strong war on both parties. But in no wise Sir Launcelot would ride out, nor go out of his castle, of long time; neither

he would none of his good knights to issue out, neither none of
the town nor of the castle, until fifteen weeks were past.

CHAPTER 11:

OF THE COMMUNICATION BETWEEN KING ARTHUR AND SIR LAUNCELOT, AND HOW KING ARTHUR REPROVED HIM

Then it befell upon a day in harvest time, Sir Launcelot looked over the walls, and spake on high unto King Arthur and
Sir Gawaine: My lords both, wit ye well all is in vain that ye make
at this siege, for here win ye no worship but maugre and dishonour;
for an it list me to come myself out and my good knights, I should
full soon make an end of this war.   Come forth, said Arthur unto
Launcelot, an thou durst, and I promise thee I shall meet thee in
middes of the field.   God defend me, said Sir Launcelot, that ever
I should encounter with the most noble king that made me knight.
Fie upon thy fair language, said the king, for wit you well and trust
it, I am thy mortal foe, and ever will to my death day; for thou hast
slain my good knights, and full noble men of my blood, that I shall
never recover again.   Also thou hast lain by my queen, and holden
her many winters, and sithen like a traitor taken her from me by
force.   My most noble lord and king, said Sir Launcelot, ye may
say what ye will, for ye wot well with yourself will I not strive; but
thereas ye say I have slain your good knights, I wot well that I
have done so, and that me sore repenteth; [356] but I was enforced
to do battle with them in saving of my life, or else I must have suffered them to have slain me.   And as for my lady, Queen Guenever,
except your person of your highness, and my lord Sir Gawaine,
there is no knight under heaven that dare make it good upon me
that ever I was traitor unto your person.   And where it please you
to say that I have holden my lady your queen years and winters,
unto that I shall ever make a large answer, and prove it upon any'
knight that beareth the life, except your person and Sir Gawaine,
that my lady, Queen Guenever, is a true lady unto your person as
any is living unto her lord, and that will I make good with my
hands.   Howbeit it hath liked her good grace to have me in charity,
and to cherish me more than any other knight; and unto my power

I again have deserved her love, for ofttimes, my lord, ye have consented that she should be brent and destroyed, in your heat, and then it fortuned me to do battle for her, and or I departed from her adversary they confessed their untruth, and she full worshipfully excused. And at such times, my lord Arthur, said Sir Launcelot, ye loved me, and thanked me when I saved your queen from the fire; and then ye promised me for ever to be my good lord; and now methinketh ye reward me full ill for my good service. And my good lord, meseemeth I had lost a great part of my worship in my knighthood an I had suffered my lady, your queen, to have been brent, and insomuch she should have been brent for my sake. For sithen I have done battles for your queen in other quarrels than in mine own, meseemeth now I had more right to do battle for her in right quarrel. And therefore my good and gracious lord, said Sir Launcelot, take your queen unto your good grace, for she is both fair, true, and good. Fie on thee, false recreant knight, said Sir Gawaine; I let thee wit my lord, mine uncle, King Arthur, shall have his queen and thee, maugre thy visage, and slay you both whether it please him. It may well be, said Sir Launcelot, but wit you well, my lord Sir Gawaine, an me list to come out of this castle ye should win me and the queen more harder than ever ye won a strong battle. Fie on thy proud words, said Sir Gawaine; as for my lady, the queen, I will never say of her shame. But thou, false and recreant knight, said Sir Gawaine, what cause hadst thou to slay my good brother Sir Gareth, that loved thee more than all my kin? Alas thou madest him [357] knight with thine own hands; why slew thou him that loved thee so well? For to excuse me, said Sir Launcelot, it helpeth me not, but by Jesu, and by the faith that I owe to the high order of knighthood, I should with as good will have slain my nephew, Sir Bors de Ganis, at that time. But alas that ever I was so unhappy, said Launcelot, that I had not seen Sir Gareth and Sir Gaheris. Thou liest, recreant knight, said Sir Gawaine, thou slewest him in despite of me; and therefore, wit thou well I shall make war to thee, and all the while that I may live. That me repenteth, said Sir Launcelot; for well I understand it helpeth not to seek none accordment while ye, Sir Gawaine, are so mischievously set. And if ye were not, I would not doubt to have the good grace of my lord Arthur. I believe it well, false recreant knight, said Sir Gawaine; for thou hast many long days overlaid me

and us all, and destroyed many of our good knights. Ye say as it
pleaseth you, said Sir Launcelot; and yet may it never be said on
me, and openly proved, that ever I by forecast of treason slew no
good knight, as my lord, Sir Gawaine, ye have done; and so did I
never, but in my defence that I was driven thereto, in saving of my
life. Ah, false knight, said Sir Gawaine, that thou meanest by Sir
Lamorak: wit thou well I slew him. Ye slew him not yourself,
said Sir Launcelot; it had been overmuch on hand for you to have
slain him, for he was one of the best knights christened of his age,
and it was great pity of his death.

CHAPTER 12:

HOW THE COUSINS AND KINSMEN OF SIR LAUNCELOT EXCITED HIM TO GO OUT TO BATTLE, AND HOW THEY MADE THEM READY

Well, well, said Sir Gawaine to Launcelot, sithen thou
upbraidest me of Sir Lamorak, wit thou well I shall never leave
thee till I have thee at such avail that thou shalt not escape my
hands. I trust you well enough, said Sir Launcelot, an ye may get
me I get but little mercy. But as the French book saith, the noble
King Arthur would have taken his queen again, and have been accorded with Sir Launcelot, but Sir Gawaine would not suffer him
by no manner of mean. And then Sir Gawaine made many men to
blow [358] upon Sir Launcelot; and all at once they called him false
recreant knight. Then when Sir Bors de Ganis, Sir Ector de Maris,
and Sir Lionel, heard this outcry, they called to them Sir Palomides,
Sir Safere's brother, and Sir Lavaine, with many more of their
blood, and all they went unto Sir Launcelot, and said thus: My lord
Sir Launcelot, wit ye well we have great scorn of the great rebukes
that we heard Gawaine say to you; wherefore we pray you, and
charge you as ye will have our service, keep us no longer within
these walls; for wit you well plainly, we will ride into the field and
do battle with them; for ye fare as a man that were afeared, and
for all your fair speech it will not avail you. For wit you well Sir
Gawaine will not suffer you to be accorded with King Arthur, and
therefore fight for your life and your right, an ye dare. Alas, said
Sir Launcelot, for to ride out of this castle, and to do battle, I am

full loath. Then Sir Launcelot spake on high unto Sir Arthur and Sir Gawaine: My lords, I require you and beseech you, sithen that I am thus required and conjured to ride into the field, that neither you, my lord King Arthur, nor you Sir Gawaine, come not into the field. What shall we do then? said Sir Gawaine, is this the king's quarrel with thee to fight? and it is my quarrel to fight with thee, Sir Launcelot, by cause of the death of my brother Sir Gareth. Then must I needs unto battle, said Sir Launcelot. Now wit you well, my lord Arthur and Sir Gawaine, ye will repent it whensomever I do battle with you. And so then they departed either from other; and then either party made them ready on the morn for to do battle, and great purveyance was made on both sides; and Sir Gawaine let purvey many knights for to wait upon Sir Launcelot, for to overset him and to slay him. And on the morn at undorne Sir Arthur was ready in the field with three great hosts. And then Sir Launcelot's fellowship came out at three gates, in a full good array; and Sir Lionel came in the foremost battle, and Sir Launcelot came in the middle, and Sir Bors came out at the third gate. Thus they came in order and rule, as full noble knights; and always Sir Launcelot charged all his knights in any wise to save King Arthur and Sir Gawaine.[359]

CHAPTER 13:

HOW SIR GAWAINE JOUSTED AND SMOTE DOWN SIR LIONEL, AND HOW SIR LAUNCELOT HORSED KING ARTHUR

Then came forth Sir Gawaine from the king's host, and he came before and proffered to joust. And Sir Lionel was a fierce knight, and lightly he encountered with Sir Gawaine; and there Sir Gawaine smote Sir Lionel throughout the body, that he dashed to the earth like as he had been dead; and then Sir Ector de Maris and other more bare him into the castle. Then there began a great stour, and much people was slain; and ever Sir Launcelot did what he might to save the people on King Arthur's party, for Sir Palomides, and Sir Bors, and Sir Safere, overthrew many knights, for they were deadly knights. And Sir Blamore de Ganis, and Sir Bleoberis de Ganis, with Sir Bellangere le Beuse, these six

knights did much harm; and ever King Arthur was nigh about Sir
Launcelot to have slain him, and Sir Launcelot suffered him, and
would not strike again. So Sir Bors encountered with King Arthur,
and there with a spear Sir Bors smote him down; and so he alit and
drew his sword, and said to Sir Launcelot: Shall I make an end of
this war? and that he meant to have slain King Arthur. Not so
hardy, said Sir Launcelot, upon pain of thy head, that thou touch
him no more, for I will never see that most noble king that made
me knight neither slain ne shamed. And therewithal Sir Launcelot
alit off his horse and took up the king and horsed him again, and
said thus: My lord Arthur, for God's love stint this strife, for ye
get here no worship, and I would do mine utterance, but always I
forbear you, and ye nor none of yours forbeareth me; my lord,
remember what I have done in many places, and now I am evil
rewarded. Then when King Arthur was on horseback, he looked
upon Sir Launcelot, and then the tears brast out of his eyen, thinking on the great courtesy that was in Sir Launcelot more than in
any other man; and therewith the king rode his way, and might no
longer behold him, and said: Alas, that ever this war began. And
then either parties of the battles withdrew [360] them to repose them,
and buried the dead, and to the wounded men they laid soft salves;
and thus they endured that night till on the morn. And on the
morn by undorne they made them ready to do battle. And then
Sir Bors led the forward. So upon the morn there came Sir
Gawaine as brym as any boar, with a great spear in his hand. And
when Sir Bors saw him he thought to revenge his brother Sir Lionel
of the despite that Sir Gawaine did him the other day. And so
they that knew either other feutred their spears, and with all their
mights of their horses and themselves, they met together so feloniously that either bare other through, and so they fell both to the
earth; and then the battles joined, and there was much slaughter
on both parties. Then Sir Launcelot rescued Sir Bors, and sent
him into the castle; but neither Sir Gawaine nor Sir Bors died not
of their wounds, for they were all holpen. Then Sir Lavaine and
Sir Urre prayed Sir Launcelot to do his pain, and fight as they had
done; For we see ye forbear and spare, and that doth much harm;
therefore we pray you spare not your enemies no more than they
do you. Alas, said Sir Launcelot, I have no heart to fight against
my lord Arthur, for ever meseemeth I do not as I ought to do. My

lord, said Sir Palomides, though ye spare them all this day they will never conne you thank; and if they may get you at avail ye are but dead. So then Sir Launcelot understood that they said him truth; and then he strained himself more than he did aforehand, and by cause his nephew Sir Bors was sore wounded. And then within a little while, by evensong time, Sir Launcelot and his party better stood, for their horses went in blood past the fetlocks, there was so much people slain. And then for pity Sir Launcelot withheld his knights, and suffered King Arthur's party for to withdraw them on side. And then Sir Launcelot's party withdrew them into his castle, and either parties buried the dead, and put salve unto the wounded men. So when Sir Gawaine was hurt, they on King Arthur's party were not so orgulous as they were toforehand to do battle. Of this war was noised through all Christendom, and at the last it was noised afroe the Pope; and he considering the great goodness of King Arthur, and of Sir Launcelot, that was called the most noblest knights of the world, wherefore the Pope called unto him a noble clerk that at that time was there present; the French book saith, it was the Bishop of Rochester; and [361] the Pope gave him bulls under lead unto King Arthur of England, charging him upon pain of interdicting of all England, that he take his queen Dame Guenever unto him again, and accord with Sir Launcelot.

CHAPTER 14:

So when this Bishop was come to Carlisle he shewed the king these bulls. And when the king understood these bulls he nyst what to do: full fain he would have been accorded with Sir Launcelot, but Sir Gawaine would not suffer him; but as for to have the queen, thereto he agreed. But in nowise Sir Gawaine would not suffer the king to accord with Sir Launcelot; but as for the queen he consented. And then the Bishop had of the king his great seal, and his assurance as he was a true anointed king that Sir Launcelot should come safe, and go safe, and that the queen should not be spoken unto of the king, nor of none other, for no thing done afore time past; and of all these appointments the Bishop brought with him sure assurance and writing, to shew Sir Launcelot. So when the Bishop was come to Joyous Gard, there he shewed Sir Launcelot how the Pope had written to Arthur and unto him, and there he told him the perils if he withheld the queen from the king. It was never in my thought, said Launcelot, to withhold the queen from my lord Arthur; but, insomuch she should have been dead for my sake, meseemeth it was my part to save her life, and put her from that danger, till better recovery might come. And now I thank God, said Sir Launcelot, that the Pope hath made her peace; for God knoweth, said Sir Launcelot, I will be a thousandfold more gladder to bring her again, than ever I was of her taking away; with this, I may be sure to come safe and go safe, and that the queen shall have her liberty as she had before; and never for no thing that hath been surmised afore this time, she never from this day stand in no peril. For else, said Sir Launcelot, I dare adventure me to keep her from [362] an harder shoure than ever I kept her. It shall not need you, said the Bishop, to dread so much; for wit you well, the Pope must be obeyed, and it were not the Pope's worship nor my poor honesty to wit you distressed, neither the queen, neither in peril, nor shamed. And then he shewed Sir Launcelot all his writing, both from the Pope and from King Arthur. This is sure enough, said Sir Launcelot, for full well I dare trust my lord's own writing and his seal, for he was never shamed of his promise. Therefore, said Sir Launcelot unto the Bishop, ye shall ride unto the king afore, and recommend me unto his good grace, and let him have knowledging that this same day eight days, by the grace of God, I myself shall bring my lady, Queen Guenever, unto him. And then say ye unto my most redoubted king, that I will say largely for the queen, that I shall none except for dread nor fear, but the king himself, and my lord Sir Gawaine; and that is more for the king's love than for himself. So the Bishop departed and came to the king at Carlisle, and told him all how Sir Launcelot answered him; and then the tears brast out of the king's eyen. Then Sir Launcelot purveyed him an hundred knights, and all were clothed in green velvet, and their horses trapped to their heels; and every knight held a branch of olive in his hand, in tokening of peace. And the queen had four and twenty gentlewomen following her in the same wise; and Sir Launcelot had twelve coursers following him, and on every courser sat a young gentleman, and all they were arrayed in green velvet, with sarpys of gold about their quarters, and the horse trapped in the same wise down to the heels, with many ouches, set with stones and pearls in gold, to the number of a thousand. And she and Sir Launcelot were clothed in white cloth of gold tissue; and right so as ye have heard, as the French book maketh mention, he rode with the queen from Joyous Gard to Carlisle. And so Sir Launcelot rode throughout Carlisle, and so in the castle, that all men might behold; and wit you well there was many a weeping eye. And then Sir Launcelot himself alit and avoided his horse, and took the Queen, and so led her where King Arthur was in his seat: and Sir Gawaine sat afore him, and many other great lords. So when Sir Launcelot saw the king and Sir Gawaine, then he led the queen by the arm, and then he kneeled down, and the queen both. Wit you well then was there many bold knight there with King Arthur that wept as ten- [363] derly as though they had seen all their kin afore them. So the king sat still, and said no word. And when Sir Launcelot saw his countenance, he arose and pulled up the queen with him, and thus he spake full knightly.

CHAPTER 15:

OF THE DELIVERANCE OF THE QUEEN TO THE KING BY SIR LAUNCELOT, AND WHAT LANGUAGE SIR GAWAINE HAD TO SIR LAUNCELOT

My most redoubted king, ye shall understand, by the Pope's commandment and yours, I have brought to you my lady the queen, as right requireth; and if there be any knight, of whatsomever degree that he be, except your person, that will say or dare say but that she is true and clene to you, I here myself, Sir Launcelot du Lake, will make it good upon his body, that she is a true lady unto you; but liars ye have listened, and that hath caused debate betwixt you and me. For time hath been, my lord Arthur, that ye have been greatly pleased with me when I did battle for my lady, your queen; and full well ye know, my most noble king, that she hath been put to great wrong or this time; and sithen it pleased you at many times that I should fight for her, meseemeth, my good lord, I had more cause to rescue her from the fire, insomuch she should have been brent for my sake. For they that told you those tales were liars, and so it fell upon them; for by likelihood had not the might of God been with me, I might never have endured fourteen knights, and they armed and afore purposed, and I unarmed and not purposed. For I was sent for unto my lady your queen, I wot not for what cause; but I was not so soon within the chamber door, but anon Sir Agravaine and Sir Mordred called me traitor and recreant knight. They called thee right, said Sir Gawaine. My lord Sir Gawaine, said Sir Launcelot, in their quarrel they proved themselves not in the right. Well well, Sir Launcelot, said the king, I have given thee no cause to do to me as thou hast done, for I have worshipped thee and thine more than any of all my knights. My good lord, said Sir Launcelot, so ye be not displeased, ye shall understand I and mine have done you oft better service than any other knights [364] have done, in many diverse places; and where ye have been full hard bestad divers times, I have myself rescued you from many dangers; and ever unto my power I was glad to please you, and my lord Sir Gawaine; both in jousts, and tournaments, and in battles set, both on horseback and on foot, I have often rescued you, and my lord Sir Gawaine, and many more of your knights in many diverse places. For now I will make avaunt, said Sir Launcelot, I will that ye all wit that yet I found never no manner of knight but that I was overhard for him, an I had done my utterance, thanked be God; howbeit I have been matched with good knights, as Sir Tristram and Sir Lamorak, but ever I had a favour unto them and a deeming what they were. And I take God to record, said Sir Launcelot, I never was wroth nor greatly heavy with no good knight an I saw him busy about to win worship; and glad I was ever when I found any knight that might endure me on horseback and on foot: howbeit Sir Carados of the Dolorous Tower was a full noble knight and a passing strong man, and that wot ye, my lord Sir Gawaine; for he might well be called a noble knight when he by fine force pulled you out of your saddle, and bound you overthwart afore him to his saddle bow; and there, my lord Sir Gawaine, I rescued you, and slew him afore your sight. Also I found his brother, Sir Turquin, in likewise leading Sir Gaheris, your brother, bounden afore him; and there I rescued your brother and slew that Turquin, and delivered three score and four of my lord Arthur's knights out of his prison. And now I dare say, said Sir Launcelot, I met never with so strong knights, nor so well fighting, as was Sir Carados and Sir Turquin, for I fought with them to the uttermost. And therefore, said Sir Launcelot unto Sir Gawaine, meseemeth ye ought of right to remember this; for, an I might have your good will, I would trust to God to have my lord Arthur's good grace.[365]

CHAPTER 16:

OF THE COMMUNICATION BETWEEN SIR GAWAINE AND SIR LAUNCELOT, WITH MUCH OTHER LANGUAGE

The king may do as he will, said Sir Gawaine, but wit thou well, Sir Launcelot, thou and I shall never be accorded while we live, for thou hast slain three of my brethren; and two of them ye slew traitorly and piteously, for they bare none harness against thee, nor none would bear. God would they had been armed, said Sir Launcelot, for then had they been on live. And wit ye well Sir Gawaine, as for Sir Gareth, I love none of my kinsmen so much as I did him; and ever while I live, said Sir Launcelot, I will bewail Sir Gareth's death, not all only for the great fear I have of you, but many causes cause me to be sorrowful. One is, for I made him knight; another is, I wot well he loved me above all other knights; and the third is, he was passing noble, true, courteous, and gentle, and well conditioned; the fourth is, I wist well, anon as I heard that Sir Gareth was dead, I should never after have your love, but everlasting war betwixt us; and also I wist well that ye would cause my noble lord Arthur for ever to be my mortal foe. And as Jesu be my help, said Sir Launcelot, I slew never Sir Gareth nor Sir Gaheris by my will; but alas that ever they were unarmed that unhappy day. But thus much I shall offer me, said Sir Launcelot, if it may please the king's good grace, and you, my lord Sir Gawaine, I shall first begin at Sandwich, and there I shall go in my shirt, bare foot; and at every ten miles' end I will found and garmake an house of religion, of what order that ye will assign me, with an whole convent, to sing and read, day and night, in especial for Sir Gareth's sake and Sir Gaheris. And this shall I perform from

Sandwich unto Carlisle; and every house shall have sufficient livelihood. And this shall I perform while I have any livelihood in
Christendom; and there nys none of all these religious places, but
they shall be performed, furnished and garnished in all things as an
holy place ought to be, I promise you faithfully. And this, Sir
Gawaine, methinketh were more fairer, holier, and more better to
their souls, than [366] ye, my most noble king, and you, Sir Gawaine,
to war upon me, for thereby shall ye get none avail. Then all
knights and ladies that were there wept as they were mad, and the
tears fell on King Arthur's cheeks. Sir Launcelot, said Sir Gawaine,
I have right well heard thy speech, and thy great proffers, but wit
thou well, let the king do as it pleased him, I will never forgive my
brothers' death, and in especial the death of my brother, Sir Gareth.
And if mine uncle, King Arthur, will accord with thee, he shall
lose my service, for wit thou well thou art both false to the king and
to me. Sir, said Launcelot, he beareth not the life that may make
that good; and if ye, Sir Gawaine, will charge me with so high a
thing, ye must pardon me, for then needs must I answer you. Nay,
said Sir Gawaine, we are past that at this time, and that caused the
Pope, for he hath charged mine uncle, the king, that he shall take
his queen again, and to accord with thee, Sir Launcelot, as for this
season, and therefore thou shalt go safe as thou camest. But in this
land thou shalt not abide past fifteen days, such summons I give
thee: so the king and we were consented and accorded or thou
camest. And else, said Sir Gawaine, wit thou well thou shouldst
not have come here, but if it were maugre thy head. And if it
were not for the Pope's commandment, said Sir Gawaine, I should
do battle with mine own body against thy body, and prove it upon
thee, that thou hast been both false unto mine uncle King Arthur,
and to me both; and that shall I prove upon thy body, when thou
art departed from hence, wheresomever I find thee.[367]

CHAPTER 18:

HOW SIR LAUNCELOT PASSED OVER THE SEA, AND HOW HE MADE GREAT LORDS OF THE KNIGHTS THAT WENT WITH HIM

. . . For ever I dread me, said Sir Launcelot, that Sir
Mordred will make trouble, for he is passing envious and applieth

him to trouble. So they were accorded to go with Sir Launcelot to
his lands; and to make short tale, they trussed, and paid all that
would ask them; and wholly an hundred knights departed with Sir
Launcelot at once, and made their avows they would never leave
him for weal nor for woe. And so they shipped at Cardiff, and
sailed unto Benwick: some men call it Bayonne, and some men call
it Beaune, where the wine of Beaune is. But to say the sooth, Sir
Launcelot and his nephews were lords of all France, and of all the
lands that longed unto France; he and his kindred rejoiced it all
through Sir Launcelot's noble prowess. And then Sir Launcelot
stuffed and furnished and garnished all his noble towns and castles.
Then all the people of those lands came to Sir Launcelot on foot
and hands. And so when he had stablished all these countries, he
shortly called a parliament; and there he crowned Sir Lionel, King
of France; and Sir Bors crowned him king of all King Claudas'
lands; and Sir Ector de Maris, that was Sir Launcelot's youngest
brother, he crowned him King of Benwick, and king of all Guienne,
that was Sir Launcelot's own land.[370] . . . Thus Sir Launcelot
rewarded his noble knights and many more, that meseemeth it were
too long to rehearse.

CHAPTER 19:

HOW KING ARTHUR AND SIR GAWAINE MADE A GREAT HOST READY TO GO OVER SEA TO MAKE WAR ON SIR LAUNCELOT

So leave we Sir Launcelot in his lands, and his noble
knights with him, and return we again unto King Arthur and to
Sir Gawaine, that made a great host ready, to the number of threescore thousand; and all thing was made ready for their shipping to
pass over the sea, and so they shipped at Cardiff. And there King
Arthur made Sir Mordred chief ruler of all England, and also he
put Queen Guenever under his governance; by cause Sir Mordred
was King Arthur's son, he gave him the rule of his land and of
his wife; and so the king passed the sea and landed upon Sir Launcelot's lands, and there he brent and wasted, through the vengeance
of Sir Gawaine, all that they might overrun. When this word came
to Sir Launcelot, that King Arthur and Sir Gawaine were landed

upon his lands, and 'made a full great destruction and waste, then spake Sir Bors, and said: My lord Sir Launcelot, it is shame that we suffer them thus to ride over our lands, for wit you well, suffer ye them as long as ye will, they will do you no favour an they may handle you. Then said Sir Lionel that was wary and wise: My lord Sir Launcelot, I will give this counsel, let us keep our strong walled towns until they have [371] hunger and cold, and blow on their nails; and then let us freshly set upon them, and shred them down as sheep in a field, that aliens may take example for ever how they land upon our lands. Then spake King Bagdemagus to Sir Launcelot: Sir, your courtesy will shende us all, and thy courtesy hath waked all this sorrow; for an they thus over our lands ride, they shall by process bring us all to nought whilst we thus in holes us hide. Then said Sir Galihud unto Sir Launcelot: Sir, here be knights come of kings' blood, that will not long droop, and they are within these walls; therefore give us leave, like as we be knights, to meet them in the field, and we shall slay them, that they shall curse the time that ever they came into this country. Then spake seven brethren of North Wales, and they were seven noble knights; a man might seek in seven kings' lands or he might find such seven knights. Then they all said at once: Sir Launcelot, for Christ's sake let us out ride with Sir Galihud, for we be never wont to cower in castles nor in noble towns. Then spake Sir Launcelot, that was master and governor of them all: My fair lords, wit you well I am full loath to ride out with my knights for shedding of Christian blood; and yet my lands I understand be full bare for to sustain any host awhile, for the mighty wars that whilom made King Claudas upon this country, upon my father King Ban, and on mine uncle King Bors; howbeit we will as at this time keep our strong walls, and I shall send a messenger unto my lord Arthur, a treaty for to take; for better is peace than always war. So Sir Launcelot sent forth a damosel and a dwarf with her, requiring King Arthur to leave his warring upon his lands; and so she start upon a palfrey, and the dwarf ran by her side. And when she came to the pavilion of King Arthur, there she alit; and there met her a gentle knight, Sir Lucan the Butler, and said: Fair damosel, come ye from Sir Launcelot du Lake? Yea sir, she said, therefore I come hither to speak with my lord the king. Alas, said Sir Lucan, my lord Arthur would love Launcelot, but Sir Gawaine will not suffer him. And then he said:

I pray to God, damosel, ye may speed well, for all we that be about
the king would Sir Launcelot did best of any knight living. And so
with this Lucan led the damosel unto the king where he sat with
Sir Gawaine, for to hear what she would say. So when she had
told her tale, the water ran out of the king's eyen, and all [372] the
lords were full glad for to advise the king as to be accorded with Sir
Launcelot, save all only Sir Gawaine, and he said: My lord mine
uncle, what will ye do? Will ye now turn again now ye are passed
thus far upon this journey? all the world will speak of your villainy.
Nay, said Arthur, wit thou well, Sir Gawaine, I will do as ye will advise me; and yet meseemeth, said Arthur, his fair proffers were not
good to be refused; but sithen I am come so far upon this journey,
I will that ye give the damosel her answer, for I may not speak to
her for pity, for her proffers be so large.

CHAPTER 20:

WHAT MESSAGE SIR GAWAINE SENT TO SIR LAUNCELOT; AND KING ARTHUR LAID SIEGE TO BENWICK, AND OTHER MATTERS

Then Sir Gawaine said to the damosel thus: Damosel,
say ye to Sir Launcelot that it is waste labour now to sue to mine
uncle; for tell him, an he would have made any labour for peace,
he should have made it or this time, for tell him now it is too late;
and say that I, Sir Gawaine, so send him word, that I promise him
by the faith I owe unto God and to knighthood, I shall never leave
him till he hath slain me or I him. So the damosel wept and departed, and there were many weeping eyen; and so Sir Lucan
brought the damosel to her palfrey, and so she came to Sir Launcelot where he was among all his knights. And when Sir Launcelot
had heard this answer, then the tears ran down by his cheeks.
And then his noble knights strode about him, and said: Sir Launcelot, wherefore make ye such cheer, think what ye are, and what men
we are, and let us noble knights match them in middes of the field.
That may be lightly done, said Sir Launcelot, but I was never so
loath to do battle, and therefore I pray you, fair sirs, as ye love me,
be ruled as I will have you, for I will always flee that noble king
that made me knight. And when I may no further, I must needs

defend me, and that will be more worship for me and us all than to compare with that noble king whom we have all served. Then they held their language, and as that night they took their rest. And upon the morn early, in the dawning of the day, as knights looked out, they saw the city of Benwick besieged round about; [373] and fast they began to set up ladders, and then they defied them out of the town, and beat them from the walls mightily. Then came forth Sir Gawaine well armed upon a stiff steed, and he came before the chief gate, with his spear in his hand, crying: Sir Launcelot, where art thou? is there none of you proud knights dare break a spear with me? Then Sir Bors made him ready, and came forth out of the town, and there Sir Gawaine encountered with Sir Bors. And at that time he smote Sir Bors down from his horse, and almost he had slain him; and so Sir Bors was rescued and borne into the town. Then came forth Sir Lionel, brother to Sir Bors, and thought to revenge him; and either feutred their spears, and ran together; and there they met spitefully, but Sir Gawaine had such grace that he smote Sir Lionel down, and wounded him there passing sore; and then Sir Lionel was rescued and borne into the town. And this Sir Gawaine came every day, and he failed not but that he smote down one knight or other. So thus they endured half a year, and much slaughter was of people on both parties. Then it befell upon a day, Sir Gawaine came afore the gates armed at all pieces on a noble horse, with a great spear in his hand; and then he cried with a loud voice: Where art thou now, thou false traitor, Sir Launcelot? Why hidest thou thyself within holes and walls like a coward? Look out now, thou false traitor knight, and here I shall revenge upon thy body the death of my three brethren. All this language heard Sir Launcelot every dele; and his kin and his knights drew about him, and all they said at once to Sir Launcelot: Sir Launcelot, now must ye defend you like a knight, or else ye be shamed for ever; for, now ye be called upon treason, it is time for you to stir, for ye have slept over-long and suffered over-much. So God me help, said Sir Launcelot, I am right heavy of Sir Gawaine's words, for now he charged me with a great charge; and therefore I wot it as well as ye, that I must defend me, or else to be recreant. Then Sir Launcelot bad saddle his strongest horse, and bad let fetch his arms, and bring all unto the gate of the tower; and then Sir Launcelot spake on high unto King Arthur, and said: My lord Arthur, and noble king that made me knight, wit you well I am right heavy for your sake, that ye thus sue upon me; and always I forbare you, for an would I have been vengeable, I might have met you in middes of the field, and there to have made your boldest knights full tame. And [374] now I have forborne half a year, and suffered you and Sir Gawaine to do what ye would do; and now may I endure it no longer, for now must I needs defend myself, insomuch Sir Gawaine hath appelled me of treason; the which is greatly against my will that ever I should fight against any of your blood, but now I may not forsake it, I am driven thereto as a beast till a bay. Then Sir Gawaine said: Sir Launcelot, an thou durst do battle, leave thy babbling and come off, and let us ease our hearts. Then Sir Launcelot armed him lightly, and mounted upon his horse, and either of the knights gat great spears in their hands, and the host without stood still all apart, and the noble knights came out of the city by a great number, insomuch that when Arthur saw the number of men and knights, he marvelled, and said to himself: Alas, that ever Sir Launcelot was against me, for now I see he hath forborne me. And so the covenant was made, there should no man nigh them, nor deal with them, till the one were dead or yelden.

CHAPTER 21:

HOW SIR GAWAINE AND SIR LAUNCELOT DID BATTLE TOGETHER, AND HOW SIR GAWAINE WAS OVERTHROWN AND HURT

Then Sir Gawaine and Sir Launcelot departed a great way in sunder, and then they came together with all their horses' might as they might run, and either smote other in middes of their shields; but the knights were so strong, and their spears so big, that their horses might not endure their buffets, and so their horses fell to the earth; and then they avoided their horses, and dressed their shields before them. Then they stood together and gave many sad strokes on divers places of their bodies, that the blood brast out on many sides and places. Then had Sir Gawaine such a grace and gift that an holy man had given to him, that every day in the year, from undern till high noon, his might increased those three hours

as much as thrice his strength, and that caused Sir Gawaine to win
great honour. And for his sake King Arthur made an ordinance,
that all manner of battles for any quarrels that should be done
afore King Arthur should begin at underne; and all was done for
Sir Gawaine's love, that by likelihood, if Sir Gawaine were on the
one part,[375] he should have the better in battle while his strength
endureth three hours; but there were but few knights that time living that knew this advantage that Sir Gawaine had, but King Arthur
all only. Thus Sir Launcelot fought with Sir Gawaine, and when
Sir Launcelot felt his might evermore increase, Sir Launcelot wondered and dread him sore to be shamed. For as the French book
saith, Sir Launcelot weened, when he felt Sir Gawaine double his
strength, that he had been a fiend and none earthly man; wherefore Sir Launcelot traced and traversed, and covered himself with
his shield, and kept his might and his braide during three hours;
and that while Sir Gawaine gave him many sad brunts, and many
sad strokes, that all the knights that beheld Sir Launcelot marvelled
how that he might endure him; but full little understood they that
travail that Sir Launcelot had for to endure him. And then when
it was past noon Sir Gawaine had no more but his own might.
When Sir Launcelot felt him so come down, then he stretched him
up and stood near Sir Gawaine, and said thus: My lord Sir Gawaine,
now I feel ye have done; now my lord Sir Gawaine, I must do my
part, for many great and grievous strokes I have endured you this
day with great pain. Then Sir Launcelot doubled his strokes and
gave Sir Gawaine such a buffet on the helmet that he fell down on
his side, and Sir Launcelot withdrew him from him. Why with-
drawest thou thee? said Sir Gawaine; now turn again, false traitor
knight, and slay me, for an thou leave me thus, when I am whole
I shall do battle with thee again. I shall endure you, Sir, by God's
grace, but wit thou well, Sir Gawaine, I will never smite a felled
knight. And so Sir Launcelot went into the city; and Sir Gawaine
was borne into King Arthur's pavilion, and leeches were brought
to him, and searched and salved with soft ointments. And then
Sir Launcelot said: Now have good day, my lord the king, for wit
you well ye win no worship at these walls; and if I would my
knights outbring, there should many a man die. Therefore, my
lord Arthur, remember you of old kindness; and however I fare,
Jesu be your guide in all places.[376]

Chapter 22:

OF THE SORROW THAT KING ARTHUR MADE FOR THE WAR, AND OF ANOTHER BATTLE WHERE ALSO SIR GAWAINE HAD THE WORSE

Alas, said the king, that ever this unhappy war was begun; for ever Sir Launcelot forbeareth me in all places, and in likewise my kin, and that is seen well this day by my nephew Sir Gawaine. Then King Arthur fell sick for sorrow of Sir Gawaine, that he was so sore hurt, and by cause of the war betwixt him and Sir Launcelot. So then they on King Arthur's part kept the siege with little war withoutforth; and they withinforth kept their walls, and defended them when need was. Thus Sir Gawaine lay sick three weeks in his tents, with all manner of leechcraft that might be had. And as soon as Sir Gawaine might go and ride, he armed him at all points, and start upon a courser, and gat a spear in his hand, and so he came riding afore the chief gate of Benwick; and there he cried on height: Where art thou, Sir Launcelot? Come forth, thou false traitor knight and recreant, for I am here, Sir Gawaine, will prove this that I say on thee. All this language Sir Launcelot heard, and then he said thus: Sir Gawaine, me repents of your foul saying, that ye will not cease of your language; for you wot well, Sir Gawaine, I know your might and all that ye may do; and well ye wot, Sir Gawaine, ye may not greatly hurt me. Come down, traitor knight, said he, and make it good the contrary with thy hands, for it mishapped me the last battle to be hurt of thy hands; therefore wit thou well I am come this day to make amends, for I ween this day to lay thee as low as thou laidest me. Jesu defend me, said Sir Launcelot, that ever I be so far in your danger as ye have been in mine, for then my days were done. But Sir Gawaine, said Sir Launcelot, ye shall not think that I tarry long, but sithen that ye so unknightly call me of treason, ye shall have both your hands full of me. And then Sir Launcelot armed him at all points, and mounted upon his horse, and gat a great spear in his hand, and rode out at the gate. And both the hosts were assembled, of them without and of them within, and stood in array full manly. And both parties were charged to hold them still, to see and behold the battle of [377] these two noble knights. And then they laid their spears in their rests, and they came together as thunder, and Sir Gawaine brake his spear upon Sir Launcelot in a hundred pieces unto his hand; and Sir Launcelot smote him with a greater might, that Sir Gawaine's horse's feet raised, and so the horse and he fell to the earth. Then Sir Gawaine deliverly avoided his horse, and put his shield afore him, and eagerly drew his sword, and bad Sir Launcelot: Alight, traitor knight, for if this mare's son hath failed me, wit thou well a king's son and a queen's son shall not fail thee. Then Sir Launcelot avoided his horse, and dressed his shield afore him, and drew his sword; and so stood they together and gave many sad strokes, that all men on both parties had thereof passing great wonder. But when Sir Launcelot felt Sir Gawaine's might so marvellously increase, he then withheld his courage and his wind, and kept himself wonder covert of his might; and under his shield he traced and traversed here and there, to break Sir Gawaine's strokes and his courage; and Sir Gawaine enforced himself with all his might and power to destroy Sir Launcelot; for as the French book saith, ever as Sir Gawaine's might increased, right so increased his wind and his evil will. Thus Sir Gawaine did great pain unto Sir Launcelot three hours, that he had right great pain for to defend him. And when the three hours were passed, that Sir Launcelot felt that Sir Gawaine was come to his own proper strength, then Sir Launcelot said unto Sir Gawaine: Now have I proved you twice, that ye are a full dangerous knight, and a wonderful man of your might; and many wonderful deeds have you done in your days, for by your might increasing you have deceived many a full noble and valiant knight; and, now I feel that ye have done your mighty deeds, now wit you well I must do my deeds. And then Sir Launcelot stood near Sir Gawaine, and then Sir Launcelot doubled his strokes; and Sir Gawaine defended him mightily, but nevertheless Sir Launcelot smote such a stroke upon Sir Gawaine's helm, and upon the old wound, that Sir Gawaine sinked down upon his one side in a swoon. And anon as he did awake he waved and foined at Sir Launcelot as he lay, and said: Traitor knight, wit thou well I am not yet slain, come thou near me and perform this battle unto the uttermost. I will no more do than I have done, said Sir Launcelot, for when I see you on foot I will do battle upon [378] you all the while I see you stand on your feet; but for to smite a wounded man that may not stand, God defend me from such a shame. And then he turned him and went his way toward the city. And Sir Gawaine evermore calling him traitor knight, and said: Wit thou well Sir Launcelot, when I am whole I shall do battle with thee again, for I shall never leave thee till that one of us be slain. Thus as this siege endured, and as Sir Gawaine lay sick near a month; and when he was well recovered and ready within three days to do battle again with Sir Launcelot, right so came tidings unto Arthur from England that made King Arthur and all his host to remove.

Book XXI, Chapter 1:

HOW SIR MORDRED PRESUMED AND TOOK ON HIM TO BE KING OF ENGLAND, AND WOULD HAVE MARRIED THE QUEEN, HIS UNCLE'S WIFE

As Sir Mordred was ruler of all England, he did do make letters as though that they came from beyond the sea, and the letters specified that King Arthur was slain in battle with Sir Launcelot. Wherefore Sir Mordred made a parliament, and called the lords together, and there he made them to choose him king; and so was he crowned at Canterbury, and held a feast there fifteen days; and afterward he drew him unto Winchester, and there he took the Queen Guenever, and said plainly that he would wed her which was his uncle's wife and his father's wife. And so he made ready for the feast, and a day prefixed that they should be wedded; wherefore Queen Guenever was passing heavy. But she durst not discover her heart, but spake fair, and agreed to Sir Mordred's will. Then she desired of Sir Mordred for to go to London, to buy all manner of things that longed unto the wedding. And by cause of her fair speech Sir Mordred trusted her well enough, and gave her leave to go. And so when she came to London she [379] took the Tower of London, and suddenly in all haste possible she stuffed it with all manner of victual, and well garnished it with men, and so kept it. Then when Sir Mordred wist and understood how he was beguiled, he was passing wroth out of measure. And a short tale for to make, he went and laid a mighty siege about the Tower of London, and made many great assaults thereat, and threw many great engines unto them, and shot great guns. But all might not prevail Sir Mordred, for Queen Guenever would never for fair speech nor for foul, would never trust to come in his hands again. Then came the Bishop of Canterbury, the which was a noble clerk and an holy man, and thus he said to Sir Mordred: Sir, what will ye do? will ye first displease God and sithen shame yourself, and all knighthood? Is not King Arthur your uncle, no farther but your mother's brother, and on her himself King Arthur begat you upon his own sister, therefore how may you wed your father's wife? Sir, said the noble clerk, leave this opinion or I shall curse you with book and bell and candle. Do thou thy worst, said Sir Mordred, wit thou well I shall defy thee. Sir, said the Bishop, and wit you well I shall not fear me to do that me ought to do. Also where ye noise where my lord Arthur is slain, and that is not so, and therefore ye will make a foul work in this land. Peace, thou false priest, said Sir Mordred, for an thou chafe me any more I shall make strike off thy head. So the Bishop departed and did the cursing in the most orgulist wise that might be done. And then Sir Mordred sought the Bishop of Canterbury, for to have slain him. Then the Bishop fled, and took part of his goods with him, and went nigh unto Glastonbury; and there he was as priest hermit in a chapel, and lived in poverty and in holy prayers, for well he understood that mischievous war was at hand. Then Sir Mordred sought on Queen Guenever by letters and sondes, and by fair means and foul means, for to have her to come out of the Tower of London; but all this availed not, for she answered him shortly, openly and privily, that she had lever slay herself than to be married with him. Then came word to Sir Mordred that King Arthur had araised the siege for Sir Launcelot, and he was coming homeward with a great host, to be avenged upon Sir Mordred; wherefore Sir Mordred made write writs to all the barony of this land, and much people drew to him. For then was the common voice among them [380] that with Arthur was none other life but war and strife, and with Sir Mordred was great joy and bliss. Thus was Sir Arthur depraved, and evil said of. And many there were that King Arthur had made up of nought, and given them lands, might not then say him a good word. Lo ye all Englishmen, see ye not what a mischief here was! for he that was the most king and knight of the world, and most loved the fellowship of noble knights, and by him they were all upholden, now might not these Englishmen hold them content with

him.   Lo thus was the old custom and usage of this land; and also
men say that we of this land have not yet lost nor forgotten that
custom and usage.   Alas, this is a great default of us Englishmen,
for there may no thing please us no term.   And so fared the people
at that time, they were better pleased with Sir Mordred than they
were with King Arthur; and much people drew unto Sir Mordred,
and said they would abide with him for better and for worse.   And
so Sir Mordred drew with a great host to Dover, for there he heard
say that Sir Arthur would arrive, and so he thought to beat his own
father from his lands; and the most part of all England held with
Sir Mordred, the people were so new fangle.

CHAPTER 2:

HOW AFTER THAT KING ARTHUR HAD TIDINGS, HE RETURNED AND CAME TO
DOVER, WHERE SIR MORDRED MET HIM TO LET HIS LANDING; AND
OF THE DEATH OF SIR GAWAINE

And so as Sir Mordred was at Dover with his host,
there came King Arthur with a great navy of ships, and galleys, and
carracks.   And there was Sir Mordred ready awaiting upon his
landing, to let his own father to land upon the land that he was
king over.   Then there was launching of great boats and small,
and full of noble men of arms; and there was much slaughter of
gentle knights, and many a full bold baron was laid full low, on
both parties.   But King Arthur was so courageous that there might
no manner of knights let him to land, and his knights fiercely followed him; and so they landed maugre Sir Mordred and all his
power, and put Sir Mordred aback, that he fled and all his people.
So when this battle was done, King Arthur let [381] bury his people
that were dead.   And then was noble Sir Gawaine found in a great
boat, lying more than half dead.   When Sir Arthur wist that Sir
Gawaine was laid so low, he went unto him; and there the king made
sorrow out of measure, and took Sir Gawaine in his arms, and thrice
he there swooned.   And then when he awaked, he said: Alas, Sir
Gawaine, my sister's son, here now thou liest, the man in the world
that I loved most; and now is my joy gone, for now, my nephew Sir
Gawaine, I will discover me unto your person: in Sir Launcelot

and you I most had my joy, and mine affiance, and now have I lost my joy of you both; wherefore all mine earthly joy is gone from me. Mine uncle King Arthur, said Sir Gawaine, wit you well my death day is come, and all is through mine own hastiness and wilfulness; for I am smitten upon the old wound the which Sir Launcelot gave me, on the which I feel well I must die; and had Sir Launcelot been with you as he was, this unhappy war had never begun; and of all this am I causer, for Sir Launcelot and his blood, through their prowess, held all your cankered enemies in subjection and daunger. And now, said Sir Gawaine, ye shall miss Sir Launcelot. But alas, I would not accord with him, and therefore, said Sir Gawaine, I pray you, fair uncle, that I may have paper, pen, and ink, that I may write to Sir Launcelot a cedle with mine own hands. And then when paper and ink was brought, then Gawaine was set up weakly by King Arthur, for he was shriven a little tofore; and then he wrote thus, as the French book maketh mention: Unto Sir Launcelot, flower of all noble knights that ever I heard of or saw by my days, I, Sir Gawaine, King Lot's son of Orkney, sister's son unto the noble King Arthur, send thee greeting, and let thee have knowledge that the tenth day of May I was smitten upon the old wound that thou gavest me afore the city of Benwick, and through the same wound that thou gavest me I am come to my death day. And I will that all the world wit, that I, Sir Gawaine, knight of the Table Round, sought my death, and not through thy deserving, but it was mine own seeking; wherefore I beseech thee, Sir Launcelot, to return again unto this realm, and see my tomb, and pray some prayer more or less for my soul. And this same day that I wrote this cedle, I was hurt to the death in the same wound, the which I had of thy hand, Sir Launcelot; for of a more nobler man might I not be slain. Also [382] Sir Launcelot, for all the love that ever was betwixt us, make no tarrying, but come over the sea in all haste, that thou mayst with thy noble knights rescue that noble king that made thee knight, that is my lord Arthur; for he is full straitly bestad with a false traitor, that is my half-brother, Sir Mordred; and he hath let crown him king, and would have wedded my lady Queen Guenever, and so had he done had she not put herself in the Tower of London. And so the tenth day of May last past, my lord Arthur and we all landed upon them at Dover; and there we put that false traitor, Sir Mordred, to flight, and there it misfortuned me to be stricken upon thy stroke. And at the date of this letter was written, but two hours and a half afore my death, written with mine own hand, and so subscribed with part of my heart's blood. And I require thee, most famous knight of the world, that thou wilt see my tomb. And then Sir Gawaine wept, and King Arthur wept; and then they swooned both. And when they awaked both, the king made Sir Gawaine to receive his Saviour. And then Sir Gawaine prayed the king for to send for Sir Launcelot, and to cherish him above all other knights. And so at the hour of noon Sir Gawaine yielded up the spirit; and then the king let inter him in a chapel within Dover Castle; and there yet all men may see the skull of him, and the same wound is seen that Sir Launcelot gave him in battle. Then was it told the king that Sir Mordred had pyghte a new field upon Barham Down. And upon the morn the king rode thither to him, and there was a great battle betwixt them, and much people was slain on both parties; but at the last Sir Arthur's party stood best, and Sir Mordred and his party fled unto Canterbury.

CHAPTER 3:

HOW AFTER, SIR GAWAINE'S GHOST APPEARED TO KING ARTHUR, AND WARNED HIM THAT HE SHOULD NOT FIGHT THAT DAY

And then the king let search all the towns for his knights that were slain, and interred them; and salved them with soft salves that so sore were wounded. Then much people drew unto King Arthur. And then they said that Sir Mordred warred upon King Arthur with wrong. And then [383] King Arthur drew him with his host down by the seaside westward toward Salisbury; and there was a day assigned betwixt King Arthur and Sir Mordred, that they should meet upon a down beside Salisbury, and not far from the seaside; and this day was assigned on a Monday after Trinity Sunday, whereof King Arthur was passing glad, that he might be avenged upon Sir Mordred. Then Sir Mordred araised much people about London, for they of Kent, Southsex, and Surrey, Estsex, and of Southfolk, and of Northfolk, held the most part with Sir Mordred; and many a full noble knight drew unto Sir Mordred and to the king: but they loved Sir Launcelot drew unto Sir Mordred. So upon Trinity Sunday at night, King Arthur dreamed a wonderful dream, and that was this: that him seemed he sat upon a chaflet in a chair, and the chair was fast to a wheel, and thereupon sat King Arthur in the richest cloth of gold that might be made; and the king thought there was under him, far from him, an hideous deep black water, and therein were all manner of serpents, and worms, and wild beasts, foul and horrible; and suddenly the king thought the wheel turned up so down, and he fell among the serpents, and every beast took him by a limb; and then the king cried as he lay in his bed and slept: Help. And then knights, squires, and yeomen, awaked the king; and then he was so amazed that he wist not where he was; and then he fell on slumbering again, not sleeping nor thoroughly waking. So the king seemed verily that there came Sir Gawaine unto him with a number of fair ladies with him. And when King Arthur saw him, then he said: Welcome, my sister's son; I weened thou hadst been dead, and now I see thee on live, much am I beholding unto almighty Jesu. O fair nephew and my sister's son, what be these ladies that hither be come with you? Sir, said Sir Gawaine, all these be ladies for whom I have foughten when I was man living, and all these are those that I did battle for in righteous quarrel; and God hath given them that grace at their great prayer, by cause I did battle for them, that they should bring me hither unto you: thus much hath God given me leave, for to warn you of your death; for an ye fight as tomorn with Sir Mordred, as ye both have assigned, doubt ye not ye must be slain, and the most part of your people on both parties. And for the great grace and goodness that almighty Jesu hath unto you, and for pity of you, and [384] many more other good men there shall be slain, God hath sent me to you of his special grace, to give you warning that in no wise ye do battle as tomorn, but that ye take a treaty for a month day; and proffer you largely, so as tomorn to be put in a delay. For within a month shall come Sir Launcelot with all his noble knights, and rescue you worshipfully, and slay Sir Mordred, and all that ever will hold with him. Then Sir Gawaine and all the ladies vanished. And anon the king called upon his knights, squires, and yeomen, and charged them wightly to fetch his noble lords and wise bishops unto him. And when they were come, the king told them his avision, what Sir Gawaine had told him, and warned him that if he fought on the morn he should be slain. Then the king commanded Sir Lucan the Butler, and his brother Sir Bedivere, with two bishops with them, and charged them in any wise, an they might, Take a treaty for a month day with Sir Mordred, and spare not, proffer him lands and goods as much as ye think best. So then they departed, and came to Sir Mordred, where he had a grim host of an hundred thousand men. And there they entreated Sir Mordred long time; and at the last Sir Mordred was agreed for to have Cornwall and Kent, by Arthur's days: after, all England, after the days of King Arthur.

CHAPTER 4:

HOW BY MISADVENTURE OF AN ADDER THE BATTLE BEGAN, WHERE MORDRED WAS SLAIN, AND ARTHUR HURT TO THE DEATH

Then were they condescended that King Arthur and Sir Mordred should meet betwixt both their hosts, and every each of them should bring fourteen persons; and they came with this word unto Arthur. Then said he: I am glad that this is done: and so he went into the field. And when Arthur should depart, he warned all his host that an they see any sword drawn: Look ye come on fiercely, and slay that traitor, Sir Mordred, for I in no wise trust him. In likewise Sir Mordred warned his host that: An ye see any sword drawn, look that ye come on fiercely, and so slay all that ever before you standeth; for in no wise I will not trust for this treaty, for I know well my father will be avenged on me. And so they met as their appointment was, and so they [385] were agreed and accorded thoroughly; and wine was fetched, and they drank. Right soon came an adder out of a little heath bush, and it stung a knight on the foot. And when the knight felt him stung, he looked down and saw the adder, and then he drew his sword to slay the adder, and thought of none other harm. And when the host on both parties saw that sword drawn, then they blew beamous, trumpets, and horns, and shouted grimly. And so both hosts dressed them together. And King Arthur took his horse, and said: Alas this unhappy day! and so rode to his party. And Sir Mordred in likewise. And never was there seen a more dolefuller battle in no Christian land; for there was but rushing and riding, foining and striking, and many a grim word was there spoken either to other, and many a deadly stroke.   But ever King Arthur rode throughout the battle of Sir Mordred many times, and did full nobly as a noble king should, and at all times he fainted never; and Sir Mordred that day put him in devoir, and in great peril.   And thus they fought all the long day, and never stinted till the noble knights were laid to the cold earth; and ever they fought still till it was near night, and by that time was there an hundred thousand laid dead upon the down.   Then was Arthur wood wroth out of measure, when he saw his people so slain from him.   Then the king looked about him, and then was he ware, of all his host and of all his good knights, were left no more on live but two knights; that one was Sir Lucan the Butler, and his brother Sir Bedivere, and they were full sore wounded.   Jesu mercy, said the king, where are all my noble knights become?   Alas that ever I should see this doleful day, for now, said Arthur, I am come to mine end.   But would to God that I wist where were that traitor Sir Mordred, that hath caused all this mischief.   Then was King Arthur ware where Sir Mordred leaned upon his sword among a great heap of dead men.   Now give me my spear, said Arthur unto Sir Lucan, for yonder I have espied the traitor that all this woe hath wrought.   Sir, let him be, said Sir Lucan, for he is unhappy; and if ye pass this unhappy day ye shall be right well revenged upon him.   Good lord, remember ye of your night's dream, and what the spirit of Sir Gawaine told you this night, yet God of his great goodness hath preserved you hitherto.   Therefore, for God's sake, my lord, leave off by this, for blessed be God ye have won the field, for here we be three on live, and with [386] Sir Mordred is none on live; and if ye leave off now this wicked day of destiny is past.   Tide me death, betide me life, saith the king, now I see him yonder alone he shall never escape mine hands, for at a better avail shall I never have him.   God speed you well, said Sir Bedivere.   Then the king gat his spear in both his hands, and ran toward Sir Mordred, crying: Traitor, now is thy death day come.   And when Sir Mordred heard Sir Arthur, he ran until him with his sword drawn in his hand.   And there King Arthur smote Sir Mordred under the shield, with a foin of his spear, throughout the body, more than a fathom.   And when Sir Mordred felt that he had his death wound he thrust himself with the might that he had up to the bur of King Arthur's spear. And right so he smote his father Arthur, with his sword holden in both his hands, on the side of the head, that the sword pierced the helmet and the brain pan, and therewithal Sir Mordred fell stark dead to the earth; and the noble Arthur fell in a swoon to the earth, and there he swooned ofttimes. And Sir Lucan the Butler and Sir Bedivere ofttimes heave him up. And so weakly they led him betwixt them both, to a little chapel not far from the seaside. And when the king was there he thought him well eased. Then heard they people cry in the field. Now go thou, Sir Lucan, said the king, and do me to wit what betokens that noise in the field. So Sir Lucan departed, for he was grievously wounded in many places. And so as he yede, he saw and hearkened by the moonlight, how that pillers and robbers were come into the field, to pill and to rob many a full noble knight of brooches, and beads, of many a good ring, and of many a rich jewel; and who that were not dead all out, there they slew them for their harness and their riches. When Sir Lucan understood this work, he came to the king as soon as he might, and told him all what he had heard and seen. Therefore by my rede, said Sir Lucan, it is best that we bring you to some town. I would it were so, said the king.[387]

Chapter 5:

HOW KING ARTHUR COMMANDED TO CAST HIS SWORD EXCALIBUR INTO THE WATER, AND HOW HE WAS DELIVERED TO LADIES IN A BARGE

But I may not stand, mine head works so. Ah Sir Launcelot, said King Arthur, this day have I sore missed thee: alas, that ever I was against thee, for now have I my death, whereof Sir Gawaine me warned in my dream. Then Sir Lucan took up the king the one part, and Sir Bedivere the other part, and in the lifting the king swooned; and Sir Lucan fell in a swoon with the lift, that the part of his guts fell out of his body, and therewith the noble knight's heart brast. And when the king awoke, he beheld Sir Lucan, how he lay foaming at the mouth, and part of his guts lay at his feet. Alas, said the king, this is to me a full heavy sight, to see this noble duke so die for my sake, for he would have holpen me, that had more need of help than I. Alas, he would not complain him, his heart was so set to help me: now Jesu have mercy upon his soul! Then Sir Bedivere wept for the death of his brother. Leave this mourning and weeping, said the king, for all this will not avail me, for wit thou well an I might live myself, the death of Sir Lucan would grieve me evermore; but my time hieth fast, said the king. Therefore, said Arthur unto Sir Bedivere, take thou Excalibur, my good sword, and go with it to yonder water side, and when thou comest there I charge thee throw my sword in that water, and come again and tell me what thou there seest. My lord, said Bedivere, your commandment shall be done, and lightly bring you word again. So Sir Bedivere departed, and by the way he beheld that noble sword, that the pommel and the haft was all of precious stones; and then he said to himself: If I throw this rich sword in the water, thereof shall never come good, but harm and loss. And then Sir Bedivere hid Excalibur under a tree. And so, as soon as he might, he came again unto the king, and said he had been at the water, and had thrown the sword in the water. What saw thou there? said the king. Sir, he said, I saw nothing but waves and winds. That is untruly said of thee, said the king, therefore go thou lightly again, and do my commandment; [388] as thou art to me lief and dear, spare not, but throw it in. Then Sir Bedivere returned again, and took the sword in his hand; and then him thought sin and shame to throw away that noble sword, and so efte he hid the sword, and returned again, and told to the king that he had been at the water, and done his commandment. What saw thou there? said the king. Sir, he said, I saw nothing but the waters wappe and waves wanne. Ah, traitor untrue, said King Arthur, now hast thou betrayed me twice. Who would have weened that, thou that hast been to me so lief and dear? and thou art named a noble knight, and would betray me for the richness of the sword. But now go again lightly, for thy long tarrying putteth me in great jeopardy of my life, for I have taken cold. And but if thou do now as I bid thee, if ever I may see thee, I shall slay thee with mine own hands; for thou wouldst for my rich sword see me dead. Then Sir Bedivere departed, and went to the sword, and lightly took it up, and went to the water side; and there he bound the girdle about the hilts, and then he threw the sword as far into the water, as he might; and there came an arm and an hand above the

water and met it, and caught it, and so shook it thrice and brandished, and then vanished away the hand with the sword in the
water. So Sir Bedivere came again to the king, and told him what
he saw. Alas, said the king, help me hence, for I dread me I have
tarried over long. Then Sir Bedivere took the king upon his back,
and so went with him to that water side. And when they were at
the water side, even fast by the bank hoved a little barge with many
fair ladies in it, and among them all was a queen, and all they had
black hoods, and all they wept and shrieked when they saw King
Arthur. Now put me into the barge, said the king. And so he did
softly; and there received him three queens with great mourning;
and so they set them down, and in one of their laps King Arthur
laid his head. And then that queen said: Ah, dear brother, why
have ye tarried so long from me? alas, this wound on your head
hath caught over-much cold. And so then they rowed from the
land, and Sir Bedivere beheld all those ladies go from him. Then
Sir Bedivere cried: Ah my lord Arthur, what shall become of me,
now ye go from me and leave me here alone among mine enemies?
Comfort thyself, said the king, and do as well as thou mayest, for
in me is no trust for to trust in; for I will into the vale of Avilion
to heal me of my [389] grievous wound: and if thou hear never more
of me, pray for my soul. But ever the queens and ladies wept and
shrieked, that it was pity to hear. And as soon as Sir Bedivere had
lost the sight of the barge, he wept and wailed, and so took the
forest; and so he went all that night, and in the morning he was
ware betwixt two holts hoar, of a chapel and an hermitage.

CHAPTER 6:

HOW SIR BEDIVERE FOUND HIM ON THE MORROW DEAD IN AN HERMITAGE, AND HOW HE ABODE THERE WITH THE HERMIT

Then was Sir Bedivere glad, and thither he went; and
when he came into the chapel, he saw where lay an hermit grovelling on all four, there fast by a tomb was new graven. When the
hermit saw Sir Bedivere he knew him well, for he was but little
tofore Bishop of Canterbury, that Sir Mordred flemed. Sir, said
Bedivere, what man is there interred that ye pray so fast for? Fair
son, said the hermit, I wot not verily, but by deeming. But this

night, at midnight, here came a number of ladies, and brought hither a dead corpse, and prayed me to bury him; and here they offered an hundred tapers, and they gave me an hundred besants. Alas, said Sir Bedivere, that was my lord King Arthur, that here lieth buried in this chapel. Then Sir Bedivere swooned; and when he awoke he prayed the hermit he might abide with him still there, to live with fasting and prayers. For from hence will I never go, said Sir Bedivere, by my will, but all the days of my life here to pray for my lord Arthur. Ye are welcome to me, said the hermit, for I know ye better than ye ween that I do. Ye are the bold Bedivere, and the full noble duke, Sir Lucan the Butler, was your brother. Then Sir Bedivere told the hermit all as ye have heard tofore. So there bode Sir Bedivere with the hermit that was tofore Bishop of Canterbury, and there Sir Bedivere put upon him poor clothes, and served the hermit full lowly in fasting and in prayers. Thus of Arthur I find never more written in books that be authorised, nor more of the very certainty of his death heard I never read, but thus was he led away in a ship wherein were three queens; that one was King Arthur's sister, Queen Morgan le Fay; the other was the Queen of Northgalis; the third was the Queen of the [390] Waste Lands. Also there was Nimue, the chief lady of the lake, that had wedded Pelleas the good knight; and this lady had done much for King Arthur, for she would never suffer Sir Pelleas to be in no place where he should be in danger of his life; and so he lived to the uttermost of his days with her in great rest. More of the death of King Arthur could I never find, but that ladies brought him to his burials; and such one was buried there, that the hermit bare witness that sometime was Bishop of Canterbury, but yet the hermit knew not in certain that he was verily the body of King Arthur: for this tale Sir Bedivere, knight of the Table Round, made it to be written.

CHAPTER 7:

OF THE OPINION OF SOME MEN OF THE DEATH OF KING ARTHUR; AND HOW QUEEN GUENEVER MADE HER A NUN IN ALMESBURY

Yet some men say in many parts of England that King Arthur is not dead, but had by the will of our Lord Jesu into another place; and men say that he shall come again, and he shall win the holy cross. I will not say it shall be so, but rather I will say, here in this world he changed his life. But many men say that there is written upon his tomb this verse: Hic jacet Arthurus Rex, quondam Rex que futurus. Thus leave I here Sir Bedivere with the hermit, that dwelled that time in a chapel beside Glastonbury, and there was his hermitage. And so they lived in their prayers, and fastings, and great abstinence. And when Queen Guenever understood that King Arthur was slain, and all the noble knights, Sir Mordred and all the remnant, then the queen stole away, and five ladies with her, and so she went to Almesbury; and there she let make herself a nun, and ware white clothes and black, and great penance she took, as ever did sinful lady in this land, and never creature could make her merry; but lived in fasting, prayers, and alms-deeds, that all manner of people marveled how virtuously she was changed.[391]

PART THREE

Criticism

KENNETH HURLSTONE JACKSON

"The Arthur of History"

From *Arthurian Literature in the Middle Ages,* ed. Roger Sherman Loomis (Oxford: at the Clarendon Press, 1959).

Did King Arthur ever really exist? The only honest answer is, 'We do not know, but he may well have existed.' The nature of the evidence is such that proof is impossible. There is a certain amount of early material dealing with him, but the difficulty lies in distinguishing what is, if anything, history from what is legend. Most scholars would agree that the Arthur of Geoffrey of Monmouth is not historical at all. Similarly the Arthur in *Culhwch and Olwen,* and the other early Welsh literary sources . . . is clearly a figure of folktale. Certain early legendary texts older than Geoffrey which mention Arthur are written in Latin, which has given them a spurious air of historicity by contrast with obviously fanciful material in Welsh like *Culhwch.* Hence, it is as well to clear these legends out of the way before discussing sources which may reasonably be regarded as historical.

The *Mirabilia* of Nennius's early ninth-century *Historia Brittonum* has two tales of Arthur. One describes a cairn in Breconshire called *Carn Cabal,* the topmost stone of which bore a footprint made by Arthur's dog Cabal while hunting the pig Troit. The other tells of the marvellous tomb of Arthur's son Amr beside the source of the Amr—the Gamber in Herefordshire. Both show that the Arthur story had already impressed itself on the landscape, in

the form of 'local legends', at least as early as the beginning of the
ninth century. Nothing else is known of Amr apart from a mention
in *Gereint*, but the other tale proves the existence already of one of
the central episodes in the Celtic legend of Arthur. None of this is
history, however. In some late eleventh- and early twelfth-century
Latin Lives of Welsh saints he appears as a king or chief, usually
troublesome to the saint at first but afterwards overcome by a
miracle. These anecdotes run true to a form common in Lives of
early Celtic saints, where wicked kings are miraculously discomfited,
repent, and grant lands or other gifts to the Church. Why is Arthur
so treated in these Lives, when in other contemporary material he
had already become the popular hero later exploited by Geoffrey? [1] Some have thought of a genuine tradition derived from
parties opposed to the Arthur of history, which is scarcely probable
considering the nature of these documents; others of monkish
writers seeking to discredit the hero of apparently semi-pagan tales.
One may suggest that the monks themselves regarded such stories
as little better than worthless fairy-tales, but saw that to introduce
such a hero in the stock part of the Recalcitrant King would give
prestige to their own heroic saints. Hence the Arthur they describe
is the typical one of early Welsh legend, overcoming monsters, having supernatural adventures with his warriors Cai and Bedwyr, and
the rest. It is idle to look here for history.

Having set aside these pre-Geoffrey Latin references to Arthur
and ignoring a few others as being trivial, or taken from Nennius,
we are left with little indeed, but that little of prime importance.
The name *Arthur* is unquestionably derived from *Artorius*, not
rare in the history of Rome since it was the title of the *gens Artoria*.
Like the many other Latin names adopted by the natives, it must
have passed into British during or soon after the period of Roman
rule. We know of one Artorius who really lived in Britain, an officer
called Lucius Artorius Castus, apparently a Dalmatian, who led the
VIth Legion on an expedition to Armorica in the middle of the
second century. He is much too early for our Arthur, and we need
not suppose . . . that the name was hereditary in Arthur's family
because some ancestor had served under him; but the fact that he
resided in Britain does prove that his name was known in Roman
Britain.

Next, Gildas, who wrote about 540, perhaps somewhere in the

west Midlands or in Wales, tells how after a struggle of varying outcome the Britons finally defeated their enemies (the Saxons are meant) at the siege of *Mons Badonicus,* in the year of his own birth, after which there had been peace. He seems to say that the battle took place forty-four years before he wrote, though this is not certain; and though the exact date has been much disputed, it must have been not far from 500. This suits remarkably the known history of southern England, from which it appears that the Anglo-Saxon penetration of the south-east during the first half-century of the invasion was stopped about 500, when it had reached the borders of Salisbury Plain in Berkshire and Hampshire, and was not resumed until another half-century later. Mount Badon must be somewhere in this area, and Badbury near [2] Swindon, Badbury Hill near Faringdon, or Badbury Rings near Blandford are possible sites. This decisive victory was credited to Arthur already by Nennius's time, and would account well for his fame as the supreme conqueror of the English. The fact that Gildas does not mention him has been urged as a serious objection, but the argument has little force. Gildas was preaching a sermon against his contemporaries, not writing a detailed history of his father's generation, and it is his general practice to avoid mentioning personal names. Besides, what English bishop, castigating the vices of his compatriots about 1860, would be so clumsy as to allude to 'the battle of Waterloo, *which was won by the Duke of Wellington'?*

There follows what may well be one of the most convincing pieces of evidence for a historical Arthur. The Welsh elegy *Gododdin,* attributed to the late sixth-century poet Aneirin, has been pretty well proved to be genuine and to date, at least in its original form, from about 600. In lines 1241-2 of Ifor Williams's edition it is said of a certain hero that 'he glutted(?) black ravens on the rampart of the city, though he was not Arthur'; that is, he slew many and did heroic deeds, so that his valour was second only to Arthur's. Arthur is treated here as a famous historical chief; Aneirin might easily have known personally old men who had met Arthur in their boyhood, if the generally accepted dates for his *floruit* are right. Unfortunately there are interpolations in the *Gododdin,* and it is impossible to prove that this is not one of them. Otherwise the historicity of Arthur would be established beyond doubt.

An important point in favour of a historical Arthur is the fact

that we know of at least four, perhaps five, people called Arthur
hailing from the Celtic areas of the British Isles who were born in
the latter part of the sixth century and early in the seventh, whereas
the name is unknown before (except for Arthur himself) and very
rare later. Some national figure called Arthur must surely have
existed at this time or a generation or two before, after whom they
were all named, either directly or because their fathers or grand-
fathers had been. It is specially significant that Aedán mac Gabráin,
king of Scottish Dál Riada, who had British connexions, christened
one of [3] his sons Arthur about 570 (and perhaps a grandson), since
he headed what was meant to be a massive attempt to drive the
English out of Northumbria.

Our fullest apparently historical reference to Arthur is contained in chapter 56 of Nennius's *Historia Brittonum*. It tells us
that after the death of Hengist his son Octha came from northern
Britain and settled in Kent, whence come the kings of Kent; the
Anglo-Saxon Chronicle dates the accession of Æsc, apparently the
same person, in 488. Nennius continues: 'tunc Arthur pugnabat
contra illos in illis diebus cum regibus Brittonum, sed ipse erat dux
bellorum'. By *illos* he seems to mean the 'Saxons' under Octha.
He then gives a list of the twelve victories won by Arthur. Some of
the sites are quite unidentifiable, though a great deal of nonsense
has been written in the attempt to identify them. The last is *Mons
Badonis*, evidently somewhere in Wessex as we have seen. . . . Of
the battle at *Castellum Guinnion* Nennius says that Arthur there
carried on his shoulders the image of the Virgin Mary, through
whose virtue and that of Jesus Christ the pagans were routed that
day; and of Badon he tells us that 960 men were slain on that one
day by Arthur himself.

Before discussing this passage it will be convenient to mention
the two remaining early 'historical' references to Arthur, in the
Annales Cambriae, which were put together in their present form
in the middle of the tenth century but may have been first compiled
early in the ninth. Where we can check this, it is a sober historical
document using good sources, not an annal- [4] ized fiction. The
first entry, 516, runs, 'The battle of Badon, in which Arthur bore
the cross of our Lord Jesus Christ three days and three nights on
his shoulders, and the Britons were victorious'; and the second, 537,
'The Battle of Camlann, in which Arthur and Medraut fell'. It is

not known how these dates were calculated, but 516 is probably too late, by as much as ten or fifteen years, so that the same may be true of 537. If Badon was fought about 500, and if Arthur really won eleven great victories before that, beginning perhaps in or after 488 (see above), he is hardly likely to have been born later than about 465, which would make him seventy-two at his last fight in 537, so that about 522-7 is more probable. It is sometimes asserted that the first of these entries has no value because it derives from Nennius. But the second proves that the compiler knew Arthurian material not quoted by Nennius, and the differences from Nennius's account of Badon are more marked than the likenesses (a cross not an image, the battle Badon not Guinnion, and three days instead of one). It is obvious that the compiler used information closely allied to but different from Nennius's source, and this makes it especially valuable; besides, the second entry is the only early reference to Camlann and to Arthur's fatal battle with Medraut, later known as Modred. Camlann is unknown . . . .[5]

It has been claimed that the words 'tunc Arthur pugnabat', &c., quoted above, form two 'Commodian' hexameters, and that the whole chapter may come from an old British work on Arthur in Latin verse. But even allowing for the fact that 'Commodian' covers a multitude of metrical sins, it is entirely foreign to the Celtic tradition to write narrative in Latin verse, and there is not the slightest evidence that the Britons ever composed Latin chronicle poems. A Latin original would surely have taken the form of annals, and the 'Arthuriana' do not look as if they were derived from annals. Others think the 'Arthuriana' are taken from a Welsh source, whether in prose or verse, oral or written. There is some internal evidence for this. . . . Scholars have noted that when Nennius says Arthur carried the image of the Virgin on his shoulders he may have had [6] scuit, 'shield', in his original, and misread it as scuid, 'shoulder'. This would be more conclusive if we knew that the Britons bore devices on their shields in the fifth century, and especially if the *Annales Cambriae* did not also give 'shoulders', which suggests an established tradition.[7]

. . . Nothing is certain about the historical Arthur, not even his existence; however, there are certain possibilities, even probabilities. There may have been a supreme British commander of genius in the late fifth century who bore the Roman-derived name of Arthur, though it would be wrong to deduce anything about his background from the name. There is little reason to think that he held any definite sub-Roman office, whether *Dux Bellorum* or otherwise, and his supposed cavalry tactics are an illusion. If we grant his existence, it seems certain that his enemies were the English, and not indeed impossible that he also fought the Picts and perhaps traitorous Britons too; but there is no ground for holding that he belonged exclusively or even predominantly to the North, whereas there is definite reason to think his greatest victory was in Wessex. The period of his campaigns seems to have been the last decade of the fifth century, culminating about 500. He may have been killed about twenty years later, possibly in one of the civil conflicts alluded to by Gildas. He was still vividly remembered towards the end of [10] the sixth century, when boys were named after him and heroes compared to him. His deeds were told in traditional Welsh oral literature, and at some time in the next two centuries may have been briefly related in a panegyric poem by an antiquarian who had heard that he won twelve victories, and knew perhaps some, but probably not all, of their real names. Badon is the most likely to be genuinely his, because it seems to have been a triumph which impressed itself deeply upon the minds of the Britons; it was fought against the English, apparently in Wessex. Nennius summarized this Welsh poem or Welsh tradition in Latin. He could hardly have *invented* Arthur himself, for Nennius was no Geoffrey [of Monmouth]; he was not capable of creating a character out of nothing at all. The *Annales Cambriae* likewise drew on Welsh traditions of a semi-historical nature, closely connected with but already divergent from those which reached Nennius. Meanwhile the historical general was already being evolved in popular story towards the miraculous 'emperor' of the later Arthurian legend.[11]

JOHN JAY PARRY

"The Historical Arthur"

From *Journal of English and Germanic Philology*, LVIII (July, 1959).

It has always seemed to me simplest to assume that behind the stories about King Arthur there must have been a real man. I knew, of course, that he could not be like the Arthur of the romances and that it was impossible to prove his existence, but I saw no reason to question it, nevertheless. Yet not everybody feels about him as I do. Lord Raglan, for example, in March of this year [1936]* published in the *Illustrated London News* an article on Arthur in which he said, "It is as certain as anything in the dim past can be, that he was not a real man." Lord Raglan considers that he must have been a war god of the Brythonic Celts because "only a god wins all his battles." He followed up this article with a book called *The Hero* . . .[367] in which he classes Arthur with other mythical heroes like Robin Hood, Zeus, Oedipus, and Siegfried. A. G. van Hamel, in his lecture before the British Academy, said, "The general likeness which links his saga to that of Finn proves that the complex was ready before it was attached to an historical person. At the very best some other British hero preceded Arthur at its head." Van Hamel goes on to say, "There is not one single testimony that can be explained exclusively by the assumption of Arthur's historicity." If he puts the matter in that way I must, of course, agree with him, but I would add: "however, there

---

* This paper was originally delivered before the Arthurian Romance Group of the Modern Language Association of America in 1936, but not published until 1959. *Editor's note.*

are many testimonies that can be explained *best* by the assumption of his historicity."

As a starting point for . . . discussion, . . . I am going to present you with the historical Arthur and his background as I see them. The problem is something like the putting together of a jigsaw puzzle; many of the pieces are missing, and those that remain are mixed with pieces of other puzzles, but I believe that enough of them fit together to justify a statement regarding the picture they present.

Let me begin with the background, about which it is possible to be fairly definite. In the century between the invasion of Julius Caesar and that of Claudius, there was an extensive, although peaceful, penetration of Roman civilization into Britain. After the Claudian invasion this Romanization proceeded at a much more rapid pace. Boudicca's rising took place less than twenty years after the beginning of the invasion, yet seventy thousand Romans and Romanized Britons fell in it, and there were undoubtedly others who escaped. The Romans made a determined attempt to plant their culture in the island, as may be seen from Tacitus' account of the measures employed by Agricola. Rome held the greater part of the island for well over three hundred years—considerably longer than the time that has elapsed between the first settlement of Jamestown and the present day. Even if we had no other evidence—and we have a great deal—we might feel justified in assuming that in so long a period as this, a people [368] like the Romans would have had a profound effect upon the civilization of the island.

Of the various factors that contributed to the Romanization of Britain, the one that most concerns us in connection with Arthur is the army. The Twentieth Legion was stationed at Chester for three hundred years, the Sixth was at York for nearly as long. The Second Augusta kept its headquarters at Caerleon for two hundred years, although many of its men were serving on Hadrian's Wall, and after that it was stationed at Richborough for a number of years. The Ninth, brought up to strength after its disaster in Boudicca's revolt, was at York for fifty years before it disappeared, and other legions were stationed in the island for shorter periods. Besides this, there were many more or less Romanized auxiliary troops permanently stationed there. It has been estimated that in the second century the regular garrison of the island was about fifty-six thousand men, nearly a third of them legionaries, which is a fairly large force if we consider that the total population of the island was probably less than a million.

Except in a few special cases, Roman citizenship was a prerequisite for enlistment in a legion; many of the auxiliaries were not citizens, although citizenship was often granted them upon the expiration of their enlistment. In any case, twenty-five years of service would be apt to fix a man firmly in Roman ways, and at the end of it he was encouraged to settle down in one of the four *coloniae,* Colchester, Gloucester, Lincoln, or York.

Technically, until the year 197, soldiers were not supposed to marry before the expiration of their enlistment. Actually this rule was not enforced, and many of them did marry; when they were discharged, such marriages were usually recognized, even if the wife was a *peregrina,* and citizenship was given to the children; sometimes the citizenship of the sons was made contingent upon enlistment in the legion, for, from the time of Hadrian onward, vacancies were filled, so far as possible, by local enlistments. A fair proportion of the recruits, instead of giving as their place of birth some city with the Roman franchise, gave simply *castris,* indicating that they were sons of veterans. I know of no evidence that the daughters of veterans married into the legion, but it is only reasonable to suppose that some [369] did. After ten generations of this sort of thing we should expect to find in the neighborhood of the Roman fortresses and of the *coloniae* a rather large population, largely British in blood but Roman in civilization and in sympathies.

When the legions were finally withdrawn and all official connection with the empire ceased, most of these people remained, and strove to keep up their Roman manner of life. Gildas tells us this very plainly, and I see no reason to doubt his statement. These "citizens," as he called them, raised troops to take the place of the legions that had gone, organizing and equipping them along Roman lines, after the patterns that the Romans had left them. In South Britain, which is the only part of the island that Gildas has any interest in, these troops were under the leadership of Ambrosius Aurelianus, a man of the Roman party, whose ancestors had held high office under the empire, and whose descendants, in the time of Gildas, were carrying on with success an offensive against the Saxon invaders. I think it a perfectly natural assump-

tion that others did the same thing in other parts of the island, and
that one named Artorius did it with such success that his name was
handed down to later generations. This assumption fits, better than
any other, the known background and the few scattered references
that remain to us, as I believe I can show by fitting a number of
them into the framework.

The first actual mention of Arthur is in the compilation of
Nennius. Nennius himself lived about three hundred years later
than Arthur, but his work seems to contain material from Latin
sources two centuries earlier than he, and from written Welsh
sources which he did not always understand; besides these he had,
as he tells us, *vetus traditio seniorum nostrorum* [the long standing
tradition of our elders]. The Arthurian *mirabilia* are fantastic,[370]
but the historical section seems reliable. Arthur here is no king but
a man of humbler birth, chosen leader because of his military
ability. He fights against the Saxons *cum militibus Bryttanicae
atque regibus,* which I think means with the levies of Romanized
Britons and with the native kings. The sites of his battles are still
in dispute, but the early ones were almost certainly in the North,
and I believe he began his career there. The persistence of the
tradition which connects him with the Southwest perhaps indicates
that he extended his sphere of operations to that district. I believe
that Badon Hill was not his victory but was inserted from Gildas,
causing a confusion in the last two battles of the original list.

The name Arthur is probably the British form of the Latin
Artorius, which would become Arthyr in Welsh. It is not a common
Latin name, but a number of people who bore it are known. One
is Lucius Artorius Castus, who appears first as centurion in the
Third Gallica Legion and after various promotions comes to be
commander of the Sixth Victrix Legion in Britain. There is no
certainty about his date, but in any event it is earlier than the
period we are considering. I see no great improbability, however,
in the suggestion that he may have left descendants in the colony
of York, one of whom inherited his military ability as well as his
name. . . .[371]

I see another connection with Rome in Arthur's title of "pendragon," which is not attested in any ancient document, but is
in such universal use later that it is probably authentic. The Old
Welsh word for a war-leader is *dragwn, dragon;* and *pendragon*

means "head war-leader." Occasionally we find *draig* (which usually means "dragon") used for "leader." Both words undoubtedly come from the Latin *dracō*. From the time of Trajan onward the dragon was the common standard of the Roman cohort, as the eagle was of the legion. Since most of the troops in Britain operated as cohorts rather than as legions, the dragon standard must have been well known in the military districts, and may even have been adopted by the native auxiliary troops. At any rate, it is not difficult to see a transfer of the name from the standard itself to the leader whom it represents. . . .[372]

. . . Welsh tradition always calls Arthur "emperor" instead of *gwledig* as it does other leaders like Ambrosius, Cunedda, and Ceredic, and I assume that Arthur took both the title and the dragon standard for the sake of the prestige they gave him as the representative of Rome. In that case he would very appropriately be called "pendragon" to distinguish him from the lesser dragons.

The famous institution of the Round Table may likewise be explained on the basis of Roman custom. In the early days of the Empire the three couches of the *triclinium* came to be replaced by a single semi-circular couch—called *sigma* because of its shape—placed about a small round table. On informal occasions—for example, when troops were in the field—this couch was replaced by a simple bolster laid upon the ground, or even by a pile of straw with a cloth laid over it. "In olden times the couch was made of straw, as it is even now in camp," says Pliny.[373] . . . If the custom was retained by the Britons after the departure of the legions, as apparently it was, the institution of the Round Table may prove to be no more than the officers' mess of Arthur's Romanized British army. The actual "table" would always have room for as many or as few as were present, yet the cloth could easily be rolled up and carried on horseback. It would not be until this manner of eating had been forgotten because men now ate at upright wooden tables that the tales the Britons told of it would seem to be fables.[374]

WINSTON S. CHURCHILL

"The Birth of Britain"

From *A History of the English-Speaking Peoples*, Volume One
(New York: Dodd, Mead & Company, 1956).

Nennius . . . tells us, what Gildas omits, the name
of the British soldier who won the crowning mercy of Mount
Badon, and that name takes us out of the mist of dimly remembered
history into the daylight of romance. There looms, large, uncertain,
dim but glittering, the legend of King Arthur and the Knights of
the Round Table. Somewhere in the Island a great [58] captain
gathered the forces of Roman Britain and fought the barbarian invaders to the death. Around him, around his name and his deeds,
shine all that romance and poetry can bestow. Twelve battles, all
located in scenes untraceable, with foes unknown, except that they
were heathen, are punctiliously set forth in the Latin of Nennius.
Other authorities say, "No Arthur; at least, no proof of any Arthur."
It was only when Geoffrey of Monmouth six hundred years later
was praising the splendours of feudalism and martial aristocracy
that chivalry, honour, the Christian faith, knights in steel and
ladies bewitching, are enshrined in a glorious circle lit by victory.
Later this would have been retold and embellished by the genius
of Mallory, Spenser, and Tennyson. True or false, they have gained
an immortal hold upon the thoughts of men. It is difficult to believe
it was all an invention of a Welsh writer. If it was he must have
been a marvellous inventor.

Modern research has not accepted the annihilation of Arthur.
Timidly but resolutely the latest and best-informed writers unite
to proclaim his reality. They cannot tell when in this dark period
he lived, or where he held sway and fought his battles. They are

ready to believe however that there was a great British warrior, who kept the light of civilisation burning against all the storms that beat, and that behind his sword there sheltered a faithful following of which the memory did not fail. All four groups of the Celtic tribes which dwelt in the tilted uplands of Britain cheered themselves with the Arthurian legend, and each claimed their own region as the scene of his exploits. From Cornwall to Cumberland a search for Arthur's realm or sphere has been pursued.

The reserve of modern assertions is sometimes pushed to extremes, in which the fear of being contradicted leads the writer to strip himself of almost all sense and meaning. One specimen of this method will suffice.[59]

It is reasonably certain that a petty chieftain named Arthur did exist, probably in South Wales. It is possible that he may have held some military command uniting the tribal forces of the Celtic or highland zone or part of it against raiders and invaders (not all of them necessarily Teutonic). It is also possible that he may have engaged in all or some of the battles attributed to him; on the other hand, this attribution may belong to a later date.

This is not much to show after so much toil and learning. None the less, to have established a basis of fact for the story of Arthur is a service which should be respected. In this account we prefer to believe that the story with which Geoffrey delighted the fiction-loving Europe of the twelfth century is not all fancy. If we could see exactly what happened we should find ourselves in the presence of a theme as well founded, as inspired, and as inalienable from the inheritance of mankind as the *Odyssey* or the Old Testament. It is all true, or it ought to be; and more and better besides. And wherever men are fighting against barbarism, tyranny, and massacre, for freedom, law, and honour, let them remember that the fame of their deeds, even though they themselves be exterminated, may perhaps be celebrated as long as the world rolls round. Let us then, declare that King Arthur and his noble knights, guarding the Sacred Flame of Christianity and the theme of a world order, sustained by valour, physical strength, and good horses and armour, slaughtered innumerable hosts of foul barbarians and set decent folk an example for all time.

We are told he was Dux Bellorum. What could be more [60]

natural or more necessary than that a commander-in-chief should be accepted—a new Count of Britain, such as the Britons had appealed to Ætius to give them fifty years before? Once Arthur is recognised as the commander of a mobile field army, moving from one part of the country to another and uniting with local forces in each district, the disputes about the scenes of his actions explain themselves. Moreover the fourth century witnessed the rise of cavalry to the dominant position in the battlefield. The day of infantry had passed for a time, and the day of the legion had passed for ever. The Saxon invaders were infantry, fighting with sword and spear, and having little armour. Against such an enemy a small force of ordinary Roman cavalry might well prove invincible. If a chief like Arthur had gathered a band of mail-clad cavalry he could have moved freely about Britain, everywhere heading the local resistance to the invader and gaining repeated victories. The memory of Arthur carried with it the hope that a deliverer would return one day. The legend lived upon the increasing tribulations of the age. Arthur has been described as the last of the Romans. He understood Roman ideas, and used them for the good of the British people. "The heritage of Rome," Professor Collingwood says, "lives on in many shapes, but of the men who created that heritage Arthur was the last, and the story of Roman Britain ends with him."

Arthur's "twelfth battle," says Nennius, "was on Mount Badon, in which there fell in one day nine hundred and sixty men from the onslaught of Arthur only, and no one laid them low save he alone. And in all his battles he was victor. But they, when in all these battles they had been overthrown, sought help from Germany and increased without intermission."

All efforts to fix the battlefield of Mount Badon have failed. A hundred learned investigations have brought no results, but [61] if, as seems most probable, it was fought in the Debatable Land to check the advance from the East, then the best claimant to the title is Liddington Camp, which looks down on Badbury, near Swindon. On the other hand, we are able to fix the date with unusual accuracy. Gildas speaks of it as having occurred forty-three years and a month from the date when he was writing, and he says that he remembers the date because it was that of his own birth. Now we know from his book that the King of North Wales, Maelgwyn, was still alive when he wrote, and the annals of Cambria tell us that he died of the plague in 547. Gildas thus wrote at the latest in this year, and the Battle of Mount Badon, forty-three years earlier, would have been fought in 503. We have also a cross-check in the Irish annals, which state that Gildas died in 569 or 570. His birth is therefore improbable before 490, and thus the date of the battle seems to be fixed between 490 and 503.[62]

JOHN J. PARRY AND ROBERT A. CALDWELL

"Geoffrey of Monmouth's *Historia Regum Britanniae*"

From *Arthurian Literature in the Middle Ages*, ed. Roger Sherman Loomis (Oxford: at the Clarendon Press, 1959).

Geoffrey's two chief contributions to the book are the stories of Merlin and Arthur. There were previous Welsh legends about Myrddin . . . , but at this time Geoffrey seems to have known little about them. Apart from the form and something of the content of the prophecies . . . , he perhaps got from oral tradition the remarkable account of the transference of the Giants' Dance from Ireland to Salisbury Plain . . . . But he took from Nennius the tale of Vortigern and his tower, the dragons in the drained pool, and the marvellous boy without a father—Nennius's Ambrosius, whom Geoffrey adopted by the simple expedient of saying that Merlin was also called Ambrosius. The rest of the Merlin story seems to have been the child of his own fertile brain.

Regarding the treatment of Arthur, much remains uncertain, but a few of the most plausible conjectures may be set down. As to Uther Pendragon, whom Geoffrey credits with the begetting of Arthur, opinion is divided as to whether there was a tradition about him or whether his name grew out of a misunderstanding of the Welsh *uthr*, 'terrible'. For the story of Arthur's begetting there are many parallels. Faral pointed to the classical myth of Jupiter and Alcmene. Nutt preferred the Irish tale of *The Birth of Mongan,* while Gruffydd took the combined evidence of this tale and of the *mabinogi* of *Pwyll* to argue the existence of a Celtic tradition of a wonder child begotten by a god who visited the mother in the shape of a king, her husband.[83] But if these stories came to Geoffrey in anything like the form in which we have them, he used his imagination freely upon them.

Nennius is the obvious source of Arthur's battles with the Saxons and of the natural marvels connected with *stagnum Lumonoi* (Loch Lomond) and Linliguan, although the possibility that Geoffrey used other traditions cannot be excluded. At any rate, from Nennius's list of battle sites he took over three. The river Dubglas, which Nennius placed in the region of Linnuis, wherever that may be, Geoffrey placed south of York, perhaps under the impression that Linnuis was Lindsey (north Lincolnshire). After interposing a siege of York and a battle at Lincoln, for which Nennius furnished no warrant, Geoffrey carried the war into Scotland and placed Arthur's next victory at the wood of Celidon, which he found in Nennius. The great historic battle of Mons Badonis, which is the climax of Nennius's list, Geoffrey arbitrarily located at Bath, and with characteristic ingenuity explained how the Saxons turned up at a place so far from their late defeat in the wood of Celidon by telling how they broke their promise to return to Germany, sailed round to Totnes, and advanced on Bath from the south.

The shield Pridwen, the sword Caliburnus, and the lance Ron which Arthur bore in the battle of Bath were derived more or less directly from Welsh sources, for in *Culhwch and Olwen* Arthur mentions his sword Caledfwch and his spear Rhongomyniad, and both in *Culhwch* and the *Spoils of Annwfn* he voyages in a ship called Prydwen. From Welsh tradition also Geoffrey took over the concept of Arthur as a king at whose court assembled the notable men of his time, for this concept had been anticipated in *Culhwch*. But, as always, he was not content merely to adopt without change the materials provided. He made of Arthur's court a glorification of the courts he knew. Instead of the fantastic warriors named and described in the Welsh tale, Geoffrey surrounded Arthur with nobles and barons assembled from many parts of Western Europe, and added others whose names he picked at random from old Welsh pedigrees.

According to the *Historia*, Arthur's victories over the Saxons were followed by his subjugation of Scotland, Ireland, Norway, and Denmark, and one may guess that this career of conquest was inspired by even wilder flights of the Welsh imagination about the military exploits of Arthur, such as one [84] finds in the speech of Glewlwyd in *Culhwch*. But these triumphs only prepared the way for greater. Frollo, tribune of Gaul, felt the weight of Caliburnus and perished in single combat; thus all Gaul was added to Arthur's dominions. The great climax, which Geoffrey carefully prepared, was the humiliation of Lucius Hiberus, Emperor of Rome. . . .

A hero as great as Arthur could not be conceived as falling except by treachery, and so Geoffrey introduced Modred. It is possible that there was a story about him, for the *Annales Cambriae*, we know, have the entry 'Battle of Camlann, in which Arthur and Medraut fell'. There is no indication whether the two were friends or enemies, but the triads and *Rhonabwy's Dream* refer to the battle in terms which show no dependence on Geoffrey's narrative.

For Geoffrey's contemporaries this story of Arthur seems to have been the high point of the book, as it is for moderns, and Geoffrey clearly intended it to be. Some of the interest in the Arthurian section was no doubt the result of the tremendous vogue of current stories, but much is also the result of the author's artistry. As Tatlock says: 'It is hard to think of a single medieval work of any extent with such foresighted, indeed classical symmetry; it recalls the structure of good tragedy.' Here, as in the work as a whole, Geoffrey employed a plain style with few deviations from classical Latin, though he could be pompous and rhetorical, as in the dedications, when the occasion seemed to demand ornament. The verses he introduced into Book I were so good that John Milton, no mean Latinist himself, could hardly believe [85] that they were authentic . . . .

Geoffrey's avowed purpose in composing his *magnum opus* was to provide the descendants of the Britons with a history of their race from the earliest times. The French, the Normans, and the Saxons had theirs, but the Welsh and Bretons had only the meagre scraps provided by Nennius and the hostile narratives of the Anglo-Saxons and the Romans, before whom there was only a blank. Here was an opportunity which a man with Geoffrey's gifts—and lack of historical conscience—could hardly miss. If the account was not true, something like it was—or should have been.

The various dedications, it is obvious, were designed to gain the more personal end of securing the favour of patrons. The complimentary portrait of Eldol, Earl of Gloucester, was surely intended to please the living Earl Robert, and the pictures of good and highly capable queens were probably written to prepare the way for rule by Matilda, whom Henry I had first designated as his heir in 1127.

Geoffrey seems also to have desired to help the English kings in their effort to assert their independence of the kings of France. As dukes of Normandy they were vassals of the French kings, who ruled as heirs of Charlemagne. But if Brutus, ravaging nearly all of Aquitaine and building Tours, had defeated the kings and peers of Gaul, if Belinus and Brennius had reduced 'the whole kingdom to submission', and if Arthur had again conquered France, all before Charlemagne's time, then the French kings should be subject to those of England. Another point brought out by the book was that all the king's subjects, no matter what their race—Geoffrey conveniently ignores the Anglo-Saxons—were kindred, for both Celts and French were descended from Trojan exiles. This would apply equally well to the subjects of Henry I or Matilda or Stephen, and when Henry II and Eleanor of Aquitaine came to the throne, its application was far broader than Geoffrey could have imagined when he first thought of the idea. . . .[86]

. . . The history proved to be a great success, even if a serious chronicler like William of Newburgh denounced its patent falsehoods, and Giraldus Cambrensis, with more humour, showed that he recognized Geoffrey's fantastic narrative for what it was. According to Giraldus, in his *Itinerarium Cambriae* . . . , there lived in the neighbourhood of Caerleon a certain Meilerius, a familiar of evil spirits, through whose aid he could predict the future, distinguish truth from falsehood, and, even though he was illiterate, pick out the [87] false passages in a book. 'It happened once, when he was being abused beyond measure by foul spirits, that the Gospel of John was placed on his breast; the spirits vanished completely, at once flying away like birds. When it was later removed and the *History of the Britons* by Geoffrey Arthur substituted for it, by way of experiment, they settled down again, not only on his entire body, but also on the book itself, for a longer time than they were accustomed to, in greater numbers, and more loathsomely.' But Giraldus could also on occasion cite the *Historia*, and for the most part it was accepted as both authoritative history and interesting reading.

The number of manuscripts (about 200) that have come down to us is exceedingly large for a work of this period, and there are few medieval historians after 1150 who do not show extensive traces of Geoffrey's influence. Even before his death Alfred of Beverley based his own history upon it, and Henry of Huntingdon, the early form of whose work Geoffrey had probably used, drew from it in the later recensions of his own *Historia Anglorum*. Prince Llywelyn ap Gruffydd justified his title to Wales by pointing out his lineal descent from Camber, to whom Brutus had given all the land west of the Severn. King Edward I, in his dispute with Pope Boniface VIII over the sovereignty of Scotland, cited, with the approval of his barons, Geoffrey's narrative as proof of his claim. A monk of St. Albans, when he came to describe the wedding feast of this King Edward and Princess Margaret of France, copied almost verbatim Geoffrey's account of Arthur's Pentecostal feast. . . .[88]

. . . In conclusion, one may say of Geoffrey of Monmouth that he was a scholar with a very wide range of reading, a stylist of high competence in both prose and verse, a bold and imaginative writer of fiction in the guise of history. With such talents it needed no Merlin to prophesy that he would be read for generations to come. But even Merlin himself could hardly have foreseen that Geoffrey's work would affect the politics of Great Britain for five centuries, and that the greatest poets of England would drink from his fountain.[93]

J. S. P. TATLOCK

"Geoffrey of Monmouth's Historiography"

From *The Legendary History of Britain* (Berkeley and Los Angeles: University of California Press, 1950).

The most original and pleasing feature of Geoffrey's manner is in the structure of the *Historia*. Here was a problem for him, which he seems to have been conscious enough to foresee. His book is not extremely long; had he written on William of Malmesbury's scale it would have been seven or eight times as long as it is. He had to cover some nineteen centuries,—was he to cover them *pari passu* in a bald and even summary like annals, or was he to attempt to enliven at frequent moments evenly throughout? Or in the midst of rapid summary with only brief slowings up was he to intersperse highly developed narratives? To perceive this last to be his solution a bird's-eye view of the narrative will be serviceable.

Brutus and his exile; becomes leader of the Trojan captives in Greece, defeats the Greeks, weds a Greek princess, and conducts his people through various adventures to found the Briton nation. His son Locrinus' marriages. This part full of exciting and romantic detail.

A long series of kings, with here and there an individual touch.

The Leir-story, detailed, romantic, touching and ethical.

A series of kings, with individual touches.

Belinus and Brennius, their relations, and conquest of Gaul and Rome; changeful and violent.

A long series of kings, here and there with striking brief incident.

Invasion of Britain by Caesar and later Romans, with exciting military and personal detail.

A series of kings, and relations to the Romans, with more incidental detail than usual, the most confusing part of the work.

The history of Vortegirnus, Uther and his brothers, the coming and struggle of the Saxons; Merlin, leading into the history of Arthur, his wars and conquests, his campaigns against the Romans and Modredus, and his passing away. The longest, and most unified and climactic part of the *Historia*.

A series of kings, as before.[392]

The romantic and pathetic histories of Caduallo and Cadualadrus, and the downfall of the Briton monarchy.

There are two notable points in the structure. First is the alternation between rapid sketches covering much but undefined time, with enough varied brief detail and incident to prevent complete baldness; and more attractive expansive slower concentration dealing with the same *dramatis personae* and connected events. The premeditation of this technique is shown by the fact that while for all the other concentrations Geoffrey made more or less use of known sources, in the Leir-story he went the length of introducing a mere folk tale because he needed some concentration between those with Locrinus and Belinus. The second point is the gradual working up to a climax three-quarters through, after Arthur's succession of triumphs, in his Pentecostal crown-wearing (IX, 12-14), picturesque, imposing, happy, described with controlled but perceptible enthusiasm; broken into dramatically by the ominous Roman threat, with the momentary relief in his following victory, but ending with a crash in Modredus' treachery and Arthur's end. This is followed by a descending action, which terminates with Cadualadrus in sad and resigned finality. The biography of Arthur itself, in composition wholly original with Geoffrey, is highly dramatic and climactic. It is hard to think of a single medieval work of any extent with such foresighted, indeed classical symmetry; it recalls the structure of good tragedy. It is thoroughly unlike medieval writers, who in structure were apt to drift; unless, that is, they fol-

lowed the stiff regimentation of the scholastics, as men like Gower
and scores of others did, including even Dante. Geoffrey's more
subtle symmetry is hard to trace to any precedent. Unlike valid historians, who were apt to become more and more detailed as they
neared their own time, and therefore found more matter, he had
little obligation to facts and sources to prevent an appropriate but
not inevitable architectonic symmetry. The structure alone would
make any keen modern suspect that the work is not genuine tradition but invention. It is also extraordinarily interesting to see what
an able medieval, free from any obligation to fact, made of his
conception of the past. He could see it fundamentally only as a
bodying-forth of his own present. And herein he was mostly wise.
Until we can see humanity past, present and future as an essence
and a whole, we shall never understand the present or determine
the future.

For the rest, much use has been made here of the very thorough
and judicious "Historiography of Geoffrey of Monmouth" by Dr.
Francis J. Colligan. After a summary of the elements and traits
which mark Geoffrey's manner as a pretended historian, he compares him with some nineteen earlier historical writers, chosen
among some fifty, dating from Livy, Florus and [393] Eutropius to
Fulcher of Chartres and Henry of Huntingdon. The result is to
confirm what might be expected in an able and rather individual
writer who wished to seem authentic as well as attractive.

Even to summarize the usages he has in common with the more
cultivated medieval historians is hardly necessary,—the quotations
from classical writers, the citation of authorities, the prophecies recorded, the pretense of precision, the chronology, the orations and
documents, the rhetorical style (less than in some). Certain traits
are due to purpose and personality,—the racial partizanship (not
uncommon elsewhere), the regnal framework, the centering on the
kings' personal histories, the exhibition of the Britons' early ad-
vancement in civilization as shown in great buildings, highways,
codes of law, art . . . ; the secular, non-ecclesiastical and usually
rationalistic spirit (a trait uncommon elsewhere), with little of the
Christian miraculous, though it has been pointed out by Dr. H.
Richter that about Geoffrey's time writers were stressing the importance of *ratio* alongside *auctoritas*. The continuity, infrequency of
digression, was called for by the immense time covered in a work by

no means long. Other appropriate elements and usages are traceable to certain works familiar to Geoffrey, or at least are paralleled in them, though found elsewhere. The statement of how he came to write, and the naming of his authorities, are in Nennius, Bede, William of Malmesbury, and Henry of Huntingdon. The last three further have dedicatory addresses, Geoffrey's two contemporaries directing them to the very men to whom he directed the whole *Historia* and the Prophecies of Merlin. The heading the history with a description of the island is in all except William (in Nennius a little later). In narrating marvelous secular events he is rather moderate, compared with many contemporaries; his account of the outlandish physical marvels in Scottish lakes (IX, 6-7,—quite in the Celtic taste) comes straight from Nennius . . . though not without parallels also in William and Henry. In Nennius too is Geoffrey's method of getting reality and solid chronology for his earlier part by means of parallel history and synchronisms,—by mentioning contemporaries of his kings among familiar classical and Hebrew worthies. The use of [394] eponymy, a frequent medieval usage, is especially noteworthy in Nennius. Geoffrey gains solidity and unity by deriving place-names from persons' names, especially where he is establishing his beginnings. His insertion of prophecies is paralleled notably in William, Henry and Nennius. As something of a parallel to his scope Henry briefly traces the Franks from the Trojan War, and William from the fourth century A.D.

No one can say from what historians he got this or that trait, for he had read many. What they omit he omits, as well as more humdrum things which they include. . . . as a model for form the chief was probably William of Malmesbury. William shows no such trimmed-down symmetrical structure as Geoffrey; he has also more grasp, philosophy and world view . . . . Nearly all Geoffrey's chief features are in William and Nennius.

The *Historia* was written not for the intellectually ablest, and assuredly not for churchmen, or the populace, but for favorable specimens of the upper-class laity, though it came more and more to appeal to those for whom it was not designed. Geoffrey's own limitations in realistic subtlety (but who else would have had so much?), and his speed, ruled out much that might have made the book more like his models,—notice of strifes of church and state, of legislation and the courts, taxation, vexatious extortions, abuses and confiscations, rebellions, shocking events. His view of the fancied past is a glazed, distant, ideal view. He undertakes to be a historian, not a chronicler, according to the highly interesting distinction between the two made a half-century later by Gervase of Canterbury; the latter being simple, condensed, modest, annalistic, the former expansive, decorative, soberly charming, life-like. This was Geoffrey's aim.[395]

ALBERT C. BAUGH

"Definition, Characteristics, and 'Matters' of Medieval Romance"

From *A Literary History of England,* ed. Albert C. Baugh (New York: Appleton-Century-Crofts, 1948).

To most people today the word *romance* suggests a love story, and because some medieval romances involve famous love stories—such as those of Lancelot and Guinevere, Tristan and Iseult, Floris and Blancheflour—they assume that a love interest is a necessary ingredient in the romance of the Middle Ages. This is not strictly true. One has only to think of the romances of Alexander, Richard the Lion-Hearted, and many lesser figures to realize that medieval romance could get along very well with little or no love element. The basic material is knightly activity and adventure, and we may best put the emphasis in the right place if we define the medieval romances as a story of adventure—fictitious and frequently marvelous or supernatural—in verse or prose. Except for the few romances in which a love story is the main feature, love, if it enters into the narrative at all, is either subordinated to the adventure *(Erec, Yvain)*, or is incidental, as when a Saracen princess conceives a desperate passion for the hero *(Bevis of Hampton)*, or is used as a motivating force, an excuse for the adventures of the hero *(Guy of Warwick)*. It may be added that the earlier romances are in verse; those in prose are generally late. The former ordinarily range in length from one thousand to six thousand lines, with occasional productions running to nearly double this limit. The commonest metres are the eight-syllable couplet and a variety of tail-rime stanzas *(aabccb, aaabcccb,* and twelve-line stanzas of more elaborate pattern).

The romance in verse, in so far as it tends to be a narrative of heroic adventure, has some things in common with the epic. But it has less unity of action and the characters are not so well defined. Although occasional romances have a simple and skilfully managed plot, many are little more than [173] a loose succession of incidents strung on a biographical thread. The characters of medieval romance are poorly differentiated. They are types rather than individuals. The hero conforms to a pattern, that of the ideal knight, and within the pattern there is little room for individual variation. Lancelot, Tristan, Gawain—they are hardly distinguishable, although we can occasionally recognize Lancelot by catching a glimpse of Guinevere in the background, or Tristan if he is contriving a secret meeting with Iseult. Since the romance deals for the most part with types and the hero is himself an idealized type, the action likewise does not admit of great variety. There is only one way in which a knight may prove himself worthy to be the hero of the story and that is by showing himself superior to other knights. Now the ways in which one may dispose of an opponent in tournament or battle are limited, and it is therefore not surprising that the poet occasionally foists in a giant or a dragon to lend variety to his hero's adventures. Yet in spite of the obvious weaknesses of the genre—weakness in plot, faintness of characterization, sameness of incident—it is surprising how interesting the individual romance, taken by itself, contrives to be.

The romance in its beginning was an aristocratic type appealing to the tastes of the upper class. As long as French remained the normal language of the English ruling classes the romances that circulated in England were French and those written in England were written in French. This means that romances in English are not to be expected until English begins to displace French as the language of polite society, that is, until the middle of the thirteenth century. There is only one English romance that can be dated with certainty earlier than 1250. Unfortunately by this time the romance in France, and indeed in Europe generally, had passed its prime. The great creative period of medieval romance was the twelfth century, and the beginning of the thirteenth. By the end of the latter century the type begins to deteriorate. Poets, chewing over the old straw, are driven to desperate measures to make it seem more palatable. Overstraining after effect replaces the easy confidence of a Chrétien de Troyes or Gottfried von Strassburg. Most of our English romances belong to the fourteenth century and nearly all of them are translations or adaptations from French originals. Yet while they seldom come up to the level of medieval romance at its best, it must not be thought that they are quite what readers of Chaucer might infer from *Sir Thopas.*

While medieval romance was at the height of its popularity a Continental poet, Jean Bodel, wrote in his *Chanson des Saisnes:*

N'en sont que trois materes a nul home entendant
De France, et de Bretaigne, et de Rome la grant.[174]

[There are only three matters for any man of understanding,
Those of France, and of Britain, and of Rome the great.]

It has been customary ever since to speak of medieval romance under these headings—the Matter of Rome, by which is meant romances based on classical history and legend, the Matter of France, meaning stories of Charlemagne and his peers, and the Matter of Britain or the Arthurian cycle. This is a fairly adequate statement of aristocratic taste on the Continent, but it needs to be supplemented in one direction for England. It leaves out of account a group of romances of great interest. These are the romances concerned with native English heroes or with a figure like Havelok the Dane, whose fortunes are tied up with England and whose principal adventures take place in the island. Later it would have been necessary for a comprehensive classification to take cognizance of many romances of Eastern and other exotic themes.[175]

GWYN JONES AND
THOMAS JONES

"Culhwch and Olwen"

From "Introduction," *The Mabinogion*, trans. Gwyn Jones and
Thomas Jones (London: J. M. Dent & Sons Ltd., 1949).

The eleven stories of the Mabinogion present a remarkable diversity within their medieval pattern. They fall into
obvious groups: the Mabinogi proper, composed of the Four
Branches of *Pwyll, Branwen, Manawydan* and *Math*; the two short
pieces, *The Dream of Macsen Wledig* and *Lludd* and *Llefelys*; the
incomparable and unclassifiable *Culhwch and Olwen*, the earliest
Arthurian tale in Welsh; *The Dream of Rhonabwy*, a romantic and
sometimes humorously appreciative looking-back to the heroic age
of Britain; and the three later Arthurian romances, *The Lady of
the Fountain, Peredur,* and *Gereint Son of Erbin,* with their abun-
dant evidence of Norman-French influences.

This diversity should not, however, tempt us to overlook a sub-
stantial unity—a unity which is imposed both by their subject matter and their social and literary milieu. The matter is primarily
mythology in decline and folklore, though it is unlikely that the
story-tellers were themselves often, if ever, aware of this. But that
such personages as Bendigeidfran, Rhiannon, Math and Mabon
son of Modron, to name but a few, are in both the literary and
mythological sense of divine origin, is so conclusively to be proved
from the Mabinogion itself, from the rich and extensive Irish
analogues, and from our knowledge of the myth-making and myth-
degrading habits of our remote world-ancestors, that the theme
needs no development at our hands. Euhemerised though they are,

they remain invested with a physical and moral grandeur which amply bespeaks their [x] godlike state and superhuman nature. The evidences of a pervading mythology are neither so numerous nor so striking in the later romances, but these too are seldom far from folklore. Other elements common to all or most of the tales are those styled onomastic, the attempts to explain place-names, and the historical in so far as the references to Arthur and heroic story of non-divine origin may be called historical.

That Wales had its bards is a circumstance known to most. So too that the bards celebrated their patrons in verse. That oftentimes these bards were also story-tellers whose medium was prose or prose and verse is an item of knowledge as well-authenticated though rather less widely diffused. The eleven tales of the Mabinogion are not the only examples of their craft which have survived, and the craft flourished during no shorter period than from the sixth century to the fifteenth. We know that the *cyfarwydd's*, or story-teller's, stock-in-trade included many elaborate saga-cycles in which prose was the medium of narrative and description, and verse, often of the englyn type, of monologue and dialogue. Other tales were entirely in prose, and we are encouraged to guess at their number when we remember that the Irish *ollamh* was required, as a professional qualification, to know three hundred and fifty such. The triads and later verse, as well as Nennius and Geoffrey of Monmouth, suggest that the Welsh story-tellers yielded to none in amplitude of material. Their tales were delivered orally, and centuries passed before some few of them were committed to writing. They had thus no fixed and inviolable form, but took shape and colour from a hundred minds, each with its human disposition to variance and mutability. . . .[xi]

The author of the Four Branches . . . was an artist who concealed his art. Not so the author of *Culhwch and Olwen*, who deploys with gusto every resource of language and style to heighten the colour and deepen the character of the fantastic and primitive world his creatures inhabit. It is a world in which birds and beasts are as important as men, a world of hunting, fighting, shape-shifting and magic. Immemorial themes of folklore are here: the jealous stepmother, the swearing of a destiny, asking a boon, the fulfilment of tasks, the helping animal, the oldest animals, the freeing of the prisoner, the hunting of the Otherworld beast, all strung along the controlling thread of Culhwch's seeking the giant's daughter for wife—itself one of the oldest themes of all. The zest of this unknown story-teller still hits one like a bursting wave; there is magnificence in his self-awareness and virtuosity. One feels how he rejoiced in being equal to all his occasions: the gallant picture of young Culhwch and his steed, the bombast of Glewlwyd Mighty-grasp, the poetic beauty of the episode of the oldest animals, the savage grotesquery of Ysbaddaden Chief Giant, the headlong rush of the hunting of Twrch Trwyth, the lyricism of the description of Olwen. Now he is bare, hard, staccato; now he luxuriates with adjectives, compounds, puns even. It is not surprising that his story is rather loosely held together: his delight in its parts has affected its unity. Twice there appears to be an attempt to bind the diverse elements together, but each time on the dubious principle that the wider you throw your net the more surely you bring things together. When Culhwch first goes to Arthur's court, the narrator supplies a list of personages which is at once an index to cycles of lost story and a glimpse into his own teeming imagination; and second, at the court of Ysbaddaden, he finds place for a list of some forty tasks, presumably each one of them the hook on which a story might be hung. Arthur's warriors and Yasbaddaden's demands are each a mytho-heroic [xxi] assemblage, and one reads them with the sensation that here, tantalizingly glimpsed, is a vast rolling panorama of lost Celtic story. Less than half the tasks are fulfilled, and of those, three do not figure in Ysbaddaden's list. It is probable that the list of tasks has been extended and not the accomplishments reduced. The personages of Arthur's court, surely the oddest retinue of any court in the world, and the list of tasks, would between them justify almost any wanderings of an author's furious fancies, but we are left with the impression of a conception too great for one man's powers. Unless indeed we have to do with a mutilated version of a masterpiece. What is left, however, is unique, a native saga hardly touched by alien influences, exciting and evocative, opening windows on great vistas of the oldest stuff of folklore and legend. After the Four Branches, it is the one story of the Mabinogion whose loss would not be made good by any other product of the medieval art of story-telling.

This is not the place to discuss the historical and pseudo-historical references to Arthur to be found in the *Historia Brittonum*

associated with the name of Nennius, and in the *Annales Cambriae.*
But it would be an omission not to stress that *Culhwch and Olwen*
is a document of the first importance for a study of the sources of
the Arthurian legend. The Arthur it portrays is, of course, remarkably unlike the gracious, glorious emperor of later tradition,
whether exemplified in the literatures of France, Germany, or
England, or for that matter in the concluding Arthurian romances
of [*The Mabinogion*], subject as they have been to Norman-French
influences. But when we recall that Arthur was not a French, German or English, but a British king, it is not unreasonable to emphasize the significance of British (which in this connexion means
Welsh) material relating to him. British material, that is, uncon-
taminated by the Cycles of Romance, though necessarily affected by
the vast complex of Celtic myth and legend. It consists for the most
part [xxii] of some exceptionally difficult poems, and of *Culhwch
and Olwen* itself.[xxiii] . . . Clearly these poems and *Culhwch and
Olwen* are much of a piece. They tell of the same people, and the
events [xxiv] described are of a kind too. . . . The feats attributed
to Arthur's followers in the Glewlwyd dialogue would not be out
of place in *Culhwch and Olwen:* the slaying of hags, monsters,
witches. Cei and Bedwyr are consistent characters throughout, the
former bearing little resemblance to the discourteous and ineffective
buffoon of later romance. And what of Arthur himself? His nature is
unmistakable: he is the folk hero, a beneficent giant, who with his
men rids the land of other giants, of witches and monsters; he undertakes journeys to the Otherworld to rescue prisoners and carry
off treasures; he is rude, savage, heroic and protective. And already
he is attracting to himself the myths of early gods and the legends
of early heroes. In other words, he is at the centre of British story;
he is the very heart of it, both for his fame as *dux bellorum* and
protector of Roman Britain against all its invaders (the historical
and pseudo-historical Arthur), and for his increasingly dominating
role in Celtic folklore and legend. It is remarkable how much of
this British Arthur has survived in the early twelfth-century *Historia* of Geoffrey of Monmouth and the mid-fifteenth-century
Morte Darthur of Malory. Arthur setting off with Kaius and Bed-
euerus to slay the swine-eating Spanish giant, and bursting out
laughing when the monster crashes like a torn-up oak, or his battle
with the beard-collecting Ritho, are cases in point. The growth may

be traced both backwards and forwards. Behind the royal features in Geoffrey and Malory may be discerned the ruder lineaments of the folk hero; in the folk hero of [xxv] *Culhwch and Olwen* one observes adumbrations of king and emperor. This is one of the three chief glories of this astonishing tale: its importance as a well-head of Arthurian romance. The other two are its richness as a repository of the early lore of Britain and its brilliance as prose narrative. For these things it is by itself, alone.[xxvi]

ERNEST HOEPFFNER

"Biket's *Lay of the Horn*"

From *Arthurian Literature in the Middle Ages*, ed. Roger Sherman Loomis (Oxford: at the Clarendon Press, 1959).

The earliest surviving lai is probably the *Lai du Cor* of Robert Biket. It is archaic in its verse form, being composed in six-syllable verses instead of the normal octosyllables; archaic also is the rather crude humour with which it treats the great King Arthur and his court. Indeed, Lucien Foulet and Bruce refused to accept the poem as a genuine lai because of its unromantic tone, and classed it as a *fabliau*. But must a Breton lai necessarily be serious and sentimental? Must it treat Arthur's fellowship with high respect? There are other poems called lais which are even more grossly cynical, and Chrétien [de Troyes] himself is by no means consistently flattering in his portrayal of Arthur.[113]

The *Lai du Cor* has been dated in the third quarter of the twelfth century, but not by conclusive criteria. Of Biket we know nothing except that his language betrays the Anglo-Norman. He

professes to have had the tale from an abbot . . . , and asserts
that the magic horn was to be seen at Cirencester—statements which
there is no more reason to doubt than that there was shown at St.
Seurin at Bordeaux what professed to be the horn of Roland.
Though Cirencester was then not more than twenty miles from the
Welsh-speaking district beyond the Severn, it is significant that the
personal names which Biket introduces are as remote from the corresponding Welsh forms as the names in any Continental French
romance. . . .

The general theme of the lai is found at different times and
under different forms in the folk-lore of many peoples. In this
poem it is a drinking-horn which is sent to Arthur's court at Caerleon by King Mangoun of Moraine and which has the property of
exposing the slightest infidelity of a wife. Arthur insists on the
experiment and, when he tries to drink, is drenched with wine from
top to toe. He would have killed the queen if his knights had not
intervened. But he recovers his good humour when he finds that all
who follow his example are similarly disillusioned by the magic
horn, and he pardons her with a kiss. Finally Garadue passes the
test triumphantly, and Arthur awards him the lordship of Cirencester.

Though stories of chastity tests are spread far and wide, and
though the *Lai du Cor* was not derived directly from the Welsh, it
may be significant that all medieval versions of the horn test are
set in Arthur's banquet hall, and that the hero bears a name renowned in Wales and Brittany.

One cannot affirm that Biket knew Chrétien's *Erec,* but he
must have known Wace. The list of royal guests, the toast 'Wesseil'
which Garadue [114] proposed to Arthur, the respectful treatment
of Keerz (Kay), and certain stylistic features assure us of the fact.
Though nearly contemporary with Chrétien's earliest work, the
Lai du Cor belongs to an older world, and its importance lies
largely in shedding light on the nature of Arthurian fiction before
the influence of Chrétien was felt. [115]

ROBERT HUNTINGTON FLETCHER

"Wace's *Roman de Brut*"

From *The Arthurian Material in the Chronicles,* Harvard Studies and Notes in Philology and Literature, X (Boston: Ginn & Company, 1906).

In general Wace's *Brut* is merely a free paraphrase of Geoffrey's *History.* It follows exactly the same order and observes practically the same proportion; in brief, it closely reproduces, in the main, the substance of its original. But Wace was very far from being a servile translator, and the great differences which distinguish his race, character, occupation, aim, language, and literary form from those of Geoffrey reappear as fully as was to be expected in his work. They are manifested partly in certain general characteristics, partly in an infinitude of minutiæ which Wace adds merely as a poet and a literary artist. For any light upon the origins of [128] the organic material of the Arthurian tradition, such characteristics and details are of no consequence; but in the literary study of the development of the tradition they assume significance. It is desirable, therefore, before taking up Wace's important changes and additions, to give attention to these others.

In the first place, Geoffrey's *History* and Wace's *Brut* stand for very different literary styles. Geoffrey put his romance into the form of an ostensibly truthful Latin chronicle. Thus he had to preserve an appearance of veracity, to maintain dignity of style, and to cultivate rhetorical elegance. Wace, though he took the story seriously enough, and was doubtless willing to be believed, employs the form of the French metrical romance. Geoffrey's sympathy with his subject was not less keen than that of Wace, and his humor was probably greater; yet the form of his work was sometimes a hindrance to him, while Wace had adopted a style and manner that were peculiarly well adapted to the material.

The most pervasive general contrast between the two styles is in vividness of narrative. Geoffrey had plenty of imagination, both dramatic and romantic, but Latin periods were not the aptest instruments for its expression. Besides, if his work was to have the air of truthful history, he could not, in general, lay claim to the detailed personal knowledge of an eyewitness or a contemporary. He could not venture to vivify and visualize the whole story. Perhaps a personal limitation entered into the case. What little we know of Geoffrey indicates that, while he was by no means a pedant, he was rather a student than a man of action; he got his ideas rather from reading than from experience. Except for a case or two like his minute description of Arthur's second coronation (which may well be taken in large part from life), and even in his accounts of battles, where he most warms to the subject and seems to wish to be thoroughly dramatic, he writes almost always, not of details but in general terms. And he is not always convincingly practical.[129] His battle speeches, too, even when they are delivered in the thick of the fight, are ornate orations, which no general could really have delivered and no soldier would have stopped to listen to.

With Wace, on the other hand, the quick-moving conversational octosyllabic couplet scarcely allows the effect of dullness, even in the least interesting parts of the narrative. And Wace himself is never afraid of seeming to know too much,—rather of not seeming to know everything. He sees whatever he writes about, and for the most part makes his readers see it too. He does not content himself, for instance, with describing the course of a battle from the point of view of a pseudo-scientific strategist: he names the various parts of the equipments of the knights and soldiers, pictures how they crashed together in the shock of the charge, how they struck and fell. He gives the impression that he is not merely imitating other metrical romances, but is reproducing what he has himself witnessed and been fired by.

One might illustrate this increase of vividness on the part of Wace by citing a large proportion of the fifteen thousand lines of his poem; but a few instances must suffice. As to the more particular details of warfare,—he speaks of foragers; describes Arthur's smallest movements in the fight with the giant; and tells how Arthur had his men advance to battle slowly, not allowing them to straggle at all. In beginning his account of Hengist's first treacherous proposals to Vortigern, he gives a lifelike setting by observing that *one day* Hengist found the king disposed to listen. In the same passage he makes Hengist say that he will send to Germany for his wife and children. Geoffrey spoke only of the warriors who were important for the immediate purposes of his narrative and whose deeds were dignified enough for the pages of history; but Wace's imagination was, or could afford to be, more practical. In telling of the escape of "Elduf" from the Saxons after his valiant [130] defense, he takes pains to explain how it was possible: Elduf got away on his horse, which was very good. When Merlin's mother was asked about her son, says Wace, she held her head down and thought a little before answering. In describing the duel between Arthur and Flollo, Wace expands Geoffrey's vague remark that the people were watching, by telling how the Parisians stood upon the walls and both sides prayed for the success of their respective champions. Longer passages of the same character occur. Thus in the account of the flight of the Saxons before Cador, we are told how they went two by two or three by three as best they could, how they had thrown down their arms, and how Cador followed, shouting his battle cry. Most prominent, though not necessarily most important, in this connection, are certain notably extended passages of original details added by Wace. When Arthur's host is embarking for the campaign against the Romans, Wace inserts a splendid picture of the scene, with plenty of nautical terms,—the memories of his boyhood serving him well. Not less spirited, though shorter, is the account of the joy with which Arthur's soldiers are received on returning from their long sojourn in France. A similar addition is the description of the bustling activity of the servants at Arthur's second coronation.

Equally original, though perhaps with rather more direct suggestion from Geoffrey, is the account of the coming of Gawain and the other envoys to the army of the Emperor; or again, that of [131] the pursuit of the envoys by the Romans after Gawain has killed Lucius's nephew, beginning as it does with the extremely effective *es vous,* so useful to the mediæval French romancers.

Another feature of Wace's style which contributes greatly to its vividness is his largely increased use of direct discourse. Sometimes he merely inserts an ejaculation or brief cry, as in Gawain's apposite exhortation to his companions when they have got into trouble in the Emperor's camp . . . . Such an undignified kind of naturalness was entirely out of the range of Geoffrey's aristocratic chronicle style. More often, however, Wace gives a whole speech in the very words of the speaker. Sometimes he enlarges a speech of Geoffrey's, as in Lucius's message to Arthur; sometimes he changes a piece of narrative into this form, as in the plea of the Scots for mercy; occasionally, as in Gawain's address after the message of Lucius, he invents the whole passage.

Wace also manifests personal feeling about the events and characters of his story. Sometimes he expresses sorrow or disgust, as at Vortigern's desire to marry Roven; he stops to curse the slayer of Bedver; he occasionally applies abusive epithets to the enemies of the Britons. He makes appeals to the reader, not only by the device of employing the second person of the verb . . . to introduce a description, but more directly, as when he asks, speaking of Hengist's treachery, "Who would have feared a traitor?" or observes, "You never saw such a fight!" or, of the death of Ambrosius, "The gentle king wished to recover, as any of you would." [132]

How thoroughly representative Wace is of his environment appears in the fact that he applies to the narrative almost universally (while Geoffrey did so only partially and in the more vivid portions) the manners and customs of his own time. This is true, for instance, of his descriptions of battles and warlike operations. He makes Vortigern's fortress a feudal castle, which Aurelius destroys by filling the moat with wood and setting this on fire. He says that Uter, on going away, intrusts the care of his army to a baron. He speaks of particular duels in the course of a main battle. He calls even the pagans "chevaliers." Mediæval customs which he inserts or emphasizes are the feudal submission of one man to another; the pledging of his land by a lord; the appointment of viscounts and provosts; the use of the dais for king and barons at a feast. . . . When he does retain the antique customs mentioned by Geoffrey, he explains that manners were different in those days. Wace has also the mediæval bigotry towards pagans, something which scarcely appears in Geoffrey. He introduces a few touches of the descriptions of love which are so pronounced a feature in a writer like Crestien de

Troyes. In one case he shows that his taste is less reserved (more Gallic, perhaps) than Geoffrey's. Once or twice he manifests the disregard for the fact of time characteristic of romances. His omissions or assumptions sometimes make it clear that he is less of a scholar than Geoffrey, or is writing for a less learned audience.

Wace was not destitute of the critical instinct. He amends certain vague or inconsistent statements; he modifies his original [133] for the sake of naturalness or probability; and in one or two details he contradicts Geoffrey flatly, merely to give variety to the narrative. Not infrequently Wace adds an explanation for some action or fact which he thinks Geoffrey has not made perfectly [134] clear. Sometimes, to be sure, no such explanation is needed, but more often it is desirable or suggestive. . . .[135]

Occasionally Wace makes changes merely in order to improve the literary effect. . . .

Wace occasionally omits things which he does not understand or does not care for. This is true of certain legendary elements which in Geoffrey's narrative have lost their significance. . . . He omits the details of the fight of the dragons (which give Geoffrey an opportunity for mystical interpretation), and also the prophecies of Merlin (except those about Vortigern), since, he says, he does not comprehend them. In telling of Arthur's dream of the fight between the dragon and the bear, Wace drops out some less important details. He also omits Geoffrey's statement that Arthur imposed silence on all those who looked on the head of the giant.

Geoffrey sometimes tries to describe the order of armies in battle, but he never succeeds in giving a consistent or comprehensible account. Wace leaves out these statements or greatly [136] changes them. He omits also various names or other geographical details relating to England, especially Welsh names, though he sometimes changes his method by explaining where a place is, his object being, of course, to be intelligible to his French-speaking readers. He regularly translates the Latin names,—almost always into French, but sometimes, in the case of a well-known town in the south of England, into English. This method, together with corruptions which have got into the manuscripts, often makes his lists of lands and countries look quite different from those of Geoffrey. On the other hand, he frequently inserts names where continental geography is concerned.

We come now to Wace's more important alterations of Geoffrey's narrative.

In the first place, it is evident that he knew—and to some extent
he introduces into his poem—a conception of Arthur, and in a less
degree of his knights, which is essentially that of the chivalric
romances, and which Geoffrey, while he felt or foreshadowed its influence, did not by any means fully represent. Wace says nothing to
necessitate the conclusion that he got from any other source than
Geoffrey the idea of Arthur as a world conqueror and a great emperor; but he makes it as plain as possible that he knew plenty of
other stories about the hero and his knights. He refers directly to
these stories as having already assumed in his own time very extravagant proportions at the hands of *conteurs,* and he refers to their
substance again when he says that while Arthur was in France
many marvels happened, and he overthrew many a proud man
and kept in restraint many a felon. This is added to Geoffrey's
statement that Arthur spent nine years [137] in conquering France.
Reference has already been made to Wace's allusion to the Breton
expectation of Arthur's second coming, on the probability of which
he refuses to pronounce.

The spirit of these independent stories has influenced the tone
of some of Wace's statements, though for the most part he follows
Geoffrey's representation of Arthur closely enough. It sounds, for
instance, like the romances when Wace calls Arthur *li bons rois,* or
says that his men remarked enthusiastically that never before was
there so valiant a king in Britain. In almost every case he takes pains
to expunge from the story certain suggestions of barbarity or lack
of chivalrousness on the part of Arthur or his knights which occur
(survive?) in Geoffrey's version. . . . Geoffrey, who, in his quiet
study, thinks of war only as a scene of pomp, and of conquest only
as a thing of glory, delights in observing that Hoel devastated Gascony with sword and flame; Wace, indeed, suggests the same thing,
but indirectly. Geoffrey says that, in the battle with Lucius, Arthur
killed a man or a horse at every stroke; Wace omits all mention of
injuring horses, which was not strictly in accordance with the ideas
of chivalry. Wace says that Arthur [138] had the body of the dead
emperor cared for with great honor; Geoffrey merely mentions his
scornful sending of it to Rome.

That Wace knew Gawain from other sources than Geoffrey is

shown by the praise of him which he adds at the first mention of his name. In one striking instance Wace introduces the characteristic romance conception of Gawain. When, in the council of Arthur's lords, Cador has made his speech in favor of war, Gawain (according to Wace) replies, praising peace. The pleasures of love, he says, are good, and for the sake of his *amie* a young man performs feats of chivalry. Geoffrey mentions no speech by Gawain.

Wace's idea of Merlin is more like that of the later romancers than is Geoffrey's. Wace represents Merlin as a great magician of unique power and position, which are recognized as a matter of course by the other characters. He has no suggestion of Geoffrey's remark that, when Aurelius was advised to send for Merlin, he did not already know of him; and states that the king at once sought him at his fountain. Geoffrey represents messengers as dispatched to all parts of the country in quest of him. According to Geoffrey, when Uther was perplexed at the appearance of the comet, he sent for wise men, among them Merlin; but Wace mentions Merlin alone, implying that, with him to rely on, no others were needed. So much for Merlin's position. As to his power, Geoffrey hesitates to admit into his narrative a wholly supernatural figure; but Wace has no scruples of the sort. So when Geoffrey, doubtless following some old magical tale, tells how Merlin transformed his own appearance and that of Uther and Ulfin, he makes Merlin observe that [139] his arts are unknown to that time,—meaning, apparently, that they belong to the mysterious past. But Wace merely takes up the expression "new arts" (by which Geoffrey seems to intend, new *to Uther*) and employs it in a non-significant way, omitting all suggestion that it was strange that Merlin should have such power. Again, when Merlin moves the great stones from Ireland, after all Uther's army have failed in the attempt, Geoffrey rationalizes the scene and makes Merlin a sixth-century Edison, who merely has far more ingenious mechanical devices than any one else. Wace, however, says that Merlin mutters something which enables the youths to handle the stones: "I do not know," observes Wace, "whether he said a prayer or not."

It is quite possible that Wace developed these ideas from the material in Geoffrey alone,—that the conception of a thoroughly supernatural wizard was perhaps for any twelfth-century French romancer a necessary substitute for the anomalous Merlin of Geoffrey. If so, Wace's change is merely another instance of the natural development of Geoffrey's story in the hands of a man of Wace's race and time. But it is also possible that, as in the case of Arthur, Wace knew independent stories about Merlin.

In the second place, there are certain definite details added by Wace which either are, or may seem to be, derived from something else than Geoffrey's narrative. On closer consideration, however, most of them prove to be merely elaborations due to Wace himself. Such are several statements that one person was cousin to another; the remark that the Emperor Lucius was born in Spain, which is evidently an inference from his surname *Hiberius;* the statement that Arthur and Genievre could not have an heir, which, indeed, is scarcely an enlargement on the mere fact that according to Geoffrey [140] they did not have any. It is interesting, however, as showing that Wace either did not know, or else disregarded, the Welsh traditions which give Arthur a son.

Certain other of Wace's additions are somewhat more doubtful. . . . Wace's statement that Modred had already loved the queen before he was left in charge of Britain may be from independent tradition, but may as easily be an inference of his own.

Perhaps traditional (but not due to Wace) are certain interpolations in one of the early manuscripts: (1) the name *Dinabuc* for the giant of Mont St. Michel; (2) the statement that Modred was brother to Genievre, which is interesting in comparison with the idea which appears in the romances that Modred was the offspring of incest between Arthur and his sister. . . .[141]

. . . Much more significant are Wace's additions about the Round Table. Into the passage which tells of the great prestige of Arthur he inserts the statement that, because each of the barons thought himself better than the others, Arthur made the Round Table, "of which the 'Bretons' tell many a fable," so that none could boast of sitting higher than any other. Twice afterwards he speaks of the table, saying once that the knights who were in the court and formed the king's bodyguard belonged to it, and in the second case that the praise of its knights was great throughout the world. This certainly indicates that Wace knew previous stories about it, which may be considered substantially proved by the nearly certain fact that round tables were a very ancient pan-Celtic institution. The antiquity of the thing being admitted, there is no reason to doubt that its close association with Arthur goes back to a stage of the tradition anterior to Wace and Geoffrey.

What has been said of Wace's *Brut* may be briefly summarized as follows. Wace paraphrases Geoffrey, but with all the freedom natural to a mediæval French poet, a freedom which leads to the insertion of plenty of mediæval local color, and the infusion of much vividness into the style and the presentation. He almost always corrects Geoffrey's inconsistencies and obscurities, and in general he tries to make everything clear to his readers. Thus he adds a great many minor details of various kinds, which are not substantially important but which contribute very largely to Wace's entire change of the literary form. He introduces something of the [142] chivalric idea of Arthur and his knights, and the conception of Merlin as a magician. This may be partly (or, in the case of Merlin, wholly) his own development from Geoffrey's story; but it is far more probable that he drew to some extent from other Celtic Arthurian stories. From such he almost or quite certainly took some additional touches about Gawain, the mention of the Britons' expectation of Arthur's return, and the institution of the Round Table.[148]

HENRY CECIL WYLD

"Layamon as an English Poet"

From *The Review of English Studies*, VI (January, 1930).

The great work known as Laȝamon's* *Brut* is not
nearly so well known as it deserves to be among students of English poetry. The reasons for this are partly its great length—it runs
to 32,241 half-lines—partly the fact that it is only available, in its
entirety, in a single edition, the splendid one of Sir Frederick
Madden, now more than eighty years old, and not always easy to
come by, and lastly the apparent uncouthness and strangeness of
the language.

And yet, and this should be said at once, the *Brut* is incom-
parably the greatest achievement in English poetry between the
Anglo-Saxon period and Chaucer. For variety of interest, vigour,
and spirit, Robert of Brunne, though greatly inferior to Laȝamon
in poetical quality, can alone be compared to him. The only other
work in verse of approximately the same date as the *Brut,* and
nearly equal to it in bulk, the *Ormulum,* is so notoriously devoid
of those graces of diction and imagery which distinguish the *Brut,*
that it is negligible as poetry, and whatever interest it may possess
for the student of literature is confined to such as attaches to an
unsuccessful metrical experiment. To borrow a phrase of Johnson's,
"it cannot be read without reluctance." The metrical version of
Genesis and Exodus which belongs to a later part of the thirteenth
century, though redeemed from the dullness of a mere paraphrase
by the occasional flashes of vividness and of genuine human feeling,
can with difficulty be brought within the sphere of poetry.

* The poet's name is properly spelled this way in its earliest form, but it
has often been modernized to Layamon or Lawman. *Editor's note.*

The outstanding quality of Laȝamon's work, and this is found on every page, almost in every line, is the essential poetical character of [1] the diction. We feel in reading the work, as we feel in reading Anglo-Saxon poetry, that it is the deliberate intention of the writer to be poetical, and to produce something which shall appeal to the imagination and the emotions. It is this consciousness that he is writing poetry, and not merely telling a story or enforcing a moral, that leads Laȝamon to employ a diction which for the men of his time was deeply tinged with heroic and romantic associations, "words," as Dr. Johnson says, "refined from the grossness of domestic use." Laȝamon's language is not merely the ancient speech of Englishmen, almost free, at least in the older text, from foreign elements, it is the language of their old poetry, as Madden well says, "at every moment reminding us of the splendid phraseology of Anglo-Saxon verse." Laȝamon is thus in the true line of succession to the old poets of his land.

His vocabulary and his spirit are theirs. His poetry has its roots, not merely in the old literary tradition, but also, like this, in the essential genius of the race.

The intensity of feeling, the wealth of imagery, the tender humanity, the love of nature, the chivalrous and romantic spirit, which distinguish the poetry of Laȝamon would give him a high place among the English poets of any age. His copious, varied, and picturesque vocabulary, so rich in association, and often so suggestive of mysterious beauty, gives his work a lasting value possessed by no other Middle-English poetry before Chaucer, disfigured as so much of of [sic] this is by an unredeemed flatness, insipidity and matter-of-factness in thought and expression.

Our knowledge of Laȝamon as a man is limited to what he himself tells us—that he was a priest, the son of one Leovenath, that he lived at Ernley (Arley) on the banks of the Severn hard by Radstone, at a noble church—the later text adds "with a good knight"; there he lived happily and "read his books," which may either mean that there he read divine service, or that there he studied. It occurred to him—he uses the Old English phrase used by King Alfred, "hit com him on mode"—and occupied his chief thought, that he would tell the noble deeds of the English, what they were called, and whence they came who first possessed the land. He enumerates the sources of his information—"the English book that St. Bede made," another in Latin which he appears to ascribe to St. Albin and St. Augustin "who brought baptism hither." Lastly, "a third book which a French clerk called Wace [2] made." The first-named authority is supposed to be the Anglo-Saxon translation of Bede's History. Regarding the identity of the second considerable doubt arises. St. Augustine died in 604, Albinus, Abbot of St. Peter's Canterbury, died in 732, so it is rather hard to understand how they can have collaborated, or which work of either can be meant. As Albinus is known to have contributed some of the material to Bede's *History*, and as the *Interrogatories* of Augustine are inserted in the first book of the *History*, Madden suggests that, by a confusion of ideas, Laȝamon attributed the English version of the *History* to Bede, and the Latin original to Augustine and Albinus. But Laȝamon's chief source is Wace's metrical Chronicle, the *Brut*, in Anglo-Norman, itself a translation and expansion of Geoffrey of Monmouth's *Historia Britonum*.

Madden says that it is "scarcely to be questioned" that for certain portions of his work which report legends or traditions not recorded either by Wace or Geoffrey, Laȝamon was indebted to Welsh souces, probably both oral and written. . . . Laȝamon, though apparently merely a parish priest, and perhaps a private chaplain to the "good knight," is revealed by his work as a man of great cultivation, steeped in the old poetry of his countrymen, versed in its history and in the ancient traditions and legends, able to read Latin and French, and probably acquainted with Welsh. . . .[3]

. . . Laȝamon's *Brut* is sometimes referred to as a translation of the Norman poem. This is true to the extent that, in the main, the episodes in the latter follow those in Wace's work, the names of persons, places, and weapons are usually faithfully preserved, though not infrequently the form of these is considerably modified; the general subject and order of the narrative are reproduced, and sometimes several lines on end are faithfully rendered. But the English poem is very far from being a line for line translation. The number of lines in Wace is 15,300, less than half that of Laȝamon.

How is it that the "translation" is double the length of the original? The extra space is accounted for in two ways: first, by the numerous episodes and scenes which Laȝamon introduces without any corresponding passages in Wace; secondly, by the innumerable touches, sometimes occupying only a few lines, with which he heightens the effect of Wace's rather bald narrative, touches that express human feeling, and reveal the sentiments and passions of the actors, which add picturesque descriptive details of an action—a fight, a carouse, the arming of a hero for battle, a sea voyage—or which show the poet's feeling for external nature.

Of the actual additions of episodes not dealt with by Wace at all, and consisting of anything from ten or twenty lines to ten or twenty pages of the printed text, Madden's list occupies about two pages of his Introduction. One of the finest of these original episodes is the splendid description of the hunting down of Childric, in which the fugitive king is compared to a fox pursued by hounds. This leads quite naturally to a highly spirited and inspiring account of a fox-hunt, so typically English in subject and feeling. . . .[5]

. . . Another passage which illustrates at once how Laȝamon expands and embellishes the text of Wace, and the way in which he introduces new matter is the noble account of Arthur's death and passage to the Valley of Avalon. . . .[6]

. . . Few will dispute the poetical value of Laȝamon's expansions and additions—the speech of Arthur to his kinsman, part of which reminds us somewhat of Beowulf's last address to Wiglaf (Beow. 2813-16); the picturesque touch whereby Arthur himself announces the manner of his passing and his expected return; the fair queen of the elves, and her healing drenches; the little ship driven by the waves in which the king is laid gently down by the two women in wondrous attire. Finally, instead of the matter-of-fact humming and hawing of "Maistre Gasse," Laȝamon contrives to create just such an atmosphere of wonder and mystery concerning the ultimate fate of Arthur as we find in the concluding lines of the account of the passing of Scyld . . . . We may compare the French and English poems almost where we will, and we shall find, here a word or two inserted, there a few lines added in the latter, which enliven the narrative and make it more picturesque and interesting. . . .[7]

. . . The love of external Nature is highly developed in Laȝamon, as in the older English poets, and there is no mistaking his keen enjoyment of it. He constantly brings in references to the sea, waves, storms, mountains, rocks, woods, animals, with a specific intimacy usually altogether absent from the corresponding passage in the French text, if indeed there be any hint there at all of such matter. How delightful and full of gaiety are the lines on the coming of summer to town! . . .

Simile is more freely used on the whole than in Anglo-Saxon poetry, and is invariably drawn from the objects or processes of Nature. There is a fine comparison of a surging host of fugitives to "a lofty wood when the wild wind shakes it violently". . . .

Arthur rushing impetuously upon his enemies is compared to "the fleet wolf when he sallies from the wood, bedecked with snow, purposing to devour such beasts as he fancies". . . .

The speed with which a man leaps upon his horse is twice compared to that of a spark flashing from the fire.[11]

. . . The most elaborate simile in the whole poem is that in which Arthur, having brought Childeric to that point of desperation when he sends envoys to sue for peace, and to promise that he will trouble Arthur and his country no more, but will sail away, compares him to a hunted fox. "Then Arthur laughed loudly. Thanks be to the Lord who rules our destinies, that Childeric has had enough of my country. He hath divided up my land among his knights, forsooth, and thought to drive me out of my country, to make me contemptible and to have my kingdom, to have destroyed my kindred, and to condemn my people". . . .[12]

There is no mistaking the gusto of all this. La3amon had evidently assisted at many a hunt, had heard the view-halloo, and the music of hounds in full cry, and had seen the fox dug out. For the moment he is much more interested in the fox than in the fate of Childeric.

The entire episode from which this passage comes is one of the most spirited and interesting in the whole of Middle English poetry, with its extraordinary variety of incident, action, scene, mood, and sentiment. Among so much that is attractive I must only mention one more passage in the present connection, the remarkable lines in which Arthur depicts Baldulf, one of Childeric's companions, standing on a hill and gazing down into the waters of the Avon. "He sees how his dead knights are lying like great steel fish below the waters of the stream, no longer able to swim indeed, their scales are gleaming as it were gold-plated shields, and their fins afloat, as it were spears. Wondrous things indeed are seen in the land—such a deer upon the hill, such fish in the water!" . . .[13]

. . . As might be expected from so spirited and romantic a

poet, Laȝamon handles the whole subject of war, and every aspect of martial action, with peculiar vigour and picturesqueness. From the arming and equipping of his hero to the final victorious rush which scatters the enemy, no detail is missing that can lend colour or majesty to the principal characters, and bring into relief their valour, their bodily strength, and their greatness of soul. The speeches of the leaders are inspiring, and we watch with growing excitement each cut and thrust and parry in the fight itself. The scene is splendidly staged, often amid romantic surroundings, and the action is carried through in true heroic manner. Laȝamon visualizes a scene and a situation, and often records the impressions of the actors in the drama with a glowing imagination and a sense of the picturesque that are quite beyond Wace. A good example of this is the sudden discovery by the Roman army of King Arthur's host ready to give battle:

The Roman people saw all the valleys, all the uplands, all the hills, dotted with helmets; they saw the lofty banners fluttering in the wind—sixty thousand warriors bore them—they saw the shields flash and the corslets gleam, the gold-embroidered cloaks, the stern men and the prancing horses. The very earth shook. The Emperor marked the king where he was encamped by the wood-shaw. . . .[18]

As in ancient heroic poetry, the arms of the hero, and the ceremony of putting them on before some momentous fight, are described with some minuteness. There are two elaborate descriptions of the arming of Arthur, the first occasion being before the fight against the Saxons at Bath, the second before Arthur's single combat with King Frolle of France. In the first of these Laȝamon follows Wace pretty closely, but adds certain important details. Perhaps the most significant is the statement that his corslet had been made by a cunning "elvish" smith. . . .

The arming of Arthur for his fight with Frolle is given with minute and splendid detail, and the account seems to be entirely Laȝamon's own. Wace's story of the combat . . . differs so much in treatment from that of Laȝamon that it is [19] very difficult to compare them. Here is his description of the process of arming:

Arthur the strong took his weapons in hand, he threw upon his back a very costly robe, a linen shirt, and a purple tunic; a precious corslet woven of steel. He set upon his head a good helmet; at his side he hung his sword Caliburne; he covered his legs with hose of steel, and put upon his feet his right good spurs. The king in his armour (weden) leapt upon his steed, and they reached him a good shield entirely made of ivory. Into his hand they gave a strong shaft at the end of which was a serviceable spearhead. This was made at Carmarthen by a smith called Griffen—Uther had owned it who was king here formerly. When he was armed the brave king rode forth, and those present could see the mighty king and how gallantly he rode. Since the world was established, no-where was it told that ever so fair a man went out upon a horse as was King Arthur the son of Uther. Behind the king there rode forty hundred valiant warriors in the first troop, noble captains in steel armour, gallant Britons busy with their weapons. . . .

There are numerous examples of leaders rallying and urging on their followers in battle—both brief cries of encouragement under stress of battle, and of more formal utterances. . . .[20]

. . . To turn from the exploits of individuals to the turmoil of general battle, there is no lack of dash and vigour in the onslaughts described in the poem. High courage and endurance in the fight are displayed by high and low alike. . . .[21]

In the various battles described by Laȝamon we find the same sort of detail as in the Anglo-Saxon poets: the mad rush of the opposing forces, the clash of sword with sword, the ringing of sword and spear against shield and helmet, the splintering of lances, the thunder of horses' hoofs, which shakes the earth and makes the welkin ring, the blare of trumpets, the hail of arrows, the fall of doomed men, the cries of agony and of triumph. The grey wolf howling over the stricken field, and the eagles and ravens eager for their prey, which play so large a part in the battle scenes of the older poets, are absent from Laȝamon. On the other hand, we have here streets and streams running with blood, which, I think, do not figure in Anglo-Saxon battle poetry. . . .[22]

. . . I now turn to consider as briefly as possible the manners and customs of the halls of princes as exhibited by Laȝamon. These bear a striking resemblance to those depicted in Beowulf. There can, I think, be little doubt that the ancient habits survived in the castles of the great, and that Laȝamon, although he may trick out his descriptions with literary graces derived from our oldest poetry, has yet given a first-hand picture of manners as he actually saw them in the early times of English chivalry. . . .[23]

The various royal banquets described in Laȝamon strongly resemble those in Hrothgar's hall. . . .[25]

Arthur gives, or is given, a great feast at Grimsby on his return to Britain from Ireland to join Guinivere. . . .

A still more gorgeous feast is described as taking place in London on Christmas Day . . . , during which, unfortunately, a serious fight breaks out through jealousy, and blood is shed. Arthur quells the disturbance, and binds all present by oaths sworn on sacred relics, to forget their differences and to behave properly for the future . . . . This, though the name is not mentioned by Laȝamon, is the virtual founding of the Order of the Table Round. The dead are carried away, the hall is cleared, and the feast proceeds as merrily as ever. . . .

Shortly afterwards the king goes into Cornwall, where he is met by a "crafty workman," who offers to make a splendid table . . . at which sixteen hundred and more knights may sit and where no more quarrels shall break out over priority of place. The table is made and inaugurated at a feast to which high and low are bidden . . . .

"This," says Laȝamon, "is the same Table . . . about which the Britons boast and tell many kinds of lies. . . ."

Wace's references to the founding of the Round Table, which he specifically calls both *Roonde Table* and *Table Roonde,* and to the members of the Order, are much briefer than those of Laȝamon,[28] and the accounts differ in various ways. Madden regards the passage . . . which deals with the events immediately leading up to the foundation of the Order, with the making of the actual Table itself, and incorporates the remarks . . . concerning the legends that had grown up concerning the Table, and about Arthur and his knights, as perhaps one of the most remarkable and curious instances which occur of the additional matter engrafted by Laȝamon on the text of Wace. . . . It is worth noting that Laȝamon never uses the French name by which the Table was afterwards known, and which he might well have taken from Wace, but contents himself with the homely English *bord.* . . .

The more we read the *Brut,* the more are we impressed by the versatility of the author. Laȝamon is gifted with an inexhaustible flow of poetical language; he has a powerful and beautiful imagination, a tender and graceful fancy, a never-failing vigour and gusto, a wide sympathy with, and enjoyment of, every phase of life and action. He never fails to interest the reader, whether his theme be drawn from his rich stores of legendary lore, from his own observation of nature, or whether it be a battle or a banquet.

Laȝamon is essentially an English poet. He is strongly moved by the old romantic stories of his native land. He loves her mountains and moors, her woods, her streams; he is in intimate touch with the wild life that stirs within them. He enters as keenly as any of his countrymen into the excitement of the chase; he loves horses, hawks, and hounds. He knows how to invest his descriptions of battles and pageants, of ceremonies and feasts and minstrelsy, with the glow and splendour of chivalry, and the glamour of romance. The colours seem as fresh to-day as when the pictures were painted. When the poet chooses to exhibit the feelings and emotions of his characters in relation to the situation in which they find themselves, he does it simply, naturally, and with a noble dignity and restraint, witness . . . the passage where Arthur learns that he is the son of Uther Pendragon:

For dead is Uther Pendragon, and thou art Arthur his son. Dead also is that other, Aurelien, his brother. Thus they told him the news,[29] and Arthur sat silent. For a while he grew pale, and weak in all his body; for a while he was flushed, and sorrowed much in his heart. At last his thoughts broke from him—it was well that he spoke. . . .

We have in the *Brut* an intensely vivid world of external nature, of human action, and of human joys and griefs; we find an untiring interest in the earthly life and affairs of men. Of strong religious and devotional feeling, or of solicitude concerning the future state of man, and his relation to eternity, I find small trace in this poem. Such a spirit, or attitude of mind, is not perceptible even as a background of the poet's thought. But if there is no expression of specific religious belief, and no avowedly moral intention, the whole atmosphere of the poem is lofty, chivalrous, and noble. Nor do we ever doubt that the writer is a man of a high and generous nature, with a true reverence for whatsoever things are lovely and of good report, and rich in every human quality which goes to make a man and a poet.[30]

IDRIS LLEWELYN FOSTER

"The Dream of Rhonabwy"

From *Arthurian Literature in the Middle Ages*, ed. Roger Sherman Loomis (Oxford: at the Clarendon Press, 1959).

Rhonabwy's Dream is manifestly the work of a talented author. It has been described as 'an artist's piece, a succession of illuminated pages, deficient in movement and character, but a *tour-de-force* of close observation and description'. The style is rich and rhetorical, and the dreamlike impression is admirably conveyed by the deliberate anachronisms, the fantastic happenings,[40] and the rapidly shifting scenes. It is probable, as Thomas Parry suggests, 'that the story was never part of the traditional stock-in-trade of the story-tellers'; this would account for the explanatory nature of the colophon.

The geographical and historical background is indicated with precision. The setting is Powys, which comprised most of central Wales, extending to the north as far as Pulford near Chester, and eastward as far as the upper Severn. Madog son of Maredudd, whose brother was being sought by Rhonabwy, ruled over Powys from 1138 to 1160, and his death was followed by much discontent and strife until his grandson, Llywelyn the Great, took possession. It is likely, then, that *Rhonabwy's Dream* was composed by an author from Powys some time during the hundred years after Madog's death, and Richards has plausibly argued that the date lay between 1220 and 1225.

The author set the main events of his narrative within the framework of a dream—a device which was certainly new in medieval Welsh literature. The fact that Rhonabwy dreams while lying on an ox-skin is probably related to an ancient Irish practice described by Keating, in which hides of bulls were spread on wattles, and presumably the diviner went to sleep on the hide for the purpose of winning knowledge. It is the nature of dreams to disregard time and space; hence the battle of Camlann is referred to as having occurred before the battle of Badon. Arthur is met by Rhonabwy on the borders of Powys, but, as in *Culhwch*, his home is in Cornwall.

The effect of unreality is intensified by the strange assortment of characters who appear in the *Dream*. Among Arthur's counsellors are numbered such figures as Nerth mab Kadarn (Strength son of Mighty), borrowed from *Culhwch*; Gilbert mab Katgyffro, who may represent Gilbert de Clare, Earl of Pembroke (d. 1147/8); Caradawg Vreichvras; March vab Meirchiawn, the husband of Essyllt, represented as leader of the men of Scandinavia; Dyrstan mab Talluch, lover of Essyllt; Edern mab Nudd, leader of the men of Denmark. Added to these counsellors are men from the Isles of Greece.

The influence of Geoffrey of Monmouth may be discerned. The presence of the hosts of Llychlyn and Denmark does not imply . . . that they had taken the place of the Saxons as traditional enemies [41] of the Britons, for they are on Arthur's side. Rather, their opportune appearance as his allies suggests the extensive dominion of the emperor Arthur. Likewise, Geoffrey's identification of Kaer Badum, the site of Arthur's great victory with Bath (Bad) seems to be reflected in the march of Arthur's host to Gweith Vaddon (the battle of Badon) and his arrival below Caer Vaddon. Geoffrey's description of Arthur's arming himself for the battle of Badon with Caliburnus may have suggested Arthur's taking his flaming sword after his arrival before Caer Vaddon; and the prominent role which Geoffrey assigned to Cador 'dux Cornubie' in this campaign may be responsible for the role of Cadwr Earl of Cornwall as Arthur's armour-bearer and counsellor in the Welsh text. The mention of Osla (or Ossa) in the same text as Arthur's prospective adversary may well represent the tradition in Nennius that Arthur's opponent was Octha son of Hengist. It should be noted, at any rate, that the Dingestow version of Geoffrey's *Historia* gives Ossa as a cousin of Otca (Octa) mab Heingyst.

Perhaps the most striking feature of *Rhonabwy's Dream* is the game of *gwyddbwyll* played by Arthur and Owain, concurrently with the conflict between Arthur's men and Owain's ravens. The game is played with gold pieces on a board of silver, and it takes place not far from Caer Vaddon. A. G. van Hamel drew attention to the basic similarity between this game in the Welsh tale and the 'game of the gods' in the Norse *Völuspá*, where also golden pieces are used. 'The golden game is the magic through which the gods keep the world in order and prevent the intrusion of war.' Arthur's game of *gwyddbwyll* and the 'divine game' in the *Völuspá* are parallel instances of the belief that the course of events may be directed by a game, and Arthur 'could not maintain his title to perpetual victory but by crushing the enchanted chessmen'.

The struggle between Arthur's men and Owain's ravens has been given various interpretations. It has been suggested that the ravens represent the Viking armies; again, that here is a form of the raven-fight which is found in early Irish literature. A more acceptable explanation is that the episode embodies the tradition that Owain was the son of Urien by Modron daughter of Avallach. Modron has her counterpart in Morgain la Fée, daughter of Avallo (or Avalloc) and mother of Yvain by Urien (in the *Suite du Merlin*).[42] In the *Didot Perceval,* a flock of large black birds swoop down upon Perceval during the combat at the ford with Urbain (probably a corrupt form of Urien) and try to tear out his eyes. Perceval kills one of them and it immediately turns into a beautiful woman; Urbain tells him that the birds were his mistress and her maidens. In Irish tradition, the fierce Morrígan, who may be said to prefigure Morgain la Fée in many ways, assumed the shape of a crow. If, therefore, the correspondence of Morrígan, Modron, and Morgain la Fée is established, then Owain's ravens in *Rhonabwy's Dream* can be recognized as the helpful forms of his mother Modron and her sisters (or companions).

The author of *Rhonabwy's Dream* brought together two traditional themes which he then handled with considerable literary skill: first, the native British tradition of Arthur's struggle against the Saxons, with its climax in the battle of Badon; and second, the older tradition, common to the Irish and the Welsh, of the wife or mistress or mother, with her companions, bringing timely assistance in the shape of birds in the stress of conflict.[43]

ROBERT W. ACKERMAN

"Arthour and Merlin"

From *Arthurian Literature in the Middle Ages*, ed. Roger Sherman Loomis (Oxford: at the Clarendon Press, 1959).

This romance is best preserved in the famous Auchinleck manuscript, where it runs to 9,938 lines, and extends from the death of Constans to the defeat of Rion immediately after the betrothal of Arthur and Guenevere. It was composed probably in Kent during the middle years or the third quarter of the thirteenth century. Though the story is obviously developed with care, there is a change of pace beginning with the events following Arthur's coronation (vs. 3133). The crown is placed on young Arthur's head by Bishop Brice (Dubricius) in the presence of the great lords, and at the feast the new king rises to distribute gifts and receive homage. At this juncture, Nentres, Lott, and other kings voice their bitter objections to the crowning of Arthur, whereupon Merlin is moved to explain just as he had done only a few lines earlier (vss. 3021-40) that Arthur is indeed their legitimate ruler. This abrupt transition, involving some doubling back of the story, introduces Arthur's struggle with his rebellious vassals, which is the most important theme in the remainder of the poem. With few relieving touches, the second part is given over to detailed accounts of single combats and of general *mêlées*.[485]

. . . the source of the Auchinleck poem must have embodied two distinct stages in the development of the history of Merlin. The first portion, up to the coronation, represents the pre-Robert [de Boron] story expanded from the chronicles; and the remainder the Vulgate sequel. Despite the gaps and the monotonous details of battle in the last two-thirds of his work, the Auchinleck poet tells his story clearly and in the second portion, at least, he abridges considerably and to advantage. Further, the four May songs and the other nature descriptions sprinkled throughout are probably his own . . . . The nature lyrics are conventional, to be sure, yet they illustrate the smooth handling of the four-stress couplet which characterizes the entire poem. The poet is self-conscious about presenting his tale in English. He observes that children who have been set early to their books have the advantage of knowing Latin and French well. As for him, he knows many an English noble who understands only English, and he will, therefore, tell his tale in that language. . . .[486]

WILLIAM MATTHEWS

"Sin and Punishment in the Alliterative *Morte Arthure*"

From *The Tragedy of Arthur: A Study of the Alliterative "Morte Arthure"* (Berkeley and Los Angeles: University of California Press, 1960).

It is while Arthur is still flushed with military triumph that report comes from Rome that he is accepted as sovereign. The bearer of news is not, as might have been expected, a Roman senator but a cardinal of the Church. A little earlier, the poet had put into Arthur's mouth an opinion that betrays political calculation about the relation of his war to the clergy—["if we spare the spiritual ones, we succeed all the better" (1. 2415)]—and now the terms of the cardinal's message make clear that Arthur had been warring not only against the pagan forces of Lucius but also, and in defiance of medieval doctrine, against the Church and the pope himself . . . [3176-3180].

Arthur's acceptance is triumphant, but this is not the end of his ambition. Once before in the poem, the phrase that is a medi- [184] eval byword for Alexander had been used of Arthur: Aungers had urged in the war council that the king ought to be overling above all other kings (1. 289). And in speaking to Gawain, Priamus had declared that the king would be Alexander's heir (1. 2634). Now, when the ambassadors have departed, Arthur sees himself as the new Alexander, the overling of everything on earth . . . [3206-3217].

It is immediately after this speech that Arthur dreams of the duchess-of-the-wheel and of Alexander and the fallen conquerors. That dream and the interpretation given to it by Arthur's philosopher are logical artistic sequels to the ruthless imperialistic warfare that the poet has depicted and to his characterization of Arthur as a latter-day Alexander, admirable in many ways but a conqueror cruel and keen, driven into ruth works by a conqueror's sin of vainglory.

The philosopher, interpreting the divine shewing of the dream, points to the king's crime of shedding innocent blood in his conquests, predicts his downfall, and urges him to confession, contrition, and acts of satisfaction. Since these are the three points that are stressed in the medieval doctrine of penitence, it might be expected that the subsequent course of the poet's adaptation of the old story would systematically follow those steps toward the salvation of Arthur's soul. But, although the poet is a moralist, he is also an artist who had an ironic understanding of the ways of men. In broad outline, the remainder of the story is the same as that in the traditional versions, but it is told freely and with the utmost originality in its details. Tragedy comes upon Arthur and the penitential mood induced by the dream dominates the narrative. But although the poetic treatment of the last part of the [135] tale is profoundly religious, how far the king has profited by his shewing and how far he moves into a state of penitence is dramatically left uncertain.

The king, who before the dream had seen himself as an avenger of Christ as well as a new Alexander, a king to be crowned on Christmas day, is certainly not made contrite by the interpreter's spiritual advice. Magnificently arrayed in jeweled garments of scarlet and gold, he stalks out of the camp in typically angry mood. . . . There he meets Sir Cradok on his way to break the news of Mordred's rebellion, and it is with Cradok's arrival that the penitential theme is introduced. Dressed in the dull, shabby array of a pilgrim, in complete contrast with Arthur's peacock magnificence, he is intent, before announcing his news to the king, on hurrying to Rome for a purpose quite different from Arthur's—to purchase pardon from the pope and to absolve himself from the pains of purgatory.

As soon as Cradok delivers, in his broad British speech, the report on Mordred's betrayal, there is a change in the king's mood. Then, for the first time in the poem, he weeps; the proud self-confidence he had displayed throughout his previous career leaves him, driven out by the despair that now darkens his mind until the day of his death. But despair is not contrition. Now and at various later times, Arthur dimly perceives some connection between his prior activities and the disaster that is bearing down on him . . . [3565-3566]. But his impulses remain the same as they had always been, and in an angry speech that ironically echoes a phrase used by the philosopher in his exhortation to repentance, Arthur threatens revenge against Mordred . . . [3559-3560].

The military decisiveness, courage, skill, and leadership also remain unchanged. Arthur rapidly makes arrangements for maintaining his foreign conquests, marches to the coast, assembles a fleet, and in the sea battle off Southampton leads his forces to [136] victory over the fleet of the traitor and his pagan allies. He retains, too, his concern for his followers. When he discovers that Gawain has waded ashore to attack the vastly superior lan.. forces of the enemy, he hastens after him, only to discover that what he had feared was true, that Gawain was dead.

It is when he is holding in his arms the corpse of Gawain that Arthur comes nearest to the state of penitence recommended by his philosopher. So overwhelmed is he by the death of the knight to whom he owed so many of his honors ["of all knights the king who lived under Christ"], that he sees his whole hope vanished and longs for death . . . [3965-3968]. To the knights who urge him to cease this womanish grief, Arthur declares that he will never cease, since it was his own sin that had led Gawain, innocent of any sin, to his death. . . . After a prayer to God for the dead saint, Arthur then makes a sacred vow. Until Gawain has been completely revenged, he will forego entirely the pleasures of hunting and regality . . . [3999-4006].

Elements of confession, contrition, and the acts of pentitence are all there. But Arthur still has no clear understanding of what was his actual offense. In exaggerated form, his grief for Gawain is similar to his grief for Kay and Bedevere when they fell in the battle with Lucius. The contrition is not for his pride of conquest nor for the carnage it had wrought abroad, upon Frollo and Feraunt, Metz and Tuscany, but rather for the loss of his own [137] men. That he holds himself responsible is a step toward self-knowledge. But he holds Mordred still more responsible, so that his response to the death of his knight is a passion for revenge on his treacherous nephew and a violence of anger which is matched only by the anger that had terrified Lucius' ambassadors earlier in the poem. . . .

The last battle in Cornwall displays an Arthur changed but still unconverted. He rushes into battle without making the preparations that his leaders advise, rashly cutting his way to a duel with Mordred. This is done with none of the old assurance, however; he works in awareness of oncoming disaster, and while displaying a deeper tenderness for his men—["the kindest creatures that ever king led"]—and comforting them that they will be ["hewed into heaven"] for their efforts against the Saracen foe, he is conscious that his own death day is near. "Wirkes now my wirchipe," he tells his knights, "to-daye my werre endys." Passionate religiosity colors his attitude toward foe and friend. The enemy being heathen as well as rebellious, he urges his men to hew them down without mercy, and through their achievements in this way he gains greater honor than any other earthly king. For the deaths of pagans he feels no more pity than did Roland at Roncesvalles, but for the deaths of his own loyal knights he expresses a Christlike compassion. It is in response to the devotion of young Idrus, determined to stay by his king to the death, that Arthur realizes his own position, midway between Alexander and Christ . . . [4155-4160].[138]

Despite this belated longing for a saviour's role, Arthur is still not free from the tragic coil of his own making, and the death duel between Mordred and the king is the occasion for the poet's most masterly exercise of his ironic imagination. The king sees the traitor lurking in the rear, disguised with arms different from those that he normally bore, awaiting his opportunity to attack. Arthur notices that he is armed with the king's own sword, Clarent. This sword, which Mordred had feloniously obtained through Guenevere, was Arthur's sword of state, kept for peaceful occasions . . . [4196-4201]. Just as significantly, it was kept in coffer at Wallingford along with the rings, relics, and regalia of France that were found upon Frollo when he met his doom at Arthur's hands. Arthur fights with his war sword Caliburn, and it is with this weapon, his companion in all the imperial campaigns, that he slays the usurper, first cutting off the sword hand that impiously bears Clarent, and then striking him down to a fairer death than such a false thief deserves. But Mordred, too, strikes a deathblow, although its effect is delayed, and he deals it with Clarent, Arthur's own sword of peace—a weapon touched with the supernatural and which is associated with Frollo, chief among the victims of Arthur's conquests who are named in the interpretation of the king's dream of fortune . . . [4236-4241].[139]

In this brilliant episode the poet rationalized and subdued to the service of his tragic climax the confusion that prevails in the Arthurian romances about Arthur's two swords—the sword-in-the-stone and the sword of the Lady of the Lake. Giving the former for dramatic contrast a name unmatched elsewhere in romance, he has also invested the two weapons with a moral significance unknown to other authors. In their own setting they are the Arthurian counterparts of the two allegorical swords that the medieval religious imagination had evoked from the weapons of Luke xxi. 38, Caliburn the sword of temporal power, Clarent the sword of spiritual life. In their typically medieval conflict Caliburn serves righteously in a role of subduing temporal crime but wrongly applied is the instrumentality of unrighteousness and a weapon that turns in the user's hand. Clarent, however, like Mordred, is the instrument of God, working through Fortune in the prosecution of divine justice and the maintenance of the spiritual arm over the temporal.

With Arthur fall almost all the knights of the Round Table, and the king, on his knees addressing Christ, laments their death in a passion of grief commensurate with his former passion of wrath. In his Tuscan campaign, Arthur's cruelty had ["made widows . . . often weary and weep and wring their hands"]. Now, in his lament over his own bereavement, Arthur's imagination calls up the same image of embittered widowhood . . . [4282-4288].

Although divine justice has done its will with Arthur in this world and although he has attained to some measure of Christian contrition, he has still, even at the point of death, not fully realized the nature of his sin nor accepted the spiritual advice of his [140] philosopher-counselor. He had not yet confessed, made no restitution, performed no voluntary act of penance. His last words on the battlefield are to thank God for giving him ["the upper hand of all other kings"]. And on his deathbed, although he calls for a confessor and forgives all grief, his dying command, just before his *in manus tuas,* is an order to bury his fallen lords and then to wreak a savage vengeance upon the innocent children of Guenevere and Mordred . . . [4318-4322].

The poet's Arthur, conceived in the context of Christian views of unjustified war and influenced by the medieval Christian opinion of Alexander the Great, is a complex figure, surely the most human of all the medieval characterizations of the British king. This is by no means the only critical portrait in medieval literature of a conquering hero: Darius, Cyrus, Alexander, Charlemagne, even Arthur himself, were all subjected to the slings and arrows of contempt of the world, scholarly scepticism, or everyday risibility. But in this poem there is no belittlement: admiration and even pity temper the poet's moral irony. Battered by divine justice, Arthur fights out his last days in a mood of despair which is only partly alleviated by his Christlike aspirations. Never clearly understanding the divine shewing of his dream or the true nature of his sin, he is spared the indignity of a groveling confession. He dies as he lived, thanking his God-of-battles for the imperial honors that had come to him and urging a last savage revenge on his enemies.

Like any other portrait that is conceived dramatically, this characterization of Arthur does not stand alone: it is enriched by related portraits of other warriors who are affected by the king's actions and whose behavior either parallels or contrasts with his. There are many such sketches in the poem: Lucius, a pagan king, a cruel emperor, but still a great warrior, the knights who make their belligerent vows at the war council, Cador whose rash eagerness for fame is rebuked by the king but matches the king's own impulse, Idrus the devoted young knight who calls forth Arthur's [141] own devotion to his men, the monster of St. Michel whose enormities may conceivably have been intended as a political caricature of an imperial conqueror. Two alone are drawn full scale, those of Mordred and Gawain, the tragic brothers; but those are done with much of the ironic humanity that determines Arthur's own portrait.

Mordred is the villain of the tale, as he is in the chronicles and romances. But the Mordred of the alliterative poem is a more human villain than any to be found in other versions of the story. Geoffrey and his followers draw a traitor pure and simple, one whose mind was on treason as soon as he was appointed to the regency. The French prose romances and their English derivatives portray him as a handsome, courageous knight, but, from the first, the only motives for his actions are envy and malice. What are his motivations in the alliterative *Morte Arthure* is not altogether certain, but for a villain he is strangely conscience-stricken. His foot had been set on the path to treason by no wish of his own. When Arthur appoints him to the regency he has no desire for the office: his intention and preparation has been to join the fight against Lucius, and his reaction to the appointment is a protest at being deprived of his chance for military glory. . . . Mordred speaks "full myldly" and with an honest sense of his own inadequacy, but it is possible that the poet, like the earlier poet who had conceived of a wronged Ganelon, intended this frustration to be the seed of his treachery. Certainly it is the seed of Arthur's disaster, for the king, in the imperious fashion that is so characteristic of him, brushes aside the protest and appoints his nephew willy-nilly. To anyone who knew the traditional story, the poet offered a rich irony in his treatment of the scene, in Arthur's commands that his nephew should never betray his trust and that [142] Guenevere should use the regent ["to do what pleases you"], in the ambiguity of the young knight's protest that the people would be deceived by his simplicity, in Guenevere's lament at being left alone to suffer her ["destiny of grief"]. But the irony is directed against neither Mordred nor Guenevere, for at this point they are sincere in their protestations. It is aimed at Arthur, whose impatience to be gone on his conquests abroad leads him to pay no heed to either Mordred's protests or Guenevere's love-inspired forebodings, and so sets two innocent people on the way to adultery and treason and betrays himself into the folly that John Gower deplored, the folly of leaving his own land in the keeping of those who will betray it.

Through his own comments and those of his characters, the poet leaves no room to question Mordred's heinousness: he is traitor, adulterer, felon, thief, warlock. Nor, when faced with the tragic results of his action, does the usurper doubt his own villainy. He proffers no explanation for what had provoked him to treason, merely cursing the fates that had caused him to wreak such misery. But after he has killed Gawain by an accident of combat, his remorse is like that of the medieval Judas who slinks away to hang himself. To King Froderick of Frisia, who asks whether he knew the dead knight, Mordred replies with a eulogy that is no less passionate than Arthur's own. Thereafter, he turns away weeping, cursing his wyrds, and, in a phrase that echoes the philosopher's advice to Arthur, repenting all his ruth works . . . [3886-3894]. The poet attempts no whitewashing of Mordred. In Cornwall he awaits Arthur's vengeance in trembling, and in the battle he fights under false colors. Yet, even in this fallen state, elements of former chivalry persist in him; almost his last act is inspired by compassion for Guenevere and her children . . . [3904-3910].[143]

In the French prose-cycles, Malory, and other romance versions of the Arthurian story, the Death of Arthur is the climax of the long series of adventures. But so romantic is its emphasis it might better be entitled the Death of Lancelot. The alliterative poet certainly knew the romance version of the story, but he was too much of an historian, too firmly interested in structure, to follow its lead. His poem is concerned with what its title proclaims, the death of Arthur. Yet, even so, there are parts of the story where Gawain commands not only the reader's interest, but also his sympathy, even to the detriment of the king. No more immune is he than Arthur from the poet's irony, but of the two it is he whom the poet admired most nearly with a whole heart. Gawain, far more than Arthur, joins the way of the soldier with the way of Christ.

At the beginning of the poem, Gawain plays a peculiarly small part. In the war council he is silent, not even giving the advice to peace that he makes in the chronicles, and in the battle with Lucius his activities are hardly important. His only vital activity in that part of the poem which closely follows the chronicles is his embassy to the Roman emperor. There and in the subsequent pursuit, he appears as a rough-tongued, overbold soldier. He is not egged into making trouble, as he is in the chronicles: he seeks it himself by bawdy insults and insolence toward Lucius and his uncle Gayous. That episode concludes with his striking off Gayous' head and an exciting pursuit, in which Gawain acts the part of a *beau sabreur*. Had the poet been content with the chronicles, his Gawain would have seemed little more than a gay braggadocio. It is, however, in those sections of the poem which are most independent that he develops his own view of the Scottish hero. He refrains from involving him in the cruelties of the Italian campaign, and in the siege of Metz he restricts his activities to the adventures of the foray for cattle. But in that exploit and in the events of Arthur's return to England, Gawain is a commanding figure, drawn in a complex moral pattern that is unmatched save in *Sir Gawain and the Green Knight*.[144]

. . . These two aspects of Gawain, his status as a soldier and his standing as a representative of Christ, are dominant in a series of brilliantly imaginative scenes which the poet has added to the last part of his tale.

In the sea battle with Mordred's forces, Gawain shares the glory of victory with Arthur and disposes of his part of the spoils with royal generosity. But, while the king welcomes this victory as an opportunity to prepare his forces cautiously for a later attack upon the vast army arrayed on the shore, Gawain is more impetuous in his desire to avenge the treason done by his brother. Taking a galley and a few men, he wades ashore, the water up to his waist. Almost single-handed, he charges upon the pagan army, kills the king of Gutland, and advances toward Mordred. The heathen surround his little company, and Gawain, upbraiding the usurper, comforts his men that should they die fighting they would sup with Our Saviour, while Mordred's soul would sink into hell. Then he rushes wildly on the enemy, clearing a bloody path toward his traitor-brother. He pierces the usurper with his lance, but as he strikes to kill with his short knife his hand slips, and Mordred cleaves him through the brain.

Characteristic as this impetuosity is of the Gawain that the poet has drawn, it is a weakness of character, a *desmesure* of generous courage, that does not escape the poet's criticism. Even in

Gawain's own mind, the foray for revenge is almost suicidal in its recklessness, for he reassures his men . . . [3802-3803].[146] And the poet, echoing the hero's own phrase, angrily breaks through his normal objectivity and condemns the gesture as madness . . . [3816-3838].

This embittered condemnation of Gawain's imbalance goes far beyond the irony with which the poet relates the failings of Arthur. Gawain is the one knight in the tale for whom the poet feels strong affection, and the bitterness of his condemnation is the bitterness of love. Of the three laments over the dead hero in the poem, the poet claims the first and most lyrical . . . [3858-3863]. The second follows almost immediately, and it is uttered by the remorse-stricken Mordred in response to Froderick of Frisia's query . . . [3875-3885].

When, after this lament over the hero he had killed, the traitor rides away grieving and repenting all his ruth works, the Christian symbolism that dominates the last part of the poem begins to [147] take on the form of an allegory of Christ's passion. For, just as Mordred sees himself in the likeness of Judas, just so Arthur, in the scene that follows, is created in the image of Joseph of Arimathea seeking Christ on the cross.

The assemblage of French prose romances called the Vulgate Cycle tends to convert the adventures of Arthur and his knights into an allegory of man's rejection of Christ, symbolized by the Holy Grail. The Cycle wanders along at vast length before it reaches the retribution depicted in *La Mort Artu*, the cataclysm of the Round Table brought on largely by the worldliness of its knights. But it begins with the story of Joseph of Arimathea. Converted and baptized, Joseph is still afraid to confess his faith openly. Deeply moved by the Saviour's death, however, he searches the house where Christ and his disciples shared their last supper, takes away the dish from which Christ ate, and then asks Pilate for permission to bury the body of Christ. Pilate is glad enough to grant this trifling request of his loyal servant, and the romance goes on to recount Joseph's dealing with the body of His Lord. . . . On the basis of some version of this celebrated scene and the related part of the Gospels, the *Morte Arthure* poet develops his episode of Arthur and the dead Gawain.

When the cautious king learns that Gawain has impetuously gone ashore to seek revenge on Mordred, he hastens after him. He gets to the battlefield too late, however, and seeks among the bodies of his knights until he finds Gawain. Weeping bitterly, he kneels down, catches up the hero's corpse, and cries . . . [3989-3992].[148] Then, in his own soldierly fashion, he does what Joseph of Arimathea had done, kneeling down and gathering up the hero's blood in a helmet . . . [3994-3996]. After making a solemn vow to forego all pleasure, never to hunt with greyhound or let goshawk fly, until he had avenged the knight who had been more worthy than himself to bear the crown, he carries the body to Winchester. Just as Joseph had been met by the three Marys and had laid Christ's body, wrapped in clean linen, in the sepulchre to await the resurrection, just so the prior and monks of Winchester greet Gawain's cortege and the hero's body is laid in state in the church, to be embalmed and await the outcome of Arthur's war and the king's return . . . [4009-4024].

The poet chose to make both his Arthur and his Mordred regard Gawain dead as Christ crucified, and from his own bitterness over Gawain's self-immolation and the passionate lyricism of his lament it may be suspected that he himself looked on his hero as [149] a type of the Saviour. But if Mordred's fear that his part in the catastrophe has been a Judas role has the poet's support, the parallelisms between Joseph of Arimathea's proceedings and Arthur's do not make the king a type of Joseph. When Arthur finds Gawain's corpse, pierced through and stained with blood, his sorrow surpasses anything proper to the death of mortal man, and his knights rebukingly suggest a more fitting object . . . [3979-3980]. But Arthur's grief is the passion of one who sees before him both an embodiment of Christ and the tragic result of his own guilt. Catching up the corpse, he kisses the leaden lips, fainting under the stress of his emotion . . . [3969-3972]. The blood guilt symbolized in this gesture is made explicit in the king's next words: ["He is innocently overcome for sin of my own!"]. And if the guiltless Gawain is a type of the sinless Christ, the sin of Arthur can only be the sin of imperial war that had brought Gawain to his death.

It is this twofold parallelism, Gawain-Christ and Arthur-Alexander, that lends to the last part of *Morte Arthure* its pitiful irony. Arthur is committed to the Alexandrian logic of his vow in the original war council, but his last prayer in battle is an anguished wish that God had cast him in the role of Christ. . . .[150]

JOHN EDWIN WELLS

"The Stanzaic *Le Morte Arthur*"

From *A Manual of the Writings in Middle English, 1050-1400* (New Haven: Yale University Press, 1916).

LE MORTE ARTHUR . . . is the Middle English poetical rendering of the love of the Maid of Astolat, and of the culmination and the end of the loves of Guinevere and Lancelot and of the rule of [48] Arthur—an admirable treatment, apparently for the first time in English, of themes that have caught and held the spirit of poet and of reader through more than five hundred years since. The poem was composed at the end of the fourteenth century, probably in the North-West Midland, the two scribes of the extant MS. being one of the North and one of the South of England. It consists of 3834 four-stress lines . . . in stanzas normally riming abababab, with extensive use of alliteration. . . . *Le Morte Arthur* deals with matter very similar to much in Malory's Books XX and XXI. Both versions seem to have had as source a lost version of the French *Mort Artu*, the last part of the French *Vulgate Lancelot*. . . . Close resemblances in phrasing at points where there is no original in the French, indicate that probably Malory was acquainted with the English poem.[49]

. . . Both its form and its matter make the poem one of the

most notable of Middle English romances. As has been indicated, its themes are in modern times among the widest known and most dearly cherished of the group of Arthurian stories. The [50] work is remarkably unified: it begins well, it ends well; it keeps to its subject, practically all its episodes contributing directly to the effect of the main theme, which cumulates as the poem advances. It is remarkably concise: the ballad manner, that is so frequently suggested in the work, is reflected in the speed with which the poet proceeds, in his omission of nonessential connective details. Stock phrases are used freely, but they are so aptly employed as to be little objectionable—indeed, often scarcely obtrusive. The expression is direct, and free from diffuseness. The poem is simple, unpretending, sincere. The writer lent himself to the human appeal of his material, and told his story with an earnestness and a sincerity of feeling that make it true and real and warm, winning a response as immediate and as profound to-day as it must have won in the fourteenth century. It is to be noted that in this poem Gawayne, though dominant over Arthur and the real champion of the King's rights after the revelation of the Queen's guilt, loses status. He is represented as attempting to beguile the Maid of Ascolot, as lying about Launcelot to the Queen, and as compelled to acknowledge his guilt. Launcelot becomes the hero.[51]

M. C. BRADBROOK

"Malory and the Heroic Tradition"

From *Sir Thomas Malory*, Writers and Their Work: No. 95
(London: Longmans, Green & Co., 1958).

Three hundred years before Malory, the poet Layamon gave an account of the founding of the Table Round.
Arthur held a great feast at which his vassals from Britain, Scotland,
Ireland and Iceland assembled. A squabble about precedence developed in which at first bread and cups were thrown and fists used.
Then a young hostage of Arthur's household snatched up the carving knives from before the King, and the killing began. It took
Arthur and a hundred armed men to quell the fight, under the most
terrifying threats of instant death for the men and mutilation for
the women of kin to those who began the brawl. If any sought revenge for what had happened, he was to be torn in pieces by wild
horses. The body of the man who began the fight was to be thrown
out to rot unburied.

As a result of these measures, the dead were carried off and the
feast went merrily on; but the cunning smith who offered to make
Arthur a wondrous table at which sixteen hundred might sit without question of precedence seems to be catering less for the vassals
of an overlord than for the members of some primitive horde. Arthur, however, appears as the dominant figure. In his words:

Sit down! sit down at once! or your lives will pay

is heard the authentic voice of command.

Precedence at feasts, and the order of service at the lord's table
was a matter of signficance throughout the Middle Ages. The long
narrow table on the dais in the opening scene of *Sir Gawayne and*

the Grene Knight is set in customary fashion with the King in the middle, and his principal guests on each side. A round table would in fact have been a great curiosity and departure from custom, in one of those ceremonious occasions which the Romans loved to depict; and in all stories, the feast which so frequently opens or closes [21] them (the symbol of good fellowship and unity) is described in the usual sort of medieval hall with the usual High Table on a dais. What generally happens is that the King is feasting his knights and declares that he will not eat till he sees a marvel. Instantly some damsel in distress or some strange apparition like the Green Knight appears and the adventure begins.

Although in most of the earlier Romances the story is concerned with the adventures of a particular knight, there is a sense of the brotherhood of the Round Table given by these feasts at the beginning and end of the story; after a series of combats, it is usual for the valiant enemy of the hero to be accepted as a member of the Round Table. By the fourteenth century it was thought of as a fellowship akin to that of some knightly order, such as the Garter, or the Bath, and certain kinds of tournament became known as 'round tables'.

The Great Tournament is in Malory the last and supreme moment of unity and good fellowship for the Round Table; it is the expression of the bond which is about to be disrupted by the quarrel between Lancelot and Gawain, Arthur's champion and his nephew and heir. Tournaments, or mock battles, in which knightly qualities were displayed wthout the risks of real battle, had become something like the Olympic Games of the fifteenth century; they were great pageants at which fortunes were spent upon equipment, and to which champions would travel from all over Europe. The last and most gorgeous occasion of this kind to be generally remembered is the encounter between Henry VIII and the King of France, known as the Field of the Cloth of Gold.

Such tournaments gave opportunity for the writer of Romance to indulge in long descriptions of splendour, with detailed accounts of the dishes at the feasts, the armour of the knights and the order of combat. Here Malory departs from the habits of the age. He is not interested in descriptions but in action; and he does not do more than note the [22] colour of the knights' armour. The foining and tracing of combat excites him, but his world lacks the stateliness and the ritual of Chaucer's and the Gawain poet's, the true courtly ceremoniousness.

He has, on the other hand, a very strong sense of the Fellowship which enables him to rise to the heights of the last books. This sense of the Fellowship dominates one or two other works; such as the poem of *Lancelot du Laik* and the alliterative *Morte Arthur* on which Malory based the first of his tales. These poems imitate the literary form of the Chronicle History. Here there is an account of the King's challenge to lordship of a foreign land; then an invasion and a series of battles are described, very closely akin to the English wars in France. In each battle, a list of the eminent warriors taking part on both sides is given, and a list of those who fell. Such poems are no longer pure Romance of adventure; they are histories. In Malory, too, there is this strong sense of history, implying the epic rather than the Romance style.

After his early tale of Arthur's conquest of Rome, Malory turned back for a time to the more primitive and wilder stories about Merlin. These belong to the oldest traditions of Romance. In general, the more primitive the stories, the larger the part played by magic; thus in the one Arthurian tale which occurs in the *Mabinogion,* all the knights are possessed of superhuman powers, and are frankly figures of magical rather than human kind.

After his excursion into the realms of magic, Malory tells a number of tales about individual knights, in the same form roughly as the Romances of adventure . . . . These are tales of wanderings, in which the hero rides away on a quest. The quest for the Sankgreal includes five such tales of individual knights. The tragic tale of *The knight with the Two Swords* and the tale of Gareth have each a strong and shapely coherence; others follow rather the interlacing and interweaving technique of the long French romances. The story of Tristram is of this kind, containing [23] in itself several minor stories, such as the tale of Alexander le Orphelin.

The adventures of individual knights in their quests show them freed from all restriction of ordinary life. Armour and tournaments may be realistic, but in a Romance there is suppression of all the usual laws of cause and effect in action. The knightly champion has to meet giants, dragons, monsters, the King's enemies, sorcerers and mysteries of all kinds. Heads that are cut off may be stuck on again;

marvels and wonders are the rule and not the exception. The appearance and manners of the knight are familiar, merely an enlargement of the everyday, but he has no responsibilities, no followers, he rides through vast and shadowy landscapes and forests, where only the cities of Caerleon and Carlisle remind the listener that this is England. The modern reader may see a parallel in the world of science fiction, in which the admired technical apparatus which commands most prestige today is used to decorate the wildest fantasy. Romance indulges in the same mixture of the fanciful and the up-to-date. It allows the listener to identify himself with a hero of almost superhuman prowess, yet matches him against forces which stress his humanity and normality. Monsters from Mars are the modern equivalent of the fairy-tale giant.

Most romances of individual knights arrive at a happy ending; feasts and weddings wind them up. When the theme is the Table Round itself, however, the story ends with the great epic battle, the unsuccessful fight against odds. Whereas incidents of the individual Romances defy cause and effect, in the epic of the Round Table morality is always felt behind the action; the ideal is a social and ethical one. It was to this graver subject that Malory finally attained at the end of his work, joining the tale of his great hero Lancelot with the fate of the whole Fellowship.

The stories of Arthur and his knights can thus be seen to undergo a development not unrelated to the society which in an idealized form they reflect. In the earliest tales, magic [24] and violence predominate; then the image of a society based on feudal ties of loyalty emerges; the adventures of individuals follow, with, in the more courtly versions, much stress on manners and on wooing, and in the popular versions, simply on adventure and marvels. In both, the ideal knight in quest of adventure undergoes a great variety of different trials, from which he usually emerges victorious. Finally, something akin to the older epic style reappears, reflecting also the form of contemporary chronicles and, in Malory, tinged with some shadowing from contemporary struggles. At his greatest, in the final passages dealing with the last battle and death of Arthur, he seems to reflect in an enlarged form all the troubles of his own society, the ruin which civil strife had brought upon him and his kind. This is imaginatively seen in the dissolution of the Table

Round, the bond and fellowship of knighthood. Conquest, like true and faithful love, belongs to the past: the first and last campaigns of Arthur represent for Malory a youthful hope of the past contrasted with a tragic present.[25]

EUGÈNE VINAVER

"Malory's Le Morte Darthur"

From *The Works of Sir Thomas Malory*, ed. Eugène Vinaver, Volume I (Oxford: at the Clarendon Press, 1947).

The text of Malory's writings preserved in the Winchester MS. throws new light on what chivalry really meant to him. The beginnings of his 'doctrine' are found in his earliest work, *The Tale of the Noble King Arthur and the Emperor Lucius,* of which the Winchester MS. alone gives a complete version. Caxton's rendering of it is a drastic abridgement. Puzzled by the archaic character of the *Tale,* Caxton, 'simple person', reduced it to less than half its size, with the result that until now it has not been possible to form an accurate idea either of the content of the story or of its position among Malory's romances. The narrative is based upon an English alliterative poem known as the *Morte Arthure.* While shortening his original and modernizing some of its vocabulary, Malory treats it with far more respect than his other sources. Its chief attraction for him lies in the record of Arthur's heroic exploits, which he expands and elaborates as best he can, so as to make Arthur appear as the true embodiment of heroic chivalry. Arthur is the 'Conquerer', the English counterpart of

Charlemagne, and he claims by right the possession of the Roman Empire. He is the champion of the weak and the oppressed, witness his fight with the giant who had caused so much distress to the people of Brittany. But he has some of the characteristics of the primitive type of warrior. He does not shrink [xxiv] from a wholesale massacre of the Romans, and his cruelty in battle is equalled only by his enormous strength. Malory is careful to emphasize, however, that in spite of this cruelty to the enemy Arthur has human qualities which endear him to his own people. The implacable conqueror of the Romans mourns the death of his own knights as an irreparable loss and forgets for a moment his grim and glorious task. The Roman Emperor's challenge grieves him because he cannot tolerate unnecessary bloodshed. He is wise and prudent, anxious to take counsel with his knights, and generous in rewarding them for their services. The noble king is thus shown in all his primitive, yet human glory: not as a mere abstract centre of the fellowship of the Round Table, but as a political and military leader, conscious of his responsibility for the welfare and the prestige of his kingdom.[xxv]

. . . Chivalry was, then, to Malory, at that initial stage of his work, the *faculté maîtresse* [chief faculty] of a brave warrior-king and of his faithful knights; it was man's heroic devotion to a great cause. As Malory's work advanced, and as he ventured deeper and deeper into the vast labyrinth of Arthurian fiction, he found himself following the tracks of innumerable 'warriors wrought in steely weeds', some of whom had distinguished themselves in Arthur's victorious campaign. But as their numbers grew their chivalric ambition, as Malory under- [xxvi] stood it, steadily decreased. They were no longer concerned with the practical business of warfare; they still wore their glittering armour and were eager to use their spears and swords; but their battles seemed to be fought in the void, and there was no discernible object in their exploits. Malory soon realized that the 'great books' of the French Arthurian Cycle failed to provide a worthy continuation of his first Arthurian work, and proceeded to supplement them with remarks and the art and meaning of chivalry. Faithful to his original conception of knighthood, he treated it not as a vague background of adventures but as the practical function of a well-established order—the 'High Order of Knighthood'—with its headquarters firmly fixed in the household of a great prince. While in the French Arthurian romances Arthur's court had been but the conventional starting-point of knightly quests and Arthur himself a fantastic character, a king of Fairyland, Malory made him into the most accomplished and dignified champion of chivalry and the real founder of its great traditions. Under Arthur's leadership chivalry becomes a useful discipline which, if properly practised, can make its adherents into 'the sternest knights to their foes'. The technique of fighting, and more particularly of single combat, is Malory's favourite topic; he speaks of it with confidence and authority. If, in addition to this, chivalry is also a matter of good breeding, gentleness, and loyalty, it is because these qualities, as shown by the example of Arthur, equip the perfect knight for his task and produce a type of warrior ready for any sacrifice and conscious of the importance of his calling. This was what Malory must have learnt both from real life and from reflection, and what he endeavoured to convey in his early work, not as a doctrine, but as a rule of conduct, more vital than ever in times of stress and struggle. The issue as he saw it was essentially a practical, not a moral one, and so far as we can judge it was in the same earnest spirit of practical heroism that in his later writings he so often attempted to commemorate in terms of imaginary knight-errantry some of the great declining traditions of his own age.[xxvii]

How so small a life was graced with true poetic vision, what miraculous play of character and circumstance brought the obscure knight-prisoner to his high theme, we may never know. But when all is said, it is enough to realize that in its varied human aspects his work does not belie what little can be inferred from the records of his strange destiny. The biographer may be tempted to go further and look for positive links between the author and his writings; the critic will more readily abide by Caxton's dictum: 'For to passe the tyme thys book shal be pleasaunte to rede in, but for to gyve fayth and byleve that al is trewe that is conteyned herin, ye be at your lyberté.' [xxviii]

. . . Next after the *Tale of Arthur and Lucius* came the *Tale of King Arthur*—a retrospective account of the early history of Arthur's kingdom, *from the maryage of Kynge Uther unto Kyng Arthure that regned aftir hym and ded many batayles.* But when Malory opened his first 'French book' in the hope of finding some material for the story, he encountered difficulties for which the simple technique he had so far acquired offered so solution. His English source was, in spite of its 'length', a straightforward account of certain pseudo-historical episodes placed in their natural order, and it was comparatively easy, by a mere process of 'reduction', to quicken its pace and remove some of the ornaments of epic style. The problem Malory now had to face was of a totally different kind.

His French romance was a combination of the prose *Merlin* with its sequel, the *Suite du Merlin*. Both were late compositions, the last in date of all the branches of the Arthurian prose Cycle. Their main attraction for Malory was that they supplied the natural beginning of the Arthur story by elaborating some of the episodes recorded in the chronicles of Wace and Geoffrey of Monmouth. But he soon found to his dismay that their treatment of the chronicle material was singularly unlike what he had seen in the *Morte Arthure;* for not only did they lengthen the pseudo-historical matter by the addition of episodes completely foreign to it, but their method of presenting these episodes was anything but normal. Adventures were piled up one upon the other without any apparent sequence or design, and innumerable personages, mostly anonymous, were introduced in a wild succession. Every now and then they stopped to lay lance in rest and overthrow one another, and then swore eternal friendship and rode away. The purpose of their encounters and pursuits was vague, and their tasks were seldom fulfilled: they met and parted and met again, each intent at first on following his particular 'quest', and [xlviii] yet prepared at any time to be diverted from it to other adventures and undertakings. As a result, 'the basic thought became subsidiary, the episode increasingly prominent, the slowing of the action defeated any attempt to reach an end, and the story lost all purpose'. In these words Gustav Gröber described half a century ago the methods used by medieval prose writers. But there is reason to believe that at a much earlier date their methods were condemned on similar grounds, and the often quoted remark of the Canon of Toledo in *Don Quixote* remains to this day the most characteristic expression of the modern view: 'I have never yet', he says, 'seen a book of chivalry complete in all its parts, so that the middle agrees with the beginning and the end with the beginning and the middle; but they seem to construct their stories with such a multitude of members as though they meant to produce a monster rather than a well-proportioned figure.' [xlix]

. . . Malory's handling of his sources shows how strongly he disliked this type of composition. With varying degrees of success, but with remarkable consistency, he endeavoured to do two things: to reduce the bulk of the stories and to alter their arrangement. Of the processes he employed the simplest was mechanical reduction: he seldom reproduced an episode in full and frequently omitted entire sections of his source. More elaborate was the device of 'telescoping': whereas the French prose writers deliberately complicated their material by duplicating episodes and inventing new characters, Malory often simplified his by making either two different scenes or two characters into one. But his most successful and historically most significant contribution to the technique of the prose tale was his attempt to substitute for the method of 'interweaving' a more modern treatment of narrative.[lii]

. . . If Malory's rejection of the theology of the *Queste* [*of the Holy Grail*] set him free to attempt a delineation of character, it led to an even [lxxviii] more striking result in his adaptation of the . . . last branch of the Cycle, the *Mort Artu*. The decisive factor in his approach to this work was his drastic simplification of the spiritual tangle in which the traditional story of Arthur had become involved. In the chronicles of Geoffrey of Monmouth and of Wace the downfall of Arthur's kingdom had no relation to any religious or moral doctrine: it was a typical epic story of the 'defence of a narrow place against odds'. But when in the second quarter of the thirteenth century French prose writers introduced it in the Arthurian Cycle and placed it immediately after the *Queste* they found it necessary to read a new meaning into it. The *Queste* condemned the Round Table in no uncertain terms: 'In this quest your knighthood will avail you nothing if the Holy Ghost does not open the way for you in all your adventures.' The knights destined to achieve the holy quest . . . were those who had hitherto had little or no part in the adventures of the Round Table: Galahad, Bors, and Perceval. The great heroes of Arthurian chivalry were disqualified either wholly, like Gawain, or partly, like Lancelot, who was permitted to enter the Grail castle, but not to see the Grail or even cross the threshold of the sanctuary. It was only natural, therefore, that the compilers of the Cycle should have imagined that in the end the Round Table perished because it had offended God. Thus a link was established between the religious teaching of the *Queste* and the events related in the *Mort Artu*. The issue was complicated rather than clarified by the addition of the 'wheel of Fortune' motif. To this the author of the *Mort Artu* gave considerable prominence. The idea of the relentless motion of the fatal wheel causing the downfall of those who rise too high—a christianized conception of *Fortuna*—had been common enough throughout the Middle Ages, but it was quite distinct from the doctrine of the *Queste*. As, however, it provided an additional reason for the fall of Arthur it was [lxxix] tacked on to the story with the result that in the *Mort Artu* the disaster was interpreted partly as a retribution for the sins of Arthur's knights and partly as a sequel to their rise. . . .

Of this elaborate attempt to give the story of Arthur's death a spiritual background nothing of importance remains in Malory's version. Despite the French Cycle he treats the *Queste* and the *Mort Artu* as self-contained works and suppresses every link between them. To understand his account of the tragedy of Lancelot and of the destruction of the Round Table it is enough to read his last two romances, *The Book of Sir Launcelot and Queen Guinevere* and the *Morte Arthur*—the only two that form together a coherent whole. The *Morte Arthur* is built round a theme which is suggested in the seemingly disconnected episodes of the *Book of Launcelot and Guinevere:* in the opening dialogue between Lancelot and Guinevere, in the story of the maid of Astolat, and in the adventure of the Knight of the Cart. On the familiar bright landscape with its smiling meadows, on the glittering armour of knights riding in search of adventure, dark and ominous shadows begin to fall. We no longer see Arthur's [lxxx] companions perform endless feats of bravery; we hear less of their glorious record, of their ultimate reward. Lancelot is still the greatest of all knights; but with each new episode he seems to lose something of his early enthusiasm, of his faith in the glory of knight-errantry. 'Do ye forthynke yourselff of youre dedis?' Guinevere asks him. There is a strange foreboding in these simple words. The last adventure in the *Book of Launcelot and Guinevere* shows Lancelot at the height of his knightly renown. Of all the knights of the Round Table he alone is privileged to heal the wounds of Sir Urry. But when the adventure is over, 'Sir Launcelot wepte as he had bene a chyld that had bene betyn'. The peripety, the 'tragic reversal of fortunes', is now upon us. It is brought to its climax in the terms of the traditional story of the downfall of Arthur's kingdom, reinterpreted and reshaped in accordance with Malory's own *sen* [spirit]. Geoffrey of Monmouth had been the first to describe how Arthur, having subdued the peoples of the British Isles, was crowned in Caerleon upon Usk, how he then extended his sway to Norway, to Gaul, and to Rome, how during the Roman campaign his nephew Mordred started a rebellion, and how on his return to England Arthur fell in the final contest with the traitor. French prose writers had endeavoured to give this story a deeper significance by complicating both its narrative content and its motivation, and above all by linking it up with the spiritual doctrine of the Grail and with the symbolism of the 'wheel of Fortune'. Malory went further. Externally, his *Most Piteous Tale of the Morte Arthur Sanz Gwerdon* may seem to be a mere abridgement of the French [lxxxi] *Mort Artu,* supplemented by drafts on the English stanzaic *Le Morte Arthur;* in actual fact it is a work of striking originality. Its dominating theme is neither a mere accident of warfare as in the Arthurian chronicles, nor a somewhat forced conclusion of a confused moral issue as in the French Cycle; it is primarily a conflict of two loyalties, both deeply rooted in the medieval conception of knightly service: on the one hand, the heroic loyalty of man to man, 'the mutual love of warriors who die together fighting against odds', a loyalty 'more passionate and less ideal than our patriotism', more sacred even than the ties of nature; on the other, the blind devotion of the knight-lover to his lady, the romantic self-denial imposed by the courtly tradition and inseparable from any form of courtly romance. The clash between these conceptions of human love and service is neither an accident nor a caprice of destiny; it is inherent in the very structure of medieval idealism. And in Malory's rendering of the story of Arthur's death it brings about, for the first time in the history of the legend, a clear and convincing interplay of emotions, infinitely more significant than any encounter with chance.

This result is achieved by subtle, though simple, means. The essential *motif*—the breach of one sacred trust through a wholehearted acceptance of another—was already implicit in the French *Mort Artu* and in the English *Le Morte Arthur*. But each of the two conflicting forces—the power of the love of man for man and the power of courtly devotion—had to be brought out more convincingly. It was not enough that in rescuing Guinevere Lancelot should have unwittingly killed Gawain's half-anonymous brothers as he does in Malory's sources; one of his victims had to be Gareth, the noble knight, who loved Lancelot 'bettir than all hys brethirn and the kynge bothe'. This is part of Malory's own narrative design, of a *sen* unknown to his models, as original as Lancelot's premonition of the coming disaster: 'And peradventure I shall there destroy som of my beste fryndis, and that shold moche repente me. And peradventure there be [lxxxii] som, and they coude wel brynge it aboute, or disobeye my lord kynge Arthur, they wold sone come to me, the which I were loth to hurte.' But Lancelot's duty is clear, even though 'that ys hard for to do'. When the news is brought to Gawain that his brothers Gaheris and Gareth have been killed by Lancelot, he at first refuses to believe it. He is bound to Lancelot by ties of friendship and comradeship which have so far stood the hardest tests. He had forgiven him the deaths of Agravain, of Florens, and of Lovell, even though Arthur had told him that he had 'no cause to love Lancelot'. But when he knows for certain that his two beloved brothers, Gaheris and Gareth, are dead he makes a vow upon which eventually the fortunes of the whole of Arthur's kingdom will break: 'From thys day forewarde I shall never fayle sir Launcelot untyll that one of us have slayne the othir.' The fratricidal struggle then begins, with each opponent keenly conscious of his profound attachment to the other. 'I requyre and bescche you', says Lancelot, 'sytthyn that I am thus requyred and conjoured to ryde into the fylde, that neyther you, my lorde kyng Arthur, nother you, sir Gawayne, com nat into the fylde.' And when he is forced to fight his dearest friend, Gawain, to throw him off his horse and wound him, he still refuses to put him to death, for it is shame 'to smite a wounded man that may not stand'. But the harm is done. Gawain dies of his old wound, repenting on his death-bed of his 'hastiness and wilfulness': 'For I am smyten upon the old wounde the whiche sir Launcelot gave me, on the which I fele well I muste dye. And had sir Launcelot bene with you, as he was, this unhappy werre had never begonne, and of all

thys I am causar.' The 'unhappy war' is not an end, and the 'piteous
tale' goes on until the Round Table becomes a mere memory.
Early in the day Arthur knows that disaster is at hand: 'Wyte you
wel, my herte was never so hevy as hit ys now. And much more
I am [lxxxiii] soryar for my good knyghtes losse than for the losse of
my fayre queen; for quenys I myght have inow, but such felyship
of good knyghtes shall never be togydirs in no company.' Only
Malory's Arthur can say with such characteristic abruptness, 'quenys
I myght have inow'; but perhaps for this very reason only Malory's
Arthur can gauge the full depth of his grief at the destruction of
his fellowship, the equal of which has not been seen in any Christian land, and the significance of his own defeat by the traitor
Mordred in that last of all battles when 'of all the good knights are
left no more alive but two', and a hundred thousand lie dead upon
the down. The action which leads to this ending is swift, inevitable,
relentless; the tragic circle of fear and pity is complete. And the
aftermath brings home the profound humanity of it. When Lancelot comes to avenge the King and the Queen he finds that the
Queen has retired from the world. To share her fate he becomes a
hermit; not for the love of God, but for the love of the Queen:
'And therefore, lady sithen you have taken you to perfection I
must needs take me to perfection of right.' A year later he is allowed
to bury her. And although it may be as a hermit that at first 'he
wepte not gretelye, but syghed', it is as her faithful lover that 'when
she was put in the erth syr Launcelot swouned and laye longe
stylle'. . . . He repents not of the sins he has committed against
God, but of the griefs he has caused his lady and King Arthur. And
so there is no relief to his pain. . . . Death [lxxxiv] alone brings him
comfort, and as he lay on his death-bed it seemed as though 'he had
smyled, and the sweetest savour aboute hym'. In the earlier scene
of Arthur's last farewell there is the same sense of unrelieved loneli-
ness. 'Comfort thyself', Arthur says to Bedwere, 'and doo as wel as
thou mayst, for in me is no truste for to truste in. For I wyl to the
vale of Avylyon to hele me of my grievous wounds.' There is no
remedy for Arthur's wounds, and no truth in the belief in his
eventual return. 'I wyl not say that it shal be so.' And when night
falls on the plain of Salisbury there is no 'trust left to trust in', no
comfort to be found in religious explanations; all doctrine shrivels
before the conflict of 'two goods' and the desolation it brings. It is

not through sin or weakness of heart that this comes about, but through the devotion of the truest friend and the truest lover, through a tragic greatness which fixes for ever the complex and delicate meaning of Arthur's epic.[lxxxv]

STUDY QUESTIONS AND TOPICS FOR INVESTIGATION

Most of the study questions included here require only brief answers. They point directly to the materials in the book so that the reader can grasp essentials quickly and go on to broader fields of research. It should be understood that some of the suggested topics are large and difficult, while others are narrow and specialized. Deciding how to deal most effectively with a research subject by extending or restricting its scope, however, is a vital part of the entire process. To assist in this matter, therefore, all topics below are arbitrarily classified as either short (*s*) or long (*l*); they may, of course, easily be enlarged or abbreviated as the teacher and student see fit.

I. HISTORY AND PSEUDO-HISTORY

A. GILDAS

1. Describe the Roman Briton resistance to the Saxons.
2. What is the state of Roman Briton morale before, during, and after the battle at Mount Badon?

Topics:

a. Leaders of the Roman Britons (*s*)
b. Roman Briton Civilization (*l*)

B. BEDE

1. Where does Bede seem to have acquired his information? Be specific.
2. How does his account differ from that of Gildas?

Topics:

a. The Anglo-Saxon Invasion of England (*s*)
b. Bede's Life, Works, and Stature as an Historian (*s*)

C. NENNIUS

1. What impression do you get of Arthur's character and achievement in this, the first historical mention of him?
2. Exactly where and how does Nennius enter the realm of pseudo-history?

Topics:

a. The Geography of Arthur's Recorded Battles (*s*)
b. Early *Mirabilia* Concerning Arthur (*s*)

D. "ANNALES CAMBRIAE"

1. What slight change in Nennius' account of Arthur is made here? What addition?
2. Is there any other new information given? If so, what?

Topics:

a. Religious Elements in Anglo-Saxon Warfare (*s*)
b. English Historical Chronicles Before the Norman Invasion (*l*)

E. WILLIAM OF MALMESBURY

1. How does William embellish the factual records you have read so far?
2. What important new aspects of Arthur are mentioned?
3. Summarize what is said about Walwen.

Topics:

a. A Brief History of Brittany from 500 A.D. to 1300 (*s*)
b. Early Celtic Civilization (*s*)
c. Welsh Arthurian Folklore to the Thirteenth Century (*l*)
d. The Norman Conquest and Its Consequences (*l*)

F. GIRALDUS CAMBRENSIS

1. What are the marvels now told of Arthur?
2. Does Giraldus give any new information which might be regarded as factual? Explain.

Topics:

a. Giraldus Cambrensis as an Historian (s)
b. Glastonbury and Avalon (s)

G. RALPH HIGDEN

1. What reasons does Higden enumerate for doubting Geoffrey of Monmouth's accounts of Arthur?
2. Are there, according to Higden, other things which might arouse an historian's suspicions?

Topics:

a. Higden's *Polychronicon* as History (s)
b. Higden and His Translators (s)

INVESTIGATIVE SUBJECTS SUGGESTED BY ALL MATERIALS IN PART I:

The Arthur of History (l)
Arthur's Stature in Early Fable and Legend (l)

II. CHRONICLE AND ROMANCE

A. "CULHWCH AND OLWEN"

1. Characterize the young hero of the tale.
2. In what ways has Arthur now become fully fictionalized?
3. Arthur has some followers and possessions which sound familiar. Name them.
4. How well is the suspense in the quests handled? Why?

5. Why do you suppose the hunting of Twrch Trwyth is so fully depicted?
6. What impression is the reader given of Olwen?

Topics:

a. The Narrative Art of *Culhwch and Olwen* (*s*)
b. *The Mabinogion* and Its Place in Welsh Literature (*s*)
c. Arthurian Stories in *The Mabinogion* (*l*)

B. GEOFFREY OF MONMOUTH

1. What impression do you get of British court life in these times?
2. Describe the character of Vortigern.
3. What is told of Merlin up to the time Arthur becomes king? Be specific.
4. How large a part does Christianity play in Geoffrey's narrative? Can you tell why?
5. Outline the Uther-Igerna-Gorlois episode. Is Uther treated sympathetically? Is Arthur's conception "shameful"?
6. What is the young Arthur like? How does the listing of his battle equipment match that in *Culhwch and Olwen?*
7. Define Arthur's attitude towards his followers and his enemies.
8. How does Arthur's march on Rome assume mounting significance?
9. Do the fights with Flollo and the giant of the mount St. Michael contribute anything to your impression of Arthur's character? Why, or why not?
10. Is the battle with the Emperor Lucius dramatic? Give specific reasons for your answer.
11. Characterize Gawain and Modred, explaining their most important functions in the chronicle.
12. Do you find that Geoffrey actually uses earlier history and pseudo-history in his narrative? If so, where?

Topics:

a. The "History" in Geoffrey of Monmouth's *Historia* (*s*)
b. Stonehenge: Fact and Myth (*s*)
c. Tintagel and Other Medieval Castles (*s*)
d. Court Life in Anglo-Norman England (*s*)

e. Merlin's Place in Geoffrey of Monmouth's *Historia* (*s*)
f. Geoffrey of Monmouth's Use of Geography (*s*)
g. Geoffrey of Monmouth's Motives in Writing the *Historia* (*s*)
h. The Theme of Conquest in Geoffrey of Monmouth's *Historia* (*l*)
i. Geoffrey of Monmouth's Narrative Art (*l*)

C. ROBERT BIKET

1. Describe the air of magic in the story.
2. How does the tone of Arthur's court differ from that in Geoffrey of Monmouth?
3. What good and bad qualities of character does Arthur reveal?
4. Is the queen's "explanation" convincing? Why, or why not?
5. What elements of humor are found in *The Lay of the Horn*? Is it dramatically told?

Topics:

a. The Medieval Fabliaux Tales (*s*)
b. The Breton Lai in Marie de France and Others (*l*)

D. WACE

1. How has Wace improved upon Geoffrey of Monmouth's story of Uther and Igerne? Be specific.
2. Does the author comment directly or indirectly on Uther's conduct with Igerne? Where?
3. What are the virtues and faults of the young Arthur according to Wace?
4. Has the poet given you a fuller picture of Guenevere? In what places?
5. Characterize Wace's Gawain. In what way does Gawain's attitude towards warfare differ from that of Cador?
6. How has the author developed Arthur's conflict with Frollo?
7. Is there a tone of moralizing in the Mordred betrayal?
8. Show how Wace has enlarged on Arthur's dream.
9. Do you think Wace has "improved" Geoffrey of Monmouth's battle scenes? Explain.
10. In what important particular does Wace contradict Nennius?

11. What genuine "additions" has Wace made to the Arthur story, particularly near the end?

Topics:

a. Medieval Sieges (s)
b. The Character of Arthur in Wace (s)
c. Courtly Elements in Wace's *Roman de Brut* (s)
d. Wace as a Translator of Geoffrey of Monmouth (l)

E. LAYAMON

1. What sources does the author claim to have used?
2. Explain what Layamon has added to the story of Arthur's birth.
3. Contrast the struggle with Childric in Layamon and Geoffrey of Monmouth.
4. Evaluate the speeches of the characters in the poem.
5. Is the dream of Arthur more or less effective now? How?
6. In what specific ways does Layamon dramatize Modred's betrayal of Arthur?
7. What, exactly, has been added to the previous descriptions of Arthur's final hours?

Topics:

a. The Development of the Round Table in Arthurian Legend (s)
b. The Legend of Arthur's Survival and Return (s)
c. The Alliterative Revival in Medieval English Poetry (l)

F. "THE DREAM OF RHONABWY"

1. What is the reason for Rhonabwy's quest?
2. Describe the opening scene specifically.
3. How does the author change the traditional story of the Arthur-Mordred conflict?
4. Try to account for the use of colors in the tale.
5. What descriptive powers does the author show? Be precise.
6. How is the game of gwyddbwyll made significant?
7. Characterize Owein.
8. Are the ravens real or metaphorical? Why?
9. What is accomplished by the ending of the story?

Topics:

a. The Characteristics of Medieval Dream Literature (s)
b. Welsh Storytelling Art in the Medieval Period (s)

G. "ARTHUR AND MERLIN"

1. Describe Kay.
2. How does Sir Antour's account of Arthur's birth differ from that of the chronicles?
3. What picture is given of young Arthur? Be exact.
4. What are the rebellious barons like?

Topics:

a. The English Coronation Ceremony in Medieval Times (s)
b. The Development of the Sword-in-the-Stone Story (s)

H. "MORTE ARTHURE"
("Alliterative Version")

1. Precisely where is Arthur campaigning at the beginning of the poem?
2. Analyze Arthur's dream carefully, concentrating on the Wheel of Fortune and the philosopher's interpretation.
3. Why is the scene with Arthur and Sir Craddock important? How are the two men contrasted?
4. What details have been added to Modred's treason which were not in Geoffrey of Monmouth, Wace, and Layamon? Be specific.
5. Describe in full Arthur's return to the shores of England.
6. Do you admire the character of Gawain in this poem? Why, or why not?
7. What is unusual in the reaction of Modred to Gawain's death? Explain.
8. Does Waynor's remorse seem genuine? In what ways does the account of her betrayal of Arthur differ from the others you have read?
9. Is Sir Ewain justified in admonishing Arthur? Comment.
10. What is new in the Arthur-Modred conflict?
11. Is there something symbolic in Caliburn and Clarent? What?

12. Who of the Round Table has perished and who has survived?
13. How truly spiritual are Arthur's final moments?
14. What is missing at the end which you found in Wace and Layamon?

Topics:

a. Dream Lore in the Middle Ages (s)
b. Medieval Naval Warfare (s)
c. Heraldry (s)
d. Battle Tactics and Dress in Fourteenth Century England (s)
e. The Functions of Gawain and Modred in the Alliterative *Morte Arthure* (s)
f. The Narrative Art of the *Morte Arthure* Poet (l)
g. Poetic Technique in Layamon and the Alliterative *Morte Arthure* (l)

I. "LE MORTE ARTHUR" ("Stanzaic Version")

1. Describe the atmosphere of Arthur's court in the opening two scenes of the poem. How is the Queen central to both?
2. Is Agravaine justified in his suspicions of Lancelot? What are the reactions of Gawain and Arthur? What is the role of Mordred here?
3. Do you notice a building up of Lancelot's character? Who is diminished? Is the author justified in treating him this way? Why, or why not?
4. Do you think Mordred's betrayal is intended by the poet as Arthur's punishment for allowing the Round Table to decline?
5. Besides treason, of what other evil is Mordred guilty? Explain.
6. Does the poet delineate the final conflict as well as the authors of previous chronicle and romance you have read? Be exact in your answer.
7. Compare and contrast Arthur's dream in the Alliterative *Morte Arthure* and the Stanzaic *Le Morte Arthur*.
8. Do you consider Arthur's bargaining with Mordred a weakness in the king? Is the tone here different from that in Geoffrey of Monmouth, Wace, and Layamon? How?
9. Why are the robbers introduced? Is tone important here also?
10. Describe the character and actions of Sir Bedivere.

11. Has the poet developed the Avalon theme in any way?
12. How is the description of Arthur's tomb like and unlike that of Giraldus Cambrensis? Be precise.

Topics:

a. The Decline of the Round Table in Romance (s)
b. King Arthur's Relatives (s)
c. The Lady of the Lake in Arthurian Romance (s)
d. Courtly Love in the Romances of Arthur (l)

J. THE PROSE *MERLIN*

1. Has the author better dramatic skills in his tale of Arthur's birth and adoption than in previous writers? What makes you say so?
2. Merlin's character has changed somewhat since the time of Geoffrey of Monmouth. How?
3. Evaluate the role of Antor as he deals with Uther Pendragon.
4. Do you have any idea who the old man is?
5. Describe the rising importance of Christianity in the story. Has this element been at all evident before? Where, and to what extent?
6. Is there greater emphasis on the barons? What, precisely, is made of the common people?
7. Describe the character of the archbishop throughout.
8. What is significant in the archbishop's sermon on Justice and the sword?
9. *Arthur and Merlin* tells essentially the same story of the Sword-in-the-Stone as the Prose *Merlin*. Which, to you, is more dramatically handled? Why?
10. Is Antor's reaction to Arthur's success too materialistic? How do you feel about Kay? Why?
11. Does the author draw out the barons' final acceptance of Arthur too much? Give reasons for your answer.
12. Does Arthur's conduct with Lot's wife diminish his stature for you? What is ironic in the whole affair? Does the author seem to be moralizing?
13. Under what conditions is Arthur's court established? Be specific.

Topics:

a. The Function of Antor in Arthurian Romance (s)
b. Kay in the Arthur Story (s)
c. Christianity in the Tales of King Arthur (l)

K. SIR THOMAS MALORY

1. What vital changes does Malory make in the Uther-Igraine-Duke of Cornwall story? Be precise.
2. Does it appear that Malory used *Arthur and Merlin* and the Prose *Merlin* for his account of Arthur's infancy? Discuss.
3. Is the Sword-in-the-Stone episode handled better in Malory or in the Prose *Merlin*? Why?
4. Does Malory make more or less of Kay's deceit over the sword?
5. How does Malory develop the story of the rebellious knights?
6. What is the purpose of Arthur's dream and the story of the "questing beast"?
7. Of what does Ulfius accuse Igraine? How is she vindicated?
8. Does Arthur's conflict with Pellinore have any significance? If so, what? Has Arthur been overcome by others this early in his career in chronicle or romance? Where?
9. Describe the scene of the Lady of the Lake.
10. Arthur's attempt to get rid of the infant Mordred may recall similar stories in myth, legend, and literature. What are they?
11. What has been added by Malory to earlier descriptions of the Arthur-Guinever relationship? What is Merlin's warning? What is the dowry?
12. What importance does Arthur's conflict with Accolon have? Be exact.
13. Has Arthur heard from the Roman ambassadors before? Where? Is their warning to Lucius found only in Malory?
14. Are Arthur's dream and his fight with the Giant of St. Michael's Mount handled differently in previous chronicles and romances? Give reasons for your answers.
15. How is the great battle with the Emperor Lucius begun?
16. Evaluate Arthur's generalship.
17. Does it appear to you that Malory embellishes the traditional accounts of the King's campaign against the Romans? Where, and in what ways?

18. Contrast Arthur's attitude at the siege of Paris in Wace with his conduct at the taking of Italian cities in Malory.

19. The end of the Roman campaign in Malory is far different from that in other accounts you have read. How?

20. What exact situation begins the fall of the Round Table? Does Malory treat it more effectively than the author of the Stanzaic *Le Morte Arthur*? Comment.

21. How is Malory vague about the supposed adultery of Launcelot and Guenever? Can you guess why?

22. Where are your sympathies in the affair—with Launcelot, Gawaine, or Arthur? Do you approve of Arthur's reaction? Explain.

23. How do Arthur's knights react to the supposed love affair, and what do they do about it? Is the function of Mordred here ironic? Why?

24. What do you think of Gawaine's reaction to the report of Launcelot's actions? What, finally, turns him against Launcelot?

25. Does Arthur, in your opinion, place the blame correctly?

26. Do you believe Launcelot's words to the King about the Queen? Evaluate his arguments.

27. In what ways does Malory build up the character of Launcelot and diminish that of Gawaine? Why was it necessary? Is there something ironic in it?

28. Does the resolution of the Arthur-Launcelot conflict satisfy you? Comment.

29. Are Launcelot's fights with Gawaine exciting? Trace Malory's art in the scenes.

30. How has Malory enlarged upon the traditional accounts of Mordred's treachery, the final struggle, and Arthur's death? Be specific.

Topics:

a. William Caxton: Printer and Author (*l*)

b. Malory's Narrative Techniques in His Story of Arthur (*s*)

c. The Stylistic Achievement of Sir Thomas Malory (*s*)

d. The Sources of Malory's *Le Morte Darthur* (*s*)

e. Morgan le Fay in Arthurian Legend (*s*)

f. The Function of Merlin in Malory's Story of Arthur (*s*)

g. The Lancelot and Guinevere of Malory (*l*)
h. Malory's Story of Tristram and Iseult (*s*)
i. Gawain and Lancelot and the Destruction of the Round Table in Malory (*l*)
j. Arthur's Death in Chronicle and Romance (*l*)

INVESTIGATIVE SUBJECTS SUGGESTED BY ALL MATERIALS IN PART II:

The Myth of Troy and Britain (*s*)
Merlin the Magician (*s*)
Arthur: King and Conqueror in Legend (*l*)
Gawain's Character in Chronicle and Romance (*l*)
French Contributions to the Character of Arthur (*s*)
Mordred the Betrayer: Man and Symbol (*s*)
The Theme of Adultery in Arthurian Romance (*s*)
Arthur's Knights: a Study in Loyalty and Prowess (*l*)

III. CRITICISM

A. JACKSON, PARRY, and CHURCHILL

1. What careful distinctions does Jackson make about all the Arthurian materials?
2. Does Parry's tone differ from Jackson's in his approach to the problem of Arthur's existence? Does he disagree with Jackson anywhere?
3. How does Churchill treat the whole matter? Is he more "believable" to you than either Jackson or Parry? Explain.

Topics:

a. Historical Views of Arthur's Existence (*l*)
b. Theory and Practice of Historical Methods in the Case of King Arthur (*s*)

B. PARRY, CALDWELL, and TATLOCK

1. Do Parry and Caldwell clear up any confusion you might have found in Geoffrey of Monmouth's story? How and where?

2. What do the authors say about Geoffrey's sources in general? about his style? about his purpose and success? Could you add more by further study?
3. Summarize Tatlock's points about the structure of Geoffrey's *Historia*.
4. How, according to Tatlock, is Geoffrey like and unlike other medieval historians? Be specific.

Topics:

a. Welsh Myrddin Legends (*s*)
b. The King Leir Story Before Shakespeare (*s*)
c. The Achievement of Geoffrey of Monmouth (*l*)

C. ALBERT C. BAUGH

1. What does Baugh make clear about the love element in medieval romance?
2. List the characteristics of medieval romance.
3. Why was the French language important to this genre?
4. What are the four "matters" of medieval romance? What are their individual subjects? Name specific examples of each.

Topics:

a. Aeneas and Arthur: from Epic to Romance (*l*)
b. French Contributions to the English Language (*s*)
c. A Study of Gottfried von Strassburg's *Tristan and Isolt* (*l*)
d. The Matter of France—or Rome—or England (*s*)

D. GWYN JONES and THOMAS JONES

1. What elements are common to the tales in *The Mabinogion?*
2. List the outstanding qualities of *Culhwch and Olwen* according to these critics.
3. Why is *Culhwch and Olwen* "a document of the first importance"?

Topics:

a. Irish Arthurian Analogues (*s*)
b. The Nature of Medieval Welsh Storytellers (*s*)
c. Celticists and Inventionists: Arthurian Critical Battleground (*s*)

E. ERNEST HOEPFFNER

1. Do you find *The Lay of the Horn* contains "rather crude humor"? Why, or why not?
2. Why, exactly, does Hoepffner think this story has some importance?

Topics:

a. The Chastity Test in Legend and Literature (*s*)
b. A Study of Chrétian de Troyes' *Erec* (*s*)

F. ROBERT HUNTINGTON FLETCHER

1. List the important differences between the styles of Wace and Geoffrey of Monmouth.
2. How, according to Fletcher, does Wace reflect his own environment in the *Roman de Brut*?
3. In what other ways is Wace's poem an "improvement"?
4. Summarize the changes Wace makes in Geoffrey's story.
5. Can you find other contrasts or alterations which Fletcher has not mentioned? What are they?

Topics:

a. The Medieval Feudal System (*l*)
b. The Role of the Medieval French Storyteller (*s*)

G. HENRY CECIL WYLD

1. List the qualities of Laȝamon as a poet. Why is the *Brut* not more popular? What rank does it have, according to the critic?
2. What does Wyld say about the sources of the poem? Why is it more than a mere "translation" of Wace?
3. How does the *Brut* remind Wyld of *Beowulf*?
4. Enumerate some of Laȝamon's poetic techniques. In what ways does the poet make his battle scenes dramatic?
5. What does Wyld say about the Round Table in Laȝamon? Be precise.

Topics:

a. Old English Poetics (s)
b. A Stylistic Analysis of Middle English Arthurian Poems (l)
c. Arthur's Ill-Fated Family in Geoffrey of Monmouth, Wace, and Layamon (l)

H. IDRIS LLEWELYN FOSTER

1. What, precisely, makes The Dream of Rhonabwy "the work of a talented author"?
2. How has Geoffrey of Monmouth influenced this work?
3. The tale, says Foster, involves traditional themes. What are they?

Topics:

a. Medieval Games (s)
b. Animal Symbolism in Medieval English Literature (l)

I. ROBERT W. ACKERMAN

1. What kind of structure does the whole of Arthur and Merlin have?
2. Ackerman makes two interesting points at the end of his essay. What are they?

Topics:

a. Arthurian Manuscripts (s)
b. The Merlin Cycle (l)

J. WILLIAM MATTHEWS

1. What does Matthews make clear about the Roman campaign in the Alliterative Morte Arthure?
2. Why is the poem "profoundly religious"?
3. How does Arthur try to fill the role of a saviour? Is he successful?
4. The Morte Arthure makes the character of Mordred complex. Exactly how?
5. In what ways, according to Matthews, does Gawain's character

grow? How do Arthur and Mordred look upon the dead Gawain? What other Biblical suggestiveness is there?

6. Define the poem's "twofold parallelism."

Topics:

a. Alexander and Arthur: Conquest and Vainglory (*l*)
b. The Medieval Doctrine of Penitence (*s*)
c. The Gawain Cycle (*l*)
d. *Sir Gawain and the Green Knight:* Critical Interpretations (*l*)

K. JOHN EDWIN WELLS

1. Why is the Stanzaic *Le Morte Arthur* significant?
2. What qualities does Wells claim for it?
3. Gawain loses status. How?

Topics:

a. The Maid of Astolat in Arthurian Romance (*s*)
b. The Reputation of Gawain in Later Arthurian Tales (*s*)

L. BRADBROOK and VINAVER

1. Miss Bradbrook stresses the fellowship of the Round Table in her discussion of Malory. Exactly why?
2. What epic qualities does Miss Bradbrook find in Malory's work? Be specific.
3. How does Malory, according to Vinaver, make Arthur the conqueror human?
4. Outline what Vinaver says about Malory's view of chivalry. How is this vital to Malory's version of the Round Table's decline?
5. Malory faced problems as he sought to simplify his story of the final catastrophe. What were they? How did he solve them?
6. How is "The Death of Arthur" original in Malory's hands? Do you feel, with Vinaver, that *Le Morte Darthur* is a book with "a complex and delicate meaning"? Why, or why not?

Topics:

a. The Winchester Manuscript of *Le Morte Darthur* (*s*)
b. Who Was Sir Thomas Malory? (*s*)

c. The Turbulent Milieu of Sir Thomas Malory (*l*)
d. Malory's Skill in the Use of His Sources (*s*)
e. The Vulgate Cycle (*s*)

INVESTIGATIVE SUBJECTS SUGGESTED BY ALL MATERIALS IN PART III:

Critical Approaches to Arthurian Literature (*l*)
The Origin and Growth of the Tristan Legend (*s*)
The Beginnings of the Grail Legend (*s*)
Chrétian de Troyes' Story of the Grail (*s*)
A Study of Wolfram von Eschenbach's *Parzival* (*l*)
The Art of *Perlesvaus* (*s*)
Percival in Arthurian Literature (*l*)
Lancelot, Galahad, and the Grail (*l*)
Arthurian Romance in Spain, Portugal, and Italy (*s*)

Bibliography
and
Glossary

BIBLIOGRAPHY

The works below represent suggestions for further reading in the Arthurian legend, but the list is highly selective. A number of these books and articles also contain bibliographies where the student can find additional guidance for research. Asterisks (*) indicate translations; paperbacks are included wherever possible.

A. GENERAL

BRUCE, James Douglas. *The Evolution of Arthurian Romance from the Beginnings Down to the Year 1300*. 2 vols. Second Edition, with a supplement by Alfons Hilka. Gloucester, Mass.: Peter Smith, Reprint, 1958.

CHAMBERS, E. K. *Arthur of Britain*. London: Sidgwick & Jackson, Ltd., 1927.

*CROSS, Tom Peete, and Clark Harris SLOVER, eds. *Ancient Irish Tales*. New York: Henry Holt and Company, 1936.

FARRAR, Clarissa P., and Austin P. EVANS. *Bibliography of English Translations from Medieval Sources*. New York: Columbia University Press, 1946.

HIBBARD, Laura A. *Medieval Romance in England:* a Study of the Sources and Analogues of the Non-Cyclic Metrical Romances. New York: Oxford University Press, 1924.

HOLMES, Urban Tigner, Jr. *A History of Old French Literature, from the Origins to 1300*. Chapel Hill: University of North Carolina Press, 1937.

KER, W. P. *Epic and Romance:* Essays on Medieval Literature. New York: Dover Publications, Inc., Reprint, 1957.

LOOMIS, Roger Sherman. *Celtic Myth and Arthurian Romance*. New York: Columbia University Press, 1927.

————, ed. *Medieval Studies in Memory of Gertrude Schoepperle Loomis*. New York: Columbia University Press, 1927.

————, ed. *Arthurian Literature in the Middle Ages:* A Collaborative History. Oxford: at the Clarendon Press, 1959.

*————, and Laura Hibbard LOOMIS, eds. *Medieval Romances*. New York: the Modern Library, 1957.

MALONE, Kemp, and Albert C. BAUGH. *The Middle Ages.* Vol. I of *A Literary History of England,* ed. Albert C. Baugh. New York: Appleton-Century-Crofts, Inc., 1948.

NEWSTEAD, Helaine H. *Bran the Blessed in Arthurian Romance.* New York: Columbia University Press, 1939.

NITZE, William A., and E. Preston DARGAN. *A History of French Literature, from the Earliest Times to the Present.* 3rd edition. New York: Henry Holt and Company, 1938.

PARRY, Thomas. *A History of Welsh Literature.* Trans. H. Idris Bell. Oxford: at the Clarendon Press, 1955.

PARRY, John J., and Margaret SCHLAUCH. *Arthurian Bibliography.* Vol. I (1922-1929), Vol. II (1930-1935). New York: Published for the Modern Language Association of America. See also the yearly bibliography published in *Modern Language Quarterly.*

PATON, Lucy Allen. *Studies in the Fairy Mythology of Arthurian Romance.* Boston: Ginn & Company, 1903.

ROBERTSON, John G. *A History of German Literature.* New and Revised Edition. New York: G. P. Putnam's Sons, 1931.

*SCHLAUCH, Margaret. *Medieval Narrative.* New York: Prentice-Hall, Inc., 1928.

SPEIRS, John. *Medieval English Poetry:* the Non-Chaucerian Tradition. New York: The Macmillan Company, 1957.

WELLS, John Edwin. *A Manual of the Writings in Middle English, 1050-1400.* With Supplements I-IX. New Haven: Yale University Press, 1916-1952.

*WESTON, Jessie L. *Romance, Vision, and Satire:* English Alliterative Poems of the Fourteenth Century. Boston and New York: Houghton Mifflin Company, 1912.

* ————. *The Chief Middle English Poets.* Boston: Houghton Mifflin Company, 1914.

ZESMER, David M. *Guide to English Literature from Beowulf through Chaucer and Medieval Drama.* With Bibliographies by Stanley B. Greenfield. College Outline Series. New York: Barnes & Noble, Inc., 1961.

B. SPECIFIC

1. GAWAIN

*BANKS, Theodore Howard, Jr. *Sir Gawain and the Green Knight.* New York: Appleton-Century-Crofts, Inc., 1929.

BLOOMFIELD, Morton W. *"Sir Gawain and the Green Knight:* An Appraisal," *Publications of the Modern Language Association of America,* LXXVI (March, 1961), 7-19.

GOLDHURST, William. "The Green and the Gold: The Major Theme of *Gawain and the Green Knight," College English,* XX (November, 1958), 61-65.

KITTREDGE, George Lyman. *A Study of Gawain and the Green Knight.* Gloucester, Mass.: Peter Smith, Reprint, 1960.

MARKMAN, Alan M. "The Meaning of *Sir Gawain and the Green Knight,"* *Publications of the Modern Language Association of America,* LXXII (September, 1957), 574-86.

*ROSENBERG, James L. *Sir Gawain and the Green Knight.* Ed. with intro. by James R. Kreuzer. Rinehart Editions. New York and Toronto: Rinehart & Co., Inc., 1959.

SAVAGE, Henry L. *The GAWAIN-Poet:* Studies in His Personality and Background. Chapel Hill: University of North Carolina Press, 1956.

2. LANCELOT

CROSS, Tom Peete, and William Albert NITZE. *Lancelot and Guenevere:* A Study on the Origins of Courtly Love. Chicago: University of Chicago Press, 1930.

*PATON, Lucy Allen. *Sir Lancelot of the Lake:* a French Prose Romance of the Thirteenth Century. London: G. Routledge & Sons, Ltd., 1929.

WESTON, Jessie L. *The Legend of Sir Lancelot du Lac:* Studies upon its Origin, Development, and Position in the Arthurian Romantic Cycle. London: David Nutt, 1901.

3. TRISTAN

*HATTO, A. T. *Gottfried von Strassburg's Tristan.* With the 'Tristran' of Thomas. The Penguin Classics. Baltimore: Penguin Books, 1960.

*LOOMIS, Roger Sherman. *The Romance of Tristram and Ysolt by Thomas of Britain.* Revised Edition. New York: Columbia University Press, 1931.

LOOMIS, Gertrude Schoepperle. *Tristan and Isolt:* a Study of the Sources of the Romance. Frankfurt: M. J. Baer & Co., 1913.

4. PERCIVAL AND THE GRAIL LEGEND

BROWN, Arthur C. L. *The Origin of the Grail Legend.* Cambridge, Mass.: Harvard University Press, 1943.

*COMFORT, William Wistar. *The Quest of the Holy Grail* [Vulgate]. Everyman's Library. London and Toronto: J. M. Dent & Sons, Ltd., 1926.

*EVANS, Sebastian. *The High History of the Holy Grail* [*Perlesvaus*]. Everyman's Library. London and Toronto: J. M. Dent & Sons, Ltd., 1910.

LOCKE, Frederick W. *The Quest for the Holy Grail:* A Literary Study of a Thirteenth-Century Prose Romance. Stanford: Stanford University Press, 1960.

*MUSTARD, Helen M., and Charles E. PASSAGE. *Wolfram von Eschenbach's Parzival.* Vintage Books. New York: Random House, 1961.

*SKEELS, Dell. *The Romance of Perceval in Prose:* A Translation of the E Manuscript of the Didot Perceval. Seattle: University of Washington Press, 1961.

WESTON, Jessie L. *The Legend of Sir Percival.* 2 vols. London: David Nutt, 1906-1909.

————. *The Quest of the Holy Grail.* London: G. Bell & Sons, Ltd., 1913.

————. *From Ritual to Romance.* Doubleday Anchor Books. Garden City, N. Y.: Doubleday & Company, Inc., Reprint, 1957.

*ZEYDEL, Edwin H., and Bayard Quincy MORGAN. *The Parzival of Wolfram von Eschenbach.* Chapel Hill: University of North Carolina Studies in the Germanic Languages and Literatures, Number Five, 1951.

5. MERLIN

See Chapters 19, 23, and 24 in Roger Sherman LOOMIS, ed., *Arthurian Literature in the Middle Ages,* for discussions of Robert de Boron's *Merlin,* the Vulgate *Merlin,* and the *Suite du Merlin.* No adequate translations of these works have been made.

6. GEOFFREY OF MONMOUTH

*EVANS, Sebastian. *History of the Kings of Britain.* Revised by Charles W. Dunn. Dutton Everyman Paperback. New York: E. P. Dutton & Co., Inc., 1958.

TATLOCK, J. S. P. *The Legendary History of Britain:* Geoffrey of Monmouth's Historia Regum Britanniae and Its Early Vernacular Versions. Berkeley and Los Angeles: University of California Press, 1950.

7. CHRÉTIEN DE TROYES

*COMFORT, W. W. *Chrétien de Troyes' Arthurian Romances.* Everyman's Library. London: J. M. Dent & Sons, Ltd., 1914.

FOWLER, David C. *Prowess and Charity in the Perceval of Chrétien de Troyes*. Seattle: University of Washington Press, 1959.

HOLMES, Urban T., Jr., and Sister M. Amelia KLENKE. *Chrétien, Troyes, and the Grail*. Chapel Hill: University of North Carolina Press, 1959.

*LINKER, Robert White. *Chrestien de Troyes' The Story of the Grail*. Second Edition. Chapel Hill: University of North Carolina Press, 1960.

LOOMIS, Roger Sherman. *Arthurian Tradition and Chrétien de Troyes*. New York: Columbia University Press, 1949.

8. MALORY

CHAMBERS, E. K. "Malory," in *English Literature at the Close of the Middle Ages*. Oxford: at the Clarendon Press, 1945, pp. 185-205.

DAVIES, R. T. "Malory's Launcelot and the Noble Way of the World," *The Review of English Studies*, New Series, VI (October, 1955), 356-64.

MOORMAN, Charles. "Malory's Treatment of the Sankgreall," *Publications of the Modern Language Association of America*, LXXI (June, 1956), 496-509.

————. "Courtly Love in Malory," *ELH*, XXVII (September, 1960), 163-76.

*RHYS, John. *Sir Thomas Malory's Le Morte D'Arthur*. 2 vols. Everyman's Library. London: J. M. Dent & Sons, Ltd., 1906.

SCUDDER, Vida. *Le Morte Darthur of Sir Thomas Malory and Its Sources*. New York: E. P. Dutton & Co., 1921.

VINAVER, Eugène. *Malory*. Oxford: at the Clarendon Press, 1929.

————, ed. *The Works of Sir Thomas Malory*. 3 vols. Oxford: at the Clarendon Press, 1947.

C. MISCELLANEOUS TRANSLATIONS

*IVES, Vernon. *Jaufry the Knight and the Fair Brunissende*. Newly Revised. New York: Holiday House, 1935.

*MASON, Eugene. *Lays of Marie de France and Other French Legends*. Everyman's Library. London: J. M. Dent & Sons, Ltd., 1911.

*————. *Arthurian Chronicles Represented by Wace and Layamon*. Everyman's Library. London: J. M. Dent & Sons, Ltd., [1912], Reprint, 1962.

*PARRY, John Jay. *The Art of Courtly Love by Andreas Capellanus.* New York: F. Ungar Publishing Co., Reprint, 1959.

*PATON, Lucy Allen. *Morte Arthur: Two Early English Romances.* Everyman's Library. London: J. M. Dent & Sons, Ltd., 1912.

*SMYTHE, Barbara. *Trobador Poets.* London: Chatto & Windus, 1929.

D. OTHER MISCELLANEOUS WORKS

ASHE, Geoffrey. *King Arthur's Avalon:* The Story of Glastonbury. New York: E. P. Dutton & Co., Inc., 1958.

BRINKLEY, Roberta Florence. *Arthurian Legend in the Seventeenth Century.* Baltimore: The Johns Hopkins Press, 1932.

KELLY, Amy. *Eleanor of Aquitaine and the Four Kings.* Vintage Books. New York: Random House, Reprint, 1959.

KIRBY, Thomas A. *Chaucer's Troilus: a Study in Courtly Love.* Gloucester, Mass.: Peter Smith, Reprint, 1958.

LEWIS, C. S. *The Allegory of Love:* a Study in Medieval Tradition. Galaxy Books. New York: Oxford University Press, Reprint, 1958.

LOOMIS, Roger Sherman, and Laura Hibbard LOOMIS. *Arthurian Legends in Medieval Art.* New York: The Modern Language Association of America, 1938.

NITZE, William Albert. *Arthurian Romance and Modern Poetry and Music.* Chicago: University of Chicago Press, 1940.

REID, Margaret J. C. *The Arthurian Legend:* Comparison of Treatment in Modern and Mediaeval Literature. Edinburgh and London: Oliver and Boyd, 1938.

WESTON, Jessie L. *The Legends of the Wagner Drama:* Studies in Mythology and Romance. New York: Charles Scribner's Sons, 1896.

Note: Especially recommended for historical and cultural backgrounds are the six volumes in the Oxford History of England series, covering from Roman Briton times to 1485.

GLOSSARY

This list is necessarily brief. Recommended for further information are Webster's unabridged dictionaries and Joseph T. Shipley, *Dictionary of Early English* (New York: Philosophical Library, 1955).

afterdele, disadvantage
Almain, Germany
alther, of all
amiral, prince
an, if
appelled, accused
appertyces, proofs of valor
araged, angered
Argante, Morgan le Fay
Argyle, w. Scotland
Armorica, Brittany
assotted, enamored of
astonied, dismayed
atheling, nobleman
August-kalends, August 1st
Autun, in Burgundy
avaunt, boast
avayled, lowered
awroke, avenged

baileys, defense courts
bale, cureless sorrow or injury
barbican, outwork of a fort
Barfleur, in Normandy
basinet, helmet
battles, armies
beamous, trumpets
beau sabreur, a dashing cavalryman
benison, benediction
bereaved, taken from
beseen, equipped
beskyfte, get rid of; avoid
bestad, situated
bezant, Byzantine coin

bisene, appointed; equipped
bitaken, entrusted; committed
bliaut, close-fitting garment
bonnets, additional canvas
boon, favor, gift
boss, knoblike ornament
bracer, arm or wrist armor
bragget, fermented ale and honey
braide, movement; vigor
brast, burst, broke
brent, burned
broached, thrust
broaches, spits
brym, angry
bushment, ambush
busk, make ready
buskins, half-boots
bustard, large game bird
byrnie, coat of chain mail

Caerleon, in Monmouthshire
Caermerdin, Carmarthen, Wales
Camelford, near Tintagel
Candlemas, February 2nd
cantel, small piece
cantrefs, territorial units
carbuncle, deep red gem
carracks, small ships
castellan, governor or warden
caul, close-fitting cap
cedle, writing, note
cere, wrap in waxed shrouds
chafe, anger
chaflet, platform

chausses, mail garment for lower limbs
cheer, facial expression
chrism, anoint; holy oil
Cirencester, in Gloucestershire
clerk, scholar, writer
Clud, Dumbarton-on-Clyde
cog, freight ship
commots, Welsh territorial units
con, know, be able
conning, learning, skill
conteur, storyteller
cordwain, cordovan leather
coronal, circlet for the head
courages, advice
covert, in reserve
creepers, grappling irons
Culhwch, Pig-run

dag, cut
dagswain, coarse shaggy cloth
damoiseau, youth
Dance of the Giants, Stonehenge
daunger, power
deem, hold
deeming, thought
dele, part, portion
delibered, resolved
deliverly, nimbly
demesnes, domains
depraved, disparaged
desmesure, excess
destrier, war horse
devoir, duty
diaper, figured cloth
dight, dress, equip
disparply, dispersed
dispenses, expenses
disperplyd, scattered
doole, pain, grief
douzepers, nobles
drag, raft
dretched, harassed
dromon, sailboat
Dumbarton, near Glasgow, Scotland

dure, endure
dyndled, quivered

efte, again
eld, old age
emprise, enterprise; boldness
endite, write, compose
englyn, short Welsh epigram
enow, enough
entente, intent, design
Ernley, Arley, n. of Worcester
ewers, wide-spouted pitchers

fain, glad; desirous
fawte, lack; fail
featly, becomingly
felly, outer rim of wheel
feutred, fixed in rest
fey, fated to die
fief, feudal estate
flemyd, fleeing; put to flight
floruit, he flourished
foin, thrust, lunge; point
forbled, weak from loss of blood
forbond, foot
fordele, advantage
forgather, encounter
fyaunce, faith, assurance

gads, goads
garnish, prepare, supply, equip
germain, closely akin
geste, tale of adventures
ghittern, guitar
ghostly, spiritual
glaive, sword
Gloucester, natural son of Henry I
gouts, heraldric elements
gramercy, many thanks
graythed, prepared
guerdon, reward
gules, red, as in heraldry
gwyddbwyll, game like chess
gyves, fetters

habergeon, short coat of mail

hackney, horse
handsel, use for the first time
hauberk, coat of mail
Hawick, town in s. Scotland
head, wishes
headland, unplowed land
Henry, 3rd son (1100-1135) of William the Conqueror
hesters, bushels
Hic jacet . . . , "Here lies King Arthur, the once and future king."
hie, hasten
hight, called, named
hippocrass, spiced wine
holt, woodland, forest
hool, whole, sound in health
hospice, inn for travelers
housel, give the Sacrament
housing, ornamental saddlecloth
hovyng, tarrying, hovering, hiding
hurdace, hurdles of wicker
husbandman, farmer

incontinent, at once
in devoir, at a disadvantage
In manus tuas, "Into thy hands I commend my spirit." Luke 23:46.
invest, lay siege to
irons, fenceposts

jesseraunt, jacket-like armor
jongleur, itinerant minstrel
jupon, close-fitting tunic

kettle-hat, helmet
kirtle, tunic

largesse, gifts; generosity
laton, brasslike metal plate
layne, conceal
leaguer, camp of besieging army
leech, physician
letted, hindered
Lettow, Lithuania
lever, more dear
lewd, ignorant

lief, welcome; dear
liege, loyal, free
list, please; wish, desire
Little Britain, Brittany
Llychlyn, Scandinavia
longed, belonged
lout, bend, stoop, bow
love-day, day for settling disputes

mal engine, evil craft
marches, borders
maugre, in spite of; ill-will
May-calends, May 1st
meet, proper
meinie, retinue
melly, melee
mesne, superior lord
mewed, molted
meyne, retinue
mickle, much
middes, midst
mischieved, harmed, injured
mishapped, chanced by mishap
Mount Snowdon, in Caernarvon, nw. Wales
myssaye, abuse, slander

natheless, nevertheless
new fangle, fond of new things
noblesse, nobility
no force, it matters not
nyst, knew not

oftsydes, often
Olwen, White-track
on live, alive
or, before
orgulous, proud
ouches, clasps
outher, or
outrageousity, outrage
Ouzel, European blackbird

paas, pace; distance, degree
par amour, for love's sake
pareylle, equal, like

pari passu, with equal pace
passant, walking; looking
paynims, pagans or heathens
peregrina, foreigner
Picts, ancient people of n. Britain
pillers, plunderers
pillion-hat, round cap
piment, wine with honey and spices
pisan, chest armor
postern, rear gate
Potestate, chief magistrate
Powys, central Wales
privily, secretly
privy, personal; aware of
purfle, purl
purvey, provide
puissance, might or force
pyght, pitched, set up
pyke, steal away

quernstones, millstones
quick, alive

ransack, examine
rase, cut
reave, strip or rob
reck, care
recounter, encounter
rede, advise, counsel
reeve, manager or bailiff
Richborough, in nw. Kent
romed, bellowed
Rood, the Cross
rout, retinue
runes, old Teutonic letters

saltire, heraldric device
samite, rich silk
sarpys, girdles
scallop, pilgrimage badge
scathe, hurt or injury
scratch, fight
scrip, small bag or wallet
seizin, possession of an estate
sendal, thin silk fabric
seneschal, major-domo

shende, harm, damage
shoure, attack
shunt, shrink aside
sieges, places, seats
Silchester, Hampshire town, long extinct
sith, since
sithence, seeing that
sondes, messages
sooth, truth
speed, success; prosper, succeed
Spruysland, Prussia
stalled, installed
sterte, sprang, started
stint, stop, pause
stound, time; moment
stour, battle
stuff, store with necessities
surcoat, tunic worn over armor
Surgenale, South Wales
swough, sound
sythen, since

Tamar, river between Cornwall and Devonshire
Tars, Tartary
taylles, taxes, reckonings
thane, warrior; follower; servant
Thanet, on ne. coast of Kent
thilk, that same
thrang, pressed forward
tierce, 9 A. M.
tilth, cultivated land
tine, antler
tofore, before
tokens, characteristics
torque, collar or neck chain
Totnes, town on Dart River, Devonshire
treats, at full length
trefoil, clover
tridents, fish spears
trow, think, believe, suppose
truage, tribute
truss, make fast; pack
trussel, furled sail

Tullian, Ciceronian
tushes, teeth

undorne, 9 A. M.
unware, unprepared
utas, eighth day after

vair, squirrel fur
varlet, knight's page or servant
vassal, royal subject or follower
vernage, Italian wine

Walwain, Gawain
wanne, lap
wappe, ebb
ware, aware
Waynor, Guinevere
wayte, watch, guard
weeds, clothing
ween, think, believe

weltered, rolled about
Wenhaver, Guinevere
whilom, formerly
wight, person; strong
Winchester, in Hampshire, old capital of Wessex
Winetland, Gwynedd, nw. Wales
wis, wot, wist, know
wise, way
withal, with it all
withe, willow twig
wone, domain
wont, custom
wood, mad, insane
worship, honor
wrake, destruction
wrung, twisted about
wyte, blame

yelden, yielded